DAVID BUSCH'S
NIKON® D90

GUIDE TO DIGITAL SLR PHOTOGRAPHY

David D. Busch

Course Technology PTR

A part of Cengage Learning

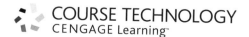

COURSE TECHNOLOGY
CENGAGE Learning™

Australia, Brazil, Japan, Korea, Mexico, Singapore, Spain, United Kingdom, United States

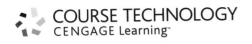
COURSE TECHNOLOGY
CENGAGE Learning™

David Busch's Nikon® D90 Guide to Digital SLR Photography
David D. Busch

Publisher and General Manager, Course Technology PTR:
Stacy L. Hiquet

Associate Director of Marketing:
Sarah Panella

Manager of Editorial Services:
Heather Talbot

Marketing Manager:
Jordan Casey

Executive Editor:
Kevin Harreld

Project Editor:
Jenny Davidson

Technical Reviewer:
Michael D. Sullivan

PTR Editorial Services Coordinator:
Jen Blaney

Interior Layout Tech:
Bill Hartman

Cover Designer:
Mike Tanamachi

Indexer:
Katherine Stimson

Proofreader:
Sandi Wilson

© 2010 David D. Busch

ALL RIGHTS RESERVED. No part of this work covered by the copyright herein may be reproduced, transmitted, stored, or used in any form or by any means graphic, electronic, or mechanical, including but not limited to photocopying, recording, scanning, digitizing, taping, Web distribution, information networks, or information storage and retrieval systems, except as permitted under Section 107 or 108 of the 1976 United States Copyright Act, without the prior written permission of the publisher.

For product information and technology assistance, contact us at
Cengage Learning Customer & Sales Support, 1-800-354-9706

For permission to use material from this text or product, submit all requests online at **cengage.com/permissions**. Further permissions questions can be e-mailed to **permissionrequest@cengage.com**.

Nikon is a registered trademark of Nikon Corporation in the United States and other countries.

All other trademarks are the property of their respective owners.

Library of Congress Control Number: 2008939943

ISBN-13: 978-1-59863-905-6

ISBN-10: 1-59863-905-6

Course Technology, a part of Cengage Learning
20 Channel Center Street
Boston, MA 02210
USA

Cengage Learning is a leading provider of customized learning solutions with office locations around the globe, including Singapore, the United Kingdom, Australia, Mexico, Brazil, and Japan. Locate your local office at: **international.cengage.com/region**.

Cengage Learning products are represented in Canada by Nelson Education, Ltd.

For your lifelong learning solutions, visit **courseptr.com**.

Visit our corporate Web site at **cengage.com**.

Printed in the United States of America
4 5 6 7 11 10

For Cathy

Acknowledgments

Once again thanks to the folks at Course Technology PTR, who recognized that a camera as popular as the Nikon D90 deserves in-depth full-color coverage at a price anyone can afford. Special thanks to executive editor Kevin Harreld, who always gives me the freedom to let my imagination run free with a topic, as well as my veteran production team including project editor Jenny Davidson and technical editor Mike Sullivan. Also thanks to Bill Hartman, layout; Katherine Stimson, indexing; Sandi Wilson, proofreading; Mike Tanamachi, cover design; and my agent, Carole Jelen, who has the amazing ability to keep both publishers and authors happy.

About the Author

With more than a million books in print, **David D. Busch** is the world's #1 selling digital camera guide author, and the originator of popular digital photography series like *David Busch's Pro Secrets* and *David Busch's Quick Snap Guides.* He has written eight hugely successful guidebooks for Nikon digital SLR models, and ten additional user guides for other camera models, as well as many popular books devoted to dSLRs, including *Mastering Digital SLR Photography, Second Edition* and *Digital SLR Pro Secrets.* As a roving photojournalist for more than 20 years, he illustrated his books, magazine articles, and newspaper reports with award-winning images. He's operated his own commercial studio, suffocated in formal dress while shooting weddings-for-hire, and shot sports for a daily newspaper and upstate New York college. His photos have been published in magazines as diverse as *Scientific American* and *Petersen's PhotoGraphic,* and his articles have appeared in *Popular Photography & Imaging, The Rangefinder, The Professional Photographer,* and hundreds of other publications. He's also reviewed dozens of digital cameras for CNet and *Computer Shopper.*

When About.com named its top five books on Beginning Digital Photography, debuting at the #1 and #2 slots were Busch's *Digital Photography All-In-One Desk Reference for Dummies* and *Mastering Digital Photography.* During the past year, he's had as many as five of his books listed in the Top 20 of Amazon.com's Digital Photography Bestseller list—simultaneously! Busch's 100-plus other books published since 1983 include bestsellers like *David Busch's Quick Snap Guide to Using Digital SLR Lenses.*

Busch earned top category honors in the Computer Press Awards the first two years they were given (for *Sorry About The Explosion* and *Secrets of MacWrite, MacPaint and MacDraw*), and he later served as Master of Ceremonies for the awards. Visit his website at http://www.nikonguides.com.

Contents

Chapter 3
Setting Up Your Nikon D90   67

Chapter 4
Fine-Tuning Exposure   163

Chapter 5
Advanced Shooting Tips for Your Nikon D90   193

Chapter 6
Working with Lenses   227

Chapter 7
Making Light Work for You   257

Chapter 8
Useful Software for the Nikon D90   297

Chapter 9
Nikon D90: Troubleshooting and Prevention   315

Preface

The Nikon D90, Nikon's latest upgrade to its compact enthusiast digital SLR camera line, includes many pace-setting features, including the first HDTV movie-making capability ever offered in a digital single lens reflex. Although easy to use, the D90 is packed with a meager black-and-white manual that is almost impossible for beginners and more experienced photographers alike to wade through. Everything is in there, but how do you find it? And what does it all *mean?* What you really need is a comprehensive guide that explains the purpose and function of every one of the D90's controls, how you should use them in specific situations, and why.

If you want a quick introduction to the D90's advanced features, including Live View and movie-making, as well as simple explanations of basics like focus controls, flash synchronization options, how to choose lenses, or which exposure modes are best, this book is for you. If you can't decide on what basic settings to use with your camera because you can't figure out how changing ISO or white balance or focus defaults will affect your pictures, you need this guide. I won't talk down to you, either; this book isn't padded with dozens of pages of checklists telling you how to take a travel picture, a sports photo, or how to take a snapshot of your kids in overly simplistic terms. There are no special sections devoted to "real world" recipes here. All of us do 100 percent of our shooting in the real world! So, I give you all the information you need to cook up great photos on your own!

Introduction

Whether you're a veteran of my previous books or a new convert, I think you'll find this introduction to the D90 quite different from the other books on the market. It's bigger, more comprehensive, and has only color illustrations, unlike the other books that are smaller, cover only the basics, and concentrate more on generalities than how to use your Nikon camera. When I first saw this exciting new camera, I scanned its list of features and realized that it deserved an entirely different approach than that offered by most so-called "guidebooks." Feedback from readers of my previous books has convinced me that a compact "field guide" doesn't really provide all the information needed to become proficient with a digital single lens reflex (dSLR) camera.

You don't need a book that devotes almost a third of its pages to little sections that provide the rudiments of shooting the most basic types of pictures. Even if you're a rank beginner, does it really help all that much to be told that you ought to use a fast shutter speed when shooting sports—you probably already have figured out that there are many different kinds of action situations when *slower* shutter speeds are superior (such as motor sports with spinning tires). But, don't worry, I provide this kind of information, too. I just don't waste dozens of pages on these basic techniques when they can be covered in the same pages that teach you enough about *photography* that you can apply to taking any kind of pictures you want. Instead of recipes, I'm going to emphasize the exciting things you can do with the Nikon D90 digital SLR. After a couple introductory chapters that help you get your bearings with this innovative camera, we're going to explore dSLR photography using a significant new tool.

Compared to offerings from other companies, the Nikon D90 has some significant advantages. For the broad range of cool features and capabilities it provides, the D90 is, first and foremost, *affordable.* Certainly, the $1,000 price neighborhood is an important price point if you're in the early throes of passion for digital photography. But, you also need a full complement of features that won't impose serious limitations on your creativity.

In that vein, it's nice to know that the Nikon D90 is also *expandable,* thanks to the huge line of Nikon AF-S lenses, and a full line of close-up attachments and other accessories that have been developed for earlier Nikon cameras. You'll find that the Nikon D90 also includes tons of *very cool features*, such as the sensor self-cleaning mode and the ability to make real HDTV movies right in the camera. There's a Retouch mode that allows you to fix up your pictures in the camera, and even create a "small picture" copy suitable for e-mailing.

I sincerely believe that this book is your best bet for learning how to use your new camera, and for learning how to use it well. If you're a Nikon D90 owner who's looking to learn more about how to use this great camera, you've probably already explored your options. There are DVDs and online tutorials—but who can learn how to use a camera by sitting in front of a television or computer screen? Do you want to watch a movie or click on HTML links, or do you want to go out and take photos with your camera? Videos and web pages are fun, but not the best answer.

Of course, there's always the manual furnished with the camera. It's compact and filled with information, but there's really very little in there about *why* you should use particular settings or features, and its organization may make it difficult to find what you need. Multiple cross-references may send you flipping back and forth between two or three sections of the book to find what you need. The basic manual is also hobbled by black-and-white line drawings and tiny monochrome pictures that aren't very good examples of what you can do.

As I mentioned earlier, I haven't been happy with the third-party guidebooks to Nikon cameras, either, especially those written for models like the D90 that are frequently purchased by new digital camera users, or those who are new to single lens reflex (SLR) cameras. The existing books range from skimpy and illustrated by black-and-white photos to lushly illustrated in full color but too generic to do much good. Photography instruction is useful, but it needs to be related directly to the Nikon D90 as much as possible.

I've tried to make *David Busch's Nikon D90 Guide to Digital SLR Photography* different from your other D90 learn-up options. The roadmap sections use larger, color pictures to show you where all the buttons and dials are, and the explanations of what they do are longer and more comprehensive. Instead of the checklists devoted to general topics like "architectural photography" or "landscape photography," you'll find tips and techniques for using all the features of your Nikon D90 to take *any kind of picture* you want.

Nor is this book a lame rewriting of the manual that came with the camera. Some folks spend five minutes with a book like this one, spot some information that also appears in the original manual, and decide "Rehash!" without really understanding the differences. Yes, you'll find information here that is also in the owner's manual, such as the parameters you can enter when changing your D90's operation in the various menus. Basic descriptions—before I dig in and start providing in-depth tips and information—may also be vaguely similar. There are only so many ways you can say, for example, "Hold the shutter release down halfway to lock in exposure and focus."

But not *everything* in the manual is included in this book. I don't include a table of error messages, for instance, because their appearance is fairly rare to begin with, and I'd expect you to go grab the manual to look one up if an error occurs. Nor do I provide advice on how to store your camera, or a complete list of memory card capacities for various file formats. I want you to *use* your D90, not store it, and you can easily figure out the capacity of any freshly formatted memory card you own from the figure displayed on the top-panel LCD. Thinking of buying a card with twice as many gigabytes as your current memory card? Multiply the figure you get with the old card by two; that will be close enough. Not *everything* should be included in a guidebook like this one.

David Busch's Nikon D90 Guide to Digital SLR Photography is aimed at both Nikon and dSLR veterans who want to learn how to use this new camera, as well as newcomers to digital photography and digital SLRs. Both groups can be overwhelmed by the options the D90 offers, while underwhelmed by the explanations they receive in their user's manual. The manuals are great if you already know what you don't know, and you can find an answer somewhere in a booklet arranged by menu listings and written by a camera vendor employee who last threw together instructions on how to operate a point-and-shoot digital camera.

Once you've read this book and are ready to learn more, I hope you pick up one of my other guides to digital SLR photography. If you've jumped right into the pool with the Nikon D90 as your first digital SLR, one of them may provide the kind of introductory material you need to get up to speed. Five of these dSLR guides are offered by Course Technology PTR, and each approaches topics from a different perspective. They include:

David Busch's Quick Snap Guide to Using Digital SLR Lenses

A bit overwhelmed by the features and controls of digital SLR lenses, and not quite sure when to use each type? This book explains lenses, their use, and lens technology in easy-to-access two- and four-page spreads, each devoted to a different topic, such as depth-of-field, lens aberrations, or using zoom lenses. If you have a friend or significant other who is less versed in photography, but who wants to borrow and use your Nikon D90 from time to time, this book can save you a ton of explanation.

David Busch's Quick Snap Guide to Lighting

This book tells you everything you need to know about using light to create the kind of images you'll be proud of. It's not Nikon-specific, and doesn't include any details on using any of the Nikon dedicated flash units, but the information you'll find applies to any digital SLR photography.

Quick Snap Guide to Digital SLR Photography

Consider this a prequel to the book you're holding in your hands. It, too, might make a good gift for a spouse or friend who may be using your D90, but who lacks even basic knowledge about digital photography, digital SLR photography, and Nikon photography. It serves as an introduction that summarizes the basic features of digital SLR cameras in general (not just the D90), and what settings to use and when, such as continuous autofocus/single autofocus, aperture/shutter priority, EV settings, and so forth. The guide also includes recipes for shooting the most common kinds of pictures, with step-by-step instructions for capturing effective sports photos, portraits, landscapes, and other types of images. (Here is where you will find those bullet-point checklists I've left out of *this* book.)

Mastering Digital SLR Photography, Second Edition

This book is an introduction to digital SLR photography, with nuts-and-bolts explanations of the technology, more in-depth coverage of settings, and whole chapters on the most common types of photography. While not specific to the Nikon D90, this book can show you how to get more from its capabilities.

Digital SLR Pro Secrets

This is my more advanced guide to dSLR photography with greater depth and detail about the topics you're most interested in. If you've already mastered the basics in *Mastering Digital SLR Photography*, this book will take you to the next level.

Who Are You?

When preparing a guidebook for a specific camera, it's always wise to consider exactly who will be reading the book. Indeed, thinking about the potential audience for *David Busch's Nikon D90 Guide to Digital SLR Photography* is what led me to taking the approach and format I use for this book. I realized that the needs of readers like you had to be addressed both from a functional level (what you will use the D90 for) as well as from a skill level (how much experience you may have with digital photography, dSLRs, or Nikon cameras specifically).

From a functional level, you probably fall into one of these categories:

- Professional photographers who understand photography and digital SLRs, and simply want to learn how to use the Nikon D90 as a backup camera, or as a camera for their personal "off-duty" use.

- Individuals who want to get better pictures, or perhaps transform their growing interest in photography into a full-fledged hobby or artistic outlet with a Nikon D90 and advanced techniques.

- Those who want to produce more professional-looking images for their personal or business website, and feel that the Nikon D90 will give them more control and capabilities.

- Small business owners with more advanced graphics capabilities who want to use the Nikon D90 to document or promote their business.

- Corporate workers who may or may not have photographic skills in their job descriptions, but who work regularly with graphics and need to learn how to use digital images taken with a Nikon D90 for reports, presentations, or other applications.

- Professional webmasters with strong skills in programming (including Java, JavaScript, HTML, Perl, etc.) but little background in photography, but who realize that the D90 can be used for sophisticated photography.

- Graphic artists and others who already may be adept in image editing with Photoshop or another program, and who may already be using a film SLR (Nikon or otherwise), but who need to learn more about digital photography and the special capabilities of the D90 dSLR.

Addressing your needs from a skills level can be a little trickier, because the D90 is such a great camera that a full spectrum of photographers will be buying it, from absolute beginners who have never owned a digital camera before up to the occasional professional with years of shooting experience who will be using the Nikon D90 as a backup body. (I have to admit I tend to carry my D90 with me everywhere, even if I intend to take most of my photos with another camera, such as my Nikon D300.)

Before tackling this book, it would be helpful for you to understand the following:

- **What a digital SLR is:** It's a camera that generally shows an optical (not LCD) view of the picture that's being taken through the (interchangeable) lens that actually takes the photo, thanks to a mirror that reflects an image to a viewfinder, but flips up out of the way to allow the sensor to be exposed. Some dSLRs (like the Nikon D90), also have a *Live View* option that flips up the mirror to allow a real-time display on the LCD.

- **How digital photography differs from film:** The image is stored not on film (which I call the *first* write-once optical media), but on a memory card as pixels that can be transferred to your computer, and then edited, corrected, and printed without the need for chemical processing.

- **What the basic tools of correct exposure are:** Don't worry if you don't understand these; I'll explain them later in this book. But if you already know something about shutter speed, aperture, and ISO sensitivity, you'll be ahead of the game. If not, you'll soon learn that shutter speed determines the amount of time the sensor is exposed to incoming light; the f/stop or aperture is like a valve that governs the quantity of light that can flow through the lens; the sensor's sensitivity (ISO setting) controls how easily the sensor responds to light. All three factors can be varied individually and proportionately to produce a picture that is properly exposed (neither too light nor too dark).

It's tough to provide something for everybody, but I am going to try to address the needs of each of the following groups and skill levels:

- **Digital photography newbies:** If you've used only point-and-shoot digital cameras, or have worked only with non-SLR film cameras, you're to be congratulated for selecting one of the very best entry-level digital SLRs available as your first dSLR camera. This book can help you understand the controls and features of your D90, and lead you down the path to better photography with your camera. I'll provide all the information you need, but if you want to do some additional reading for extra credit, you can also try one of the other books I mentioned earlier. They complement this book well.

- **Advanced point-and-shooters moving on up:** There are some quite sophisticated pocket-sized digital cameras available, including those with many user-definable options and settings, so it's possible you are already a knowledgeable photographer, even though you're new to the world of the digital SLR. You've recognized the limitations of the point-and-shoot camera: even the best of them have more noise at higher sensitivity (ISO) settings than a camera like the Nikon D90; the speediest still have an unacceptable delay between the time you press the shutter and the photo is actually taken; even a non-interchangeable super-zoom camera with 12X to 20X magnification often won't focus close enough, include an aperture suitable for low-light photography, or take in the really wide view you must have. Interchangeable lenses and other accessories available for the Nikon D90 are another one of the reasons you moved up. Because you're an avid photographer already, you should pick up the finer points of using the D90 from this book with no trouble.

- **Film SLR veterans new to the digital world:** You understand photography, you know about f/stops and shutter speeds, and thrive on interchangeable lenses. If you have used a newer film SLR, it probably has lots of electronic features already, including autofocus and sophisticated exposure metering. Perhaps you've even been using a Nikon film SLR and understand many of the available accessories that work with both film and digital cameras. All you need is information on using digital-specific features, working with the D90 itself, and how to match—and exceed—the capabilities of your film camera with your new Nikon D90.

- **Experienced dSLR users broadening their experience to include the D90:** Perhaps you started out with the Nikon D70 back in 2004, or a D100 before that. It's very likely that some of you used the 6-megapixel Nikon D40 before the bug to advance to more megapixels bit you. You may have used a digital SLR from Canon or another vendor and are making the switch. You understand basic photography, and want to learn more. And, most of all, you want to transfer the skills you already have to the Nikon D90, as quickly and seamlessly as possible.

■ **Pro photographers and other advanced shooters:** I expect my most discerning readers will be those who already have extensive experience with Nikon intermediate and pro-level cameras. I may not be able to teach you folks much about photography. But, even so, an amazing number of D90 cameras have been purchased by those who feel it is a good complement to their favorite advanced dSLR. Others (like myself) own a camera like the Nikon D300 and find that the D90 fills a specific niche incredibly well, and, is useful as a backup camera; because the D90's 12-megapixel images are often just as good as those produced by more "advanced" models. You pros and semi-pros, despite your depth of knowledge, should find this book useful for learning about the features the D90 has that your previous cameras lack or implement in a different way.

Who Am I?

After spending years as the world's most successful unknown author, I've become slightly less obscure in the past few years, thanks to a horde of camera guidebooks and other photographically oriented tomes. You may have seen my photography articles in *Popular Photography & Imaging* magazine. I've also written about 2,000 articles for magazines like *Petersen's PhotoGraphic* (which is now defunct through no fault of my own), plus *The Rangefinder, Professional Photographer,* and dozens of other photographic publications. But, first, and foremost, I'm a photojournalist and made my living in the field until I began devoting most of my time to writing books. Although I love writing, I'm happiest when I'm out taking pictures, which is why I took off 11 days right in the middle of writing this book to travel out West to Zion National Park in Utah, the Sedona "red rocks" area and Grand Canyon in Arizona, and, for a few days, in Las Vegas (although I did a lot more shooting than gambling in Sin City). You'll find photos of all these visual treasures within the pages of this book.

Like all my digital photography books, this one was written by a Nikon devotee with an incurable photography bug. My first Nikon SLR was a venerable Nikon F back in the 1960s, and I've owned most of the newer digital models since then.

Over the years, I've worked as a sports photographer for an Ohio newspaper and for an upstate New York college. I've operated my own commercial studio and photo lab, cranking out product shots on demand and then printing a few hundred glossy 8 × 10s on a tight deadline for a press kit. I've served as a photo-posing instructor for a modeling agency. People have actually paid me to shoot their weddings and immortalize them with portraits. I even prepared press kits and articles on photography as a PR consultant for a large Rochester, N.Y., company, which shall remain nameless. My trials and travails with imaging and computer technology have made their way into print in book form an alarming number of times, including a few dozen on scanners and photography.

Like you, I love photography for its own merits, and I view technology as just another tool to help me get the images I see in my mind's eye. But, also like you, I had to master this technology before I could apply it to my work. This book is the result of what I've learned, and I hope it will help you master your Nikon D90 digital SLR, too.

As I write this, I'm currently in the throes of upgrading my website, which you can find at www.nikonguides.com, adding tutorials and information about my other books. There's a lot of information about several Nikon models right now, but I'll be adding tips and recommendations about the Nikon D90 (included a list of equipment and accessories that I can't live without) in the next few months. I hope you'll stop by for a visit. I've also set up a wish list of Nikon cameras, lenses, and accessories on Amazon.com for those who want to begin shopping now. I hope you'll stop by for a visit to http://astore.amazon.com/nikonphoto-20.

1

Setting Up Your Nikon D90

Although the Nikon D90 may be your first exposure to some advanced features—particularly Live View or movie-making—Nikon has retained enough "turn it on and shoot" ease of operation that you can, with about 60 seconds' worth of prep, go out and begin taking great pictures.

As is my custom, my first photo with this camera was a snapshot of the owner of the photo store where I bought my D90. As a long-time Nikon owner, I could have purchased just the D90 body (sans lens), but the new 18-105mm kit lens with vibration reduction (anti-shake) was too tempting, so I got that. I remembered to take a memory card with me when I picked up the camera. Because the D90 had just been introduced, there was enough of a maintenance charge in the fresh-off-the-boat battery to allow capturing a few images on the spot, even before the ink on my check was dry.

Try it. Insert a memory card and mount the lens (if you bought the D90 at a store, they probably did that for you). Charge the battery and insert it into the camera. Remove the lens cap, turn the camera on (the button's concentric with the shutter release button), and then set the big ol' dial on the top-left edge to the green AUTO icon. Point the D90 at something interesting and press the shutter release. Presto! A pretty good picture will pop up on the color LCD on the back of the camera. Wasn't that easy?

But if you purchased this book, you're probably not going to be satisfied with pretty good photos. You want to shoot *incredible* images. The D90 can do that, too. All you need is this book and some practice. The first step is to familiarize yourself with your camera. The first three chapters of this book will take care of that. Then, as you gain experience and skills, you'll want to learn more about how to improve your exposures, fine-tune the color, or use the essential tools of photography, such as electronic flash and available light. You'll want to learn how to choose and use lenses, too. All that information can be found in the second part of this book. The Nikon D90 is not only easy to use, it's easy to *learn* to use.

I'm going to divide my introduction to the Nikon D90 into three parts. The first part will cover what you absolutely *need* to know just to get started using the camera (you'll find that in this chapter). The second part offers a more comprehensive look at what you *should* know about the camera and its controls to use its features effectively (that'll be found in Chapter 2). Finally, you'll learn how to make key settings using the menu system, so you'll be able to fine-tune and tweak the D90 to operate exactly the way you want, in Chapter 3. While you probably should master everything in the first two chapters right away, you can take more time to learn about the settings described in Chapter 3, because you won't need to use all those options right away. I've included everything about menus and settings in that chapter so you'll find what you need, when you need it, all in one place.

Some of you may have owned a Nikon digital SLR before. Perhaps you owned a Nikon D50 or D70/D70s, or even the D90's immediate predecessor, the D80, for some time and were eager to upgrade to a more modern 12-megapixel model with more features. It's even possible you owned a Nikon D40/D40x, or D60, enjoyed using it, and wanted more megapixels and some of the added features the D90 offers, such as automatic sensor cleaning and that handy shake-resistant (*vibration reduction*) 18-105mm lens I found so tempting. A few of you may even be someone like me, who uses a more advanced Nikon dSLR, such as the D300, as a "main" camera, but finds the more compact D90 an alluring walk-about camera and backup.

If you fall into any of those categories, you may be able to skim through this chapter quickly and move on to the two that follow. The next few pages are designed to get your camera fired up and ready for shooting as quickly as possible. If you're new to digital SLRs, Nikon dSLRs, or even digital photography, you'll want to read through this introduction more carefully. After all, the Nikon D90 is not a point-and-shoot camera, although, as I said, you can easily set it up in fully automated Auto mode, or use the semi-automated Program exposure mode and a basic autofocus setting for easy capture of grab shots. But, if you want a little more control over your shooting, you'll need to know more. So I'm going to provide a basic pre-flight checklist that you need to complete before you really spread your wings and take off. You won't find a lot of detail in this chapter. Indeed, I'm going to tell you just what you absolutely *must* understand, accompanied by some interesting tidbits that will help you become acclimated to your D90. I'll go into more depth and even repeat some of what I explain here in later chapters, so you don't have to memorize everything you see. Just relax, follow a few easy steps, and then go out and begin taking your best shots—ever.

First Things First

The Nikon D90 comes in an impressive box filled with stuff, including connecting cords, booklets, a CD, and lots of paperwork. The most important components are the camera and lens (unlike some other Nikon models, the D90 is most often sold in a kit with a lens), battery, battery charger, and, if you're the nervous type, the neck strap. You'll also need a Secure Digital memory card, as one is not included. If you purchased your D90 from a camera shop, as I did, the store personnel probably attached the neck strap for you, ran through some basic operational advice that you've already forgotten, tried to sell you a Secure Digital card, and then, after they'd given you all the help you could absorb, sent you on your way with a handshake.

Perhaps you purchased your D90 from one of those mass merchandisers that also sell washing machines and vacuum cleaners. In that case, you might have been sent on your way with only the handshake, or, maybe, not even that if you resisted the hard-sell efforts to sell you an extended warranty. You save a few bucks at the big-box stores, but you don't get the personal service a professional photo retailer provides. It's your choice. There's a third alternative, of course. You might have purchased your camera from a mail order or Internet source, and your D90 arrived in a big brown (or purple/red or yellow/red) truck. Your only interaction when you took possession of your camera was to scrawl your signature on an electronic clipboard.

In all three cases, the first thing to do is to carefully unpack the camera and double-check the contents with the checklist on one end of the box, helpfully designated under the [Supplied Accessories] bracketed heading. While this level of setup detail may seem as superfluous as the instructions on a bottle of shampoo, checking the contents *first* is always a good idea. No matter who sells a camera, it's common to open boxes, use a particular camera for a demonstration, and then repack the box without replacing all the pieces and parts afterwards. Someone might actually have helpfully checked out your camera on your behalf—and then mispacked the box. It's better to know *now* that something is missing so you can seek redress immediately, rather than discover two months from now that the video cable you thought you'd never use (but now *must* have) was never in the box. I once purchased a brand-new Nikon dSLR kit that was supposed to include a second focusing screen; it wasn't in the box, but because I discovered the deficiency right away, the dealer ordered a replacement for me post haste.

At a minimum, the box should hold the following:

■ **Nikon D90 digital camera.** It almost goes without saying that you should check out the camera immediately, making sure the color LCD on the back isn't scratched or cracked, the Secure Digital and battery doors open properly, and, when a charged battery is inserted and lens mounted, the camera powers up and reports for duty. Out-of-the-box defects like these are rare, but they can happen. It's probably more common that your dealer played with the camera or, perhaps, it was a customer return. That's why it's best to buy your D90 from a retailer you trust to supply a factory-fresh camera.

■ **Rechargeable Li-ion battery EN-EL3e.** You'll need to charge this 7.4V, 1500mAh (milliampere hour) battery before using it. I'll offer instructions later in this chapter.

■ **Quick charger MH-18a.** This charger is required to vitalize the EN-EL3e battery.

■ **Video cable EG-D2.** Use this cable to connect your D90 to a standard definition (analog) television through the set's yellow RCA video jack when you want to view the camera's output on a larger screen.

■ **USB cable UC-E4.** You can use this cable to transfer photos from the camera to your computer (I don't recommend that because direct transfer uses a lot of battery power), to upload and download settings between the camera and your computer (highly recommended), and to operate your camera remotely using Nikon Camera Control Pro software (not included in the box). This cable is a standard one that works with the majority of digital cameras—Nikon and otherwise—so if you already own one, you now have a spare.

■ **Neck strap.** Nikon provides you with an AN-DC1 "steal me" neck strap emblazoned with your camera model, and while useful for showing off to your friends exactly which nifty new camera you bought, it's not very adjustable. I never attach the Nikon strap to my cameras, and instead opt for a more serviceable strap from UPstrap (www.upstrap-pro.com) or Op-Tech (www.optechusa.com). If you carry your camera over one shoulder, as many do, I particularly recommend UPstrap (shown in Figure 1.1). It has a patented non-slip pad that offers reassuring traction and eliminates the contortions we sometimes go through to keep the camera from slipping off. I know several photographers who refuse to use anything else. If you do purchase an UPstrap, be sure to mention that I sent you hence. You won't get a discount, but I may get another free UPstrap from photographer-inventor Al Stegmeyer.

■ **BF-1A body cap/rear lens cap.** The body cap keeps dust from infiltrating your camera when a lens is not mounted. Always carry a body cap (and rear lens cap, also supplied with the D90) in your camera bag for those times when you need to

Figure 1.1
Third-party
neck straps like
this UPstrap
model, are
often preferable
to the Nikon-
supplied strap.

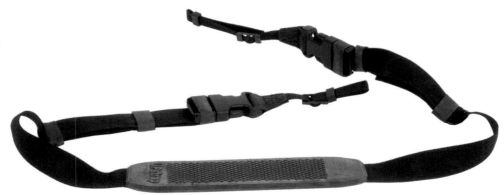

have the camera bare of optics for more than a minute or two. (That usually happens when repacking a bag efficiently for transport, or when you are carrying an extra body or two for backup.) The body cap/lens cap nest together for compact storage.

- **DK-21 rubber eyecup.** This is the square rubber eyecup that comes installed on the D90. It slides on and off the viewfinder.

- **DK-5 eyepiece cap.** This small piece can be clipped over the viewfinder window to prevent strong light sources from entering the viewing system when your eye is not pressed up against it, potentially affecting exposure measurement. That can be a special problem when the camera is mounted on a tripod, because additional illumination from the rear can make its way to the 1005-segment CCD that interprets light reaching the focusing screen. I pack this widget away to keep from losing it. As a practical matter, you'll never find it when you really need it, and covering the viewfinder with your hand (hover *near* the viewfinder window rather than touch it, to avoid shaking a tripod-mounted camera) works almost as well.

- **BM-10 monitor cover.** This plastic cover protects the color LCD on the back of the camera. I prefer the tempered glass GGS covers that seem to be available only on eBay, as they are thinner and provide less distortion of the LCD image.

- **BS-1 accessory shoe cover.** This is a sliding plastic piece that fits into the accessory shoe on top of the camera, and protects its contents from damage. You can remove it (and probably lose it) when you attach an optional external electronic flash to the shoe. I always, without fail, tuck it into the same place each time (in my case, my right front pants pocket), and have yet to lose one.

- **User manual.** Even if you have this book, you'll probably want to check the user's guide that Nikon provides, if only to confirm the actual nomenclature for some obscure accessory, or to double-check an error code. Google "Nikon D90 manual PDF" to find a downloadable, non-printable version that you can store on your laptop, a CD-ROM, or other media in case you want to access this reference when the paper version isn't handy. If you have an old Secure Digital card that's too small to be usable on a modern dSLR (I still have some 128MB and 256MB cards), you can store the PDF on that. But an even better choice is to put the manual on a low-capacity USB "thumb" drive, which you can buy for less than $10. You'll then be able to access the reference anywhere you are, because you can always find someone with a computer that has a USB port and Adobe Acrobat Reader available. You might not be lucky enough to locate a computer with a Secure Digital reader.

- **Quick guide.** This little booklet tucked away in the camera's paperwork offers a reasonable summary of the Nikon D90's basic commands and settings, and can be stowed in your camera bag more easily than a "field guide" or even this book.

- **Software CD-ROM.** Here you'll find the Nikon Software Suite, which includes various drivers required by some operating systems; Nikon Transfer (to move your files from camera or memory card to your computer); Nikon ViewNX (a useful image management program); as well as various third-party utilities (some of which you may already have installed on your computer). I'll cover all the Nikon software offerings later in this book.

- **Warranty and registration card.** Don't lose these! (But don't panic if you do; you can still register your camera without them.) You can register your Nikon D90 by mail or online (in the USA, the URL is www.nikonusa.com/register) and may need the information in this paperwork (plus the purchase receipt/invoice from your retailer) should you require Nikon service support.

Don't bother rooting around in the box for anything beyond what I've listed previously. There are a few things Nikon classifies as optional accessories, even though you (and I) might consider some of them essential. Here's a list of what you *don't* get in the box, but might want to think about as an impending purchase. I'll list them roughly in the order of importance:

- **Secure Digital card.** First-time digital camera buyers are sometimes shocked that their new tool doesn't come with a memory card. Why should it? The manufacturer doesn't have the slightest idea of how much storage you require, or whether you want a slow/inexpensive card or one that's faster/more expensive, so why should they pack one in the box and charge you for it? You'll want to buy one of your own that is 4GB in size, at the minimum.

- **Extra EN-EL3e battery.** Even though you might get 500 to more than 1,000 shots from a single battery, it's easy to exceed that figure in a few hours of shooting sports at up to 4.5 fps. Batteries can unexpectedly fail, too, or simply lose their charge from sitting around unused for a week or two. Buy an extra. I own five, in total, because they also work just fine in my old Nikon D70, my D300, and D700 cameras. Keep one or more charged at all times, and free your mind from worry.

- **Add-on speedlight.** One of the best uses for your Nikon D90's built-in electronic flash is as a remote trigger for an off-camera speedlight such as the SB-900. Your built-in flash can function as the main illumination for your photo, or softened and used to fill in shadows. But, you'll have to own one or more external flash units to gain that flexibility. If you do much flash photography at all, consider an add-on speedlight as an important accessory.

- **Wireless Remote Control ML-L3.** Use this infrared trigger (see Figure 1.2) to take a picture without the need to touch the camera itself. In a pinch, you can use the D90's self-timer to minimize vibration when triggering the camera. But when you want to take a photo at the exact moment you desire (and not when the self-timer happens to trip), or need to eliminate all possibility of human-induced camera shake, you need this infrared control.

Figure 1.2
The Nikon Wireless Remote Control ML-L3 lets you trigger your camera remotely.

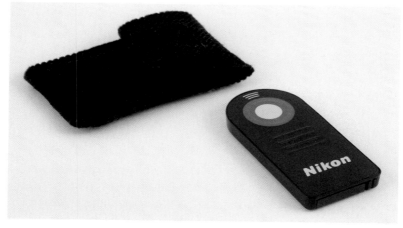

- **Nikon GP-1 global positioning system (GPS) device.** This accessory attaches to the accessory shoe on top of the Nikon D90 and captures latitude, longitude, and altitude information that is imprinted in a special data area of your image files. The "geotagging" data can be plotted on a map in Nikon ViewNX or other software programs. I'll explain more about this feature in Chapter 5.

- **Remote Release Cable MC-DC2.** This is a new cable release, currently used only with the Nikon D90, that allows triggering the shutter without touching the camera itself. It plugs into the GPS port at the bottom-left edge of the camera. You can use this release at the same time as the GP-1 accessory; the GPS cable has a pass-through that allows plugging in the MC-DC2.

- **AC adapter EH-5a.** These two optional devices are used together to power the Nikon D90 independently of the batteries. There are several typical situations where this capability can come in handy: when you're cleaning the sensor manually and want to totally eliminate the possibility that a lack of juice will cause the fragile shutter and mirror to spring to life during the process; when indoors shooting tabletop photos, portraits, class pictures, and so forth for hours on end; when using your D90 for remote shooting as well as time-lapse photography; for extensive review of images on your television; or for file transfer to your computer. These all use prodigious amounts of power, which can be provided by this AC adapter. (Beware of power outages and blackouts when cleaning your sensor, however!)

- **Multi-power battery pack MB-D80.** Lots of photographers consider this battery pack/vertical grip to be an essential item. The price is reasonable at less than $170. Unfortunately, it is delivered "bare," with no extra power sources at all. You'll need to purchase six AA batteries (alkalines or rechargeables) for the supplied AA battery tray, or have an extra EN-EL3e battery or two to use this accessory. (I *told* you that you'd need that extra battery.)

- **MH-19 multiple battery charger.** If you own several EN-EL3e batteries, you can charge two at once using this charger.

- **DR-6 right-angle viewer.** Used with the Nikon Eyepiece Adapter DK-22, it fastens in place of the standard square rubber eyecup and provides a 90-degree view for framing and composing your image at right angles to the original viewfinder. It's useful for low-level (or high-level) shooting. (Or, maybe, shooting around corners!)

- **SC-28 TTL flash cord.** Allows using Nikon speedlights off-camera, while retaining all the automated features.

- **SC-29 TTL flash cord.** Similar to the SC-28, this unit has its own AF-assist lamp, which can provide extra illumination for the D90's autofocus system in dim light (which, not coincidentally, is when you'll probably be using an electronic flash).

- **Nikon Capture NX 2 software.** Nikon's NEF (RAW) conversion and image tweaking software is an extra-cost option that most D90 owners won't need until they progress into extensive image editing. I'll describe this utility's functions in Chapter 8.

- **Camera Control Pro 2 software.** This is the utility you'll use to operate your camera remotely from your computer. Nikon charges extra for this software, too, but you'll find it invaluable if you're hiding near a tethered, tripod-mounted camera while shooting, say, close-ups of hummingbirds. There are lots of applications for remote shooting, and you'll need Camera Control Pro to operate your camera.

Initial Setup

Once you've unpacked and inspected your camera, the initial setup of your Nikon D90 is fast and easy. Basically, you just need to charge the battery, attach a lens, and insert a Secure Digital card. I'll address each of these steps separately, but if you already are confident you can manage these setup tasks without further instructions, feel free to skip this section entirely. I realize that some readers are ambitious, if inexperienced, and should, at the minimum, skim the contents of the next section, because I'm going to list a few options that you might not be aware of.

Mastering the Multi-Selector

I'll be saving descriptions of most of the controls used with the Nikon D90 until Chapter 2, which provides a complete "roadmap" of the camera's buttons and dials and switches. However, you may need to perform a few tasks during this initial setup process, and most of them will require the Menu button and the multi-selector pad. The Menu button is easy to find: it's located to the left of the LCD, the second button from the top. It requires almost no explanation; when you want to access a menu, press it. To exit most menus, press it again.

The multi-selector pad may remind you of the similar control found on many point-and-shoot cameras, and other digital SLRs. It consists of a thumbpad-sized button with indentations at the North, South, East, and West positions, plus a button in the center marked "OK" (see Figure 1.3).

The multi-selector on the D90 functions slightly differently than its counterpart on some other cameras. For example, some point-and-shoot models assign a function, such as white balance or ISO setting, to one of the directional buttons (usually in conjunction with a function key of some sort). The use of the multi-selector varies, even within the Nikon dSLR line up. For example, many Nikon digital SLRs, such as the Nikon

Figure 1.3
The multi-selector pad has four directional buttons for navigating up/down/left/right, and an OK button to confirm your selection.

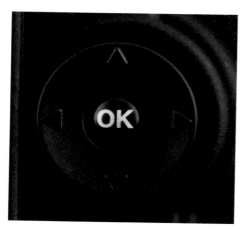

D50/D70/D80/ have no center button in the multi-selector at all. (Their OK/Enter button is located elsewhere.) Other Nikon cameras (such as the D300 and D3/D3x) allow assigning a function of your choice to the multi-selector center button.

With the D90, the multi-selector is used exclusively for navigation; for example, to navigate among menus on the LCD or to choose one of the 11 focus points, to advance or reverse display of a series of images during picture review, or to change the kind of photo information displayed on the screen. The OK button is used to confirm your choices, and also to enter movie-shooting mode when using Live View.

So, from time to time in this chapter (and throughout this book), I'll be referring to the multi-selector and its left/right/up/down buttons, and center OK button.

Setting the Clock

It's likely that your Nikon D90's internal clock hasn't been set to your local time, so you may need to do that first. (The in-camera clock might have been set for you by someone checking out your camera prior to delivery.) If you do need to set the clock, the flashing CLOCK indicator roughly in the center of the monochrome top panel LCD will be the giveaway. You'll find complete instructions for setting the four options for the date/time (time zone, actual date and time, the date format, and whether you want the D90 to conform to Daylight Savings Time) in Chapter 3. However, if you think you can handle this step without instruction, press the Menu button to the left of the LCD, and then use the multi-selector to scroll down to the Setup menu (it's marked with a wrench icon), press the multi-selector button to the right, and then press the down button to scroll down to World Time, and press the right button again. The options will appear on the screen that appears next. Keep in mind that you'll need to reset your camera's internal clock from time to time, as it is not 100 percent accurate. Of course, your camera will not explode if the internal clock is inaccurate, but your images will have the wrong time stamped on them. You may also need to reset your camera's internal clock if you travel and you want the time stamp on your pictures to reflect the time where the images were shot, and not the time back home.

Battery Included

Your Nikon D90 is a sophisticated hunk of machinery and electronics, but it needs a charged battery to function, so rejuvenating the EN-EL3e lithium-ion battery pack furnished with the camera should be your first step. A fully charged power source should be good for a minimum of 500 shots, based on standard tests defined by the Camera & Imaging Products Association (CIPA) document DC-002. In the real world, of course, the life of the battery will depend on how often you review the shots you've taken on the LCD screen, how many pictures you take with the built-in flash, and many other factors. You'll want to keep track of how many pictures *you* are able to take in your own typical circumstances, and use that figure as a guideline, instead.

A BATTERY AND A SPARE

I always recommend purchasing Nikon brand batteries (for about $40) over less-expensive third-party packs, even though the $30 substitute batteries may offer more capacity at a lower price (some top the 1,500 mAh offered by the Nikon battery). My reasoning is that it doesn't make sense to save $10 on a component for a sophisticated camera, especially since batteries have been known to fail in potentially harmful ways. You need only look as far as Nikon's own recall of its earlier EN-EL3 batteries, which forced the company to ship out thousands of free replacement cells. You're unlikely to get the same support from a third-party battery supplier that sells under a half-dozen or more different brand names, and may not even have an easy way to get the word out that a recall has been issued.

If your pictures are important to you, always have at least one spare battery available, and make sure it is an authentic Nikon product.

All rechargeable batteries undergo some degree of self-discharge just sitting idle in the camera or in the original packaging. Lithium-ion power packs of this type typically lose a small amount of their charge every day, even when the camera isn't turned on. Li-ion cells lose their power through a chemical reaction that continues when the camera is switched off. So, it's very likely that the battery purchased with your camera is at least partially pooped out, so you'll want to revive it before going out for some serious shooting.

Charging the Battery

When the battery is inserted into the MH-18a charger properly (it's impossible to insert it incorrectly), an orange Charge light begins flashing, and remains flashing until the status lamp glows steadily indicating that charging is finished (see Figure 1.4). When the battery is charged, slide the latch on the bottom of the camera and ease the battery in, as shown in Figure 1.5.

Figure 1.4
When the charger is plugged in, the flashing status light will illuminate while the battery is being charged.

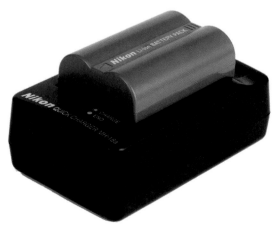

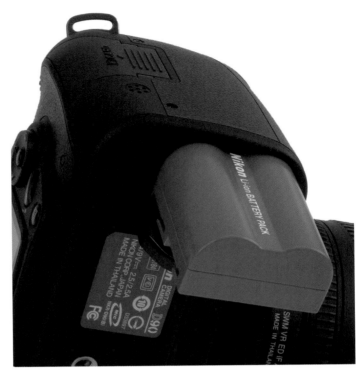

Figure 1.5
Insert the battery in the camera; it only fits one way.

Final Steps

Your Nikon D90 is almost ready to fire up and shoot. You'll need to select and mount a lens, adjust the viewfinder for your vision, and insert a Secure Digital card. Each of these steps is easy, and if you've used any Nikon before, you already know exactly what to do. I'm going to provide a little extra detail for those of you who are new to the Nikon or SLR worlds.

Mounting the Lens

As you'll see, my recommended lens mounting procedure emphasizes protecting your equipment from accidental damage and minimizing the intrusion of dust. If your D90 has no lens attached, select the lens you want to use and loosen (but do not remove) the rear lens cap. I generally place the lens I am planning to mount vertically in a slot in my camera bag, where it's protected from mishaps, but ready to pick up quickly. By loosening the rear lens cap, you'll be able to lift it off the back of the lens at the last instant, so the rear element of the lens is covered until then.

After that, remove the body cap by rotating the cap towards the release button. You should always mount the body cap when there is no lens on the camera, because it helps keep dust out of the interior of the camera. (While the D90's automatic sensor cleaning mechanism works fine, the less dust it has to contend with, the better.) The body cap also protects the camera's innards from damage caused by intruding objects (including your fingers, if you're not cautious).

Once the body cap has been removed, remove the rear lens cap from the lens, set it aside, and then mount the lens on the camera by matching the alignment indicator on the lens barrel with the white dot on the camera's lens mount (see Figure 1.6). Rotate the lens toward the shutter release until it seats securely. Some lenses are trickier to mount than others, especially telephoto lenses with special collars for attaching the lens itself to a tripod.

Figure 1.6
Match the indicator on the lens with the white dot on the camera mount to properly align the lens with the bayonet mount.

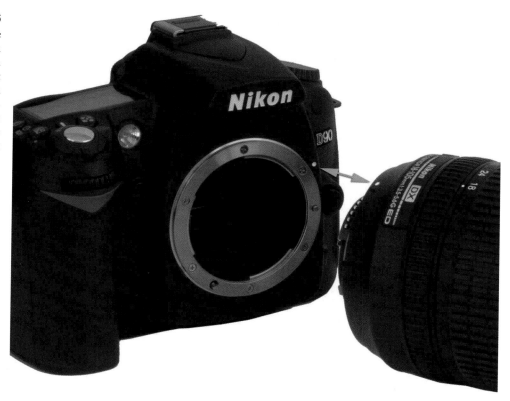

Set the focus mode switch on the lens to AF or M/A (Autofocus). If the lens hood is bayoneted on the lens in the reversed position (which makes the lens/hood combination more compact for transport), twist it off and remount with the "petals" (if present) facing outward (see Figure 1.7). A lens hood protects the front of the lens from accidental bumps, and reduces flare caused by extraneous light arriving at the front of the lens from outside the picture area.

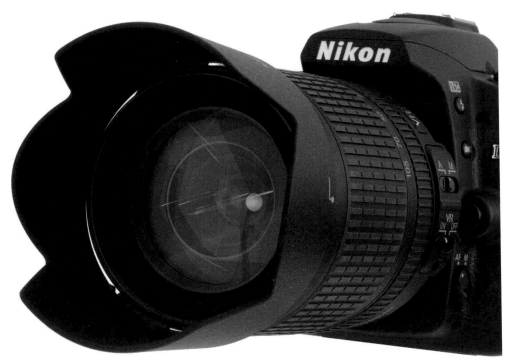

Figure 1.7
A lens hood protects the lens from extraneous light and accidental bumps.

Adjusting Diopter Correction

Those of us with less than perfect eyesight can often benefit from a little optical correction in the viewfinder. Your contact lenses or glasses may provide all the correction you need, but if you are a glasses wearer and want to use the D90 without your glasses, or to add further correction, you can take advantage of the camera's built-in diopter adjustment, which can be varied from −1.7 to +0.5 correction. Press the shutter release halfway to illuminate the indicators in the viewfinder, then rotate the diopter adjustment knob next to the viewfinder (see Figure 1.8) while looking through the viewfinder until the indicators appear sharp. Should the available correction be insufficient, Nikon offers nine different Diopter-Adjustment Viewfinder Correction lenses for the viewfinder window, ranging from -5 to +3, at a cost of $15-$20 each.

Inserting a Secure Digital Card

You may have set up your D90 so you can't take photos without a Secure Digital card inserted. (There is a No memory card entry, Custom Setting menu CSM #f6 that enables/disables shutter release functions when a memory card is absent—learn about that in Chapter 3.) So, your final step will be to insert a Secure Digital card. Slide the cover on the right side of the camera towards the back, and then open it. You should only remove the memory card when the camera is switched off, or, at the very least, the yellow-green card access light (just to the right of the LCD and INFO button on the back of the camera) that indicates the D90 is writing to the card is not illuminated.

Figure 1.8
Viewfinder diopter correction from −1.7 to +0.5 can be dialed in.

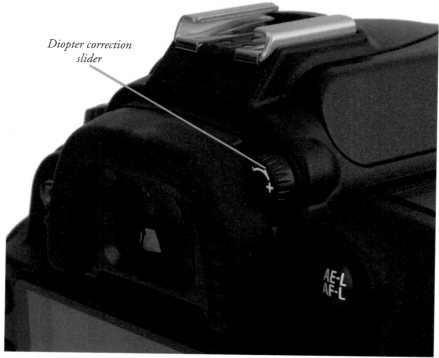

Diopter correction slider

MORE ABOUT CSM OPTIONS IN CHAPTER 3

You'll find a complete list of Custom Setting menu options and parameters in Chapter 3.

Insert the memory card with the label facing the back of the camera oriented so the edge with the gold edge connectors goes into the slot first (see Figure 1.9). Close the door, and, if this is your first use of the card, format it (described next). When you want to remove the memory card later, press the card inwards, and it will pop right out.

Formatting a Memory Card

There are four ways to create a blank Secure Digital card for your D90, and two of them are at least partially wrong. Here are your options, both correct and incorrect:

- **Transfer (move) files to your computer.** When you transfer (rather than copy) all the image files to your computer from the Secure Digital card (either using a direct cable transfer or with a card reader and appropriate software, as described later in this chapter), the old image files can, at your option, be erased from the card, leaving the card blank. Theoretically. Unfortunately, this method does *not* remove files that you've labeled as Protected (by pressing the Protect button to the right of the

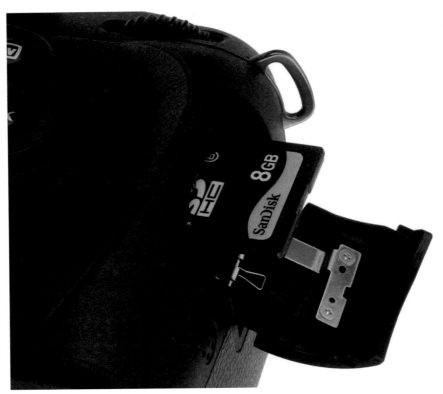

Figure 1.9
The Secure Digital card is inserted with the label facing the back of the camera.

viewfinder window [it's marked with a key icon] while viewing the image on the LCD), nor does it identify and lock out parts of your SD card that have become corrupted or unusable since the last time you formatted the card. Therefore, I recommend always formatting the card, rather than simply moving the image files, each time you want to make a blank card. The only exception is when you *want* to leave the protected/unerased images on the card for awhile longer, say, to share with friends, family, and colleagues.

- **(Don't) Format in your computer.** With the SD card inserted in a card reader or card slot in your computer, you can use Windows or Mac OS to reformat the memory card. Don't! The operating system won't necessarily arrange the structure of the card the way the D90 likes to see it (in computer terms, an incorrect *file system* may be installed). The only way to ensure that the card has been properly formatted for your camera is to perform the format in the camera itself. The only exception to this rule is when you have a seriously corrupted memory card that your camera refuses to format. Sometimes it is possible to revive such a corrupted card by allowing the operating system to reformat it first, then trying again in the camera.

■ **Setup menu format.** To use one of the recommended methods to format a memory card, press the Menu button, use the up/down buttons of the multi-selector (that thumb-pad-sized control to the right of the LCD) to choose the Setup menu (which is represented by that wrench icon), navigate to the Format memory card entry with the right button of the multi-selector, and select Yes from the screen that appears. Press OK (in the center of the multi-selector pad) to begin the format process.

■ **Format buttons.** To bypass the menus, you can hold down the two buttons labeled with the red Format indicator for about two seconds, until you see the For indicator on the top monochrome LCD. Then, press the buttons again to start the process. The buttons are located on top of the camera to the southwest of the shutter release, and on the upper-back edge (the "Trash" button). (See Figure 1.10.) You'll see the indicator For flash on the top monochrome LCD while the card is being formatted.

Figure 1.10
Press and hold down the Format button on top of the camera, and the second Format button on the back left side of the camera twice to format a memory card.

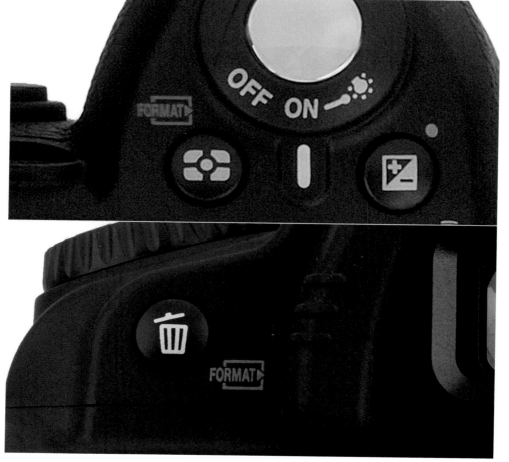

HOW MANY SHOTS?

The D90 provides a fairly accurate estimate of the number of shots remaining on the LCD, as well as at the lower-right edge of the viewfinder display when the display is active. (Tap the shutter release button to activate it.)

It is only an estimate, because the actual number will vary, depending on the capacity of your memory card, the file format(s) you've selected (more on those later), and the content of the image itself. (Some photos may contain large areas that can be more efficiently squeezed down to a smaller size.)

For example, a 2GB card can hold about 270 shots in the format known as JPEG Fine at the D90's maximum resolution (Large) format; 536 shots using the Normal JPEG setting; or more than 1,000 shots with Basic JPEG setting. When numbers exceed 1,000, the D90 displays a figure and decimal point, followed by a K superscript, so that 1,900 shots (or thereabouts) is represented by [1.9]^K on the LCD and viewfinder.

Table 1.1 shows the typical number of shots you can expect using a moderately-sized 8GB SD memory card (which I expect will be a popular size card among D90 users as prices continue to plummet during the life of this book). All figures are by actual count with my own 8GB SD card. Take those numbers and cut them in half if you're using a 4GB SD card; multiply by 25 percent if you're using a 2GB card, or by 12.5 percent if you're working with a 1GB SD card. (You can hold down the QUAL button on the left back side of the camera and rotate the main command dial to change the file/formats in column 1, and the sub command dial to change the image sizes in columns 2, 3, and 4.)

Table 1.1 Typical Shots with an 8GB Memory Card

	Large	Medium	Small
JPEG Fine	1,080	1908	4,200
JPEG Normal	2,144	3,704	7,725
JPEG Basic	4,000	7300	13,123
RAW	528	N/A	N/A
RAW+JPEG Fine	352	N/A	N/A
RAW+JPEG Normal	424	N/A	N/A
RAW+JPEF Basic	468	N/A	N/A

Release/Drive Modes

This shooting mode determines when (and how often) the D90 makes an exposure. If you're coming to the dSLR world from a point-and-shoot camera, you might have used a model that labels these options as Drive modes, dating back to the film era when cameras could be set for single-shot or "motor drive" (continuous) shooting modes. Your D90 has five release (shooting) modes: Single Shot, Continuous Shooting High (4.5 frames per second), Continuous Shooting Low (1 to 4 frames per second, chosen by the user), Self-Timer, Two-Second Delayed Remote, and Quick Response Remote. (The latter two require the use of the ML-L3 infrared remote control.) You'll find more on setting these modes in Chapter 2.

Selecting an Exposure Mode

The Nikon D90 has two types of exposure modes, Advanced modes, and a second set, which Nikon now labels Scene modes (originally they called Digital Vari-Program modes or DVP modes). The first two, Auto and Auto (Flash Off) are referred to as point-and-shoot modes by Nikon, but I've lumped them in with the other Scene modes.

The Advanced modes include Programmed-Auto (or Program mode), Aperture Priority Auto, Shutter Priority Auto, and Manual exposure mode. (I'll call these advanced modes PASM, for their initials, from time to time in this book.) These are the modes you'll use most often after you've learned all your D90's features, because they allow you to specify how the camera chooses its settings when making an exposure, for greater creative control.

The Scene modes take full control of the camera, make all the decisions for you, and don't allow you to override the D90's settings. They are most useful while you're learning to use the camera, because you can select an appropriate mode (Auto, Auto/No Flash, Portrait, Landscape, Sports, Close-up, or Night Portrait) and fire away. You'll end up with decent photos using appropriate settings, but your opportunities to use a little creativity (say, to overexpose an image to create a silhouette, or to deliberately use a slow shutter speed to add a little blur to an action shot) are minimal.

Choosing a Scene Mode

The seven Scene modes can be selected by rotating the mode dial on the top left of the Nikon D90 to the appropriate icon (shown in Figure 1.11):

■ **Auto.** In this mode, the D90 makes all the exposure decisions for you, and will pop up the internal flash if necessary under low-light conditions. The camera automatically focuses on the subject closest to the camera (unless you've set the lens to Manual focus), and the autofocus assist illuminator lamp on the front of the camera will light up to help the camera focus in low-light conditions.

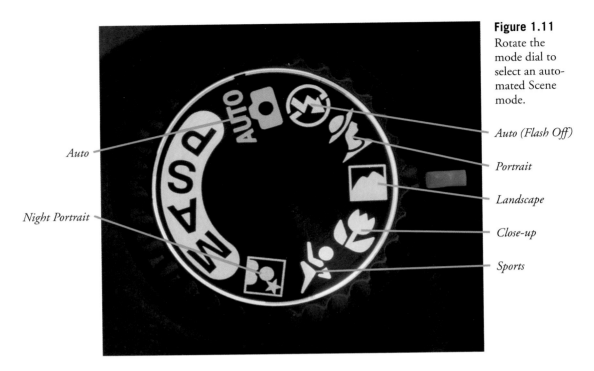

Figure 1.11
Rotate the mode dial to select an automated Scene mode.

Auto

Night Portrait

Auto (Flash Off)

Portrait

Landscape

Close-up

Sports

- **Auto (Flash Off).** Identical to Auto mode, except that the flash will not pop up under any circumstances. You'd want to use this in a museum, during religious ceremonies, concerts, or any environment where flash is forbidden or distracting.

- **Portrait.** Use this mode when you're taking a portrait of a subject standing relatively close to the camera and want to de-emphasize the background, maximize sharpness, and produce flattering skin tones. The built-in flash will pop up if needed.

- **Landscape.** Select this mode when you want extra sharpness and rich colors of distant scenes. The built-in flash and AF-assist illuminator are disabled.

- **Sports.** Use this mode to freeze fast-moving subjects. The D90 selects a fast shutter speed to stop action, and focuses continuously on the center focus point while you have the shutter release button pressed halfway. However, you can select one of the other two focus points to the left or right of the center by pressing the multi-selector left/right buttons. The built-in electronic flash and focus assist illuminator lamp are disabled.

- **Close-up.** This mode is helpful when you are shooting close-up pictures of a subject from about one foot away or less, such as flowers, bugs, and small items. The D90 focuses on the closest subject in the center of the frame, but you can use the multi-selector right and left buttons to focus on a different point. Use a tripod in this mode, as exposures may be long enough to cause blurring from camera movement. The built-in flash will pop up if needed.

■ **Night Portrait.** Choose this mode when you want to illuminate a subject in the foreground with flash (it will pop up automatically, if needed), but still allow the background to be exposed properly by the available light. The camera focuses on the closest main subject. Be prepared to use a tripod or a vibration-resistant lens like the 18-105mm VR kit lens to reduce the effects of camera shake. (You'll find more about VR and camera shake in Chapter 6.)

Choosing an Advanced Mode

If you're very new to digital photography, you might want to set the camera to P (Program mode) and start snapping away. That mode will make all the appropriate settings for you for many shooting situations. If you have more photographic experience, you might want to opt for one of the semi-automatic modes, or even Manual mode. These are described in more detail in Chapter 4. These advanced modes all let you apply a little more creativity to your camera's settings. Figure 1.12 shows the position of the modes described next.

■ **M (Manual).** Select when you want full control over the shutter speed and lens opening, either for creative effects or because you are using a studio flash or other flash unit not compatible with the D90's automatic flash metering.

Figure 1.12
Rotate the mode dial to select an advanced mode.

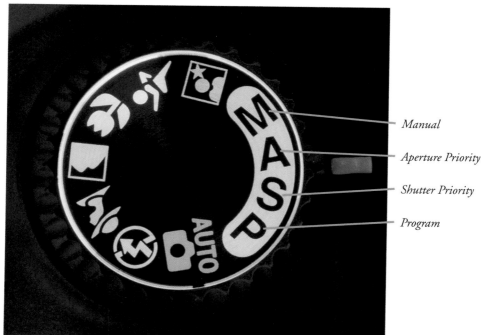

Manual

Aperture Priority

Shutter Priority

Program

- **A (Aperture Priority).** Choose when you want to use a particular lens opening, especially to control sharpness or how much of your image is in focus. Specify the f/stop you want, and the D90 will select the appropriate shutter speed for you.

- **S (Shutter Priority).** This mode is useful when you want to use a particular shutter speed to stop action or produce creative blur effects. Choose your preferred shutter speed, and the D90 will select the appropriate f/stop for you.

- **P (Program).** This mode allows the D90 to select the basic exposure settings, but you can still override the camera's choices to fine-tune your image, while maintaining metered exposure.

Choosing a Metering Mode

The metering mode you select while using one of the advanced modes determines how the D90 calculates exposure. You might want to select a particular metering mode for your first shots, although the default Matrix metering is probably the best choice as you get to know your camera. (It is used automatically in any of the D90's Scene modes.) I'll explain when and how to use each of the three metering modes later. To change metering modes, hold down the Metering Mode button (located on the top of the camera, just southwest of the shutter release button) and rotate the main command dial (see Figure 1.13).

- **Matrix metering.** The standard metering mode; the D90 attempts to intelligently classify your image and choose the best exposure based on readings from a 420-segment color CCD sensor that interprets light reaching the viewfinder using a database of hundreds of thousands of patterns.

- **Center-Weighted Averaging metering.** The D90 meters the entire scene, but gives the most emphasis to the central area of the frame, measuring about 8mm.

- **Spot metering.** Exposure is calculated from a smaller 3.5 mm central spot, about 2.5 percent of the image area.

You'll find a detailed description of each of these modes in Chapter 4.

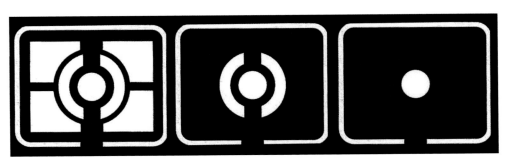

Figure 1.13
Metering modes are (left to right): Matrix, Center-Weighted, Spot.

Choosing Focus Options

The Nikon D90 can focus your pictures for you, or allow you to manually focus the image using the focus ring on the lens. (I'll help you locate this ring in Chapter 2.) Switching between Automatic and Manual focus is easy. You can move the AF/MF (Autofocus/Manual focus) or M/A-M (Manual Fine-tune Autofocus/Manual) switch on the lens mounted on your camera.

When using autofocus, you have additional choices. The D90 has 11 autofocus zones that can be used to focus in on a particular subject area in your image. (See Figure 1.14.) In addition, you can select *when* the D90 applies its focusing information to your image prior to exposure.

Figure 1.14
The D90 has 11 different autofocus points, here highlighted in red.

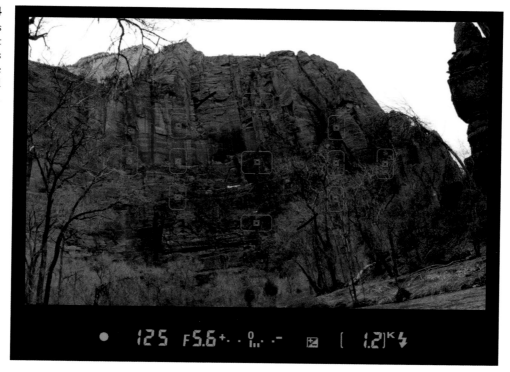

Selecting a Focus Mode

When you are using Program, Aperture Priority, Shutter Priority, or Manual exposure mode, you can select *when* the D90 measures and locks in focus prior to pressing the shutter release down all the way and taking the picture. Just follow these steps:

1. Press and hold the AF button (located on top of the camera, to the lower right of the monochrome status LCD).

2. Rotate the main command dial.

3. Select AF-A, AF-C, or AF-S, which will appear on the monochrome LCD on top of the camera.

Or, you can select Manual focus by sliding the AF/MF button on the front left of the camera body to the MF position, or by moving the M/A-M or AF/MF slider on the lens to M or MF. The four focus modes are as follows:

- **Automatic Autofocus (AF-A).** This default setting switches between AF-C and AF-S, as described below.

- **Continuous-Servo Autofocus (AF-C).** This mode, sometimes called *Continuous Autofocus*, sets focus when you partially depress the shutter button (or other autofocus activation button), but continues to monitor the frame and refocuses if the camera or subject is moved. This is a useful mode for photographing sports and moving subjects.

- **Single-Servo Autofocus (AF-S).** This mode, sometimes called *Single Autofocus*, locks in a focus point when the shutter button is pressed down halfway, and the focus confirmation light glows at bottom left in the viewfinder. The focus will remain locked until you release the button or take the picture. This mode is best when your subject is relatively motionless.

- **Manual focus (M).** When focus is set to Manual, you always focus manually using the focus ring on the lens. The focus confirmation indicator in the viewfinder provides an indicator when correct focus is achieved.

Note

Note that the Autofocus/Manual focus switch on the lens and the setting made in camera body must agree; if either is set to Manual focus, then the D90 defaults to Manual focus regardless of how the other is set.

Choosing Autofocus-Area Mode

I'll explain autofocus in more depth in Chapter 5, but you can still learn to set the AF-Area mode now.

1. Press the Menu button, and press the left multi-selector button to highlight the column of icons down the left side of the menu screen.

2. Press the up/down keys to navigate to the Custom Menu (indicated by a Pencil icon).

3. Press the right multi-selector key twice to choose Autofocus, and then the down key to select Custom Menu Setting a1 (CSM #a1), AF-Area mode. Press the right key to view the four selections available.

4. Choose the AF-Area Mode (described next), and press the OK button to select the option.

5. Press the Menu button again (or just tap the shutter release button) to exit the menu.

The four modes, described in more detail in Chapter 5, are as follows:

- **Single point.** You always choose which of the 11 points are used, and the Nikon D90 sticks with that focus bracket, no matter what. This mode is best for non-moving subjects.

- **Dynamic area.** You can choose which of the 11 focus zones to use, but the D90 will switch to another focus mode when using AF-C or AF-A mode (described next) and the subject moves. This mode is great for sports or active children.

- **Auto-Area.** This default mode chooses the focus point for you, and can use distance information when working with a lens that has a G or D suffix in its name. (See Chapter 6 for more on the difference between G/D lenses and other kinds of lenses.)

- **3D Tracking (11 points).** You can select the focus zone, but when not using AF-S mode, the camera refocuses on the subject if you reframe the image.

Adjusting White Balance and ISO

There are a few other settings you can make if you're feeling ambitious, but don't feel ashamed if you postpone using these features until you've racked up a little more experience with your D90.

If you like, you can custom-tailor your white balance (color balance) and ISO (sensitivity) settings. I'll explain more about what these settings are, and why you might want to change them, in Chapter 3. To start out, it's best to set white balance (WB) to Auto, and ISO to ISO 200 for daylight photos, and ISO 400 for pictures in dimmer light. (Don't be afraid of ISO 1600, however; the D90 does a *much* better job of producing low-noise photos at higher ISOs than most other cameras.) You'll find complete recommendations for both these settings in Chapter 4. You can adjust either one now by holding down the ISO or WB buttons on the left side of the back of the camera, and rotating the main command dial until the setting you want to use is displayed on the top panel monochrome LCD.

Reviewing the Images You've Taken

The Nikon D90 has a broad range of playback and image review options, and I'll cover them in more detail in Chapter 3. For now, you'll want to learn just the basics. Here is all you really need to know at this time, as shown in Figure 1.15:

- Press the Playback button (marked with a white right-pointing triangle) at the upper-left corner of the back of the camera to display the most recent image on the LCD.

- Spin the main command dial left or right to review additional images. You can also use the multi-selector left/right buttons. Press right to advance to the next image, or left to go back to a previous image.

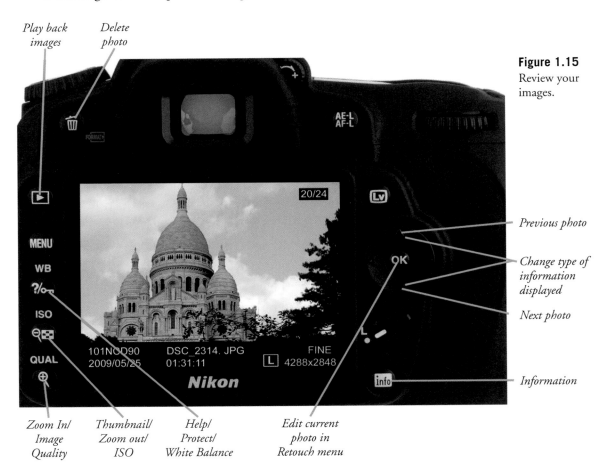

Figure 1.15
Review your images.

Play back images

Delete photo

Previous photo

Change type of information displayed

Next photo

Information

Zoom In/ Image Quality

Thumbnail/ Zoom out/ ISO

Help/ Protect/ White Balance

Edit current photo in Retouch menu

- Press the multi-selector button up or down to change among overlays of basic image information or detailed shooting information.

- Press the Zoom button repeatedly to zoom in on the image displayed; the Zoom Out button reduces the image. A thumbnail representation of the whole image appears in the lower-right corner with a yellow rectangle showing the relative level of zoom. At intermediate zoom positions, the yellow rectangle can be moved around within the frame using the multi-selector.

- Press the Protect button to mark an image and shield it from accidental erasure (but not from reformatting of the memory card).

- Press the Trash button twice to remove the photo currently being displayed.

- Press the Playback button again, or just tap the shutter release button to exit playback view.

You'll find information on viewing thumbnail indexes of images, automated playback, and other options in Chapter 3.

Using the Built-in Flash

Working with the D90's built-in flash (as well as external flash units like the Nikon SB-400) deserves a chapter of its own, and I'm providing one (see Chapter 7). But the built-in flash is easy enough to work with that you can begin using it right away, either to provide the main lighting of a scene or as supplementary illumination to fill in the shadows.

The built-in flash will pop up automatically as required in Auto, Portrait, Close-up, and Night Portrait DVP/Scene modes. To use the built-in flash in Manual, Aperture Priority, Shutter Priority, or Program modes, just press the flash pop-up button (shown in Figure 1.16). When the flash is fully charged, a lightning bolt symbol will flash at the right side of the viewfinder display. When using P (Program) and A (Aperture Priority) exposure modes, the D90 will select a shutter speed for you automatically from the range 1/200 to 1/60 seconds. In S (Shutter Priority) and M (Manual) modes, you select the shutter speed from 1/200 to 30 seconds.

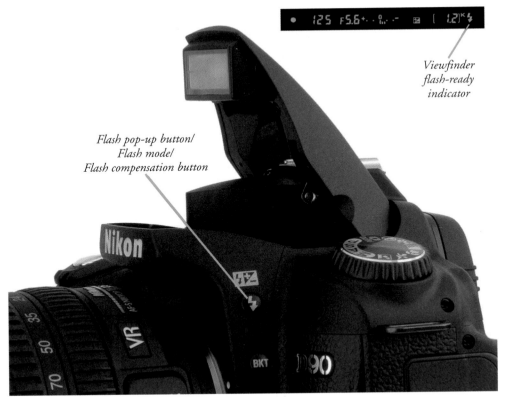

Figure 1.16
The pop-up
electronic flash
can be used as
the main light
source or for
supplemental
illumination.

*Viewfinder
flash-ready
indicator*

*Flash pop-up button/
Flash mode/
Flash compensation button*

Transferring Photos to Your Computer

The final step in your picture-taking session will be to transfer the photos you've taken to your computer for printing, further review, or image editing. Your D90 allows you to print directly to PictBridge-compatible printers and to create print orders right in the camera, plus you can select which images to transfer to your computer. I'll outline those options in Chapter 3.

I always recommend using a card reader attached to your computer to transfer files, because that process is generally a lot faster and doesn't drain the D90's battery. However, you can also use a cable for direct transfer, which may be your only option when you have the cable and a computer, but no card reader (perhaps you're using the computer of a friend or colleague, or at an Internet café).

To transfer images from the camera to a Mac or PC computer using the USB cable:

1. Turn off the camera.

2. Pry back the rubber cover that protects the D90's USB port, and plug the USB cable furnished with the camera into the USB port (see Figure 1.17).

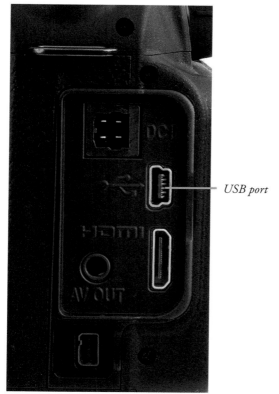

USB port

3. Connect the other end of the USB cable to a USB port on your computer.

4. Turn on the camera. The operating system itself, or installed software such as Nikon Transfer or Adobe Photoshop Elements Transfer usually detects the camera and offers to copy or move the pictures. Or, the camera appears on your desktop as a mass storage device, enabling you to drag and drop the files to your computer.

To transfer images from a Secure Digital card to the computer using a card reader, as shown in Figure 1.18, do the following:

1. Turn off the camera.

2. Slide open the memory card door, press the edge of the card in, and it will pop out so you can remove the SD card from the camera.

3. Insert the Secure Digital card into your memory card reader. Your installed software detects the files on the card and offers to transfer them. The card can also appear as a mass storage device on your desktop, which you can open and then drag and drop the files to your computer.

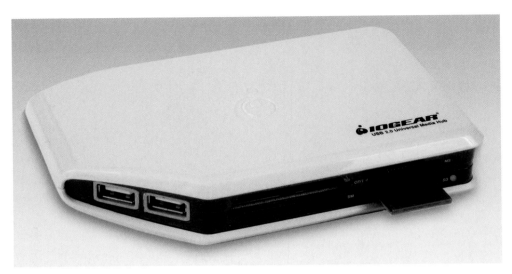

Figure 1.18
A card reader is
the fastest way
to transfer
photos.

2

Nikon D90 Roadmap

With the D90, Nikon has done a rather amazing job of creating a super-compact digital SLR that retains the convenience and easy access to essential controls. Its layout simplifies options through a clever arrangement of two dials, a thumb pad, and about a dozen logically laid out buttons. Most of the Nikon D90's key functions and settings that are changed frequently can be accessed directly using the array of dials, buttons, and knobs that populate the camera's surface, or through the Quick Settings screen on the LCD. With so many quick-access controls available, you'll find that the bulk of your shooting won't be slowed down by a visit to the vast thicket of text options called Menu-land.

If you want to operate your D90 efficiently, you'll need to learn the location, function, and application of all these controls. What you really need is a street-level roadmap that shows where everything is, and how it's used. But what Nikon gives you in the user's manual is akin to a world globe with an overall view and many cross-references to the pages that will tell you what you really need to know. Check out the Getting to Know the Camera pages in Nikon's manual, which compress views of the front, back, top, and bottom of the D90 into tiny drawings with more than 57 callouts pointing to various buttons and dials crammed into the illustrations. If you can find the control you want within this cramped layout, you'll still need to flip back and forth among multiple pages (individual buttons can have several different cross-references!) to locate the information.

Most other third-party books follow this format, featuring black-and-white photos or line drawings of front, back, and top views, and many labels. I originated the up-close-and-personal, full-color, street-level roadmap (rather than a satellite view) that I use in this book and my previous camera guidebooks. I provide you with many different views, like the one shown in Figure 2.1, and lots of explanation accompanying each zone of the camera, so that by the time you finish this chapter, you'll have a basic understanding of every control and what it does. I'm not going to delve into menu functions here—you'll find a discussion of your setup, shooting, and playback menu options in Chapter 3. Everything here is devoted to the button pusher and dial twirler in you.

You'll also find this "roadmap" chapter a good guide to the rest of the book, as well. I'll try to provide as much detail here about the use of the main controls as I can, but some topics (such as autofocus and exposure) are too complex to address in depth right away. So, I'll point you to the relevant chapters that discuss things like setup options, exposure, use of electronic flash, and working with lenses with the occasional cross-reference.

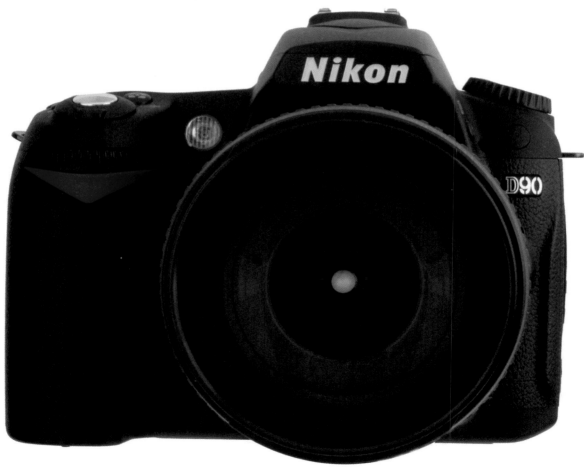

Figure 2.1

Nikon D90: Front View

This is the side of the D90 seen by your victims as you snap away. For the photographer, though, the front is the surface your fingers curl around as you hold the camera, and there are really only a few buttons to press, all within easy reach of the fingers of your left and right hands. There are additional controls on the lens itself. You'll need to look at several different views to see everything.

Figure 2.2 shows a front view of the Nikon D90 from a 45-degree angle. The main components you need to know about are as follows:

- **Shutter release.** Angled on top of the handgrip is the shutter release button, which has multiple functions. Press this button down halfway to lock exposure and focus. Press it down all the way to actually take a photo or sequence of photos if you're using the Continuous Shooting mode. Tapping the shutter button when the D90's exposure meters have turned themselves off reactivates them, and a tap can be used to remove the display of a menu or image from the rear color LCD.

- **On/Off switch.** Turns the D90 on or off. When rotated all the way towards the outer edge of the camera, turns on a lamp that illuminates the top-panel monochrome control panel LCD for a few seconds.

Figure 2.2

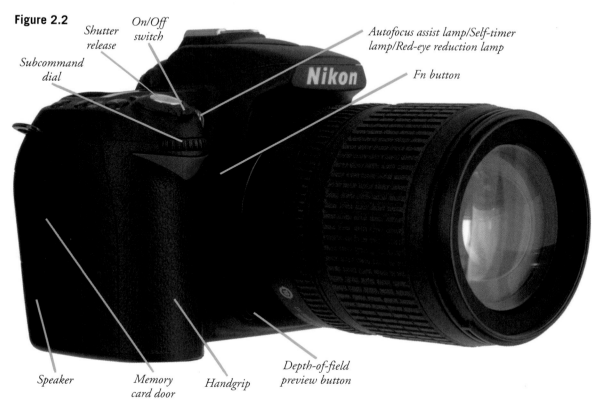

Shutter release

On/Off switch

Autofocus assist lamp/Self-timer lamp/Red-eye reduction lamp

Subcommand dial

Fn button

Speaker

Memory card door

Handgrip

Depth-of-field preview button

■ **Red-eye reduction/Self-timer/Autofocus assist lamp.** This LED provides a blip of light shortly before a flash exposure to cause the subjects' pupils to close down, reducing the effect of red-eye reflections off their retinas. When using the self-timer, this lamp also flashes to mark the countdown until the photo is taken, and serves to provide some extra illumination in dark environments to assist the autofocus system.

■ **Subcommand dial.** Provides secondary adjustments for functions with two settings. For example, when using the main command dial (on the back of the camera) to change the shutter speed in Manual exposure mode, the subcommand dial is used to adjust the aperture.

■ **Handgrip.** This provides a comfortable handhold, and also contains the D90's battery.

■ **Memory card door.** Slide this door toward the back of the camera to provide access to the SD memory card slot.

■ **Speaker.** Plays back monaural sound from movies.

■ **Fn (Function) button.** This conveniently located button can be programmed to perform any one of several functions (including changing the metering mode, disabling the built-in electronic flash, or changing the autofocus area mode).

■ **Depth-of-Field (DOF) Preview button.** When held down, closes the lens opening to the aperture that will be used to take the picture, so you can better see the approximate range of sharpness in your final image.

You'll find more controls on the other side of the D90, shown in Figures 2.3 and 2.4. The main points of interest shown include:

■ **Infrared sensor.** You can trigger the D90 remotely using the optional ML-L3 infrared remote control, which is detected by this sensor.

■ **Lens release button.** Press this button to unlock the lens, and then rotate it away from the shutter release button to dismount your optics.

■ **Microphone.** Records monaural sound when shooting movies.

■ **Bracket button.** Hold down this button to choose the number of shots to be bracketed (rotate the main command dial) and the bracket increment (rotate the subcommand dial). You can shoot two or three images with bracketed settings for exposure, flash exposure, white balance, and Active D-Lighting. Chapters 3 and 4 explain this feature in more detail.

■ **Autofocus/Manual focus switch.** Changes from Autofocus to Manual focus.

Figure 2.3

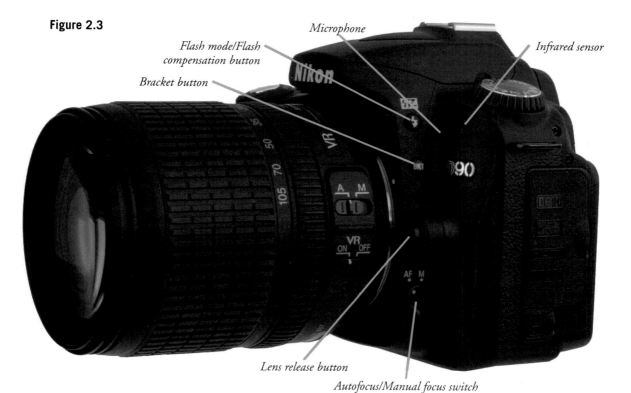

Microphone

Flash mode/Flash
compensation button

Bracket button

Infrared sensor

Lens release button

Autofocus/Manual focus switch

- **Flash mode/Flash compensation button.** This button releases the built-in flash so it can flip up and start the charging process. If you decide you do not want to use the flash, you can turn it off by pressing the flash head back down. Hold down this button while spinning the command dial to chose a flash mode. I'll explain how to use the various flash modes (red-eye reduction, front/rear curtain sync, and slow sync) in Chapter 7, along with some tips for adjusting flash exposure.

- **Pop-up flash.** The flash elevates from the top of the camera (see Figure 2.4), theoretically reducing the chances of red-eye reflections, because the higher light source is less likely to reflect back from your subjects' eyes into the camera lens. In practice, the red-eye effect is still possible (and likely), and can be further minimized with the D90's red-eye reduction lamp (which flashes before the exposure, causing the subjects' pupils to contract), and the after-shot, red-eye elimination offered in the Retouch menu. (Your image editor may also have anti-red-eye tools.) Of course, the best strategy is to use an external speedlight that mounts on the accessory shoe on top of the camera (and thus is even higher) or a flash that is off-camera entirely.

Figure 2.4

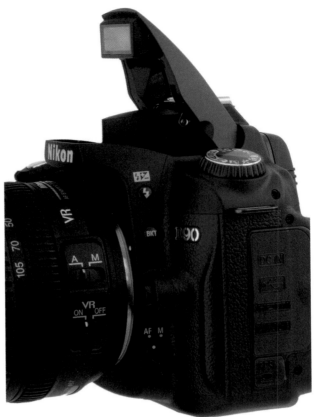

The main feature on the side of the Nikon D90 is a rubber cover (see Figure 2.5) that protects the two connector ports and reset button underneath from dust and moisture. The features, shown in Figure 2.6, with the rubber cover removed, are as follows:

- **DC power.** Connect the optional EH-5a DC power connector plugs in here, for use when you want to operate the D90 for extended periods without relying on battery power.

- **USB port.** Plug in the USB cable furnished with your Nikon D90 and connect the other end to a USB port in your computer to transfer photos, or to interface with the Nikon Camera Control Pro software described in Chapter 8.

- **HDMI port.** You need to buy an accessory cable (a C mini-pin HDMI cable available from third-party suppliers) to connect your D90 to an HDTV, as one to fit this port is not provided with the camera. If you have a high-resolution television, it's worth the expenditure to be able to view your camera's output in all its glory.

- **Video port.** You can link this connector with a television to view your photos on a large screen.

Figure 2.5

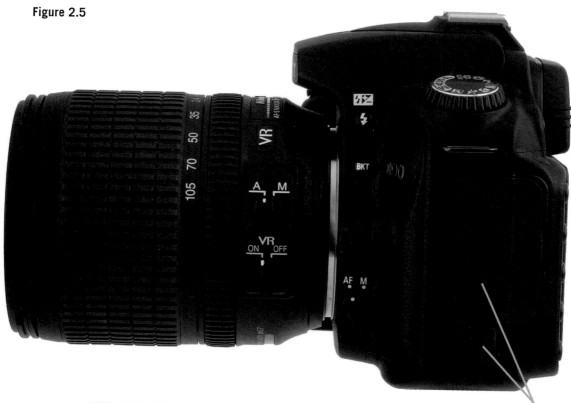

*Covers for power,
USB, HDMI, AV,
remote release, and
GPS connectors*

Figure 2.6

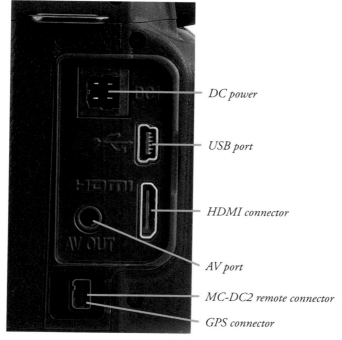

DC power

USB port

HDMI connector

AV port

MC-DC2 remote connector

GPS connector

- **GPS/Remote release connector.** You can plug in the GP-1CA90 cable from the Nikon GPS-1 geotagging accessory here to embed latitude, longitude, and altitude information in your images. The Nikon MC-DC2 remote release also can be plugged in here, or into the GP-1CA90 cable, which has a pass-through connection to allow use of both devices at once.

The Nikon D90's Business End

The back panel of the Nikon D90 (see Figure 2.7) bristles with almost a dozen different controls, buttons, and knobs. That might seem like a lot of controls to learn, but you'll find that it's a lot easier to press a dedicated button and spin a dial than to jump to a menu every time you want to access one of these features.

Figure 2.7

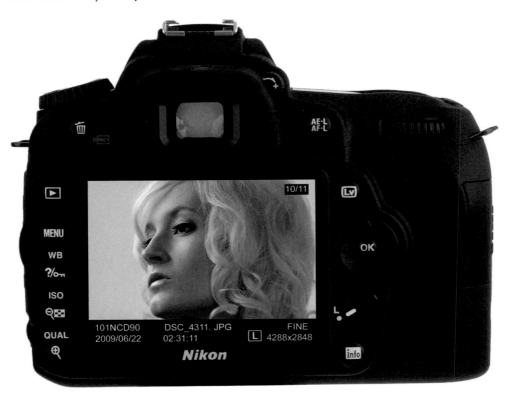

You can see the controls clustered along the top edge of the back panel in Figure 2.8. The key buttons and components and their functions are as follows:

- **Viewfinder eyecup.** You can frame your composition by peering into the viewfinder. It's surrounded by a soft rubber eyecup that seals out extraneous light when pressing your eye tightly up to the viewfinder, and it also protects your eyeglass lenses (if worn) from scratching. It can be removed and replaced by the

DK-5 eyepiece cap when you use the camera on a tripod, to ensure that light coming from the back of the camera doesn't venture inside and possibly affect the exposure reading. Shielding the viewfinder with your hand may be more convenient (unless you're using the self-timer to get in the photo yourself).

■ **Diopter adjustment knob.** Rotate this wheel to adjust the diopter correction for your eyesight, as described in Chapter 1.

■ **AE-L/AF-L lock.** When shooting pictures, the button locks the exposure or focus that the camera sets when you partially depress the shutter button. The exposure lock indication (AE-L icon) appears at bottom left in the viewfinder. If you want to recalculate exposure or autofocus with the shutter button still partially depressed, press the button again. The exposure/autofocus will be unlocked when you release the shutter button or take the picture. To retain the exposure/autofocus lock for subsequent photos, keep the button pressed while shooting.

■ **Main command dial.** The command dial is used to set or adjust many functions, such as shutter speed, ISO value, or image quality. It is used in conjunction with the subcommand dial on the front of the camera when adjusting features with two parameters, such as shutter speed/aperture, number of bracketed shots/bracket increment, and so forth.

■ **Trash/Format #1 button.** Press twice when viewing an image on the LCD to erase that image. Hold down this button and the Format #2 button (the Metering Mode button on top of the camera) for about two seconds, then release when the For message flashes on the top LCD, then hold down again to reformat your memory card.

Figure 2.8

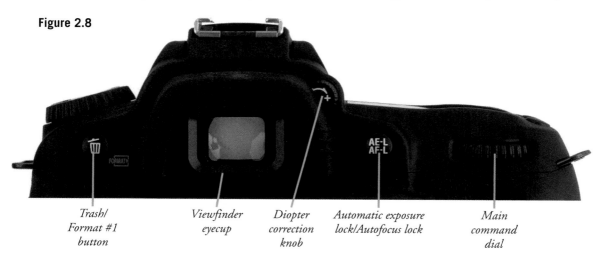

Trash/
Format #1
button

Viewfinder
eyecup

Diopter
correction
knob

Automatic exposure
lock/Autofocus lock

Main
command
dial

You'll be using the five buttons to the left of the LCD monitor (shown in Figure 2.9) quite frequently, so learn their functions now.

- **Playback button.** Press this button to review images you've taken, using the controls and options I'll explain in the next section. To remove the displayed image, press the Playback button again, or simply tap the shutter release button.

- **Menu button.** Summons/exits the menu displayed on the rear LCD of the D90. When you're working with submenus, this button also serves to exit a submenu and return to the main menu.

- **White balance/Help/Protect Image.** Hold down this button and rotate the main command dial to change the white balance settings shown on the top-panel monochrome control panel LCD. Press the button when a menu item is highlighted to produce a brief screen that describes the function of that item. When reviewing a picture on the LCD, press once to protect the image, and a second time to unprotect it. A key symbol appears when the image is displayed to show that it is protected. (This feature safeguards an image from erasure when deleting or transferring pictures only; when you format a card, protected images are removed along with all the others.)

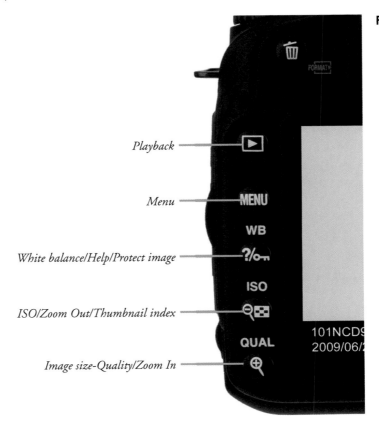

Figure 2.9

Playback

Menu

White balance/Help/Protect image

ISO/Zoom Out/Thumbnail index

Image size-Quality/Zoom In

- **ISO/Thumbnail/Zoom Out.** Hold down this button and rotate the main command dial to change the ISO sensitivity settings, shown on the top-panel monochrome control panel LCD. In Playback mode, use this button to zoom out of an image that is magnified, or to change from full-screen view to six or nine thumbnails. I'll explain zooming and other playback options in the next section.

- **QUAL/Zoom In button.** Hold down this button and rotate the main dial to change the Image Quality settings. An indicator on the top-panel monochrome control panel LCD will cycle among RAW, JPEG Fine, JPEG Normal, JPEG Basic, RAW+Fine, RAW+Normal, and RAW+Basic. Rotate the subcommand dial to cycle among Large, Medium, and Small resolutions. In Playback mode, press to zoom in on an image.

More controls reside on the right side of the back panel, as shown in Figure 2.10. The key controls and their functions are as follows:

- **LCD.** View your images and navigate through the menus on this screen.

- **Live View button.** Press this button to activate Live View; press a second time to turn off Live View.

- **Multi-selector.** This joypad-like button can be shifted up/down and side to side to provide several functions, including AF point selection, scrolling around a magnified image, or trimming a photo. Within menus, pressing the up/down buttons moves the on-screen cursor up or down; pressing towards the right selects the highlighted item and displays its options; pressing left cancels and returns to the previous menu.

- **OK button.** Use this button to confirm a selection. When working with menus, press the Menu button instead to back out without making a selection. When using Live View mode, this button activates the movie-making feature; press a second time to stop motion picture capture.

- **Memory card access lamp.** When lit or blinking, this lamp indicates that the memory card is being accessed.

- **Lock/unlock focus point selection.** Turn to the L setting to lock the focus point at its current position. Turn to the • position, and you can then move the active focus point around among the 11 available points when using Single Point, Dynamic Area, or 3D Tracking (11 points) focus zone selection (as described in Chapter 5).

- **Info display/Quick Settings Display button.** Use this button to show/hide basic shooting information on the color LCD, and to make some settings changes, such as noise reduction, picture controls, and button assignments.

Figure 2.10

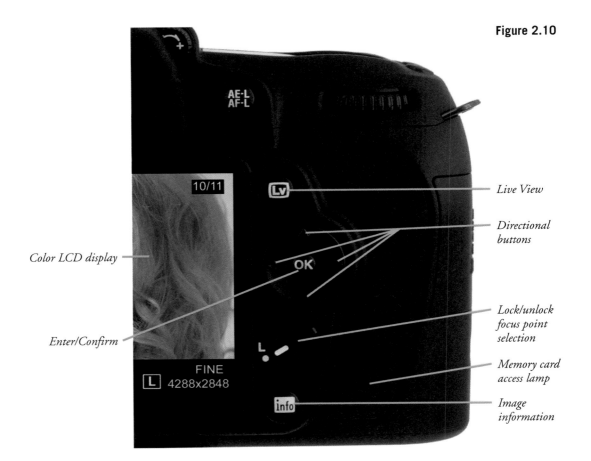

Live View

Directional buttons

Color LCD display

Enter/Confirm

Lock/unlock focus point selection

Memory card access lamp

Image information

Playing Back Images

Reviewing images is a joy on the Nikon D90's big three-inch LCD. Here are the basics involved in reviewing images on the LCD screen (or on a television screen you have connected with a cable). You'll find more details about some of these functions later in this chapter, or, for more complex capabilities, in the chapters that I point you to. This section just lists the must-know information.

- **Start review.** To begin review, press the Playback button at the upper-left corner of the back of the D90. The most-recently viewed image will appear on the LCD.

- **Playback folder.** Image review generally shows you the images in the currently selected folder on your memory card. A given card can contain several folders (a new one is created anytime you exceed 999 images in the current folder). You can use the Playback folder menu option in the Playback menu (as I'll explain in Chapter 3) to select a specific folder, or direct the D90 to display images from all the folders on the memory card.

■ **View thumbnail images.** To change the view from a single image to four or nine thumbnails, follow the instructions in the "Viewing Thumbnails" section that follows.

■ **Zoom in and out.** To zoom in or out, press the Zoom button, following the instructions in the "Zooming the Nikon D90 Playback Display" in the next section. (It also shows you how to move the zoomed area around using the multi-selector pad.)

■ **Move back and forth.** To advance to the next image, press the right edge of the multi-selector pad; to go back to a previous shot, press the left edge. When you reach the beginning/end of the photos in your folder, the display "wraps around" to the end/beginning of the available shots.

■ **See different types of data.** To change the type of information about the displayed image that is shown, press the up and down portions of the multi-selector pad. To learn what data is available, read the "Working with Photo Information" section later in this chapter.

■ **Retouch image.** Press the OK button while a single image is displayed on the screen to jump to the Retouch menu to modify that photograph. (I'll explain the workings of the Retouch menu in Chapter 3.)

■ **Remove images.** To delete an image that's currently on the screen, press the Trash button once, and then press it again to confirm the deletion. To select and delete a group of images, use the Delete option in the Playback menu to specify particular photos to remove, as described in more detail in Chapter 3.

■ **Cancel playback.** To cancel image review, press the Playback button again, or simply tap the shutter release button.

Zooming the Nikon D90 Playback Display

Here's how to zoom in and out on your images during picture review:

1. When an image is displayed (use the Playback button to start), press the Zoom In button to fill the screen with a slightly magnified version of the image. You can keep pressing the Zoom In button to magnify a portion of the image up to 6.7X.

2. A navigation window appears in the lower-right corner of the LCD showing the entire image. Keep pressing to continue zooming in.

3. A yellow box in the navigation window shows the zoomed area within the full image. The entire navigation window vanishes from the screen after a few seconds, leaving you with a full-screen view of the zoomed portion of the image.

4. Use the command dial to move to the same zoomed area of the next/previous image.

5. Use the Zoom Out/Thumbnail button to zoom back out of the image.

6. Use the multi-selector buttons to move the zoomed area around within the image. The navigation window will reappear for reference when zooming or scrolling around within the display.

7. The display will place white borders around up to 10 faces detected while zooming. The white boxes will appear within the yellow box that indicates the zoomed area. You can rotate the subcommand dial to scroll among the detected faces (see Figure 2.11).

8. To exit Zoom In/Zoom Out display, keep pressing the Zoom Out button until the full-screen/full-image/information display appears again. If you continue pressing the Zoom Out button from the full-screen view, you'll be shown four, nine, and 72 thumbnails, plus a Calendar view. These are all described in the next section.

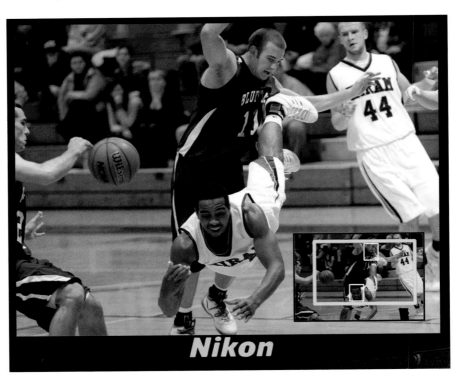

Figure 2.11
The D90 incorporates a small thumbnail image with a yellow box showing the current zoom area.

Viewing Thumbnails

The Nikon D90 provides other options for reviewing images in addition to zooming in and out. You can switch between single image view and either four, nine, or 72 reduced-size thumbnail images on a single LCD screen.

Pages of thumbnail images offer a quick way to scroll through a large number of pictures quickly to find the one you want to examine in more detail. The D90 lets you switch quickly from single- to four- to nine- to 72-image views, with a scroll bar displayed at the right side of the screen to show you the relative position of the displayed thumbnails within the full collection of images in the active folder on your memory card. Figure 2.12 offers a comparison between the three levels of thumbnail views. The Zoom In and Zoom Out/Thumbnail buttons are used.

- **Add thumbnails.** To increase the number of thumbnails on the screen, press the Zoom Out button. The D90 will switch from single image to four thumbnails to nine thumbnails to 72 thumbnails, and then to Calendar view (discussed next). Additional presses in Calendar view toggles back and forth between highlighting calendar dates, or showing pictures taken on that date (see "Working with Calendar View," next). (The display doesn't cycle back to single image again).

- **Reduce number of thumbnails.** To decrease the number of thumbnails on the screen, press the Zoom In button to change from Calendar view to 72 to nine thumbnails to four thumbnails, or from four to single-image display. Continuing to press the Zoom In button once you've returned to single-image display starts the zoom process described in the previous section.

- **Change highlighted thumbnail area.** Use the multi-selector (or the main and sub-command dials) to move the yellow highlight box around among the thumbnails.

- **Protect and delete images.** When viewing thumbnails or a single-page image, press the Protect button to preserve the image against accidental deletion (a key icon is overlaid over the full-page image) or the Trash button (twice) to erase it.

- **Exit image review.** Tap the shutter release button or press the Playback button to exit image review. You don't have to worry about missing a shot because you were reviewing images; a half-press of the shutter release automatically brings back the D90's exposure meters, the autofocus system, and cancels image review.

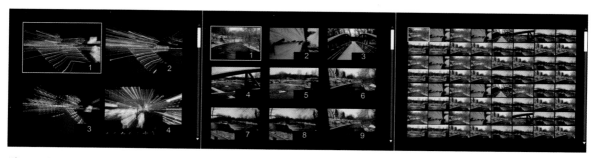

Figure 2.12 Switch between four thumbnails (left),nine thumbnails (center), or 72 thumbnails (right), by pressing the Zoom Out and Zoom In buttons.

Working with Calendar View

Once in Calendar view, you can sort through images arranged by the date they were taken. This feature is especially useful when you're traveling and want to see only the pictures you took in, say, a particular city on a certain day.

- **Change dates.** Use the multi-selector keys or main dial and subcommand dial to move through the date list. If your memory card has pictures taken on a highlighted date, they will be arrayed in a scrolling list at the right side of the screen (see Figure 2.13).

- **View a date's images.** Press the Zoom In button to toggle between the date list to the scrolling Thumbnail List of images taken on that date. When viewing the Thumbnail List, you can use the multi-selector up/down keys to scroll through the available images.

- **Preview an image.** In the Thumbnail List, when you've highlighted an image you want to look at, press the Zoom In button to see an enlarged view of that image without leaving the Calendar View mode. The zoomed image replaces the date list.

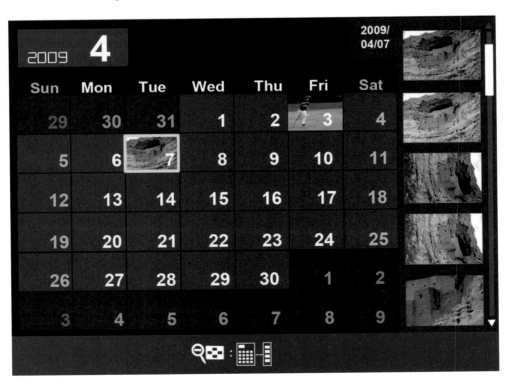

Figure 2.13
Calendar view allows you to browse through all images on your memory card taken on a certain date.

- **Delete images.** Pressing the Trash button deletes a highlighted image in the Thumbnail List. In the Date List view, pressing the Trash button removes all the images taken on that date (use with caution!).

- **Exit Calendar view.** In Thumbnail view, if you highlight an image and press the OK button, you'll exit Calendar view and the highlighted image will be shown on the LCD in the display mode you've chosen. (See "Working with Photo Information" to learn about the various display modes.) In Date List view, pressing the Zoom In button exits Calendar view and returns to 72 thumbnails view. You can also exit Calendar view by tapping the shutter release (to turn off the LCD for shooting) or by pressing the Menu button.

Working with Photo Information

When reviewing an image on the screen, your D90 can supplement the image itself with a variety of shooting data, ranging from basic information presented at the bottom of the LCD display, to three text overlays that detail virtually every shooting option you've selected. This section will show you the type of information available. Most of the data is self-explanatory, so the labels in the accompanying figures should tell you most of what you need to know. To change to any of these views while an image is on the screen in Playback mode, press the multi-selector up/down buttons (unless you've swapped the up/down functions with the left/right functions in the Custom Settings menu). Here's the order in which the screens are displayed when you press the multi-selector down button:

- **File information.** The basic full-image review display is officially called the File Information screen, and looks like Figure 2.14.

- **RGB histogram.** This shows the image accompanied by a brightness histogram, as well as red, green, and blue histograms, which you can see in Figure 2.15. The histogram is a kind of chart that represents an image's exposure, and how the darkest areas, brightest areas, and middle tones have been captured. Histograms are easy to work with, and I'll show you how in Chapter 4.

- **Highlights.** When the Highlights display is active (see Figure 2.16), any overexposed areas will be indicated by a flashing black border. As I am unable to make the printed page flash, you'll have to check out this effect for yourself.

- **Shooting Data 1.** This screen tells you everything else you might want to know about a picture you've taken, including metering mode, exposure mode, exposure compensation, lens information, and all the details of any built-in or external dedicated flash units you might have used. I'm not providing any labels in Figure 2.17, because the information in the first eight lines in the screen should be obvious as you read about metering, exposure modes, lens focal lengths, and flash modes in this book.

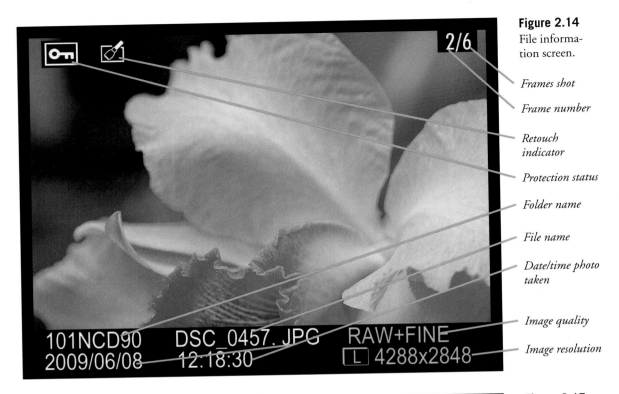

Figure 2.14
File informa-
tion screen.

Frames shot

Frame number

*Retouch
indicator*

Protection status

Folder name

File name

*Date/time photo
taken*

Image quality

Image resolution

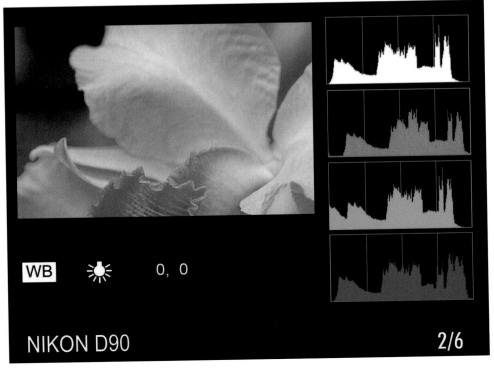

Figure 2.15
Brightness/
RGB histograms
screen.

Figure 2.16
Highlights
screen.

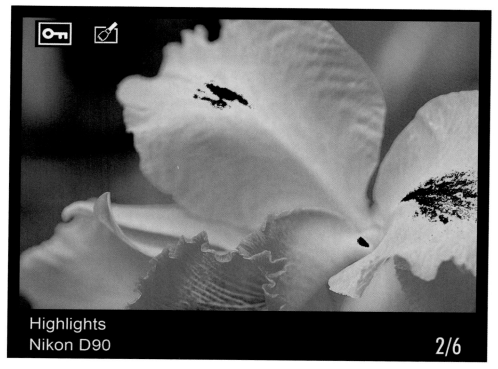

Highlights
Nikon D90   2/6

Figure 2.17
Shooting Data
1 screen.

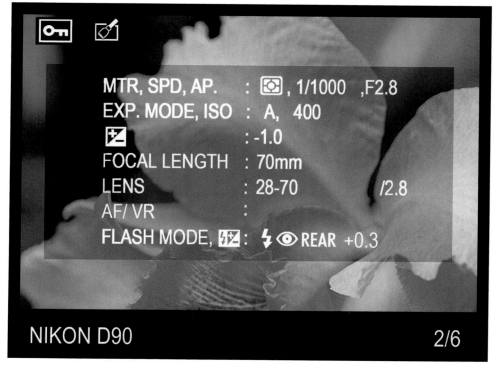

MTR, SPD, AP.	: ▣ , 1/1000 ,F2.8
EXP. MODE, ISO	: A, 400
🔲	: -1.0
FOCAL LENGTH	: 70mm
LENS	: 28-70 /2.8
AF/ VR	:
FLASH MODE, 🔲	: ⚡ ◉ REAR +0.3

NIKON D90   2/6

- **Shooting Data 2.** This screen shows white balance data and adjustments, sharpness and saturation settings, and other parameters (see Figure 2.18).

- **Shooting Data 3.** This screen shows noise reduction information, Active D-Lighting, Retouching effects that have been applied, and your user comments, as shown in Figure 2.19.

- **GPS data.** This screen appears *only* if the image was taken using the GPS device. It includes latitude, longitude, altitude, and time information, as shown in Figure 2.20.

- **Overview data.** This screen adds more data, including metering mode, shutter speed, f/stop, and ISO setting, and looks like Figure 2.21

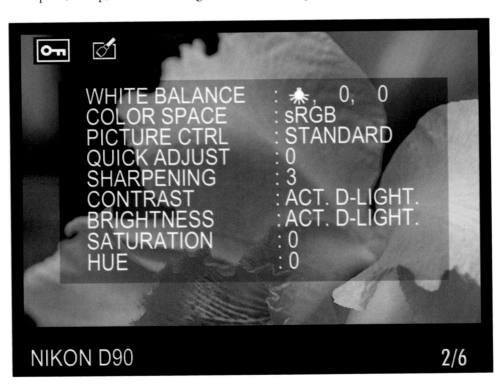

Figure 2.18
Shooting Data 2 screen.

Figure 2.19
Shooting Data
3 screen.

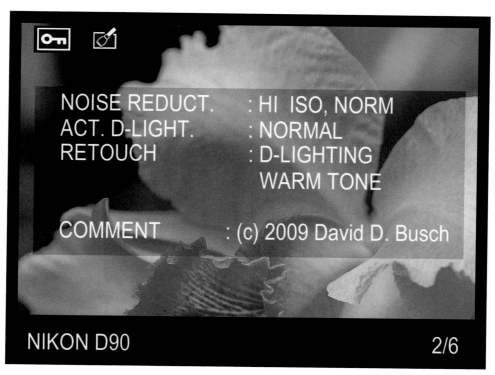

Figure 2.20
GPS data
screen.

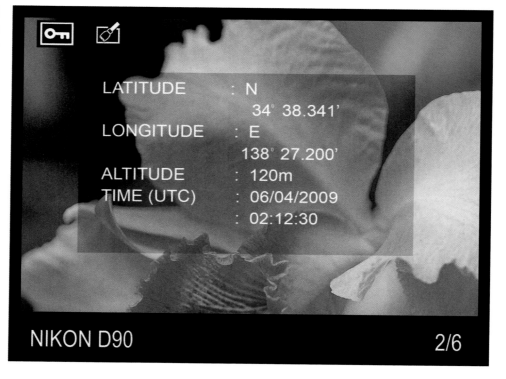

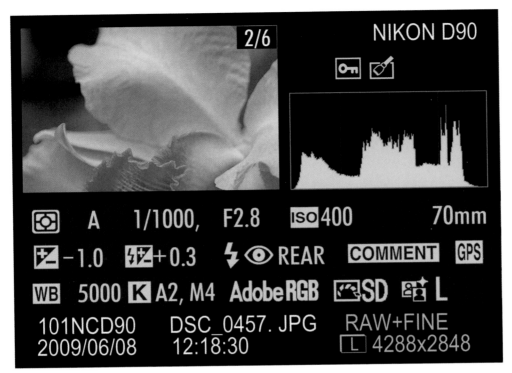

Figure 2.21
Overview data
screen.

Shooting Information Display/Quick Settings Screen

Although the Nikon D90 has an informative monochrome control panel LCD on top (I'll explain the features of that part of your camera next), the back panel color LCD can be used to provide a wealth of the same type of information (the Shooting Information Display) and access to a number of settings (the Quick Settings Screen). The Shooting Information Display is especially useful when the D90 is mounted high on a tripod, as you can conveniently view the camera's settings from the back when the monochrome control panel LCD is too high to see. The Quick Settings Screen can help you avoid some trips to Menu-land, by making some basic adjustments available using the color LCD's speedy settings view.

To activate the Shooting Information Display, press the INFO button on the back of the camera, near the bottom-right corner of the color LCD. You'll see settings like those shown in Figure 2.22. Use Custom Settings Menu entry CSM #d8 (described in Chapter 3) to switch from a dark text on light background, or light text on dark background display. Or, you can choose AUTO and let the D90 decide which color scheme to use, based on the amount of ambient light (light-on-dark is usually easier to read in dim lighting conditions, while the reverse scheme is better under bright lighting).

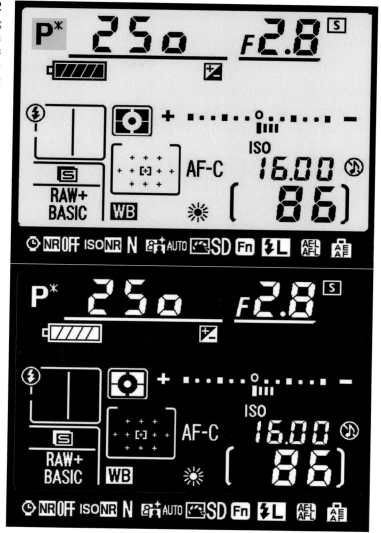

Figure 2.22
The Shooting Information Display shows basic information on the color LCD.

Figure 2.23 shows the full Shooting Information Display/Quick Settings Screen, color-coded for easy reference. Not all of the information is shown at once.

When the Shooting Information Display is shown, press the INFO button a second time to activate the Quick Settings menu at the bottom of the screen, shown in Figure 2.24. Use the multi-selector left/right buttons to highlight one of the adjustments, then press the OK button to produce a screen of options for that setting. You'll find the Quick Settings Screen can be much faster to use for setting ISO Noise Reduction, adjusting Active D-Lighting, accessing a Picture Control, or changing the definition of the Fn and AE-L/AF-L buttons. You'll find full explanations of these features in Chapter 3.

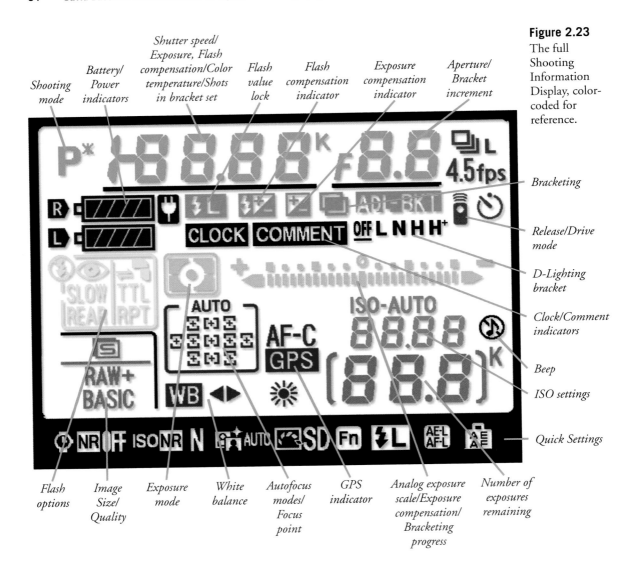

Figure 2.23
The full Shooting Information Display, color-coded for reference.

Shooting mode

Battery/ Power indicators

Shutter speed/ Exposure, Flash compensation/Color temperature/Shots in bracket set

Flash value lock

Flash compensation indicator

Exposure compensation indicator

Aperture/ Bracket increment

Bracketing

Release/Drive mode

D-Lighting bracket

Clock/Comment indicators

Beep

ISO settings

Quick Settings

Flash options

Image Size/ Quality

Exposure mode

White balance

Autofocus modes/ Focus point

GPS indicator

Analog exposure scale/Exposure compensation/ Bracketing progress

Number of exposures remaining

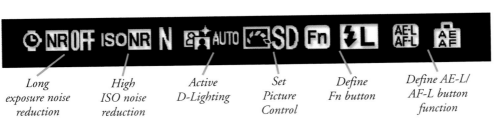

Figure 2.24
Quick Settings can be accessed by a second press of the INFO button.

Long exposure noise reduction

High ISO noise reduction

Active D-Lighting

Set Picture Control

Define Fn button

Define AE-L/ AF-L button function

Going Topside

The top surface of the Nikon D90 (see Figure 2.25) has its own set of frequently accessed controls.

- **Accessory shoe.** Slide an electronic flash into this mount when you need a more powerful speedlight. A dedicated flash unit, like the Nikon SB-400, SB-600, or SB-900, can use the multiple contact points shown to communicate exposure, zoom setting, white balance information, and other data between the flash and the camera. There's more on using electronic flash in Chapter 8.

- **Power switch.** Rotate this switch clockwise to turn on the Nikon D90 (and virtually all other Nikon dSLRs). Rotate all the way clockwise to turn on backlighting for the monochrome control panel status LCD.

- **Shutter release button.** Partially depress this button to lock in exposure and focus. Press all the way to take the picture. Tapping the shutter release when the camera has turned off the autoexposure and autofocus mechanisms reactivates both. When a review image is displayed on the back-panel color LCD, tapping this button removes the image from the display and reactivates the autoexposure and autofocus mechanisms.

Figure 2.25

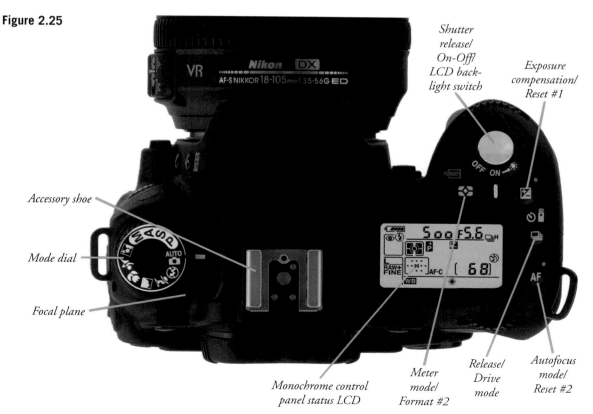

Shutter release/ On-Off/ LCD back-light switch

Exposure compensation/ Reset #1

Accessory shoe

Mode dial

Focal plane

Monochrome control panel status LCD

Meter mode/ Format #2

Release/ Drive mode

Autofocus mode/ Reset #2

- **Meter mode/Format #2 button.** Hold down this button while rotating the main command dial to switch among Matrix, Center-Weighted, and Spot metering. Hold this button while pressing the Format #1 button (the Trash button) for about two seconds, then release when the For message appears on the top LCD, and press again to reformat your memory card.

- **Exposure compensation/Reset #1 button.** Press this button while spinning the command dial to add or subtract exposure when using Program, Aperture Priority, or Shutter Priority modes. This facility allows you to "override" the settings the camera has made and create a picture that is lighter or darker. This is called *exposure compensation.* You can "apply" exposure compensation in Manual mode, too, but in that case the exposure isn't really changed. The D90 simply tells you how much extra or reduced exposure you are requesting, using the analog exposure scale display in the viewfinder and color LCD. Hold down this button while pressing the AF/Reset #2 button to reset the camera's values.

- **Autofocus mode.** Hold down this button while spinning the main command dial to change autofocus settings from among AF-S, AF-C, and AF-A.

- **Focal plane indicator.** This indicator shows the *plane* of the sensor, for use in applications where exact measurement of the distance from the focal plane to the subject is necessary. (These are mostly scientific/close-up applications.)

- **Mode dial.** Rotate the mode dial to choose between Program, Aperture Priority, Shutter Priority, and Manual exposure modes, as well as the Scene modes Auto, Auto (No Flash), Portrait, Landscape, Sports, Close-up, and Night Portrait. Your choice will be displayed on the LCD and in the viewfinder, both described in the next sections. You can read more about the Scene modes in Chapter 1.

LCD Control Panel Readouts

The top panel of the Nikon D90 (see Figure 2.26) contains a monochrome status LCD readout (the "control panel") that displays status information about most of the shooting settings. All of the information segments available are shown in Figure 2.27. I've color-coded the display to make it easier to differentiate them; the information does *not* appear in color on the actual D90. Many of the information items are mutually exclusive (that is, in the White Balance area at lower right, only one of the possible settings illustrated will appear).

Some of the items on the status LCD also appear in the viewfinder and Shooting Information Display, such as the shutter speed and aperture. This is a thicket of information, but I'll spell out what the categories of data include:

- **Battery status.** Five segments show the approximate battery power remaining. A better indicator is the Battery Info entry in the Setup menu.

Figure 2.26
The monochrome status LCD ("control panel") displays shooting information.

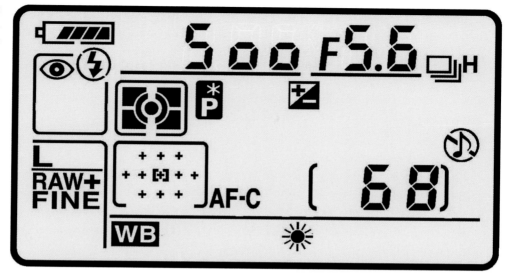

Figure 2.27
Color-coded top-panel LCD readouts.

Shutter speed/Exposure compensation value/Flash compensation value/White balance fine-tuning/White balance preset number/Number of shots in bracket sequence

Exposure compensation/Flash exposure compensation

Aperture/Bracketing increment

Bracketing

Release/Drive mode

Battery status

Program shift indicator

Flash options

Metering mode

Clock reminder

Autofocus options

Image size/Image quality

White balance settings

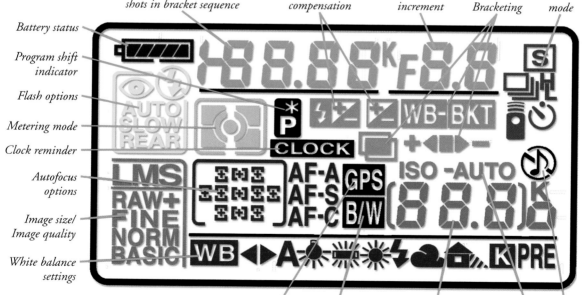

GPS indicator

Black-and-white indicator

Exposures remaining/Buffer shots remaining/White balance recording/Capture mode indicator/ISO sensitivity

ISO setting

Beep

- **Image size.** Shows whether the D90 is shooting Large (4288 × 2848 pixels), Medium (3216 × 2136 pixels), or Small (2144 × 1424 pixels) sizes.

- **Image quality.** Shows current image quality, including TIFF, JPEG, RAW, and any of the several RAW+JPEG combinations.

- **Autofocus-area/AF mode indicator.** Displays the autofocus area status, with the active focus zone shown from among the 11 available points.

- **Clock not set.** This indicator is displayed when your clock needs to be reset. You'll see it when your camera is activated for the first time, any time that the internal clock battery runs down (say, when you've removed the main battery for a few days), and when your internal clock battery wears out and will no longer hold a charge.

- **ISO indicator.** Displayed when you've set the D90 to adjust ISO for you automatically. It flashes when the exposure meters are active, as a way to warn you that the camera may be adjusting the ISO setting.

- **Exposure compensation.** Appears when you've dialed in exposure compensation. Monitor this indicator, as it's easy to forget that you've told the Nikon D90 to use more or less exposure than what its (reasonably intelligent) metering system would otherwise select.

- **Flash compensation active.** Reminds you that you've tweaked the D90's electronic flash exposure system with more or less exposure requested.

- **White balance settings.** One of the white balance settings will appear here, depending on the selection you've made.

- **Bracketing indicator.** Shows that exposure, flash, Active D-Lighting, or white balance bracketing is underway.

- **Number of exposures/additional functions.** This indicator shows the number of exposures remaining on your memory card, as well as other functions, such as the number of shots remaining until your memory buffer fills.

- **GPS active.** If you have a GPS device attached and working, you'll know it when this indicator shows up.

- **Electronic flash settings.** The current mode for the D90's built-in electronic flash unit is shown here.

- **Beep indicator.** Indicates that a helpful beep will sound when using the self-timer or when the D90 successfully focuses when in Single-Servo Autofocus mode (AF-S).

- **Aperture/additional functions.** The selected f/stop appears here, along with a lot of other alternate information, as shown in the label in the figure.

- **Shutter speed/additional functions.** Here you'll find the shutter speed, ISO setting, color temperature, and other useful data.

Lens Components

The lens shown at left in Figure 2.28 is a typical lens that might be mounted on the Nikon D90. It is, in fact, the 18-55mm VR "kit" lens sometimes sold with the camera body. Unfortunately, this particular lens doesn't include all the common features found on the various Nikon lenses available for your camera, so I am including a second lens (shown at right in the figure) that *does* have more features and components. It's not a typical lens that a D90 user might work with, however. This 17-35mm zoom is a pricey "pro" lens that costs about 1.5X as much as the entire D90 camera. Nevertheless, it makes a good example. Components found on this pair of lenses include:

■ **Filter thread.** Most lenses have a thread on the front for attaching filters and other add-ons. Some, like the 18-55 VR kit lens, also use this thread for attaching a lens hood (you screw on the filter first, and then attach the hood to the screw thread on the front of the filter). Some lenses, such as the AF-S Nikkor 14-24mm f/2.8G ED lens, have no front filter thread, either because their front elements are too curved to allow mounting a filter and/or because the front element is so large that huge filters would be prohibitively expensive. Some of these front-filter-hostile lenses allow using smaller filters that drop into a slot at the back of the lens.

Figure 2.28

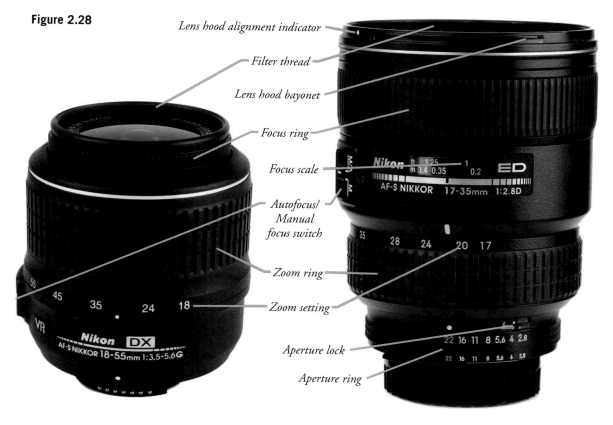

- **Lens hood bayonet.** Lenses like the 17-35mm zoom shown in the figure use this bayonet to mount the lens hood. Such lenses generally will have a dot on the edge showing how to align the lens hood with the bayonet mount.

- **Focus ring.** This is the ring you turn when you manually focus the lens, or fine-tune autofocus adjustment. It's a narrow ring at the very front of the lens (on the 18-55mm kit lens), or a wider ring located somewhere else.

- **Focus scale.** This is a readout found on many lenses that rotates in unison with the lens' focus mechanism to show the distance at which the lens has been focused. It's a useful indicator for double-checking autofocus, roughly evaluating depth-of-field, and for setting manual focus guesstimates. Chapter 6 deals with the mysteries of lenses and their controls in more detail.

- **Zoom setting.** These markings on the lens show the current focal length selected.

- **Zoom ring.** Turn this ring to change the zoom setting.

- **Autofocus/Manual switch.** Allows you to change from Automatic focus to Manual focus.

- **Aperture ring.** Some lenses have a ring that allows you to set a specific f/stop manually, rather than use the camera's internal electronic aperture control. An aperture ring is useful when a lens is mounted on a non-automatic extension ring, bellows, or other accessory that doesn't couple electronically with the camera. Aperture rings also allow using a lens on an older camera that lacks electronic control. In recent years, Nikon has been replacing lenses that have aperture rings with versions that only allow setting the aperture with camera controls.

- **Aperture lock.** If you want your D90 (or other Nikon dSLR) to control the aperture electronically, you must set the lens to its smallest aperture (usually f/22 or f/32) and lock it with this control.

- **Focus limit switch.** Some lenses have this switch (shown in Figure 2.29), which limits the focus range of the lens, thus potentially reducing focus seeking when shooting distant subjects. The limiter stops the lens from trying to focus at closer distances (in this case, closer than 2.5 meters).

- **Vibration reduction switch.** Lenses with Nikon's Vibration Reduction (VR) feature include a switch for turning the stabilization feature on and off, and, in some cases, for changing from normal vibration reduction to a more aggressive "active" VR mode useful for, say, shooting from moving vehicles. More on VR and other lens topics in Chapter 6.

Figure 2.29

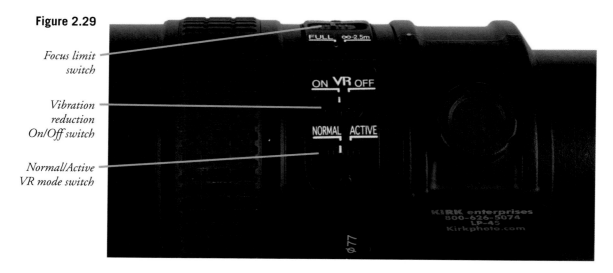

Focus limit switch

Vibration reduction On/Off switch

Normal/Active VR mode switch

The back end of a lens intended for use on a Nikon camera has other components that you seldom see (except when you swap lenses), shown in Figure 2.30, but still should know about:

■ **Lens bayonet mount.** This is the mounting mechanism that attaches to a matching mount on the camera. Although the lens bayonet is usually metal, some lenses use a rugged plastic for this key component.

Figure 2.30

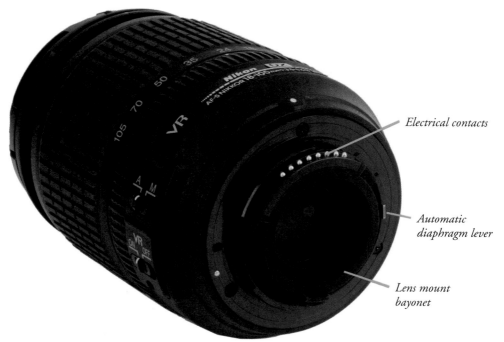

Electrical contacts

Automatic diaphragm lever

Lens mount bayonet

- **Automatic diaphragm lever.** This lever is moved by a matching lever in the camera to adjust the f/stop from wide open (which makes for the brightest view) to the *taking aperture*, which is the f/stop that will be used to take the picture. The actual taking aperture is determined by the camera's metering system (or by you when the D90 is in Manual mode), and is communicated to the lens through the electronic contacts described next. (An exception is when the aperture ring on the lens itself is unlocked and used to specify the f/stop.) However, the spring-loaded physical levers are what actually push the aperture to the selected f/stop.

- **Electronic contacts.** These metal contacts pass information to matching contacts in the camera body allowing a firm electrical connection so that exposure, distance, and other information can be exchanged between the camera and lens.

Looking Inside the Viewfinder

Much of the important shooting status information is shown inside the viewfinder of the Nikon D90. Not all of this information will be shown at any one time. Figure 2.31 shows what you can expect to see. These readouts include:

- **Focus points.** Can display the 11 areas used by the D90 to focus. The camera can select the appropriate focus zone for you, or you can manually select one or all of the zones, as described in Chapters 1 and 5.

- **Active focus point.** The currently selected focus point can be highlighted with red illumination, depending on focus mode.

- **Battery indicator.** Appears when the D90's battery becomes depleted.

- **Focus indicator.** This green dot stops blinking when the subject covered by the active autofocus zone is in sharp focus, whether focus was achieved by the AF system, or by you using manual focusing.

- **Autoexposure lock.** Shows that exposure has been locked.

- **Shutter speed.** Displays the current shutter speed selected by the camera, or by you in Manual exposure mode.

- **Aperture.** Shows the current aperture chosen by the D90's autoexposure system, or specified by you when using Manual exposure mode.

- **Automatic ISO indicator.** Shown as a reminder that the D90 has been set to adjust ISO sensitivity automatically. It flashes when the exposure meters are active as a warning to you that the camera may be adjusting the ISO setting.

- **Electronic analog exposure display.** This scale shows the current exposure level, with the bottom indicator centered when the exposure is correct as metered. The indicator may also move to the left or right to indicate over- or underexposure (respectively). The scale is also used to show the amount of exposure compensation dialed in.

Figure 2.31

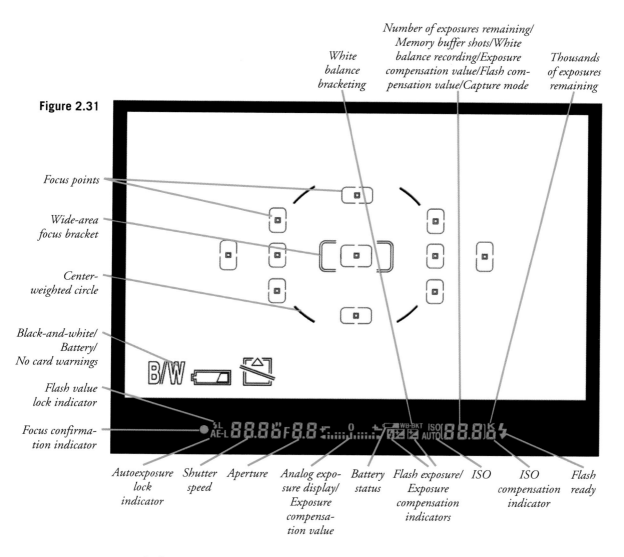

White balance bracketing

Number of exposures remaining/ Memory buffer shots/White balance recording/Exposure compensation value/Flash compensation value/Capture mode

Thousands of exposures remaining

Focus points

Wide-area focus bracket

Center-weighted circle

Black-and-white/ Battery/ No card warnings

Flash value lock indicator

Focus confirmation indicator

Autoexposure lock indicator

Shutter speed

Aperture

Analog exposure display/ Exposure compensation value

Battery status

Flash exposure/ Exposure compensation indicators

ISO

ISO compensation indicator

Flash ready

- **Flash compensation indicator.** Appears when flash EV changes have been made.

- **Exposure compensation indicator.** This is shown when exposure compensation (EV) changes have been made. It's easy to forget you've dialed in a little more or less exposure, and then shoot a whole series of pictures of a different scene that doesn't require such compensation. Beware!

- **Flash ready indicator.** This icon appears when the flash is fully charged.

■ **Exposures remaining/maximum burst available.** Normally displays the number of exposures remaining on your memory card, but while shooting it changes to show a number that indicates the number of frames that can be taken in Continuous Shooting mode using the current settings. This indicator also shows other information, such as exposure/flash compensation values, and whether the D90 is connected to a PC through a USB cable.

Underneath Your Nikon D90

There's not a lot going on with the bottom panel of your Nikon D90. You'll find the battery compartment access door and a tripod socket, which secures the camera to a tripod. The socket accepts other accessories, such as flash brackets and quick release plates that allow rapid attaching and detaching of the D90 from a matching platform affixed to your tripod.

Figure 2.32 shows the underside view of the camera.

Figure 2.32

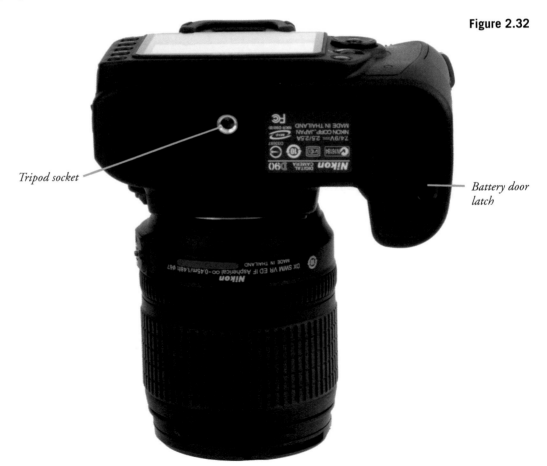

Tripod socket

Battery door latch

Using the MB-D80 Multi-Power Battery Pack/Vertical Grip

One optional accessory that you might want to consider is the Nikon MB-D80 battery pack/vertical grip, which attaches to the underside the D90 and provides extra power for those long shooting sessions, as well as convenient shutter release, main and sub-command dials, and an AF-ON button, all arranged for easy access when the camera is rotated to shoot pictures in a vertical orientation. This accessory is available for about $160—but you may already own one. Nikon was smart enough to make the D90 compatible with the exact same grip designed for the previous Nikon D80, so if you're upgrading to the D90 and have already purchased the MB-D80, you can continue to use it with your new camera.

To use the MB-D80, just follow these steps:

1. Open the battery compartment door on the bottom of the D90, and remove the EN-EL3e battery.

2. Rotate the battery compartment door at approximately a 35-45 degree angle. That lines up the hinge with a slot that allows you to pull the door straight out at that angle to remove it from the camera body. This step feels wrong the first time you do it, but if you have the door angled properly, it will snap right out. (To replace the door, position it at the same angle and press inward evenly.)

3. Slide the extension of the MB-D80 into the empty battery compartment, where it will connect with the electrical contacts inside.

4. When the grip and D90 are fit snugly together, rotate the large wheel under the base of the MB-D80 to lock the device onto the D90, as shown in Figure 2.33.

5. Take the battery you removed from the camera and insert it into the compartment in the grip. You can add a second EN-EL3e battery to double your available power. Or you can use six AA batteries with the supplied holder.

6. To use the shutter release on the vertical grip, you must turn the rotating knob so the dot aligns with the line on the grip, indicating that the shutter release is unlocked. If you're holding the camera in horizontal orientation and using the regular shutter release, it's easy to accidentally trip the vertical release with the palm of your right hand. (This accounts for the "phantom" shutter releases that mystify new users of this grip.)

7. To remove the grip, reverse these steps.

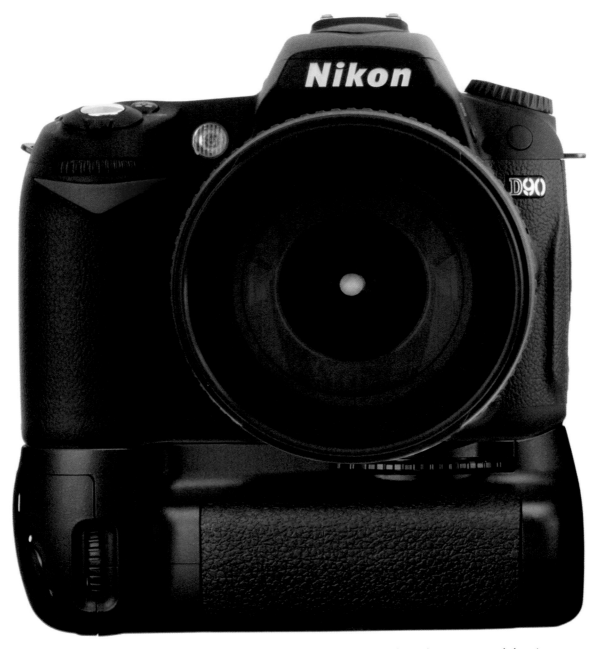

Figure 2.33 The Nikon MB-D80 Multi-Power Grip can double the length of your battery-powered shooting session, while adding convenient vertically oriented controls.

3

Setting Up Your Nikon D90

The Nikon D90 has a remarkable number of options and settings you can use to customize the way your camera operates. Not only can you change shooting settings used at the time the picture is taken, but you can adjust the way your camera behaves. Indeed, if your D90 doesn't operate in exactly the way you'd like, chances are you can make a small change in the Playback, Shooting, Custom Setting, and Setup menus that will tailor the D90 to your needs. If you don't like the menus themselves, you can customize which items appear using the D90's My Menu option.

This chapter will help you sort out the settings for all the D90's menus. These include the Playback and Shooting menus, which determine how the D90 displays images on review, and how it uses many of its shooting features to take a photo. Later in the chapter, I'll show you how to use the Custom Setting menu to set power-saving timers, choose a metering mode, and set other functions. In the section on the Setup menu, you'll discover how to format a memory card, set the date/time and LCD brightness, and do other maintenance tasks. You'll learn how to use the Retouch menu to remove red-eye and fix up photos right in your camera.

As I've mentioned before, this book isn't intended to replace the manual you received with your D90, nor have I any interest in rehashing its contents. You'll still find the original manual useful as a standby reference that lists every possible option in exhaustive (if mind-numbing) detail—without really telling you how to use those options to take better pictures. There is, however, some unavoidable duplication between the Nikon manual and this chapter, because I'm going to explain all the key menu choices and the options you may have in using them. You should find, though, that I will give you the information you need in a much more helpful format, with plenty of detail on why you should make some settings that are particularly cryptic.

I'm not going to waste a lot of space on some of the more obvious menu choices in these chapters. For example, you can probably figure out, even without my help, that the Beep option in Custom Setting Menu CSM #d1 deals with the solid-state beeper in your camera that sounds off during various activities (such as the self-timer countdown). You can certainly decipher the import of the two options available for the Beep entry (On and Off). In this chapter, I'll devote no more than a sentence or two to the blatantly obvious settings and concentrate on the more confusing aspects of D90 setup, such as autofocus. I'll start with an overview of using the D90's menus themselves.

Anatomy of the Nikon D90's Menus

The D90 has one of the best-designed menu systems of any digital SLR in its price class, with a remarkable amount of consistency with other cameras in the Nikon product line. In fact, if you used any other Nikon dSLR before you purchased your Nikon D90, you're probably already familiar with the basic menu lineup. Press the Menu button, located fourth from the bottom at the left side of the LCD. As you explore the menus and submenus, note that when the D90 is set on Auto or Scene modes, some submenu choices, such as Picture Controls, are not available. There are three columns of information in each menu screen.

- The left-hand column includes an icon representing each of the top-level menu screens. From the top in Figure 3.1, they are Playback (right-pointing triangle icon), Shooting (camera icon), Custom Setting (pencil icon), Setup (wrench), and Retouch (a paintbrush), and either an icon representing Recent Settings or My Menu, depending on which tab you've selected for that slot. (The My Menu icon is like the Recent Settings icon shown in the figure, but with a check mark.) At the bottom of the column is question mark icon representing Help access.

- The center column includes the name representing the function of each choice in the currently selected menu. For example, Delete represents the menu entry for removing individual photos or multiple images, while Playback folder indicates the menu entry used for choosing which of the folders on your memory card will be accessed when reviewing pictures.

- The right-hand column has an icon or text that shows either the current setting for that menu item or text or an icon that represents the function of that menu entry. In Figure 3.1, a trash can icon shows that you can use the Delete entry for removing images, while the text Off appears next to the Rotate tall entry, indicating that the D90 has been set to not rotate vertical images to display them in their proper orientation on the LCD.

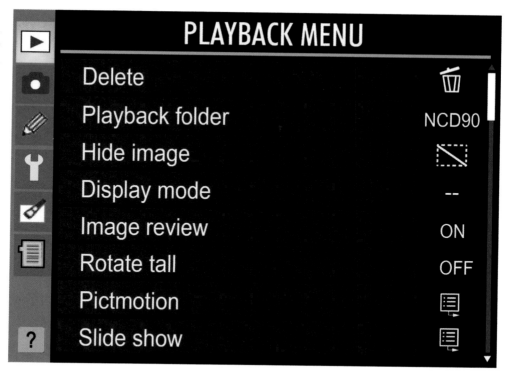

Navigating among the various menus is easy and follows a consistent set of rules.

- **Press Menu to start.** Press the Menu button to display the main menu screens.

- **Navigate with the multi-selector pad.** The multi-selector pad, located to the right of the LCD, has indents at the up/down/left/right positions. Press these "buttons" to navigate among the menu selections. Press the left button to move highlighting to the left column; then press the up/down buttons to scroll up or down among the five top-level menus.

- **Highlighting indicates active choice.** As each top-level menu is highlighted, its icon will first change from black and white to yellow/amber, white, and black. As you use the multi-selector's right button to move into the column containing that menu's choices, you can then use the up/down buttons to scroll among the individual entries. If more than one screen full of choices is available, a scroll bar appears at the far right of the screen, with a position slider showing the relative position of the currently highlighted entry. (You'll see the scroll bar in an upcoming menu screen.)

- **Select a menu item.** To work with a highlighted menu entry, press the OK button in the center of the multi-selector on the back of the D90 or just press the right button on the multi-selector. Any additional screens of choices will appear. You can move among them using the same multi-selector movements.

- **Choose your menu option.** You can confirm a selection by pressing the OK button or, frequently, by pressing the right button on the multi-selector once again. Some functions require scrolling to a Done menu choice, or include an instruction to Set a choice using some other button.

- **Leaving the menu system.** Pressing the multi-selector left button usually backs you out of the current screen, and pressing the Menu button again usually does the same thing. You can exit the menu system at any time by tapping the shutter release button. If you haven't confirmed your choice for a particular option, no changes will be made.

- **Quick return.** The Nikon D90 "remembers" the top-level menu and specific menu entry you were using (but not any submenus) the last time the menu system was accessed (even if you have subsequently turned off the camera), so pressing the Menu button brings you back to where you left off. So, if you were working with, say, the Delete option in the Playback menu, the next time you press the Menu button, the Playback menu and Delete entry will be highlighted, but not the specific submenu that you might have selected.

The top-level menus are color-coded, and a bar in that color is displayed underneath the menu title when one of those menus is highlighted. The colors are Playback menu (blue); Shooting menu (green); Custom Setting menu (red); Setup menu (orange); Retouch menu (purple); and My Menu (gray).

Playback Menu Options

The blue-coded Playback menu has nine entries used to select options related to the display, review, and printing of the photos you've taken. (The ninth, Print set (DPOF) is not visible in Figure 3.1; it's scrolled off the bottom of the screen.) The choices you'll find include:

- Delete
- Playback folder
- Hide image
- Display mode
- Image review
- Rotate tall
- Pictmotion
- Slide show
- Print set (DPOF)

Delete

Choose this menu entry and you'll be given three choices: Selected, Select Date, and All. The ability to select images by date the picture was taken is new to the Nikon D90. You first saw this feature in action in Chapter 2, specifically in Figure 2.13, which showed the Calendar view information screen. Previous Nikon cameras allowed you to work with selected images and all images.

If you choose Selected, you'll see an image selection screen like the one shown in Figure 3.2. Then, follow these instructions:

1. **Review thumbnails.** Use the multi-selector left/right and up/down buttons to scroll among the available images.

2. **Examine image.** When you highlight an image you think you might want to delete, press the Zoom In button to temporarily enlarge that image so you can evaluate it further. When you release the button, the selection screen returns.

3. **Mark/unmark images.** To mark an image for deletion, press the Zoom Out/Index button (*not* the Trash button). A trash can icon will appear overlaid on that image's thumbnail. To unmark an image, press the Zoom Out/Index button again.

4. **Remove images.** When you've finished marking images to delete, press OK. A final screen will appear asking you to confirm the removal of the image(s). Choose Yes to delete the image(s) or No to cancel deletion, and then press OK. If you selected Yes, then you'll return to the Playback menu; if you chose No, you'll be taken back to the selection screen to mark/unmark images.

5. To back out of the selection screen, press the Menu button.

Figure 3.2
Images selected for deletion are marked with a trash can icon.

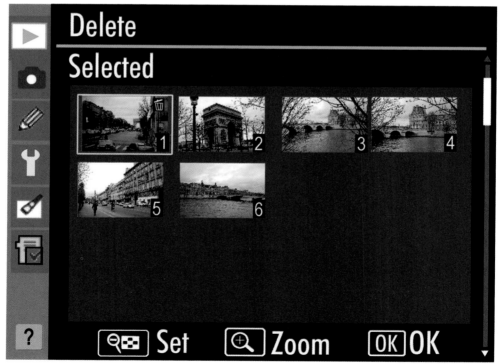

In the main Delete screen you can also choose Select Date. Highlight any of the available dates that have pictures, and press the multi-selector right button to add a check mark to that date. Press the Zoom Out/Index button to view/confirm that the images for the date you've marked are those you want to delete, and press the button again to return to the Select Date screen. When you're finished choosing dates, press OK to delete the images from the confirmation screen.

Your final choice from the main Delete screen is All, which removes all the images from your memory card, except for those marked as Protected. Keep in mind that deleting images though the Delete process is slower than just wiping out the whole card with the Format command, so using Format is generally much faster than choosing Delete: All, and also is a safer way of returning your memory card to a fresh, blank state.

Playback Folder

Images created by your Nikon D90 are deposited into folders on your memory card. These folders have names like 100NCD90 or 101NCD90, but you can change those default names to something else using the Folders option in the Setup menu, described later in this chapter.

With a freshly formatted memory card (formatting is covered under the Setup menu), the D90 starts with a default name: 100NCD90. When that folder fills with the maximum of 999 images, the camera automatically creates a new folder numbered one higher, such as 101NCD90. If you use the same memory card in another camera, that camera will also create its own folder (say, 102NCD60 for a Nikon D60). Thus you can end up with several folders on the same memory card, at least one for each camera the card is used in, until you eventually reformat the card and folder creation starts anew. Later in this chapter, in the section on the Setup menu, I'll show you how to create folders with names you select yourself.

This menu item allows you to choose which folders are accessed when displaying images using the D90's Playback facility. Your choices are as follows:

■ **Current.** The D90 will display only images in the current folder, as specified in the Setup menu (described later in this chapter). For example, if you have been shooting heavily at an event and have already accumulated more than 999 shots and the D90 has created a new folder for the overflow, you'd use this setting to view only the most recent photos, which reside in that new current folder. You can change the current folder to any other specific folder on your memory card using the Folders option in the Setup menu, described later in this chapter.

- **All.** All folders containing images that the D90 can read will be accessed, regardless of which camera created them. You might want to use this setting if you swap memory cards among several cameras and want to be able to review all the photos. You will be able to view images even if they were created by a non-Nikon camera *if* those images conform to a specification called the Design Rule for Camera File systems (DCF).

NOT ALL IMAGES CAN BE DISPLAYED

Even when you specify All, the D90 may not be able to show every image on your memory card, particularly if that photo was not taken with a D90. The camera may not be able to display photos taken with non-Nikon cameras, especially if the image was captured at a higher resolution than the D90's 12 megapixels. This happened to me recently when I discovered that I could view an image, but not zoom in during picture review. It turns out that the photo was taken with a non-Nikon at a higher resolution. My camera could show the embedded JPEG image, but was unable to process the full picture to magnify the photo.

Hide Image

Use this menu option to protect *and* hide images. When you choose Hide Image, you'll be given three choices: Select/Set, Select Date, and (Deselect)All. These use a selection process virtually identical to the one used with Delete Images and shown in Figure 3.2. You can select individual images, select images by date, or select/deselect all images.

Unlike the Protect option, which just marks images to keep them from accidental deletion, this feature also hides them from view using the regular Playback functions. Pictures that have been hidden can only be viewed from the Hide Image selection screen. I use this facility in two different ways:

- Sometimes I have a memory card filled with images and I want to show some of the images, perhaps as a slide show, or sometimes just by handing the camera to someone and asking them to browse through the photo. I can hide the non-relevant images so only the relevant pictures appear.

- Hiding images is a good way to make your real stinkers invisible if you haven't quite made up your mind to delete them.

Remember that if you "unhide" an image you are also removing the Protect attribute. If you want the photo to be visible, but still protected, press the Protect button while viewing the image on the LCD. The key icon will be superimposed on the image, showing you that it is now protected from accidental erasure. Reformatting the card removes the Hidden and Protected attributes, of course—because it removes those images as well!

Display Mode

You'll recall from Chapter 2 that a great deal of information, available on multiple screens, can be displayed when reviewing images. This menu item helps you reduce/increase the clutter by specifying which information and screens will be available. To activate or deactivate an info option, scroll to that option and press the right multi-selector button to add a check mark to the box next to that item. Press the right button to unmark an item that has previously been checked. **Important:** When you're finished, you must scroll up to Done and press OK or the right multi-selector button to confirm your choices. Exiting the Display mode menu any other way will cause any changes you may have made to be ignored. Your info options include:

- **Highlights.** When enabled, overexposed highlight areas in your image will blink with a black border during picture review. That's your cue to consider using exposure compensation to reduce exposure, unless a minus-EV setting will cause loss of shadow detail that you want to preserve. You can read more about correcting exposure in Chapter 4.

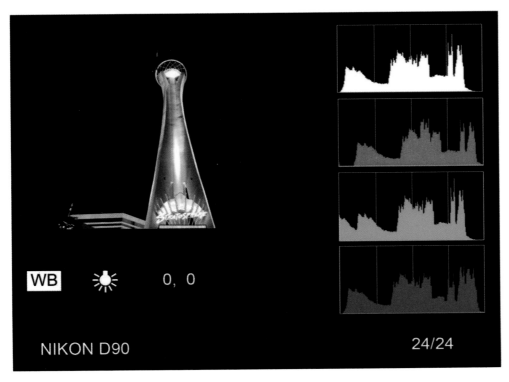

Figure 3.3
Use the Display mode menu entry to activate various data displays, like the RGB display shown here.

- **RGB histogram.** Displays both luminance (brightness) and RGB histograms on a screen that can be displayed using the up/down multi-selector buttons, as described in Chapter 2. When unmarked, this histogram screen is disabled, and only the Overview Data screen, with the Brightness histogram, is displayed.

- **Data.** Activates the pages of shooting data shown in Chapter 2.

Image Review

There are certain shooting situations in which it's useful to have the picture you've just shot pop up on the LCD automatically for review. Perhaps you're fine-tuning exposure or autofocus and want to be able to see whether your most recent image is acceptable. Or, maybe you're the nervous type and just want confirmation that you actually took a picture. Instant review has saved my bacon a few times; for example, when I was shooting with studio flash in Manual mode and didn't notice that the shutter speed had been set to a (non-syncing) 1/320th second by mistake.

A lot of the time, however, it's a better idea to *not* automatically review your shots in order to conserve battery power (the LCD is one of the major juice drains in the camera) or to speed up or simplify operations. For example, if you've just fired off a burst of eight shots at 4.5 fps during a football game do you *really* need to have each and every frame display as the D90 clears its buffer and stores the photos on your memory card? Or, when you're shooting at an acoustic concert, wouldn't it be smart to disable image review so the folks behind you aren't hit with a blast of light from that giant three-inch LCD every time you take a picture? This menu operation allows you to choose which mode to use:

- **On.** At this default setting, image review is automatic after every shot is taken.

- **Off.** Images are displayed only when you press the Playback button.

Rotate Tall

When you rotate the D90 to photograph vertical subjects in portrait (tall), rather than landscape (wide) orientation, you probably don't want to view them tilted onto their sides later on, either on the camera LCD or within your image viewing/editing application on your computer. The D90 is way ahead of you. It has a directional sensor built in that can detect whether the camera was rotated when the photo was taken and hide this information in the image file itself.

The orientation data is applied in two different ways. It can be used by the D90 to automatically rotate images when they are displayed on the camera's LCD monitor, or you can ignore the data and let the images display in non-rotated fashion (so you have to rotate the camera to view them in their proper orientation). Your image-editing application, such as Adobe Photoshop Elements, can also use the embedded file data to automatically rotate images on your computer screen.

But either feature works only if you've told the D90 to place orientation information in the image file so it can be retrieved when the image is displayed. You must set Auto image rotation to On in the Setup menu (I'll show you how to do that later in this chapter). Once you've done that, the D90 will embed information about orientation in the image file, and both your D90 and your image editor can rotate the images for you as the files are displayed.

This menu choice deals only with whether the image should be rotated when displayed on the *camera LCD monitor*. (If you de-activate this option, your image-editing software can still read the embedded rotation data and properly display your images.) When Rotate Tall is turned off, the Nikon D90 does not rotate pictures taken in vertical orientation, displaying them as shown in Figure 3.4. The image is large on your LCD screen, but you must rotate the camera to view it upright.

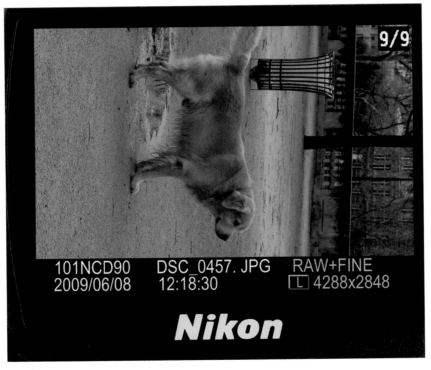

Figure 3.4
With Rotate Tall turned off, vertical images appear large on the LCD, but you must turn the camera to view them upright.

When Rotate Tall is turned on, the D90 rotates pictures taken in vertical orientation on the LCD screen so you don't have to turn the camera to view them comfortably. However, this orientation also means that the longest dimension of the image is shown using the shortest dimension of the LCD, so the picture is reduced in size, as you can see in Figure 3.5.

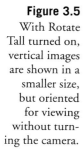

Figure 3.5
With Rotate Tall turned on, vertical images are shown in a smaller size, but oriented for viewing without turning the camera.

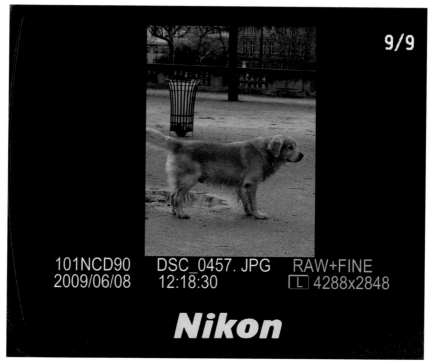

So, leave this feature at the default On setting (as well as Auto image rotation in the Setup menu), if you'd rather not turn your camera to view vertical shots in their natural orientation, and don't mind the smaller image. Turn the feature Off if, as I do, you'd rather see a larger image and are willing to rotate the camera to do so.

Pictmotion

If you've used the Slide Show capability found in lesser Nikon cameras (or even the Slide Show feature still available in the D90), Pictmotion will be a revelation. Slide Show pretty much limits you to displaying all the non-hidden pictures in a folder one after another, with the only options the interval between photos and the ability to pause. Pictmotion, on the other hand, allows you to choose the photos you want to use, add background music, and generate special effects transitions between shots. It's a much more flexible and interesting tool. It even has the capability of integrating the first few seconds of those HDTV movies you can shoot with the D90 into your Pictmotion shows.

You build shows using the screen shown in Figure 3.6, which has four options:

- **Start.** Use this option to view your finished show on the three-inch color LCD, on a television monitor connected to the AV port on the side of the D90, or on an HDTV connected to the HDML port.

- **Select pictures.** Highlight this option and press the multi-selector right button to produce the Select Pictures screen. Use the same picture selection process I first described in the Delete Pictures menu entry at the beginning of this chapter. That is, you can choose Selected (you choose individual photos), Select Date (all pictures taken on a given date will be displayed), or All (all pictures in the currently active folder(s) will be shown). Use the Playback Folder option (also described earlier in this chapter) to specify which folder (or all folders) are to be used.

- **Background music.** You can select one of five canned music selections as background for your epic slide show. Your choices are High-Speed, Emotional, Natural, Up-Tempo, and Relaxed. These don't give you a full range of moods (maybe a Salsa or Bossa Nova clip, a few Metal moments, a Country twang or two, or some Hip Hop beat would be nice), but the provided clips are a great improvement over the sounds of silence.

- **Effects.** You can flow between shots using five different transitional effects, including Zoom Bounce, Zoom In/Out, Blend, Wipe, and Zoom Out Fade. Having been tortured by more than a few PowerPoint and Photoshop Elements slide shows in which wildly varying transitions seemed to be mandatory, I recommend you use these, but stick to one or perhaps two for your entire show. There's nothing wrong with using a wipe between almost every shot, then switching to a zoom in to emphasize a detail as a change of pace. But if you find your audience guessing which effect will come next, you've probably overdone it.

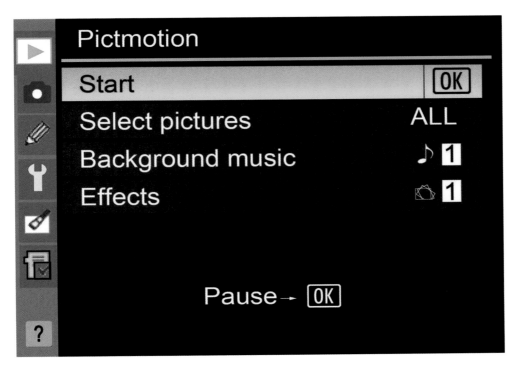

Figure 3.6
Use this menu to select Pictmotion options.

GETTING CLEVER WITH CLIPS

Pictmotion shows only the first few seconds of your D90's movie clips, but there's no reason why you couldn't assemble some HDTV movies expressly for a Pictmotion production. If you limit each clip to a couple seconds, they'll be shown exactly as you made them. Quick cuts are exciting, anyway, right?

When it comes time to view your show, select Start from the Pictmotion menu and press OK. Then, control your production using the following keys:

- **Pause.** Press OK to pause; press again to resume.

- **Increase volume.** Press the Zoom In button.

- **Decrease volume.** Press the Zoom Out button.

- **Return to the Playback menu.** Press the Menu button.

- **End the show.** Press the Playback button to stop the show and return to Playback mode.

- **Take a picture.** You won't lose any photos while your show is on display. As always, when something is on the screen, you can exit and go to shooting mode by pressing the shutter release halfway.

Slide Show

The D90's Slide Show feature is a convenient way to review images in the current playback folder one after another, without the need to manually switch between them. It's faster to set up and use than Pictmotion, but doesn't have much in the way of options.

To activate a slide show, just choose Start from this entry in the Playback menu. If you like, you can choose Frame interval before commencing the show in order to select an interval of 2, 3, 5, or 10 seconds between "slides." During playback, you can press the OK button to pause the "slide show" (in case you want to examine an image more closely). When the show is paused, a menu pops up, as shown in Figure 3.7, with choices to restart the show (by pressing the OK button again); change the interval between frames; or to exit the show entirely.

As the images are displayed, press the up/down multi-selector buttons to change the amount of information presented on the screen with each image. For example, you might want to review a set of images and the settings used to shoot them. At any time during the show, press the up/down buttons until the informational screen you want is overlaid on the images.

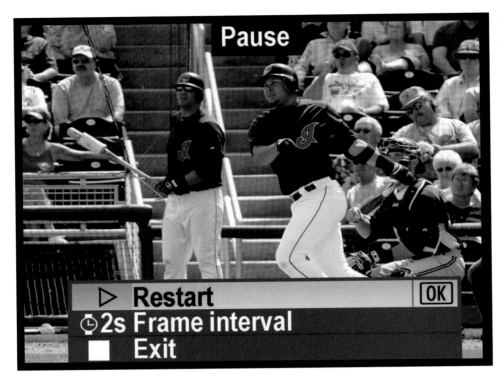

Figure 3.7
Press the OK
button to pause
the slide show,
change the
interval
between slides,
or to exit the
presentation.

As the slide show progresses, you can press the left/right multi-selector buttons to move back to a previous frame or jump ahead to the next one. The slide show will then proceed as before. Press the Menu button to exit the slide show and return to the menu, or the Playback button to exit the menu system totally. As always, while reviewing images you can tap the Menu button to exit the show and return to the menus, or tap the shutter release button if you want to remove everything from the screen and return to shooting mode.

At the end of the slide show, as when you've paused it, you'll be offered the choice of restarting the sequence, changing the frame interval, or exiting the slide show feature completely.

Print Set (DPOF)

You can print directly from your camera to a printer compatible with a specification called *PictBridge* (most recent printers are, and have a connector for that mode). You can also move your memory card and give it to your retailer for printing in their lab or in-store printing machine, or insert the card into a stand-alone picture kiosk and make prints yourself. In all these cases, you can easily specify exactly which photos you want printed, and how many copies you'd like of each picture. This menu item does all the work for you.

The Nikon D90 supports the DPOF (Digital Print Order Format) that is now almost universally used by digital cameras to specify which images on your memory card should be printed, and the number of prints desired of each image. This information is recorded on the memory card and can be interpreted by a compatible printer when the camera is linked to the printer using the USB cable, or when the memory card is inserted into a card reader slot on the printer itself. Photo labs and stand-alone kiosks are also equipped to read this data and make prints when you supply your memory card to them.

When you choose this menu item, you're presented with a set of screens that looks very much like the Delete photos screens described earlier (I used the same set of example pictures for the illustration), only you're selecting pictures for printing rather than deleting them. The first screen you see when you choose Print Set (DPOF) asks if you'd like to Select/Set Pictures for Printing, or Deselect All? images that have already been marked.

Choose Select/set to choose photos and specify how many prints of each you'd like. Choose Deselect All? to cancel any existing print order and start over. If you want to select photos for printing, follow these steps when the screen shown in Figure 3.8 appears:

1. **View images on your card.** Use the multi-selector keys to scroll among the available images.

2. **Evaluate specific photos.** When you highlight an image you might want to print, press the Zoom button to temporarily enlarge that image so you can evaluate it further. When you release the button, the selection screen returns.

Figure 3.8
Select images for printing.

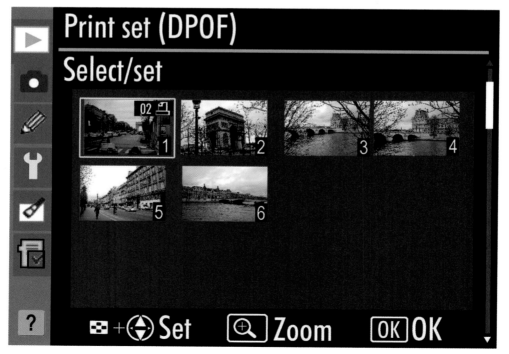

3. **Mark images for printing and specify number of copies.** To mark a highlighted image for printing, hold the Zoom Out/Thumbnail button and press the multi-selector up/down buttons to choose the number of prints you want, up to 99 per image. The up button increases the number of prints; the down button decreases the amount. A printer icon and the number specified will appear overlaid on that image's thumbnail.

4. **Unmark images if you change your mind.** To unmark an image for printing, highlight and press the Zoom Out/Thumbnail button and multi-selector down button until the number of prints reaches zero. The printer icon will vanish.

5. **Finish selecting and marking images.** When you've finished marking images to print, press OK.

6. **Specify date or shooting information on the print.** A final screen will appear in which you can request a data imprint (shutter speed and aperture) or imprint date (the date the photos were taken). Use the up/down buttons to select one or both of these options, if desired, and press the left/right buttons to mark or unmark the check boxes. When a box is marked, the imprint information for that option will be included on *all* prints in the print order.

7. **Exit the Print Set screens.** Scroll up to Done when finished, and press OK or the right cursor button.

Shooting Menu Options

This menu has just 13 settings. Taken together, these are likely to be the most common settings changes you make, with changes made to one or more of them during a particular session fairly common. You might make such adjustments as you begin a shooting session, or when you move from one type of subject to another. Nikon makes accessing these changes very easy.

This section explains the options of the Shooting menu and how to use them. The options you'll find in these green-coded menus include the following. The first eight choices are shown in Figure 3.9.

- Set Picture Control
- Manage Picture Control
- Image quality
- Image size
- White balance
- ISO sensitivity settings
- Active D-Lighting

- Color space
- Long exposure noise reduction
- High ISO noise reduction
- Active folder
- Multiple exposure
- Movie settings

Figure 3.9
This is the first
page of the
Shooting
menu.

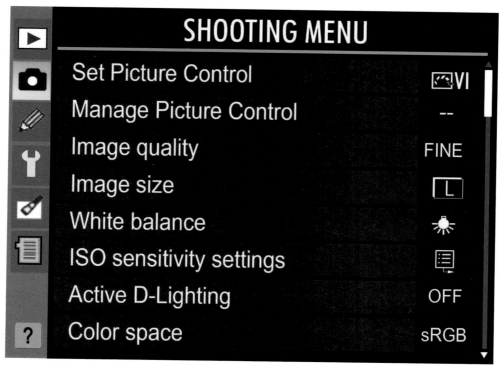

Set Picture Control

Nikon's Picture Control styles are a major improvement over the Optimize Image feature found in some earlier Nikon cameras when it comes to choosing your own sharpness, contrast, color saturation, and hue settings applied to your images. If you have used a camera with the Optimize Image option, you'll recall that it offered five fixed settings to choose from (Normal, Softer, Vivid, More Vivid, Portrait), plus Black-and-White, and a single Custom entry that allowed you to specify sharpening, tone compensation (contrast), color mode, saturation, and hue. Yes, that's right—you got *one* custom settings slot, and although you could create your own custom settings on your computer and upload them to the camera, the five predefined settings and single set of custom parameters was quite a limitation.

Happily, the Nikon D90 sweeps those limitations aside with the Picture Control styles. There are only six predefined styles offered: (Standard, Neutral, Vivid, Monochrome, Portrait, and Landscape). However, you can *edit* the settings of any of those styles (but not rename them) so they better suit your taste. But that's only the beginning, the D90 also offers *nine* (count 'em) user-definable Picture Control styles that you can edit to your heart's content, assign descriptive names, and deploy at the press of a few buttons. Even better, you can *copy* these styles to a memory card, edit them on your computer, and reload them into your camera at any time. So, effectively, you can have a lot more than nine custom Picture Control styles available: the nine in your camera, as well as a virtually unlimited library of user-defined styles that you have stored on memory cards. Custom Picture Controls can be created in Nikon View NX or Capture NX2, described in Chapter 8.

Moreover, Nikon insists that these styles have been standardized to the extent that if you re-use a style created for one camera (say, your D90) and load it into a different compatible camera (such as a Nikon D3), you'll get substantially the same rendition. In a way, Picture Control styles are a bit like using a particular film. Do you want the look of Kodak Ektachrome or Fujifilm Velvia? Load the appropriate style created by you—or anyone else.

Using and managing Picture Control styles is accomplished using two different menu entries, Set Picture Control, which allows you to choose an existing style and to edit the predefined styles that Nikon provides, and Manage Picture Control, discussed in the next section, which gives you the capability of creating and editing user-defined styles.

Choosing a Picture Control Style

In Set Picture Control, choose from one of the predefined styles (Standard, Neutral, Vivid, or Monochrome) or select a user-defined style that has previously been created (numbered C-1 to C-9)—you can't create a new Picture Control here—and follow these steps:

1. Choose Set Picture Control from the Shooting menu. The screen shown in Figure 3.10 appears. Note that Picture Controls that have been modified from their standard settings have an asterisk next to their name.

2. Scroll down to the Picture Control you'd like to use.

3. Press OK to activate the highlighted style. (Although you can usually select a menu item by pressing the multi-selector right button; in this case, that button activates editing instead.)

4. Press the Menu button or tap the shutter release to exit the menu system.

Editing a Picture Control Style

You can change the parameters of any of Nikon's predefined Picture Controls, or any of the nine user-defined styles you create. You are given the choice of using the quick adjust/fine-tune facility to modify a Picture Control with a few sliders, or to view the relationship of your Picture Controls on a grid.

Figure 3.10
You can choose from the six predefined Picture Controls, or select a user-defined style, such as *C-1 My Landscapes* shown here.

Original Picture Controls

User-defined Picture Control

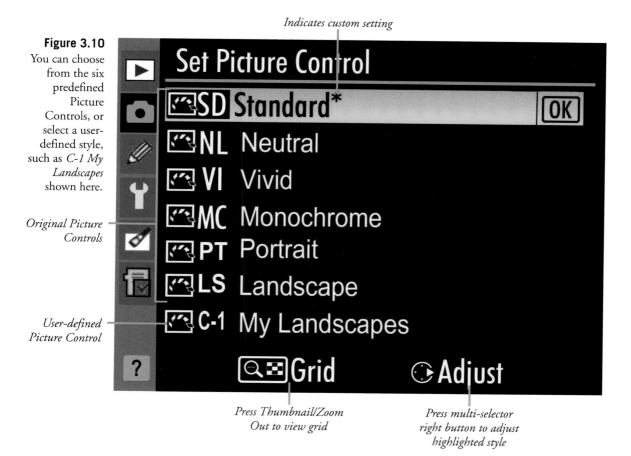

Indicates custom setting

Press Thumbnail/Zoom Out to view grid

Press multi-selector right button to adjust highlighted style

To make quick adjustments to any Picture Control except the Monochrome style, follow these steps:

1. Choose Set Picture Control from the Shooting menu.

2. Scroll down to the Picture Control you'd like to edit.

3. Press the multi-selector right button to produce the adjustment screen shown in Figure 3.11.

4. Use the Quick Adjust slider to exaggerate the attributes of the Standard, Vivid, Portrait, or Landscape styles (Quick Adjustments are not available with other predefined styles).

5. Scroll down to the Sharpening, Contrast, Brightness, Saturation, and Hue sliders with the multi-selector up/down buttons, then use the left/right buttons to decrease or increase the effects. A line will appear under the original setting in the slider whenever you've made a change from the defaults.

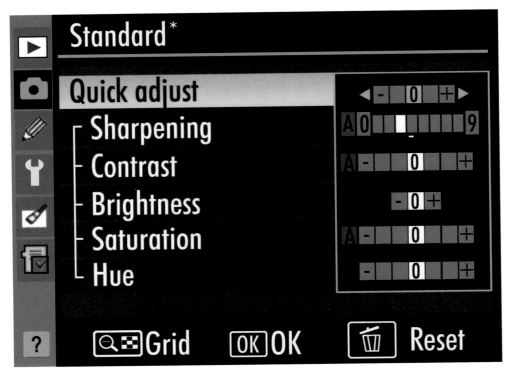

6. Instead of making changes with the slider's scale, you can move the cursor to the far left and choose A (for auto) instead when working with the Sharpening, Contrast, and Saturation sliders. The D90 will adjust these parameters automatically, depending on the type of scene it detects.

7. Press the Trash button to reset the values to their defaults.

8. Press the Thumbnail/Zoom Out button to view an adjustment grid (discussed next).

9. Press OK when you're finishing making adjustments.

Editing the Monochrome style is similar, except that the parameters differ slightly. Sharpening, Contrast, and Brightness are available, but instead of Saturation and Hue, you can choose a filter effect (Yellow, Orange, Red, Green, or none) and choose a toning effect (black-and-white, plus seven levels of Sepia, Cyanotype, Red, Yellow, Green, Blue Green, Blue, Purple Blue, and Red Purple). (Keep in mind that once you've taken a JPEG photo using a Monochrome style, you can't convert the image back to full color. Shoot using RAW+JPEG, and you'll get a monochrome JPEG, plus the RAW file that retains all the color information.)

FILTERS VS. TONING

Although some of the color choices seem to overlap, you'll get very different looks when choosing between Filter Effects and Toning. Filter Effects add no color to the monochrome image. Instead, they reproduce the look of black-and-white film that has been shot through a color filter. That is, Yellow will make the sky darker and the clouds will stand out more, while Orange makes the sky even darker and sunsets more full of detail. The Red filter produces the darkest sky of all and darkens green objects, such as leaves. Human skin may appear lighter than normal. The Green filter has the opposite effect on leaves, making them appear lighter in tone. Figure 3.12 shows the same scene shot with no filter, then Yellow, Green, and Red filters.

The Sepia, Blue, Green, and other toning effects, on the other hand, all add a color cast to your monochrome image. Use these when you want an old-time look or a special effect, without bothering to recolor your shots in an image editor.

Figure 3.12
No filter (upper left); Yellow filter (upper right); Green filter (lower left); and Red filter (lower right).

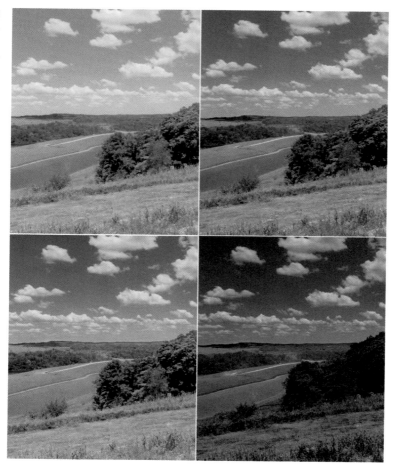

When you press the Thumbnail/Zoom Out button, a grid display, like the one shown in Figure 3.13, appears showing the relative contrast and saturation of each of the pre-defined Picture Controls. If you've created your own custom Picture Controls, they will appear on this grid, too, represented by the numbers 1-9. Because the values for auto-contrast and autosaturation may vary, the icons for any Picture Control that uses the Auto feature will be shown on the grid in green, with lines extending up and down from the icon to tip you off that the position within the coordinates may vary from the one shown.

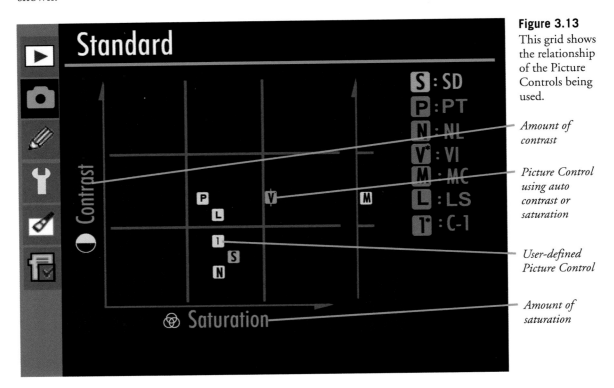

Figure 3.13
This grid shows the relationship of the Picture Controls being used.

Amount of contrast

Picture Control using auto contrast or saturation

User-defined Picture Control

Amount of saturation

Manage Picture Control

The Manage Picture Control menu entry can be used to create new styles, edit existing styles, rename or delete them, and store/retrieve them from the memory card. Here are the basic functions of this menu item, which can be found on the Shooting menu directly below the Set Picture Control entry:

- **Make a copy.** Choose Save/edit, select from the list of available Picture Controls, and press OK to store that style in one of the user-defined slots C-1 to C-9, as shown in Figure 3.14.

- **Save an edited copy.** Choose Save/edit, select from the list of available Picture Controls, and then press the multi-selector right button to edit the style, as

Figure 3.14
Picture
Controls that
you define can
be stored in
your D90's
settings.

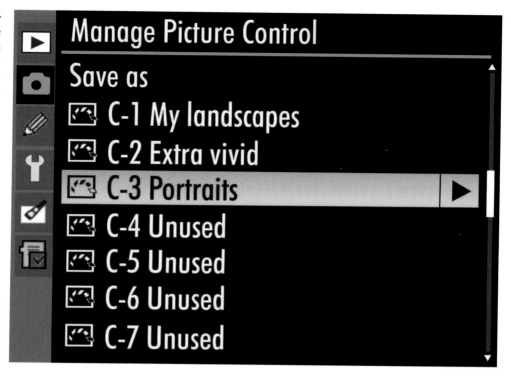

described in the previous section. Press OK when finished editing, and then save the modified style in one of the user-defined slots C-1 to C-9.

■ **Rename a style.** Choose Rename, select from the list of user-defined Picture Controls (you cannot rename the default styles), and then enter the text used as the new label for the style, using the standard D90 text entry screen shown in Figure 3.15. You may use up to 19 characters for the name.

■ **Remove a style.** Select Delete, choose from the list of user-defined Picture Controls (you can't remove one of the default styles), press the multi-selector right button, then highlight Yes in the screen that follows and press OK to remove that Picture Control.

■ **Store/retrieve style on card.** Choose Load/Save, then select Copy to Camera to locate a Picture Control on your Secure Digital card and copy it to the D90; Delete from Card to select a Picture Control on your memory card and remove it; or Copy to Card to duplicate a style currently in your camera onto the Secure Digital card. This last option allows you to create and save Picture Controls in excess of the nine that can be loaded into the camera at one time. Once you've copied a style to your memory card, you can modify the version in the camera, give it a new name, and, in effect, create a whole new Picture Control.

Entering Text on the Nikon D90

The Nikon D90 uses a fairly standardized text entry screen to name Picture Controls, create new folder names, and enter Image Comments and other text. Now is a good time to master text entry, because you'll be using it with other functions that I'll describe later in this book. The screen looks like the one shown in Figure 3.15, with some variations (for example, some functions have a less diverse character set, or offer more or fewer spaces for your entries). To name a Picture Control, just use the multi-selector navigational buttons to scroll around within the array of alphanumerics, as shown in Figure 3.15. Then, enter your text:

- **Highlight a character.** Use the multi-selector keys to scroll around within the array of characters.

- **Insert highlighted character.** Press the Zoom In button to insert the highlighted character. The cursor will move one place to the right to accept the next character.

- **Non-destructively backspace.** Hold down the Thumbnail/Zoom Out button and use the left/right buttons to move the cursor within the line of characters you've entered. This allows you to backspace and replace a character without disturbing the others you've entered.

- **Erase a highlighted character.** To remove a character you've already input, move the cursor to highlight that character, and then press the Trash button.

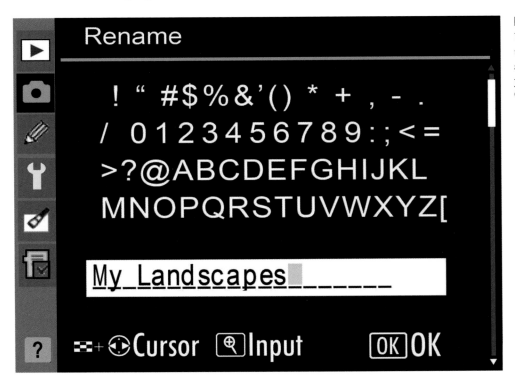

Figure 3.15
Use the D90's text entry screen to label your Picture Controls.

■ **Confirm your entry.** When you're finished entering text, press the OK button to confirm your entry, then press the left button twice to return to the Shooting menu, or just tap the shutter release to exit the menu system entirely.

Image Quality

As I noted in Chapter 2, you can choose the image quality settings used by the D90 to store its files. Just press the QUAL button and rotate the main command dial to scroll through the image quality (JPEG compression level) settings and the subcommand dial to choose the image size (resolution). You can also use this menu option and the next one, if you prefer. There is no real advantage to using these menus instead of the QUAL button and command dials. You have two choices to make:

■ **Level of JPEG compression.** To reduce the size of your image files and allow more photos to be stored on a given memory card, the D90 uses JPEG compression to squeeze the images down to a smaller size. This compacting reduces the image quality a little, so you're offered your choice of Fine (a 1:4 reduction), Normal (1:8 reduction), and Basic (1:16) compression. You can see an exaggerated version of the effects of JPEG compression in Figure 3.16. I'll explain more about JPEG compression later in this section.

■ **JPEG, RAW, or both.** You can elect to store only JPEG versions of the images you shoot, or you can save your photos as RAW images, which Nikon calls NEF, for Nikon Electronic Format files. RAW images consume more than twice as much space on your memory card. Or, you can store both RAW and a JPEG Basic files at once as you shoot. Many photographers elect to save *both* JPEG and a RAW, so they'll have a JPEG Basic version that might be usable as-is, as well as the original "digital negative" RAW file in case they want to do some processing of the image later. You'll end up with two different versions of the same file: one with a .jpg extension, and one with the .nef extension that signifies a Nikon RAW file.

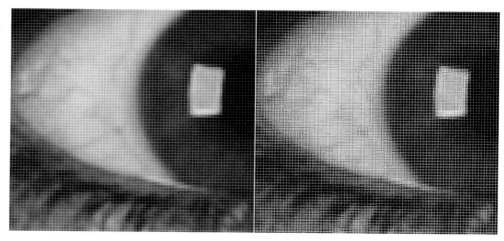

Figure 3.16
At low levels of JPEG compression the image looks sharp even when you enlarge it enough to see the actual pixels (left); when using extreme JPEG compression (right), an image obviously loses quality.

To choose the combination you want, access the Shooting menu, scroll to Image Quality, and select it by pressing OK or the multi-selector right button. Scroll to highlight the setting you want, and either press OK or push the multi-selector right button to confirm your selection (see Figure 3.17).

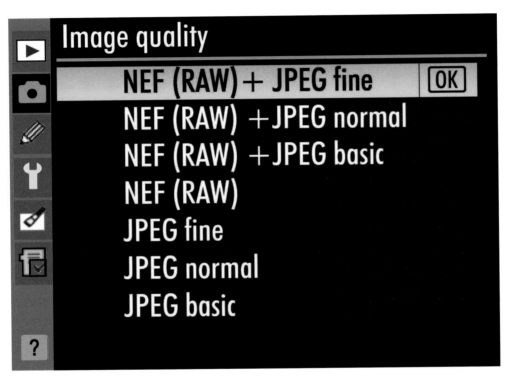

Figure 3.17
Choose from seven different combinations of RAW, JPEG, and RAW+JPEG formats.

In practice, you'll probably use the JPEG Fine or NEF (RAW)+JPEG Fine selections most often. Why so many choices, then? There are some advantages to using the JPEG Normal and JPEG Basic settings. Settings that are less than max allow stretching the capacity of your memory card so you can shoehorn quite a few more pictures onto a single memory card. That can come in useful when on vacation and you're running out of storage, or when you're shooting non-critical work that doesn't require 12 megapixels of resolution (such as photos taken for real-estate listings, web page display, photo ID cards, or similar applications). Some photographers like to record RAW+JPEG Normal so they'll have a moderate quality JPEG file for review only and no intention of using for editing purposes, while retaining access to the original RAW file for serious editing.

For most work, using lower resolution and extra compression is false economy. You never know when you might actually need that extra bit of picture detail. Your best bet is to have enough memory cards to handle all the shooting you want to do until you have the chance to transfer your photos to your computer or a personal storage device.

However, reduced image quality can sometimes be beneficial if you're shooting sequences of photos rapidly, as the D90 is able to hold more of them in its internal memory buffer before transferring to the memory card. Still, for most sports and other applications, you'd probably rather have better, sharper pictures than longer periods of continuous shooting. Do you really need 10 shots of a pass reception in a football game, or six slightly different versions of your local basketball star driving in for a lay-up?

JPEG vs. RAW

You'll sometimes be told that Nikon's NEF or RAW files are the "unprocessed" image information your camera produces, before it's been modified. That's nonsense. RAW files are no more unprocessed than camera film is after it's been through the chemicals to produce a negative or transparency. Your digital image undergoes a significant amount of processing before it is saved as a RAW file.

A RAW file is more similar to a film camera's processed negative. It contains all the information captured by the sensor, but with no sharpening and no application of any special filters or other settings you might have specified when you took the picture. Those settings are *stored* with the RAW file so they can be applied when the image is converted to a form compatible with your favorite image editor. However, using RAW conversion software such as Adobe Camera Raw or Nikon Capture NX, you can override those settings and apply settings of your own. You can select essentially the same changes there that you might have specified in your camera's picture-taking options.

RAW exists because sometimes we want to have access to all the information captured by the camera, before the camera's internal logic has processed it and converted the image to a standard file format. RAW doesn't save as much space as JPEG. What it does do is preserve all the information captured by your camera after it's been converted from analog to digital form.

So, why don't we always use RAW? Some photographers avoid using Nikon's RAW NEF files on the misguided conviction that they don't want to spend time in an image editor. But, if your basic settings are okay, such work is *optional*, and needs to be applied only when a particular image needs to be fine-tuned.

Although some photographers do save *only* in RAW format, it's common to use RAW+JPEG Basic, or, if you're confident about your settings, just shoot JPEG and eschew RAW altogether. In some situations, working with a RAW file can slow you down a little. RAW images take longer to store on the memory card, and must be converted from RAW to a format your image editor can handle, whether you elect to go with the default settings in force when the picture was taken, or make minor adjustments to the settings you specified in the camera.

As a result, those who depend on speedy access to images or who shoot large numbers of photos at once may prefer JPEG over RAW. These photographers include wedding and sports shooters, who may take hundreds to more than a thousand pictures within a few hours.

JPEG was invented as a more compact file format that can store most of the information in a digital image, but in a much smaller size. JPEG predates most digital SLRs and was initially used to squeeze down files for transmission over slow dial-up connections. JPEG provides smaller files by compressing the information in a way that loses some image data. JPEG remains a viable alternative because it offers several different quality levels. At the highest-quality Fine level, you might not be able to tell the difference between the original RAW file and the JPEG version. If you don't mind losing some quality, you can use more aggressive Normal compression with JPEG to cut the size again.

HIDDEN JPEGS

You may not be aware that your RAW file contains an embedded JPEG file, hidden inside in the JPEG Basic format. It's used to provide thumbnail previews of JPEG files, which is why you may notice an interesting phenomenon when loading a RAW image into a program like Nikon Capture NX or Adobe Lightroom. When the software first starts interpreting the RAW image, it may immediately display this hidden JPEG view which has, as you might expect, all the settings applied that you dialed into the camera. Then, as it finishes loading the RAW file, the application (Lightroom in particular) uses its own intelligence to fine-tune the image and display what it thinks is a decent version of the image, replacing the embedded JPEG. That's why you may see complaints that Lightroom or another program is behaving oddly: the initial embedded JPEG may look better than the final version, so it looks as if the application is degrading the image quality as the file loads. Of course, in all cases, once the RAW file is available, you can make your own changes to optimize it to your taste.

There is a second use for these hidden JPEG files. If you shoot RAW without creating JPEG files and later decide you want a JPEG version, there are dozens of utility programs that will extract the embedded JPEG and save it as a separate file. (Google "JPEG extractor" to locate a freeware program that will perform this step for your Mac, PC, or other computer.)

Image Size

The next menu command in the Shooting menu lets you select the resolution, or number of pixels captured as you shoot with your Nikon D90. Your choices range from Large (L—4,288×2,848, 12 megapixels), Medium (M—3,216×2,136, 6.8 megapixels), and Small (S—2,144×1424, 3 megapixels). There are no additional options available from the Image Size menu screen. Keep in mind that if you choose NEF (RAW) or NEF (RAW)+JPEG Basic, only the Large image size can be selected. The other size options are unavailable.

White Balance

The Shooting menu's White Balance settings are considerably more flexible than those available by pressing the WB button on the back of the D90, so you might want to use this menu entry instead. The button lets you choose one of six predefined settings, plus Auto and PRE (which is a user-definable white balance you can base on the lighting in a scene of your choice). The White Balance menu, on the other hand, gives you the additional option of fine-tuning the white balance precisely.

Different light sources have different "colors," at least as perceived by your D90's sensor. Indoor illumination tends to be somewhat reddish, while daylight has, in comparison, a more bluish tinge. If the color balance the camera is using doesn't match the light source, you can end up with a color rendition that is off-kilter, as you can see in Figure 3.18.

This menu entry allows you to choose one of the white balance values from among Auto, incandescent, seven varieties of fluorescent illumination, direct sunlight, flash, cloudy, shade, a specific color temperature of your choice, or a preset value taken from an existing photograph or a measurement you make.

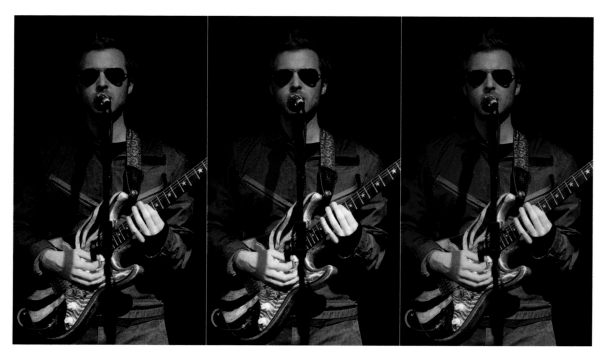

Figure 3.18 Adjusting color temperature can provide different results of the same subject at settings of 3,400K (left), 5,000K (middle), and 2,800K (right).

When you select the White Balance entry on the Shooting menu, you'll see an array of choices like those shown in Figure 3.19. (One additional choice, PRE Preset Manual is not visible until you scroll down to it.) Choose the predefined value you want by pressing the multi-selector right button, or press OK.

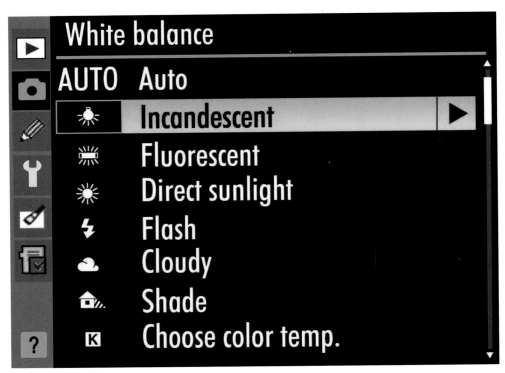

Figure 3.19
The White Balance menu has predefined values, plus the option of setting a preset you measure yourself.

If you choose Fluorescent, you'll be taken to another screen that presents seven different types of lamps, from sodium-vapor through warm-white fluorescent down to high-temperature mercury vapor. If you know the exact type of non-incandescent lighting being used, you can select it, or settle on a likely compromise (probably Cool-White, or shoot RAW and change the color balance when you import the image to your image editor). Press the multi-selector right button again or press OK to select the fluorescent lamp variation you want to use.

The Choose color temp. selection allows you to select from an array of color temperatures in degrees Kelvin from 2,500K to 10,000K, and then further fine-tune the color bias using the fine-tuning feature. Select Preset Manual to record or recall custom white balance settings suitable for environments with unusual lighting or mixed lighting, as described later in this section.

When you've finished choosing a fluorescent light source *and for all other predefined values* (Auto, incandescent, direct sunlight, flash, cloudy, or shade), you'll next be taken to the fine-tuning screen shown in Figure 3.20 (and which uses the incandescent setting as an example). The screen shows a grid with two axes, a blue/amber axis extending left/right, and a green/magenta axis extending up and down the grid. By default, the grid's cursor is positioned in the middle, and a readout to the right of the grid shows the cursor's coordinates on the A-B axis (yes, I know the display has the end points reversed) and G-M axis at 0,0.

Figure 3.20
Specific white balance settings can be fine-tuned by changing their bias in the amber/blue, magenta/green directions—or along both axes simultaneously.

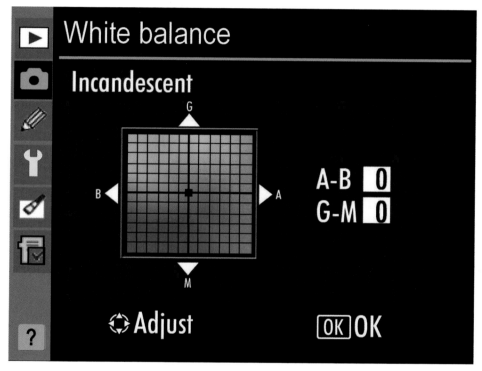

You can use the multi-selector's up/down and right/left buttons to move the cursor to any coordinate in the grid, thereby biasing the white balance in the direction(s) you choose. The amber-blue axis makes the image warmer or colder (but not actually yellow or blue). Similarly, the green/magenta axis preserves all the colors in the original image, but gives them a tinge biased toward green or magenta. Each increment equals about five mired units, but you should know that mired values aren't linear; five mireds at 2,500K produces a much stronger effect than five mireds at 6,000K. If you really want to fine-tune your color balance, you're better off experimenting and evaluating the results of a particular change.

When you've fine-tuned white balance, an asterisk appears next to the white balance icon in both the Shooting menu and Shooting Information screen shown on the LCD, as a tip-off that this tweaking has taken place.

Using Preset Manual White Balance

If automatic white balance or one of the predefined settings available aren't suitable, you can set a custom white balance using the Preset Manual menu option. You can apply the white balance from a scene, either by shooting a new picture on the spot and using the resulting white balance (Measure), or using an image you have already shot (Use photo). To perform direct measurement from your current scene using a reference object (preferably a neutral gray or white object), follow these steps:

1. Place the neutral reference under the lighting you want to measure.

2. Press the WB button and rotate the main command dial to display PRE on the top panel LCD.

3. Release the WB button momentarily.   Then press the button again until the PRE icon in the top panel LCD and viewfinder starts flashing.

4. While the indicators are flashing, fill the frame with the neutral reference subject.

5. Press the shutter release to measure the white balance.

6. After you've taken the photo, if the D90 was able to capture the white balance data, a message Good will flash on the top   panel LCD, and Gd will appear in the viewfinder.   Otherwise, no Gd   will be shown in both locations.   Thereafter, the captured white balance value will appear in the Preset section of the White Balance entry in the Shooting menu (see Figure 3.21).

The preset value you've captured will remain in the D90's memory until you replace that white balance with a new captured value. You can also use the white balance information from a picture you've already taken, using the Use photo option, as described next:

1. Choose Preset Manual from the White Balance menu.

2. Select Use Photo.

3. The most recently shot picture will appear, with a menu offering to use This Image or Select Image.

4. Press OK to use the displayed image, or choose Select Image to specify another picture on your memory card.

5. If you want to select a different image, you can choose which folder on your memory card, then navigate through the selected images, using the standard D90 image selection screen shown several times previously in this chapter. (See Figure 3.15 for a refresher.)

Figure 3.21
When you capture a scene's white balance, it will be stored in the D90's white balance preset.

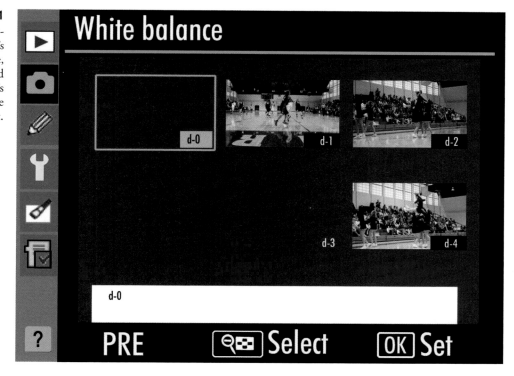

6. When the photo you'd like to use is highlighted, press OK to select it.

7. You'll be returned to the Shooting menu, where you can press the Menu button to exit, or just tap the shutter release.

A WHITE BALANCE LIBRARY

Consider dedicating a low-capacity memory card to stow a selection of images taken under a variety of lighting conditions. If you want to "recycle" one of the color temperatures you've stored, insert the card and select it with the Use Photo option.

ISO Sensitivity Settings

This is the first entry in the second page of the Shooting menu (see Figure 3.22). ISO governs how sensitive your Nikon D90 is to light. Low ISO settings, such as ISO 200 mean that the camera must have more light available to take a picture, or that you must use wider lens openings or slower shutter speeds. Faster ISO settings, on the other hand, let you take pictures in lower light levels, with faster shutter speeds (say, to freeze action) or with smaller lens openings (to produce a larger range in which objects are in sharp focus). I'll explain all these factors in more detail in Chapter 4.

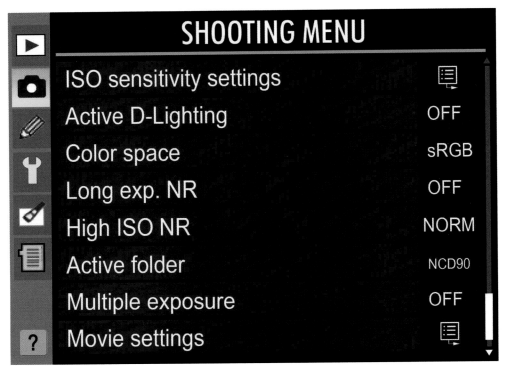

This menu entry has two parts, ISO Sensitivity (available with all exposure modes) and ISO Sensitivity Auto Control (available only in PAS modes). The former is simply a screen that allows you to specify the ISO setting, just as you would by spinning the main command dial while holding down the ISO button on the back the D90. The available settings range from LO 1 (ISO 100 equivalent) through ISO 3200 to HI 1 (ISO 6400 equivalent). Use the ISO sensitivity menu when you find it more convenient to set ISO using the three-inch color LCD.

The ISO sensitivity auto control menu used with Program, Aperture Priority, and Shutter Priority (but not Manual) exposure modes lets you specify how and when the D90 will adjust the ISO value for you automatically under certain conditions. This capability can be potentially useful, although experienced photographers tend to shy away from any feature that allows the camera to change basic settings like ISO that have been carefully selected. Fortunately, you can set some boundaries so the D90 will use this adjustment in a fairly intelligent way.

When Auto ISO is activated, the camera can bump up the ISO sensitivity, if necessary, whenever an optimal exposure cannot be achieved at the current ISO setting. Of course, it can be disconcerting to think you're shooting at ISO 400 and then see a grainier ISO 1600 shot during LCD review. While the D90 provides a flashing ISO-Auto alert in the viewfinder and top-panel status LCD, the warning is easy to miss.

Here are the important considerations to keep in mind when using the options available for this feature:

- **Off.** Set ISO sensitivity auto control to off, and the ISO setting will not budge from whatever value you have specified. Use this setting when you don't want any ISO surprises, or when ISO increases are not needed to counter slow shutter speeds. For example, if the D90 is mounted on a tripod, you can safely use slower shutter speeds at a relatively low ISO setting, so there is no need for a speed bump. On the other hand, if you're handholding the camera and the D90 set for Program (P) or Aperture Priority (A) mode wants to use a shutter speed slower than, say, 1/30th second, it's probably a good idea to increase the ISO to avoid the effects of camera shake. If you're using a longer lens, a shutter speed of 1/125th second or higher might be the point where an ISO bump would be a good idea. In that case, you can turn the ISO sensitivity auto control on, or remember to boost the ISO setting yourself.

- **Maximum sensitivity.** Use this parameter to indicate the highest ISO setting you're comfortable having the D90 set on its own. You can choose from ISO 400, 800, 1600, 3200, and HI 1 (ISO 6400 equivalent) as the max ISO setting the camera will use. Use a low number if you'd rather not take any photos at a high ISO without manually setting that value yourself. Dial in a higher ISO number if getting the photo at any sensitivity setting is more important than worrying about noise.

- **Minimum shutter speed.** This setting allows you to tell the D90 how slow the shutter speed must be before the ISO boost kicks in, within the range 1 second to 1/250th second. The default value is 1/30th second, because for most shooters in most situations, any shutter speed longer than 1/30th is to be avoided, unless you're using a tripod, monopod, or looking for a special effect. If you have steady hands, or the camera is partially braced against movement (say, you're using that monopod), a slower shutter speed, down to 1 full second, can be specified. Similarly, if you're working with a telephoto lens and find even a relatively brief shutter speed "dangerous," you can set a minimum shutter speed threshold of 1/250th second. When the shutter speed is faster than the minimum you enter, auto ISO will not take effect.

Active D-Lighting

D-Lighting is a feature that improves the rendition of detail in highlights and shadows when you're photographing high contrast scenes (those that have dramatic differences between the brightest areas and the darkest areas that hold detail). It's been available as an internal retouching option that could be used *after* the picture has been taken, and has been found in Nikon's lower-end cameras (by that I mean the CoolPix point-and-shoot line) for some time, and has gradually worked its way up through the company's dSLR products, most recently becoming available in the Nikon D60, D90, D90, D3, and D3x. You'll find this post-shot feature in the Retouch menu, which I'll describe later in the chapter.

A new wrinkle, however, is the *Active D-Lighting* capability introduced with Nikon's newest cameras, which, unlike the Retouch menu post-processing feature, applies its improvements *while you are actually taking the photo.* That's good news and bad news. It means that, if you're taking photos in a contrasty environment, Active D-Lighting can automatically improve the apparent dynamic range of your image as you shoot, without additional effort on your part. However, you'll need to disable the feature once you leave the high contrast lighting behind, and the process does take some time to apply as you shoot. You wouldn't want to use Active D-Lighting for continuous shooting of sports subjects, for example. There are many situations in which the selective application of D-Lighting using the Retouch menu is a better choice. Figure 3.23 shows a typical example.

For best results, use your D90's Matrix metering mode (described in more detail in Chapter 4), so the Active D-Lighting feature can work with a full range of exposure information from multiple points in the image. Active D-Lighting works its magic by subtly *underexposing* your image so that details in the highlights (which would normally be overexposed and become featureless white pixels) are not lost. At the same time, it adjusts the values of pixels located in midtone and shadow areas so they don't become

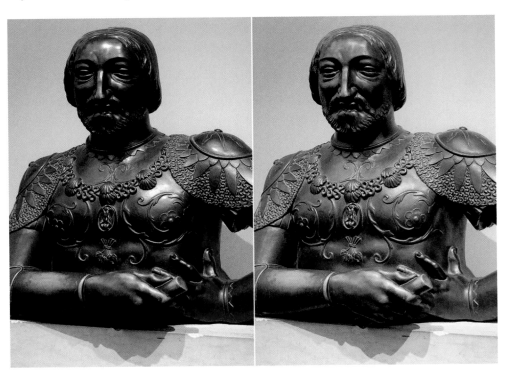

Figure 3.23
No D-Lighting (left); Active D-Lighting (right).

too dark because of the underexposure. Highlight tones will be preserved, while shadows will eventually be allowed to go dark more readily. Bright beach or snow scenes, especially those with few shadows (think high noon, when the shadows are smaller) can benefit from using Active D-Lighting.

You have just two choices: Off and On. You'll want to experiment to see which types of situations can benefit your shooting the most.

Color Space

The Nikon D60's Color Space option gives you two different color spaces (also called *color gamuts*), named Adobe RGB (because it was developed by Adobe Systems in 1998), and sRGB (supposedly because it is the *standard* RGB color space). These two color gamuts define a specific set of colors that can be applied to the images your D90 captures.

You're probably surprised that the Nikon D90 doesn't automatically capture *all* the colors we see. Unfortunately, that's impossible because of the limitations of the sensor and the filters used to capture the fundamental red, green, and blue colors, as well as that of the phosphors used to display those colors on your camera and computer monitors. Nor is it possible to *print* every color our eyes detect, because the inks or pigments used don't absorb and reflect colors perfectly.

On the other hand, the D90 does capture quite a few more colors than we need. The original 12-bit RAW image contains a possible 68 *billion* different hues, which are condensed down to a mere 16.8 million possible colors when converted to a 24-bit (eight bits per channel) image. While 16.8 million colors may seem like a lot, it's a small subset of 68 billion captured, and an even smaller subset of all the possible colors we can see.

The set of colors, or gamut, that can be reproduced or captured by a given device (scanner, digital camera, monitor, printer, or some other piece of equipment) are represented as a color space that exists within the larger full range of colors. That full range is represented by the odd-shaped splotch of color shown in Figure 3.24, as defined by scientists at an international organization back in 1931. The colors possible with Adobe RGB are represented by the larger, black triangle in the figure, while the sRGB gamut is represented by the smaller white triangle.

Regardless of which triangle—or color space—is used by the D90, you end up with some combination of 16.8 million different colors that can be used in your photograph. (No one image will contain all 16.8 million! If each and every pixel in a D90's 12-megapixel image were a different color—which is extremely unlikely—you'd need only 12 million different colors.) But, as you can see from the figure, the colors available will be *different*.

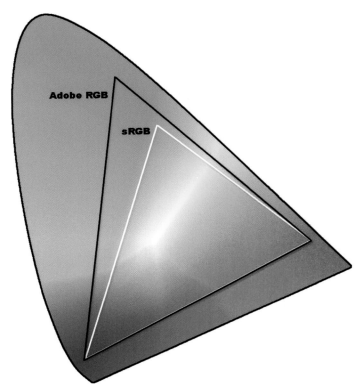

Figure 3.24
The outer figure shows all the colors we can see; the two inner outlines show the boundaries of Adobe RGB (black triangle) and sRGB (white triangle).

Adobe RGB is an expanded color space useful for commercial and professional printing, and it can reproduce a wider range of colors. It can also come in useful if an image is going to be extensively retouched, especially within an advanced image editor, like Adobe Photoshop, which has sophisticated color management capabilities that can be tailored to specific color spaces. As an advanced user, you don't need to automatically "upgrade" your D90 to Adobe RGB, because images tend to look less saturated on your monitor and, it is likely, significantly different from what you will get if you output the photo to your personal inkjet. (You can *profile* your monitor for the Adobe RGB color space to improve your on-screen rendition.)

While both Adobe RGB and sRGB can reproduce the exact same 16.8 million absolute colors, Adobe RGB spreads those colors over a larger portion of the visible spectrum, as you can see in the figure. Think of a box of crayons (the jumbo 16.8 million crayon variety). Some of the basic crayons from the original sRGB set have been removed and replaced with new hues not contained in the original box. Your "new" box contains colors that can't be reproduced by your computer monitor, but which work just fine with a commercial printing press. For example, Adobe RGB has more "crayons" available in the cyan-green portion of the box, compared to sRGB, which is unlikely to be an advantage unless your image's final destination are the cyan, magenta, yellow, and black inks of a printing press.

The other color space, sRGB is recommended for images that will be output locally on the user's own printer, as this color space matches that of the typical inkjet printer fairly closely. You might prefer sRGB, which is the default for the Nikon D90 and most other cameras, as it is well suited for the range of colors that can be displayed on a computer screen and viewed over the Internet. If you plan to take your image file to a retailer's kiosk for printing, sRGB is your best choice, because those automated output devices are calibrated for the sRGB color space that consumers use.

BEST OF BOTH WORLDS

If you plan to use RAW+JPEG for most of your photos, go ahead and set sRGB as your color space. You'll end up with JPEGs suitable for output on your own printer, but you can still extract an Adobe RGB version from the RAW file at any time. It's like shooting two different color spaces at once—sRGB and Adobe RGB—and getting the best of both worlds.

Of course, choosing the right color space doesn't solve the problems that result from having each device in the image chain manipulating or producing a slightly different set of colors. To that end, you'll need to investigate the wonderful world of *color management*, which uses hardware and software tools to match or *calibrate* all your devices, as closely as possible, so that what you see more closely resembles what you capture, what you see on your computer display, and what ends up on a printed hardcopy. Entire books have been devoted to color management, and most of what you need to know doesn't directly involve your Nikon D90, so I won't detail the nuts and bolts here.

To manage your color, you'll need, at the bare minimum, some sort of calibration system for your computer display, so that your monitor can be adjusted to show a standardized set of colors that is repeatable over time. (What you see on the screen can vary as the monitor ages, or even when the room light changes.) I use Pantone's Huey monitor color correction system for my computer's main 26-inch wide-screen LCD display, as well as for the smaller 20-inch wide-screen secondary display that flanks it. The Huey checks room light levels every five minutes, and reminds me to recalibrate every week or two, using the small sensor device shown in Figure 3.25, which attaches temporarily to the front of screen with tiny suction cups, and interprets test patches that the Huey software displays during calibration. The rest of the time, the Huey sensor sits in the stand shown, measuring the room illumination, and adjusting my monitors for higher or lower ambient light levels.

The Huey (www.pantone.com) is an inexpensive (under $100) system that does a good job of calibrating a single monitor. You can upgrade it, as I did, for use with multiple monitors using a $40 software download. If you're serious about accurate color and make prints, you'll want a more advanced system (up to $500) like the various Spyder products from Datacolor (www.datacolor.com), or Colormunki from X-Rite (www.colormunki.com).

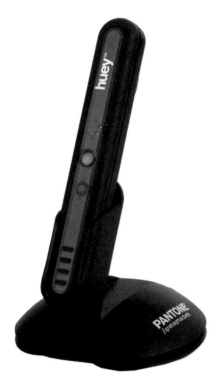

Long Exp. NR

Visual noise is that awful graininess caused by long exposures and high ISO settings, and which shows up as multicolored specks in images. This setting helps you manage the kind of noise caused by lengthy exposure times. In some ways, noise is like the excessive grain found in some high-speed photographic films. However, while photographic grain is sometimes used as a special effect, it's rarely desirable in a digital photograph. There are easier ways to add texture to your photos.

Some noise is created when you're using shutter speeds longer than eight seconds to create a longer exposure. Extended exposure times allow more photons to reach the sensor, but increase the likelihood that some photosites will react randomly even though not struck by a particle of light. Moreover, as the sensor remains switched on for the longer exposure, it heats, and this heat can be mistakenly recorded as if it were a barrage of photons. This menu setting can be used to switch the D90's long exposure noise-canceling operation performed by the EXPEED digital signal processor.

■ **Off.** This default setting disables long exposure noise reduction. Use it when you want the maximum amount of detail present in your photograph, even though higher noise levels will result. This setting also eliminates the extra time needed to take a picture caused by the noise reduction process. If you plan to use only lower ISO settings (thereby reducing the noise caused by ISO amplification), the noise levels produced by longer exposures may be acceptable. For example, you might be shooting a waterfall at ISO 100 (L 1.0) with the camera mounted on a tripod, using a neutral density filter and a long exposure to cause the water to blur. (Try exposures of 2 to 16 seconds, depending on the intensity of the light and how much blur you want.) To maximize detail in the non-moving portions of your photos for the exposures that are eight seconds or longer, you can switch off long exposure noise reduction, as was done for Figure 3.26.

- **On.** When exposures are eight seconds or longer, the Nikon D90 takes a second, blank exposure and compares that to the first image. (While the second image is taken, the warning Job nr appears on the monochrome LCD panel and in the viewfinder.) Noise (pixels that are bright in a frame that *should* be completely black) in the "dark frame" image is subtracted from your original picture, and only the noise-corrected image is saved to your memory card. Because the noise-reduction process effectively doubles the time required to take a picture, you won't want to use this setting when you're rushed. Some noise can be removed later on, using tools like Bibble Pro or the noise reduction features built into Nikon Capture NX.

Figure 3.26
No long exposure noise correction was needed for this shot.

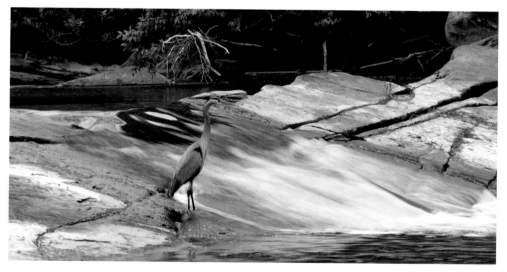

High ISO NR

Noise can also be caused by higher ISO sensitivity settings, and the Nikon D90, which offers settings up to ISO 3200 (and thence up to the equivalent of ISO 6400 with the H 1.0 setting) has a loftier ISO ceiling than most cameras. Indeed, the D90 uses a reduced-noise CMOS sensor (instead of the CCD sensor found in the Nikon D80) and gives you results that are at least one or two stops better than its immediate predecessor. That is, you can expect the Nikon D90 to produce results at ISO 3200 that you might have expected from the D80 at ISO 800 to ISO 1600. Even so, high ISO noise reduction, which can be set with this menu option, may be a good option in many cases. You can choose Off when you want to preserve detail at the cost of some noise graininess, and the D90 will apply high ISO NR only at the "boosted" settings of HI 0.3, HI 0.6, and HI 1.0. Or, you can select Low, Normal, and High noise reduction, which is applied when ISO sensitivity has been set to ISO 800 or higher.

The effects of high ISO noise are something like listening to a CD in your car, and then rolling down all the windows. You're adding sonic noise to the audio signal, and while increasing the CD player's volume may help a bit, you're still contending with an unfavorable signal to noise ratio that probably mutes tones (especially higher treble notes) that you really want to hear.

The same thing happens when the analog image signal is amplified: You're increasing the image information in the signal, but boosting the background fuzziness at the same time. Tune in a very faint or distant AM radio station on your car stereo. Then turn up the volume. After a certain point, turning up the volume further no longer helps you hear better. There's a similar point of diminishing returns for digital sensor ISO increases and signal amplification as well.

As the captured information is amplified to produce higher ISO sensitivities, some random noise in the signal is amplified along with the photon information. Increasing the ISO setting of your camera raises the threshold of sensitivity so that fewer and fewer photons are needed to register as an exposed pixel. Yet, that also increases the chances of one of those phantom photons being counted among the real-life light particles, too.

Fortunately, the Nikon D90's CMOS sensor and its EXPEED digital processing chip are optimized to produce low noise levels, so ratings as high as ISO 1600 to ISO 3200 can be used routinely (although there will be some noise, of course), and even HI 1.0 (ISO 6400 equivalent) can generate good results. Some kinds of subjects may not require this kind of noise cancellation, particularly with images that have a texture of their own that tends to hide or mask the noise.

Active Folder

If you want to store images in a folder other than the one created and selected by the Nikon D90, you can switch among available folders on your Compact Flash card, or create your own folder. Remember that any folders you create will be deleted when you reformat your memory card.

To change the currently active folder:

■ Choose Active Folder in the Shooting menu.

■ Scroll down to Select Folder and press the multi-selector right button.

- From among the available folders shown, scroll to the one that you want to become active for image storage and playback. (This capability can be handy when displaying images using the Slide Show feature.)

- Press the OK button to confirm your choice, or press the multi-selector right button to return to the Shooting menu.

Why create your own folders? Perhaps you're traveling and have a high-capacity memory card and want to store the images for each day (or for each city that you visit) in a separate folder. Maybe you'd like to separate those wedding photos you snapped at the ceremony from those taken at the reception. As I mentioned earlier, the Nikon D90 automatically creates a folder on a newly formatted memory card with a name like 100ND90, and when it fills with 999 images, it will automatically create a new folder with a number incremented by one (such as 101ND90). To create, delete, or rename a folder:

- Choose Active Folder in the Shooting menu.

- Scroll down to New, Rename, or Delete and press the multi-selector right button.

- To name a new folder or rename an existing folder, use the text entry screen, first shown in Figure 3.15, and key in a name.

- Press OK when finished to create and activate the new folder.

Multiple Exposure

This option, available only in PSAM modes, lets you combine two exposures into one image without the need for an image editor like Photoshop, and can be an entertaining way to return to those thrilling days of yesteryear, when complex photos were created in the camera itself. In truth, prior to the digital age, multiple exposures were a cool, groovy, far-out, hep/hip, phat, sick, fabulous way of producing composite images. Today, it's more common to take the lazy way out, snap two or more pictures, and then assemble them in an image editor like Photoshop.

However, if you're willing to spend the time planning a multiple exposure (or are open to some happy accidents), there is a lot to recommend about the multiple exposure capability that Nikon has bestowed on the D90. For one thing, the camera is able to combine two or more images using the RAW data from the sensor, producing photos that are blended together more smoothly than is likely for anyone who's not a Photoshop guru.

Figure 3.27 shows an odd double exposure created by shooting two pictures about 20 feet apart, directly in front of the stage at a concert.

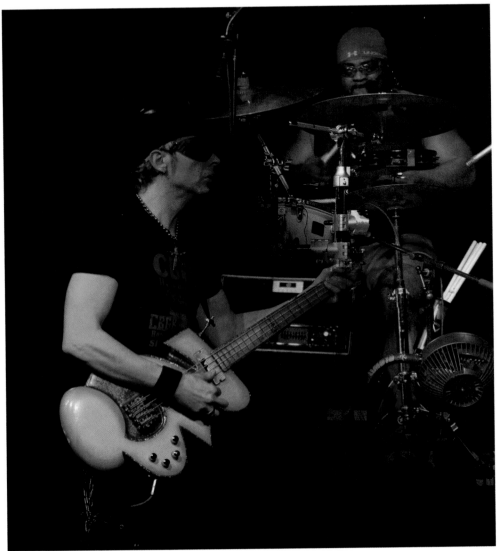

To take your own multiple exposures, just follow these steps (although it's probably a good idea to do a little planning and maybe even some sketching on paper first):

1. Choose Multiple Exposure from the Shooting menu.

2. Select Number of Shots, choose a value from 2 to 10 with the multi-selector up/down buttons, and press OK.

3. Choose Auto Gain and specify either On (the default) or Off. When On is selected, the D90 will divide the total exposure of the image by the number of shots speci-fied, for example applying 1/4 of the exposure time to each shot in a four-image

series. Choose Off, and the full exposure is applied to each picture. You'd want to use Off when using a dark background that would allow successive exposures to add details, and On to avoid the risk of overlapping images washing each other out.

4. Press OK to set the gain.

5. Move the cursor up to Done and press OK. The multiple exposure icon appears in the monochrome LCD status panel.

6. Take the photo by pressing the shutter release button multiple times until all the exposures in the series have been taken. (In Continuous Shooting mode, the entire series will be shot in a single burst.) The blinking multiple exposure icon vanishes when the series is finished, and the camera reverts to Multiple Exposure: Off.

Keep in mind if you wait longer than 30 seconds between any two photos in the series, the sequence will terminate and combine the images taken so far. If you want a longer elapsed time between exposures, go to the Playback menu and make sure On has been specified for Image Review, and then extend the monitor display time using CSM #c4 (described later in this chapter) to an appropriate maximum interval. The Multiple Exposure feature will then use the monitor-off delay as its maximum interval between shots.

Movie Settings

There aren't too many options in this menu entry. You can select image quality (frame size) and whether to use sound. All clips are shot at the same 24 frames per second rate. Your choices are as follows:

- **Quality—1280×720 (16:9).** Select this option to shoot HDTV-quality movies in the 16:9 aspect ratio. This mode uses the most space on your memory card, and limits your recording time to five minutes (about 2GB in size). Use this mode when you want to make clips that you can view on a television.

- **Quality—640×424 (3:2).** This mode shoots movies roughly comparable to what you'd get with a non-HDTV camcorder, such as a VHS recording. You can use this mode to get movies that look good on a standard television, or on a computer monitor as part of a presentation or web page. You can shoot sequences up to 20 minutes long.

- **Quality—320×216 (3:2).** This mode produces more compact movies that can be used on smaller screens and web pages. Your sequences at this setting can be up to 20 minutes long.

- **Sound—On/Off.** Use On to record movies with monaural sound. If you want silent movies, or plan to add your own narration, music, or soundtrack later, or are working in a very noisy environment with lousy ambient sound, use the Off setting.

The Custom Setting Menu

The Custom Setting menus consist of a series of six color-coded menu categories, plus Reset Custom Settings. The categories include:

- a Autofocus (red)
- b Metering/exposure (yellow)
- c Timers/AE lock (green)
- d Shooting/display (cyan)
- e Bracketing/flash (blue)
- f Controls (purple)

Unlike the Shooting menu options, which you are likely to modify frequently as your picture-taking environment changes, the Custom Setting menus (see Figure 3.28) provides a roster of slightly more stable groups of preferences that let you tailor the behavior of your camera in a variety of different ways for longer-term use.

Some options are minor tweaks useful for specific shooting situations. You can turn off the D90's built-in beeper when you are shooting an acoustic music concert, when you'd rather not disrupt the environment. Others make the camera more convenient to use. Perhaps you'd like to assign a frequently used feature to the Fn button.

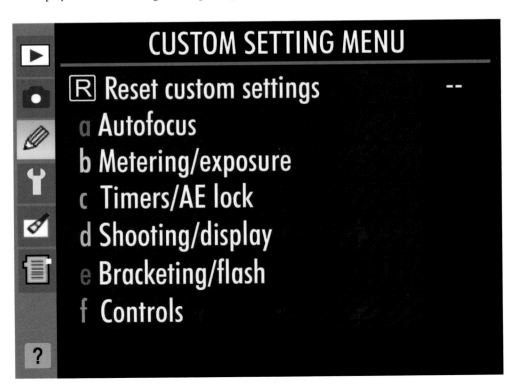

Figure 3.28
The Custom Setting menu.

This section concentrates on explaining all the options of the Custom Setting menu and, most importantly, when and why you might want to use each setting.

Reset

If you select Yes, all the Custom Setting options will be reset to their default values. It has no effect on the settings in other menus, or any of the other camera settings. If that's what you want, try the two-button reset described in Chapter 1, holding down the EV (+/-) button (just southwest of the shutter release) and the AF button (the bottom button to the right of the top panel LCD), both marked with green dots, for about two seconds.

You'd want to use this Reset option when you've made a bunch of changes to your Custom Setting (say, while playing around with them as you read this chapter), and now want to put them back to the factory defaults. Your choices are Yes and No.

a. Autofocus Options

The red-coded Autofocus options (see Figure 3.29) deal with some of the potentially most vexing settings available with the Nikon D90. After all, incorrect focus is one of the most damaging picture-killers of all the attributes in an image. You may be able to compensate for bad exposure, partially fix errant color balance, and perhaps even incorporate motion blur into an image as a creative element. But if focus is wrong, the

Figure 3.29
The Autofocus
Custom Setting
menu.

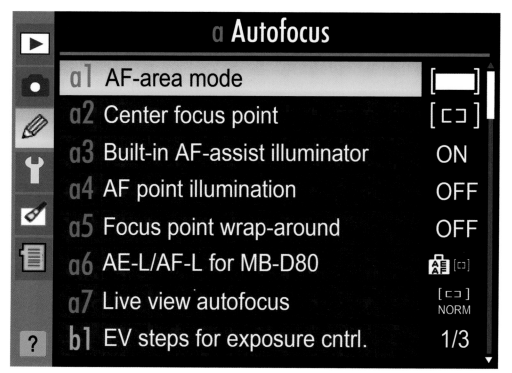

photograph doesn't look right, and no amount of "I meant to do that!" pleas are likely to work. The D90's autofocus options enable you to choose how and when focus is applied, the controls used to activate the feature, and the way focus points are selected from the available 11 zones. This submenu has seven choices that control how your D90 uses its autofocus system. They are as follows:

- a1 AF-area mode
- a2 Center focus point
- a3 Built-in AF-assist illuminator
- a4 AF point illumination
- a5 Focus point wrap-around
- a6 AE-L/AF-L for MB-D80
- a7 Live View autofocus

a1 AF-area mode

Autofocus Area parameter tells your Nikon D90 how to choose which of the 11 focus points in the viewfinder should be used to evaluate and lock in focus. The D90 can choose a focus point itself, and does so automatically when using Auto, No-Flash, Portrait, Landscape, Night Portrait, and in PASM (Program, Aperture Priority, Shutter Priority, Manual) when you select Auto Area. You must rotate the Focus Selector lever on the back of the camera (to the right of the LCD) from the L (locked) position to the * (unlocked) position. When the focus point is unlocked, you can use the multi-selector pad to shift the active point to any of the 11 focus points seen in the viewfinder. Then, choose either Single Point or Dynamic Area from the list below.

- **Single Point.** You choose which of the 11 points is used, with the multi-selector buttons. Good for stationary subjects, Single Point is used automatically in Close-up scene mode.

- **Dynamic Area.** You can select the focus point, but the D90 can use other focus points as well. Good for objects that are moving, the D90 will use the area you choose in Single-Servo autofocus mode (AF-S), or, when using Continuous autofocus mode (AF-C) or Automatic autofocus mode (AF-A), the D90 will refocus using other focus zones if the subject begins moving. Use for sports and active children.

- **Auto-Area.** This default mode chooses the focus point for you, and can use distance information when working with a G or D lens that supplies that data to the camera.

- **3D Tracking (11 points).** In this mode, you select the focus point using the multi-selector, but if you subsequently reframe the picture slightly, the D90 uses distance information when in AF-C or AF-A modes to refocus on the original subject if necessary. (When using AF-S, this mode functions the same as Single Point focus area mode.) This mode is useful if you need to reframe a relatively static subject from time to time. If your subject leaves the frame entirely, you'll need to release the shutter button and refocus.

a2 Center focus point

You have two choices here. (Chapter 5 explains all these focus options in more detail.)

- **Normal Zone.** This default setting is useful for non-moving objects that can be captured within the center focus point on the viewfinder screen.

- **Wide Zone.** Used with moving objects, it provides a wider focus area that does a better job of tracking active subjects. This setting is not available when Auto-Area autofocus is used.

a3 Built-in AF-assist illuminator

Use this setting to control whether the AF-assist lamp built into the Nikon D90, or the more powerful AF-assist lamp built into Nikon electronic flash units (like the Nikon SB-900) and the Nikon SC-29 coiled remote flash cord (for firing the flash when not mounted on the camera) are used to provide an extra pre-exposure burst of light to aid in automatic focusing.

- **On.** This default value will cause the AF-assist illuminator lamp to flash when lighting is poor, but only if Single-Servo autofocus (AF-S) is active, or you have selected the center focus point manually and either Single Point or Dynamic Area autofocus (rather than Auto-Area autofocus) has been chosen.

- **Off.** Use this to disable the AF-assist illuminator. You'd find that useful when the lamp might be distracting or discourteous (say, at a religious ceremony or acoustic music concert), or your subject is located closer than 1 foot, eight inches or farther than about 10 feet.

a4 AF point illumination

It's usually helpful to have the active focus point highlighted in red in the viewfinder, although the flashing indicator does use a minuscule amount of power. This setting lets you specify when/if this highlighting happens. Your choices:

- **Auto.** With this default setting, the D90 will illuminate the selected focus point if it determines that highlighting is needed to sufficiently contrast the focus zone from the background.

- **On.** The selected focus point is always highlighted.

- **Off.** The selected focus point is never highlighted in red.

a5 Focus point wrap-around

This setting is purely a personal preference parameter. When you press the multi-selector left/right and up/down buttons to choose a focus point, the D90 can be told to stop when the selection reaches the edge of the 11-point array—or, it can continue, wrapping around to the opposite edge, like Pac-Man leaving the playing area on one side or top/bottom to re-emerge on the other. (I hope I'm not revealing my age, here.) Your choices are simple; decide which behavior you prefer:

- **Wrap.** Pressing the left/right or up/down buttons when you've reached the edge of the focus point display wraps the selection to the opposite side, still moving in the same direction.

- **No Wrap.** The focus point selection stops at the edge of the focus zone array. This is the default setting.

a6 AE-L/AF-L for MB-D80

You can use the AF-ON button included in the MB-D10 battery pack/grip for its intended purpose when firing the camera in vertical orientation, or you can redefine the button to a related function, depending on your working preferences. This setting changes *only* the behavior of the AF-ON button on the MB-D80; the AF-ON button on the D90 camera body may be set up to do something different (which can be *very* confusing). Your choices are as follows:

- **AE/AF lock.** With this default setting, both focus and exposure are locked when the AE-L/AF-L button on the MB-D80 is held down.

- **AE lock only.** Exposure is locked while the AE-L/AF-L button on the MB-D80 is held down.

- **AF lock only.** This setting locks autofocus as long as the button on the MB-D80 is pressed.

- **AE lock (Hold).** Exposure locks when the AE-L/AF-L button is pressed, and remains locked at that exposure until the button is pressed again, or the meters turn off.

- **AF-ON.** Autofocus is initiated when the AE-L/AF-L button on the MB-D80 is pressed.

- **FV Lock.** Flash value for the built-in flash or an attached dedicated flash is locked when the AE-L/AF-L button on the MB-D80 is pressed. The flash setting remains locked until you press the button again, or the exposure meters turn off.

- **Focus point selection.** When this option is selected, you can choose a focus point (except in Auto-Area mode) by pressing the AE-L/AF-L button on the MB-D80 and rotating the grip's subcommand dial.

a7 Live View autofocus

Although you can select any of the three Live View autofocus modes while using Live View (just press the AF button and rotate the main command dial), you can specify a default mode for Live View here. You'll find more tips on using Live View in Chapter 5. Your choices are as follows:

■ **Wide-Area.** A large red box appears on the LCD when using this mode.

■ **Normal Area.** A smaller red box appears.

■ **Face Priority.** No box is shown.

b. Metering/Exposure Options

The orange-coded metering/exposure Custom Setting (see Figure 3.30) let you define four different parameters that affect exposure metering in the Nikon D90. Your choices are as follows:

■ b1 EV steps for exposure cntrl

■ b2 Easy exposure compensation

■ b3 Center-weighted area

■ b4 Fine-tune optimal exposure

Figure 3.30
There are four metering/ exposure options.

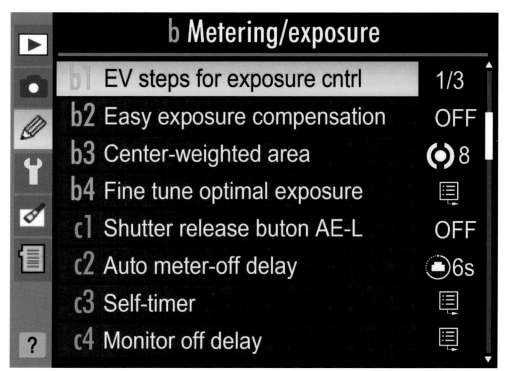

b1 EV steps for exposure cntrl

This setting tells the Nikon D90 the size of the "jumps" it should use when making exposure adjustments, exposure compensation, and bracketing—either one-third, one-half, or one full stop. The increment you specify here applies to f/stops, shutter speeds, EV changes, and autoexposure bracketing. As with ISO sensitivity step value, you can select from 1/3 step (the default); 1/2 step; and 1 step increments.

Choose the 1/3 stop setting when you want the finest increments between shutter speeds and/or f/stops. For example, the D90 will use shutter speeds such as 1/60th, 1/80th, 1/100th, 1/125th, and 1/160th second and f/stops such as f/5.6, f/6.3, f/7.1, and f/8, giving you (and the autoexposure system) maximum flexibility.

With 1/2 stop increments, you will have larger and more noticeable changes between settings. The D90 will apply shutter speeds such as 1/60th, 1/125th, 1/250th, and 1/500th second, and f/stops including f/5.6, f/6.7, f/8, f/9.5, and f/11. These coarser adjustments are useful when you want more dramatic changes between different exposures.

b2 Easy exposure compensation

This setting potentially simplifies dialing in EV (exposure value compensation) adjustments when using PSAM modes by specifying whether the exposure compensation button must be pressed while adding or subtracting EV compensation. Because of the possibility of confusion or error, I tend to leave this setting turned off. Your choices are as follows:

- **On.** This setting allows you to add or subtract exposure by rotating the subcommand dial when in Program (P) or Shutter Priority (S) exposure modes, or by rotating the main command dial when using Aperture Priority (A) mode. Rotating either dial has no effect in Manual (M) exposure mode. (If you've reversed the behavior of the command dials using CSM #f5, the "opposite" command dial must be used to make the changes.) Any adjustments you've made are canceled when the camera is shut off, or the meter-off time expires and the D90's exposure meters go back to sleep. That's a useful mode, because most of us have made an EV adjustment and then forgotten about it, only to expose a whole series of improperly exposed photos. You can still have "sticky" EV settings when Easy Exposure Compensation is turned on: just hold down the exposure compensation button when you make your changes.

- **Off.** With this default setting (and my strong preference), you must always press the exposure compensation button while rotating the main command dial to add or subtract exposure. Use this choice when you don't want any EV changes unless you deliberately make them by pressing the button.

b3 Center-weighted area

This setting changes the size of the center-weighted exposure spot when the D90 is used with a non-CPU (generally older AI and AI-S and earlier lenses that haven't been updated with a "computer" chip). Your choices include 6mm, 8mm, or 10mm. If you're using a non-CPU lens (see Chapter 6 for a description of non-CPU lenses—which are generally older manual-focus optics), the center-weighted area is fixed at 8mm, which is indicated by the round brackets in the viewfinder.

b4 Fine-tune optimal exposure

This setting is a powerful adjustment that allows you to dial in a specific amount of exposure compensation that will be applied, invisibly, to every photo you take using each of the three metering modes. No more can you complain, "My D90 always under-exposes by 1/3 stop!" If that is actually the case, and the phenomenon is consistent, you can use this Custom menu adjustment to compensate.

While exposure compensation is usually a better idea (does your camera *really* under-expose that consistently?) this setting does allow you to "recalibrate" your D90 yourself. Your dialed-in modifications will survive a two-button reset. However, you have no indication that fine-tuning has been made, so you'll need to remember what you've done. After all, you someday might discover that your camera is consistently *over*exposing images by 1/3 stop, not realizing that your CSM #b4 adjustment is the culprit.

In practice, it's rare that the Nikon D90 will *consistently* provide the wrong exposure in any of the three metering modes, especially Matrix metering, which can alter exposure dramatically based on the D90's internal database of typical scenes. This feature may be most useful for Spot metering, if you always take a reading off the same type of subject, such as a human face or 18-percent gray card. Should you find that the gray card readings, for example, always differ from what you would prefer, go ahead and fine-tune optimal exposure for Spot metering, and use that to read your gray cards. To use this feature:

1. Choose b4 Fine-tune optimal exposure from the Custom settings menu.

2. In the screen that appears, choose Yes after carefully reading the warning that Nikon insists on showing you each and every time this option is activated.

3. Choose Matrix metering, Center-Weighted, or Spot metering in the screen that follows by highlighting your choice and pressing the multi-selector right button.

4. Press the up/down buttons to dial in the exposure compensation you want to apply. You can specify compensation in increments of 1/6 stop, half as large a change as conventional exposure compensation. This is truly *fine-tuning*.

5. Press OK when finished. You can repeat the action to fine-tune the other two exposure modes if you wish.

NIKON GOOFED

On Page 178 of the D90 manual, Nikon reminds you that exposure can be fine-tuned for each of the Custom Setting banks. That's impossible to do, because the Nikon D90 does not have multiple Custom Setting banks. Ignore this reference to a feature the D90 does not have. (The D300 and other more advanced cameras do have four different Custom Setting banks, which is where this language came from.)

---

c. Timers/AE Lock

The green-coded Timers/AE Lock Custom Setting (see Figure 3.31) lets you define five different parameters that affect exposure metering in the Nikon D90. This category is a mixed bag of settings, covering both entries that adjust delay times and how the shutter release and AE-L buttons interact. I think the latter setting should have been placed in the purple f-coded Controls section. Go figure. Your choices are as follows:

- c1 Shutter release button AE-L
- c2 Auto meter-off delay
- c3 Self-timer
- c4 Monitor off delay
- c5 Remote on duration

c1 Shutter release button AE-L

This is another of Nikon's easily confusing options for controlling how and when autofocus and exposure are activated and locked. The intent is to allow you to separate autofocus and autoexposure activation and locking.

- **Off.** Exposure is locked *only* when the AE-L/AF-L button is pressed.
- **On.** Exposure locks when either the shutter release button is depressed halfway or the AE-L/AF-L button is held down.

Figure 3.31
There are five Timers/AE Lock options.

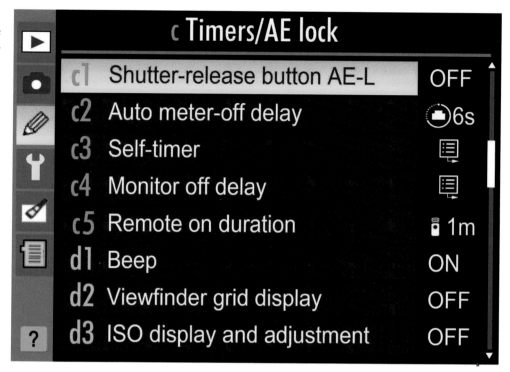

c2 Auto meter-off delay

Use this setting to determine how long the D90's exposure meter continues to operate after the last operation, such as autofocusing, focus point selection, and so forth, was performed. The default value is 6 seconds, but you can also select 4, 8, 16, and 30 seconds, as well as 1, 5, 10, and 30 minutes.

To save power, you should select an intermediate value, such as 8, 16, or 30 seconds if the default 6 seconds is not long enough. When the Nikon EH5a or EH-5 AC adapter is connected to the D90, the exposure meter will remain on indefinitely. Absent an external power source, any setting longer than 8 seconds will definitely eat up power.

Even so, sports shooters and some others prefer a longer delay, because they are able to keep their camera always "at the ready" with no delay to interfere with taking an action shot that unexpectedly presents itself. Extra battery consumption is just part of the price paid. For example, when I am shooting football, a meter-off delay of 16 seconds is plenty, because the players lining up for the snap is my signal to get ready to shoot. But for basketball or soccer, I usually set the meter-off delay for 30 minutes, because action is virtually continuous. I typically use the MB-D80 battery pack/grip at these events, so my D90 has plenty of power, and I carry two sets of spares. I rarely shoot much more than 1,000-1,200 shots at any sports event, so that's sufficient juice even with meter-off delay set for 30 minutes.

Of course, even if the meters have shut off, if the power switch remains in the On position, you can bring the camera back to life by tapping the shutter button.

c3 Self-timer delay

This setting lets you choose the length of the self-timer shutter release delay. The default value is 10 seconds. You can also choose 2, 5, or 20 seconds. If I have the camera mounted on a tripod or other support and am too lazy to attach the MC-D2 cable release, I can set a 2-second delay that is sufficient to let the camera stop vibrating after I've pressed the shutter release. I use a longer delay time if I am racing to get into the picture myself and am not sure I can make it in 10 seconds.

SAVING POWER WITH THE NIKON D90

There are six settings and several techniques you can use to stretch the longevity of your D90's battery. To get the most from each charge, consider these steps:

- **Playback menu: Image Review.** Turn Off image review after each shot. You can still review your images by pressing the Playback button.

- **Auto meter-off-delay (CSM #c2).** Set to 4 seconds if you can tolerate such a brief active time.

- **Monitor off Delay (CSM #c4).** Set for the minimum, 4 seconds, or 10 seconds if you find that too speedy. That big three-inch LCD uses a lot of juice, so reducing the amount of time it is used (either for automatic review or for manually playing back your images) can boost the effectiveness of your battery.

- **Reduce LCD illumination (CSM #d9).** Set to Off, so the monochrome LCD status panel will be backlit only when you manually use the switch around the shutter release. It will then shut off automatically after about six seconds.

- **Shorten IR Remote Duration (CSM #c5).** Set for 1 minute, so the IR sensor isn't constantly monitoring for a signal as the camera remains in standby mode.

- **Reduce LCD brightness.** In the Setup menu, select the lowest of the seven brightness settings that work for you under most conditions. If you're willing to shade the LCD with your hand, you can often get away with lower brightness settings outdoors, which will further increase the useful life of your battery.

- **Turn off modeling flash (CSM #e3).** Set to Off.

- **Reduce internal flash use.** No flash at all or fill flash use less power than a full blast.

- **Cancel VR.** Turn off vibration reduction using the switch on your lens (if your lens has that feature) if you feel you don't need it.

- **Use a card reader.** When transferring pictures from your D90 to your computer, use a card reader instead of the USB cable. Linking your camera to your computer and transferring images using the cable takes longer and uses a lot more power.

You can also choose the number of shots that will be taken each time the self-timer is triggered. Choose from 1-9 shots. They'll be snapped off at the rate you select for Continuous L mode (1 to 4 frames per second).

c4 Monitor off delay

You can adjust the amount of time the monitor remains on when no other operations are being performed. As with the meter-off delay, if the EH-5a or EH-5 AC adapter is attached, the monitor will remain on for the maximum amount, about 10 minutes. On battery power, the default value is 20 seconds, but you can also select 10 seconds, plus 1, 5, or the full 10 minutes. Choosing a brief duration can help preserve battery power. However, the D90 will always override the review display when the shutter button is partially or fully depressed, so you'll never miss a shot because a previous image was on the screen.

c5 Remote on duration

The default value is 1 minute, but you can also choose 5, 10, or 15 minutes. Use the longer times only if you know there will be a delay before you activate the shutter when using the IR remote control.

d. Shooting/Display

The cyan-coded Shooting/Display section (see Figure 3.32) has 12 settings that let you define five different parameters that affect exposure metering in the Nikon D90. There are a variety of mostly unrelated shooting and display options not found elsewhere, but which are not frequently changed, making them suitable for a Custom Setting entry.

Your choices are as follows:

- d1 Beep
- d2 Viewfinder grid display
- d3 ISO display and adjustment
- d4 Viewfinder warning display
- d5 Screen tips
- d6 CL mode shooting speed
- d7 File number sequence
- d8 Shooting info display
- d9 LCD illumination
- d10 Exposure delay mode
- d11 Flash warning
- d12 MB-D80 battery type

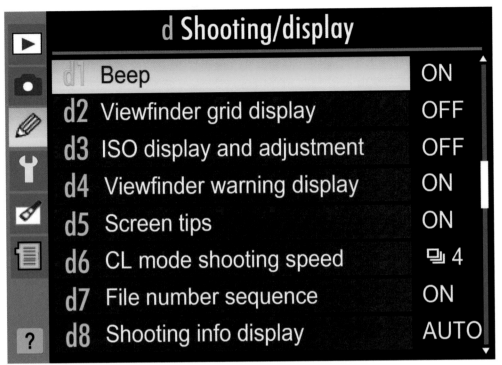

Figure 3.32
There are 12
options in the
Shooting/
Display
Custom Setting
menu.

d1 Beep

The Nikon D90's internal beeper provides a (usually) superfluous chirp to signify various functions, such as the countdown of your camera's self-timer/delayed remote or autofocus confirmation in AF-S mode or AF-A mode with a static subject. You can (and probably should) switch it off if you want to avoid the beep because it's annoying, impolite, or distracting (at a concert or museum), or undesired for any other reason. It's one of the few ways to make the D90 a bit quieter. (I've actually had new dSLR owners ask me how to turn off the "shutter sound" the camera makes; such an option was available in the point-and-shoot camera they'd used previously.) Your choices are On and Off. When the beeper is active, a musical note icon is shown in the monochrome LCD control panel.

d2 Viewfinder grid display

The D90 can display a grid of lines overlaid on the viewfinder, offering some help when you want to align vertical or horizontal lines. Note that the intersections of these lines do *not* follow the Rule of Thirds convention, and so are less useful for composition, assuming you want to follow the Rule of Thirds guideline in the first place. If you happen to subscribe to the Rule of Quarters, you're all set. Note that for critical applications, it's possible that your D90's viewfinder isn't absolutely accurate. I sometimes have to rotate images slightly in Photoshop because the grid is not perfectly aligned. Your options for this grid display are On and Off (the default).

d3 ISO display and adjustment

It's useful to have the current ISO sensitivity displayed in the monochrome LCD control panel and viewfinder, and to be able to adjust ISO settings quickly. Decide whether you would rather have a frame counter or ISO setting displayed, and then choose one of this menu entry's three options:

- **Show frame count.** With this default setting active, the frame counter area of the monochrome control panel LCD and the viewfinder shows the frame count only.

- **Show ISO sensitivity.** When this option is selected, the current ISO setting is shown in the frame counter displays in the monochrome control panel LCD and at right in the lower-edge display of the viewfinder.

- **Show ISO/Easy ISO.** This option also shows the ISO sensitivity instead of the frame count, along with the Easy ISO icon, which indicates you can adjust the ISO sensitivity by spinning the subcommand dial when using Program (P) or Shutter Priority (S) exposure modes, or by spinning the main command dial when using Aperture Priority (A) mode.

d4 Viewfinder warning display

The D90 has a low-battery, black-and-white (Monochrome Picture Control) warning, and a "no card loaded" advisory. Your options are On (the default) and Off. I find the B/W and No Card warnings obtrusive or superfluous, respectively, but the low-battery warning can be helpful, so I recommend leaving this feature turned on.

d5 Screen tips

Your Nikon D90 can display tips for items that are highlighted in the Shooting Information Display. The default setting is On, but if you feel you don't need any prompting, you can switch to Off.

d6 CL mode shooting speed

While the frames per second shooting rate at the High-Speed Continuous Shooting mode (C_H) is fixed at 4.5 fps, you can adjust the speed for the low-speed mode (C_L). You can select 1 to 4 fps rates. Choose a firing speed suitable for the kind of shooting environment you're in:

- **Normal Continuous Shooting.** I set my D90 to the 1 fps rate most of the time, so that I can take multiple shots quickly without needing to press the shutter release repeatedly. A 1-second rate isn't so fast that I end up taking a bunch of shots that I don't want, but it is fast enough that I can shoot a series.

- **Bracketing.** When I'm using bracketing, I generally have the D90 set to shoot a bracketed set of three pictures: normal, over-, and underexposure. With the camera set to 3 fps, I can press the shutter once and take all three bracketed shots, with basically the same framing, within about one second.

- **Slower action sequences.** The 4.5 fps and faster rates available for sports photography often produce an embarrassing plethora of pictures that are a pain to wade through after the event is over. For some types of action, such as long distance running, golf, swimming, or routine baseball plays, a rate of 3 fps might be sufficient. You can make this more reasonable speed available by defining it here.

d7 File number sequence

The Nikon D90 will automatically apply a file number to each picture you take, using consecutive numbering for all your photos over a long period of time, spanning many different memory cards, starting over from scratch when you insert a new card, or when you manually reset the numbers. Numbers are applied from 0001 to 9999, at which time the D90 "rolls over" to 0001 again.

The camera keeps track of the last number used in its internal memory and, if File Number Sequence is turned On, will apply a number that's one higher, or a number that's one higher than the largest number in the current folder on the memory card inserted in the camera. You can also start over each time a new folder has been created on the memory card, or reset the current counter back to 0001 at any time. Here's how it works:

- **On.** At this default setting, the D90 will use the number stored in its internal memory any time a new folder is created, a new memory card inserted, or an existing memory card formatted. If the card is not blank and contains images, then the next number will be one greater than the highest number on the card *or* in internal memory (whichever is higher). Here are some examples.

  - You've taken 1,235 shots with the camera, and you insert a blank/reformatted memory card. The next number assigned will be 1,236, based on the value stored in internal memory.

  - You've taken 1,235 shots with the camera, and you insert an old memory card you previously used with the D90, but which has a picture numbered 0728. The next picture will be numbered 1,236.

  - You've taken more than 9,999 shots with the camera and the counter has rolled over to 0001 again, and your new total is 1,235 shots. You insert an old memory card with a picture from before the rollover that's numbered 8,281. The next picture will be numbered 8,282, and that value will be stored in the camera's menu as the "high" shot number (and will be applied when you next insert a blank card). This misnumbering makes it a good idea to always reformat your memory cards before taking a photo, if at all possible.

- **Off.** If you're using a blank/reformatted memory card, or a new folder is created, the next photo taken will be numbered 0001. File number sequences will be reset every time you use or format a card, or a new folder is created (which happens when an existing folder on the card contains 999 shots).

- **Reset.** The D90 assigns a file number that's one larger than the largest file number in the current folder, unless the folder is empty, in which case numbering is reset to 0001. At this setting, new or reformatted memory cards will always have 0001 as the first file number.

HOW MANY SHOTS, REALLY?

The file numbers produced by the D90 don't provide information about the actual number of times the camera's shutter has been tripped—called actuations. For that data, you'll need a third-party software solution, such as the free Opanda iExif (www.opanda.com) for Windows or the non-free ($34.95) GraphicConverter for Macintosh (www.lemkesoft.com). These utilities can be used to extract the true number of actuations from the Exif information embedded in a JPEG file.

d8 Shooting info display

The Shooting Info Display that appears when you press the INFO button can be set to change automatically from dark lettering on a light background to light lettering on a dark background, or you can select one or the other to be used all the time. The color LCD monitor will automatically change its brightness to provide the best contrast for the selected text display. Your choices are as follows:

- **Auto.** If the scene as viewed through the lens indicates a bright environment, the Shooting Info Display will appear as black letters on a white background, producing an improved view in full daylight. If the scene appears dark, the display will have lighter letters on a dark background. Note that it's easy to "fool" the camera. Until you take the lens cap off, you'll see the dark background display regardless of your shooting environment. If you're standing in a darkened location, but point the camera at a bright scene, the D90 will show you the "daylight" display.

- **Manual.** Select this option and you can choose B (Dark on light) or W (Light on dark).

d9 LCD illumination

This is the first entry on the second page of the Shooting/Display menu. (See Figure 3.33.) When set to Off (the default), the monochrome LCD status/control panel (and the status LCDs on any attached compatible Nikon speedlight, such as the Nikon SB-900) will illuminate for as long as the exposure meters are active, but only when the

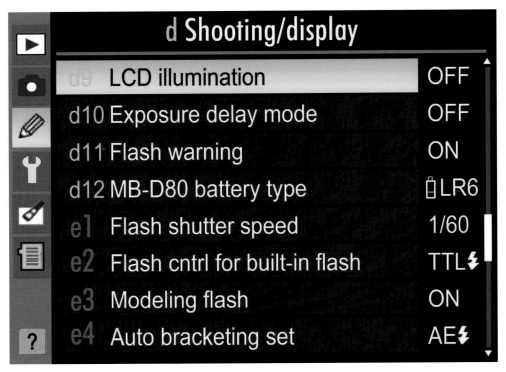

Figure 3.33
The last four Shooting/Display menu options appear when you scroll down far enough.

switch around the shutter release is pressed towards the maximum clockwise direction, just past the On indicator. Choose On, and the panel will be illuminated any time the exposure meters are active (and thus using more power), without the need to press the switch.

d10 Exposure delay mode

This is a marginally useful feature you can use to force the Nikon D90 to snap a picture about one second after you've pressed the shutter release button all the way. It's useful when you are using shutter speeds of about 1/8 to 1/60th second handheld and want to minimize the effects of the vibration that results when you depress the shutter button. It can also be used when the camera is mounted on a tripod, although the self-timer function, set to a two-second delay, is more useful in that scenario. When switched On, the camera will pause while you steady your steely grip on the camera, taking the picture about one second later. When turned Off, the picture is taken when the shutter release is pressed, as normal. One interesting side-effect of this mode is that it separates the normally invisible preflash produced by the D90's internal flash (or any external flash that's connected) with the delay, so, if you're shooting living subjects (human or animal) they may be startled by the initial flash and close their eyes just before the main flash fires 1,000 milliseconds later.

d11 Flash warning

You'll need to raise the D90's built-in electronic flash manually by pressing the Flash button when using PSAM (Program, Shutter Priority, Aperture Priority, Manual) exposure modes. With this option's default On setting, if lighting is low and flash needed, the flash-ready light (lightning bolt) indicator in the viewfinder will flicker when the shutter release button is pressed halfway. Choose Off, and no warning is displayed. This feature operates in PSAM modes only.

d12 MB-D80 battery type

This option is needed to communicate to the D90 what type of AA batteries are being used in the MB-D80 battery pack/grip, because the different varieties of AA batteries provide slightly different voltages, and change voltages at different rates as they are used up. The D90 automatically detects and accommodates the EN-EL3e battery, which you may use singly or in a pair. Your choices include:

- **LR6 (AA alkaline).** For ordinary alkaline batteries

- **HR6 (AA NiMH).** For Nickel-Metal Hydride batteries

- **FR6 (AA lithium).** For non-rechargeable lithium batteries

- **ZR6 (AA NiMn).** For Nickel-Manganese batteries

Because of their limited capacity, you'll want to use conventional AA alkaline batteries or nickel-manganese batteries only as a last resort, and then only when the weather is warmer than 68 degrees Fahrenheit, because the chemical reactions that provide power decline at lower temperatures.

e. Bracketing/Flash

The blue-coded Shooting/Display section (see Figure 3.34) has six settings that let you define parameters that control four flash functions, plus two bracketing functions. Your choices are as follows:

- e1 Flash shutter speed

- e2 Flash cntrl for built-in flash

- e3 Modeling flash

- e4 Auto bracketing set

- e5 Auto FP

- e6 Bracketing order

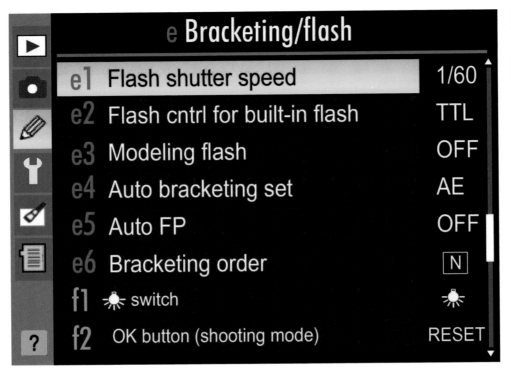

Figure 3.34
There are six options in the Bracketing/ Flash Custom Setting menu.

e1 Flash shutter speed

This setting, which functions only in Program and Aperture Priority modes, determines the *slowest* shutter speed that is available for electronic flash synchronization when you're not using a "slow-sync" mode (described in Chapter 7). As you may know, when you're using flash, the flash itself provides virtually all of the illumination that makes the main exposure, and the shutter speed determines how much, if any, of the ambient light contributes to that second, non-flash exposure. Indeed, if the camera or subject is moving, you can end up with two distinct exposures in the same frame: the sharply defined flash exposure, and a second, blurry "ghost" picture created by the ambient light.

If you *don't* want that second exposure, you should use the highest shutter speed that will synchronize with your flash. This setting prevents Program or Aperture Priority modes (which both select the shutter speed for you) from inadvertently selecting a "too slow" shutter speed. You can select a value from 30 s to 1/60 s, and the D90 will avoid using speeds slower than the one you specify with electronic flash (unless you've selected slow sync, slow rear-curtain sync, or red-eye reduction with slow sync). The "slow-sync" modes do permit the ambient light to contribute to the exposure (say, to allow the background to register in night shots, or to use the ghost image as a special effect). For brighter backgrounds, you'll need to put the camera on a tripod or other support to avoid the blurry ghosts that can occur from camera shake, even if the subject is stationary.

If you are able to hold the D90 steady, a value of 1/30 s is a good compromise; if you have shaky hands, use 1/60 s or higher. Those with extraordinarily solid grips or who are using a VR lens can try the 1/15 s setting. Remember that this setting only determines the slowest shutter speed that will be used, not the default shutter speed.

e2 Flash cntrl for built-in flash

The Nikon D90's built-in flash has four modes, which I'll describe in a lot more detail in Chapter 7. Your four options are as follows:

■ **TTL.** When the built-in flash is triggered, the D90 first fires a pre-flash and measures the light reflected back and through the lens to calculate the proper exposure when the full flash is emitted a fraction of a second later.

■ **Manual.** You can set the level of the built-in flash from full power to 1/128 power.

■ **Repeating flash.** The flash fires multiple bursts, producing a stroboscopic lighting effect. As I'll describe in Chapter 7, when you choose repeating flash you'll be asked to select Output (flash power level), Times (the number of times the flash is fired at the output level you specify), and Frequency (how often the flash fires per second). Note that these factors are interdependent. For example, if you tell the flash to fire at 1/8 output power, you can select from 2 to 5 flashes, at a rate of 1 to 50 flashes per second. That's because the flash has only enough power for a maximum of five flashes at the 1/8 output setting. At 1/128 power, there's enough juice for 2 to 35 individual flashes, at a rate of no more than 50 flashes per second.

■ **Commander mode.** If you never use external flash, you can safely ignore this setting. If you do, you'll want to set up the D90 for your most frequently used options, to avoid having to fiddle with the camera if you decide to pull your SB-900 out of your bag for some impromptu multi-flash shooting. In Commander mode, the built-in flash emits preflashes that can be used to wirelessly control one or more remote external flash units. **Note:** If the Nikon SB-400 flash unit is attached and turned on, this menu choice is not available, because the SB-400 unit, unlike the D90's built-in flash and other external flash units, cannot function in Commander mode. You'll be able to set flash compensation and flash mode for the built-in flash as well as individual "groups" of flashes (Groups A and B) and the triggering channels. As you'll see, using electronic flash with the Nikon D90 is worth a book of its own, but I'll do my best to explain the vagaries in Chapter 7.

e3 Modeling flash

The Nikon D90, and certain compatible external flash units (like the SB-R200, SB-600, SB-900, and the discontinued SB-800) have the capability of simulating a modeling lamp when using PSAM exposure modes. The modeling flash feature gives you the limited capability of previewing how your flash illumination is going to look in the finished photo. The modeling flash is not a perfect substitute for a real incandescent or fluorescent modeling lamp, but it does help you see how your subject is illuminated, and spot any potential problems with shadows.

When this feature is activated (On), pressing the Depth-of-Field button on the D90 briefly triggers the modeling flash for your preview. Selecting Off (the default) disables the feature. Turning the modeling flash off saves some power if you're using flash a lot, and can be useful if you anticipate using the Depth-of-Field preview button for depth-of-field purposes (imagine that) and do *not* want the modeling flash to fire when the flash unit is charged and ready. Some external flash units, such as the SB-800 and SB-900, have their own modeling flash buttons. Although the SB-600 does not have this button, it works fine with the D90's modeling flash feature.

e4 Auto bracketing set

The Nikon D90 can automatically take several pictures using slightly different settings within a range that you specify, and apply the changes to automatic exposure, electronic flash, or white balance. This setting allows you to specify whether bracketing is used for both automatic exposure *and* flash (AE & flash), automatic exposure only (AE), flash bracketing only (Flash only), white balance color bracketing alone (WB bracketing), or Active D-Lighting bracketing alone. (With ADL bracketing the D90 takes two pictures, one with ADL turned off, and a second using your currently selected ADL setting, as described in the Shooting menu discussion earlier in this chapter.)

No autoexposure or flash bracketing will be performed when white balance bracketing is activated. Because you can specify white balance manually when importing a RAW file, WB bracketing is not available when Quality has been set to NEF (RAW) or NEF (RAW)+JPEG. The results you get with flash bracketing can vary quite a bit, depending on the amount of ambient illumination and flash mode you've chosen, but exposure bracketing is fairly consistent. I tend to leave this option set to AE most of the time. White balance bracketing is useful when you're not quite sure of the color balance of your illumination. ADL bracketing is chiefly useful when you're first learning to use this feature and want to compare shots with/without Active D-Lighting.

e5 Auto FP

Use this option to enable electronic flash at shutter speeds of 1/200-1/4,000th second with compatible external flash. Although your D90 is ordinarily limited to using flash at shutter speeds of 1/200th second or slower, some external flash units, such as the Nikon SB-900, include a high-speed sync mode that can deliver a reduced-power burst over a longer period. That longer burst allows exposing an image during the time the partially open shutter passes over the sensor, making the flash useful for filling in shadows when shooting under bright light or with larger f/stops (both of which call for faster shutter speeds). This option enables that Auto FP High-Speed Sync option. You'll find a detailed explanation of the feature in Chapter 7.

e6 Bracketing order

Use this setting to define the sequence in which bracketing (available only in PASM modes) is carried out. Your choices are the default: MTR>Under>Over (metered exposure, followed by version receiving less exposure, and finishing with the picture receiving the most exposure); and Under>MTR>Over, which orders the exposures from least exposed to most exposed (for both ambient and flash exposures). The same order is applied to white balance bracketing, too, but the values are Normal>More Yellow>More Blue and More Yellow>Normal>More Blue. (Nikon actually calls "yellow" by the term "amber," but I've found "yellow" easier to understand.) You'll find lots more about bracketing in Chapter 4.

f. Controls

The purple-coded Controls section (see Figure 3.35) has seven settings that let you modify the way various control buttons and dials perform by using the options in this submenu, shown in Figure 3.35.

- f1 backlight switch
- f2 OK button (shooting mode)
- f3 Assign FUNC. button
- f4 Assign AE-L/AF-L button
- f5 Customize command dials
- f6 No memory card?
- f7 Reverse indicators

f1 LCD backlight switch

The monochrome LCD control panel has a backlight, which can be activated by rotating the power switch (concentric with the shutter release button) to the full clockwise position. When this option is set to the default LCD backlight choice, the lamp illuminates for about six seconds when activated. Choose Both, and shooting data is shown in the Shooting Information Display on the color LCD monitor as well. (Press the INFO button to illuminate only the Shooting Information Display, or use the Backlight switch concentric with the shutter release to illuminate both the Shooting Information Display and monochrome LCD status/control panel.)

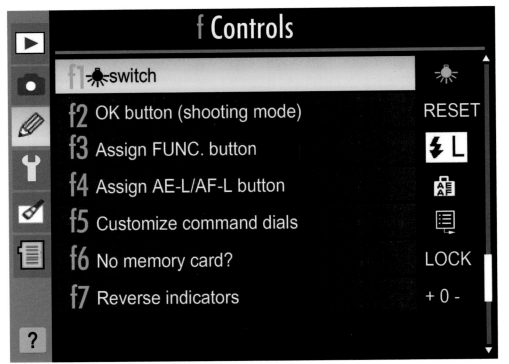

Figure 3.35
There are seven options in the Controls Custom Setting menu.

f2 OK button (shooting mode)

The OK button in the center of the multi-selector pad can be assigned its own function.

- **Select center focus point.** The default setting moves the center focus point to the middle of the 11-point cluster when the OK button is pressed. Especially useful when you've moved the focus point to an edge and then, in a fast-moving situation, you want to return it to the center spot, either because that zone is more appropriate or because you want to move the spot to the opposite edge of the viewfinder.

- **Highlight active focus point.** If you sometimes wonder which focus point has been selected, this choice and an OK press will light up the active point in red.

- **Not used.** If you'd rather have the OK button do nothing when shooting photos, select this option.

f3 Assign FUNC. button

You can define the action that the Function (Fn) button performs when pressed. There are 10 different actions you can define for the button:

- **Framing grid.** This activates/deactivates the viewfinder framing grid when the Fn button is pressed and the main command dial is rotated.

- **AF-Area mode.** With this option, hold the Fn button while rotating the main command dial to select one of the AF area modes.

- **Center Focus Point.** Hold down the Fn button while rotating the main command dial to flip between normal and wide center focus points when this option is active.

- **FV lock.** This default configuration lets you lock the flash value of the built-in flash or compatible dedicated external flash when the Fn button is pressed once. Press again to unlock the flash lock.

- **Flash off.** If you frequently find yourself in situations where you want to temporarily disable the flash, this setting will let you do it for as long as the Fn button is held down.

- **Matrix metering.** Switches from the current metering mode to Matrix metering while the Fn button is held down. You might appreciate this capability during a session where you're using, say, Spot metering, and decide you want to use Matrix metering for a shot or two.

- **Center-Weighted metering.** Switches from the current metering mode to Center-Weighted metering while the Fn button is held down.

- **Spot metering.** Switches from the current metering mode to Spot metering while the Fn button is held down.

- **Access First Item in My Menu.** This feature is quite flexible, as it allows you to quickly access whichever menu entry you've placed at the top of your My Menu list (described later in this chapter) by pressing the Fn button. Because you can easily add items to My Menu and/or move particular entries to the top of the My Menu list, this feature gives instant access to whatever menu item you currently have as a favorite.

- **+NEF (RAW).** You've optimized your JPEG settings so your images look good. Then, suddenly, you encounter a situation that you recognize might require some post-processing touch up, preferably with a RAW image. If you've set this option, you can press the Fn button to take the next picture as a JPEG+RAW. I've used this setting while photographing under a fairly constant light source, only to find a different light source (say, a spotlight that somebody turned on unexpectedly) that differs from my chosen color balance. Press Fn, shoot a RAW+JPEG combo, then adjust the RAW picture later for the right color balance.

f4 Assign AE-L/AF-L button

When the Nikon D90 is set to its default values, a half-press of the shutter release locks in the current autofocus setting in AF-S mode, or in AF-A mode if your subject is not moving. (The camera will refocus if the subject moves and the D90 is set for AF-C or AF-A mode.) That half-press also activates the exposure meter, but, ordinarily, the exposure changes as the lighting conditions in the frame change.

You can change that behavior to something else. For example, sometimes you want to lock in focus and/or exposure, and then reframe your photo. For that, and for other focus/exposure locking options, Nikon gives you the AE-L/AF-L button (located on the back of the camera to the right of the viewfinder window), and a variety of behavior combinations for it. This CSM setting allows you to define whether the Nikon D90 locks exposure, focus, or both when the button is pressed, so the AE-L/AF-L button can be used for these functions in addition to, or instead of a half-press of the shutter release. It can also be set so that autofocus starts *only* when the button is pressed; in that case, a half-press of the shutter release initiates autoexposure, but the AE-L/AF-L button *must* be pressed to start the autofocusing process. These options can be a little confusing, so I'll offer some clarification:

- **AE/AF lock.** Locks both focus and exposure while the AE-L/AF-L button is pressed and held down, even if the shutter release button has not been pressed. This is the default value, and is useful when you want to activate and lock in exposure and focus independently of the shutter release button. Perhaps your main subject is off-center; place that subject in the middle of the frame, lock in exposure and focus, and then reframe the picture while holding the AE-L/AF-L button.

- **AE lock only.** Lock only the exposure while the AE-L/AF-L button is pressed. The exposure is fixed when you press and hold the button, but autofocus continues to operate (say, when you press the shutter release halfway) using the AF-A, AF-S, or AF-C mode you've chosen.

- **AF lock only.** Focus is locked in while the AE-L/AF-L button is held down, but exposure will continue to vary as you compose the photo and press the shutter release button.

- **AE lock (Hold).** Exposure is locked when the AE-L/AF-L button is pressed, and remains locked until the button is pressed again, or the exposure meter-off delay expires. Use this option when you want to lock exposure at some point, but don't want to keep your thumb on the AE-L/AF-L button.

- **AF (AF-ON).** The AE-L/AF-L button is used to initiate autofocus. A half-press of the shutter release button does not activate or change focus. This setting is useful when you want to frame your photo, press the shutter release halfway to lock in exposure, but don't want the D90 to autofocus until you tell it to. I use this for sports photography when I am waiting for some action to move into the frame before starting autofocus. For example, I might press the AE-L/AF-L button just before a racehorse crosses the finish line.

- **FV Lock.** Pressing the AE-L/AF-L button locks the flash value for the built-in flash or a compatible external dedicated flash unit. Press a second time to cancel FV lock.

f5 Customize command dials

You can use the options in this menu entry to change the behavior of the command dials. Use the available tweaks to change the behavior of the dials to better suit your preferences, or if you're coming to the Nikon world from another vendor's product that uses a different operational scheme. Keep in mind that redefining basic controls in this way can prove confusing if someone other than yourself uses your camera, or if you find yourself working with other Nikon cameras that have retained the normal command dial behavior. Your options include:

- **Reverse rotation.** Rotating the main command dial (on both the camera and MB-D80 battery pack) counterclockwise causes shutter speeds to become shorter in Manual and Shutter Priority modes; rotating the subcommand dial counterclockwise selects larger f/stops. If you want to reverse the directional orientation of the dials (so you'll need to rotate the main command dial clockwise to specify shorter shutter speeds, etc.), set this option to Yes. Set to No to return to the original D90 scheme of things.

- **Change main/sub.** Select On to exchange the functions of the main and subcommand dials on the camera and MB-D80 battery pack. When activated, the main dial will set the aperture in Manual and Aperture Priority modes, and the subcommand dial will adjust the shutter speed in Manual and Shutter Priority modes. All other normal functions are swapped, as well. Select Off to return to the Nikon D90's default arrangement.

- **Menus and playback.** This option has three choices:

  - **On.** With this default setting, the main command dial is used to choose the picture shown during full-frame playback, to relocate the cursor left or right during thumbnail view, or move the menu highlight up or down. The subcommand dial shows additional information in full-frame review, moves the cursor up or down when viewing thumbnails, and displays submenus/previous menus.

  - **On (Image Review Excluded).** Functions the same as On, except the main command dial can't be used during image review.

  - **Off.** Only the multi-selector can be used to select pictures, thumbnails, and to navigate through menus.

f6 No memory card?

This entry gives you the ability to snap off "pictures" without a memory card installed—or, alternatively, to lock the camera shutter release if no card is present. It is sometimes informally called Play mode, because you can experiment with your camera's features or even hand your D90 to a friend to let them fool around, without any danger of pictures actually being taken.

Back in our film days, we'd sometimes finish a roll, rewind the film back into its cassette surreptitiously, and then hand the camera to a child to take a few pictures—without actually wasting any film. It's hard to waste digital film, but "shoot without card" mode is still appreciated by some, especially camera vendors who want to be able to demo a camera at a store or trade show, but don't want to have to equip each and every demonstrator model with a memory card. Choose Enable release to activate "play" mode or Release locked to disable it.

The pictures you actually "take" are displayed on the LCD with the legend "Demo" superimposed on the screen, and they are, of course, not saved. Note that if you are using the optional Camera Control Pro 2 software to record photos from a USB-tethered D90 directly to a computer, no memory card is required to unlock the shutter even if Release locked has been selected.

f7 Reverse indicators

Refugees from the Canon world or other dSLR product lines are sometimes put off that Nikon cameras place the plus exposure values on the left side of the analog exposure display in the control panel, viewfinder, and Shooting Information Display, with the negative values on the right. This default setting (+0-) can be swapped for the opposite orientation (-0+) to change the display to the other orientation. My take is that if you've fled to Nikonland, you might as well get used to it. I suppose this setting is useful for a dedicated Canon shooter who sometimes uses a Nikon dSLR.

Setup Menu Options

The orange-coded Setup menu (see Figure 3.36 for its first page) has a long list of 14 entries. In this menu you can make additional adjustments on how your camera *behaves* before or during your shooting session, as differentiated from the Shooting menu, which adjusts how the pictures are actually taken. Your choices include:

- Format memory card
- LCD brightness
- Clean image sensor
- Lock up mirror for cleaning
- Video mode
- HDMI
- World Time

- Language
- Image comment
- Auto image rotation
- Image Dust Off ref photo
- Battery info
- GPS
- Firmware version

Figure 3.36
The first page
of the Setup
menu has eight
entries.

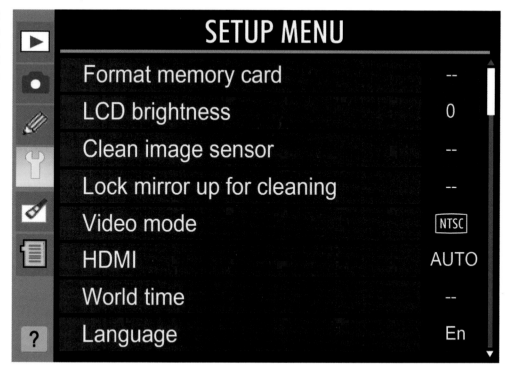

Format Memory Card

I recommend using this menu entry to reformat your memory card after each shoot. While you can move files from the memory card to your computer, leaving behind a blank card, or delete files using the Playback menu's Delete feature, both of those options can leave behind stray files (such as those that have been marked as Protected). Format removes those files completely and beyond retrieval (unless you use a special utility program as described in Chapter 9) and establishes a spanking new fresh file system on the card, with all the file allocation table (FAT) pointers (which tell the camera and your computer's operating system where all the images reside) efficiently pointing where they are supposed to on a blank card.

To format a memory card, choose this entry from the Setup menu, highlight Yes on the screen that appears, and press OK. You can also format a memory card by pressing the Format #1 and Format #2 buttons as described in Chapter 2. I prefer not to use that option, because it's too easy to get into the habit, and potentially reformat a card by mistake. If you're someone, like me, who goes into a room to get something, and forgets what it was by the time you get there, it's a better idea to go through Menu-land to give you a little more time to think. Do not turn off your camera while formatting is underway.

LCD Brightness

You can also choose to adjust the intensity of the display using the LCD brightness option. A grayscale strip appears on the LCD, as shown in Figure 3.37. Use the multi-selector up/down keys to adjust the brightness to a comfortable viewing level over a range of +3 to −3. Under the lighting conditions that exist when you make this adjustment, you should be able to see all 10 swatches from black to white. If the two end swatches blend together, the brightness has been set too low. If the two whitest swatches on the right end of the strip blend together, the brightness is too high. Brighter settings use more battery power, but can allow you to view an image on the LCD outdoors in bright sunlight. When you have the brightness you want, press OK to lock it in and return to the menu.

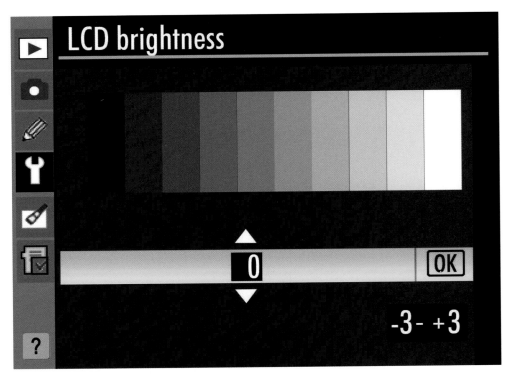

Figure 3.37
Adjust the LCD brightness so that all the grayscale strips are visible.

Clean Image Sensor

This entry gives you some control over the Nikon D90's automatic sensor cleaning feature, which removes dust through a vibration cycle that shakes the sensor until dust, presumably, falls off and is captured by a sticky surface at the bottom of the sensor area. If you happen to take a picture and notice an artifact in an area that contains little detail (such as the sky or a blank wall), you can access this menu choice, place the camera with its base downward, choose Clean now, and press OK. A message Image sensor cleaning appears, and the dust you noticed has probably been shaken off.

You can also tell the D90 when you'd like it to perform automatic cleaning without specific instructions from you. Choose Clean at and select from:

- **On. Clean at startup.** This allows you to start off a particular shooting session with a clean sensor.

- **Off. Clean at shutdown.** This removes any dust that may have accumulated since the camera has been turned on, say, from dust infiltration while changing lenses. Note that this choice does not turn off automatic cleaning; it simply moves the operation to the camera power-down sequence.

- **On/Off. Clean at both startup and shutdown.** Use this setting if you're paranoid about dust and don't mind the extra battery power consumed each time the camera is turned on or off. If you only turn off the D90 when you're finished shooting, the power penalty is not large, but if you're the sort who turns off the camera every time you pause in shooting, the extra power consumed by the dust removal may exceed any savings you get from leaving the camera off.

- **Cleaning Off.** No automatic dust removal will be performed. Use this to preserve battery power, or if you prefer to use automatic dust removal only when you explicitly want to apply it.

Mirror Lockup

You can also clean the sensor manually. Use this menu entry to raise the mirror and open the shutter so you'll have access to the sensor for cleaning with a blower, brush, or swab, as described in Chapter 9. You don't want power to fail while you're poking around inside the camera, so this option is available only when sufficient battery power (at least 60 percent) is available. Using a fully charged battery or connecting the D90 to an EH-5/EH5a AC adapter is an even better idea.

Video Mode

This controls the output of the Nikon D90 when directed to a conventional video system through the video cable when you're displaying images on a monitor or connected to a VCR through the external device's yellow video input jack. You can select either NTSC, used in the United States, Canada, Mexico, many Central, South American, and Caribbean countries, much of Asia, and other countries; or PAL, which is used in the UK, much of Europe, Africa, India, China, and parts of the Middle East.

HDMI

Use this setting to control the HDMI format used to play back camera images and movies on a High Density Television (HDTV) using a special cable not supplied by Nikon. You can choose Auto, in which case the camera selects the right format, or, to suit your particular HDTV, one of three progressive scan options (480p—640×480 pixels; 576p—720×576 pixels; 720p—1280×720 pixels), and one interlaced scan option (1080i—1920×1080 pixels).

Note that this setting controls *only* the output from your D90 to the HDTV. It has no effect on the resolution of your images or your movie clips.

World Time

Use this menu entry to adjust the D90's internal clock. (See Figure 3.38.) Your options include:

- **Time zone.** A small map will pop up on the setting screen and you can choose your local time zone. I sometimes forget to change the time zone when I travel (especially when going to Europe), so my pictures are all time-stamped incorrectly. I like to use the time stamp to recall exactly when a photo was taken, so keeping this setting correct is important.
- **Date.** Use this setting to enter the exact year, month, day, hour, minute, and second.
- **Date format.** Choose from Year/month/day (Y/M/D), Month/day/year (M/D/Y), or Day/month/year (D/M/Y) formats.
- **Daylight saving time.** Use this to turn daylight saving time On or Off. Because the date on which DST takes effect has been changed from time to time, if you turn this feature on you may need to monitor your camera to make sure DST has been implemented correctly.

Language

Choose from 17 languages for menu display, choosing from Danish, German, English, Spanish, Finnish, French, Italian, Dutch, Norwegian, Polish, Portuguese, Russian, Swedish, Traditional Chinese, Simplified Chinese, Japanese, or Korean.

Image Comment

The Image Comment entry is your opportunity to add a copyright notice, personal information about yourself (including contact info), or even a description of where the image was taken (e.g., Seville Photos 2009), although text entry with the Nikon D90 is a bit too clumsy for doing a lot of individual annotation of your photos. (But you still might want to change the comment each time, say, you change cities during your travels.) The embedded comments can be read by many software programs, including Nikon ViewNX or Capture NX.

Figure 3.38
The second page of the Setup menu.

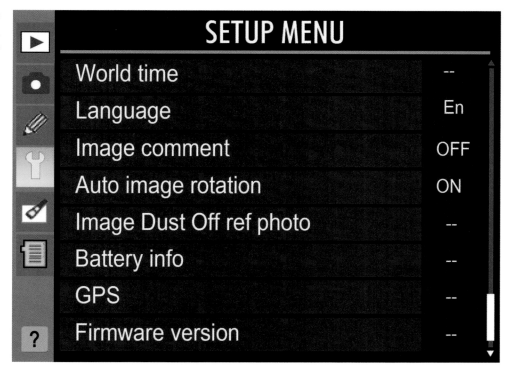

The standard text entry screen described earlier in this chapter can be used to enter your comment, with up to 36 characters available. For the copyright symbol, embed a lowercase "c" within opening and closing parentheses: (c). You can enter text by choosing Input comment, turn attachment of the comment On or Off using the Attach Comment entry, and select Done when you're finished working with comments. If you find typing with a cursor too tedious, you can enter your comment in Nikon Capture NX and upload it to the camera though a USB cable.

Auto Image Rotation

Turning this setting On tells the Nikon D90 to include camera orientation information in the image file. The orientation can be read by many software applications, including Adobe Photoshop, Nikon ViewNX, and Capture NX, as well as the Rotate Tall setting in the Playback menu. Turn this feature Off, and none of the software applications or Playback's Rotate Tall will be able to determine the correct orientation for the image. Nikon notes that only the first image's orientation is used when shooting continuous bursts; subsequent photos will be assigned the same orientation, even if you rotate the camera during the sequence (which is something I have been known to do myself when shooting sports like basketball).

Image Dust Off Ref Photo

This menu choice lets you "take a picture" of any dust or other particles that may be adhering to your sensor. The D90 will then append information about the location of this dust to your photos, so that the Image Dust Off option in Capture NX can be used to mask the dust in the NEF image.

To use this feature, select Image Dust Off ref photo, choose either Start or Clean sensor, then start, and then press OK. If directed to do so, the camera will first perform a self-cleaning operation by applying ultrasonic vibration to the low-pass filter that resides on top of the sensor. Then, a screen will appear asking you to take a photo of a bright featureless white object 10 cm from the lens. Nikon recommends using a lens with a focal length of at least 50mm. Point the D90 at a solid-white card and press the shutter release. An image with the extension .ndf will be created, and can be used by Nikon Capture NX as a reference photo if the "dust off" picture is placed in the same folder as an image to be processed for dust removal.

Battery Info

This screen is purely informational; there are no settings to be made. If you're using the MB-D80 battery pack with two EN-EL3e batteries, info for each battery will be displayed separately. When invoked, you can see the following information:

- **Bat. Meter.** The current battery level, shown as a percentage from 100 to 0 percent.

- **Pic. Meter.** This shows the number of actuations with the current battery since it was last recharged. This number can be larger than the number of photos taken, because other functions, such as white balance presetting, can cause the shutter to be tripped. This display is not shown when the MB-D80 battery pack is attached and loaded with AA batteries.

- **Charging life.** Eventually, a battery will no longer accept a charge as well as it did when it was new, and must be replaced. This indicator shows when a battery is considered new (0); has begun to degrade slightly (1,2,3); or has reached the end of its charging life and is ready for replacement (4). Batteries charged at temperatures lower than 41 degrees F may display an impaired charging life temporarily, but return to their true "health" when recharged above 68 degrees F. This display is not shown when the MB-D10 battery pack is attached and loaded with AA batteries.

GPS

This menu entry has options for using the Nikon GP-1 Global Positioning System (GPS) device, described in Chapter 5. It has three options, none of which turn GPS features on or off, despite the misleading "Enable" and "Disable" nomenclature (what you're enabling and disabling is the automatic exposure meter turn-off):

- **Enable.** Reduces battery drain by enabling turning off exposure meters while using the GP-1 after the time specified in CSM #c2 (Auto meter-off delay, discussed earlier in this chapter) has elapsed. When the meters turn off, the GP-1 becomes inactive and must reacquire at least three satellite signals before it can begin recording GPS data once more.

- **Disable.** Causes exposure meters to remain on while using the GP-1, so that GPS data can be recorded at any time, despite increased battery drain.

- **Position.** This is an information display, rather than a selectable option. It appears when the GP-1 is connected and receiving satellite positioning data. It shows the latitude, longitude, altitude, and Coordinated Universal Time (UTC) values.

Eye-Fi Upload

This option (not shown in the figure) is shown only when a compatible Eye-Fi memory card is being used in the D90. The Eye-Fi card looks like an ordinary SDHC memory card, but has built-in WiFi capabilities, so it can be used to transmit your photos as they are taken directly to a computer over a WiFi network. You'll find more about using Eye-Fi in Chapter 9.

Firmware Version

You can see the current firmware release in use in this menu listing, which you must scroll to view. You can learn how to update firmware in Chapter 9.

Retouch Menu

The Retouch menu has 13 entries, with eight shown on its first screen (see Figure 3.39). These include:

- D-Lighting
- Red-eye correction
- Trim
- Monochrome
- Filter effects
- Color balance
- Small picture
- Image overlay
- NEF (RAW) Processing
- Quick retouch
- Straighten
- Distortion control
- Fisheye

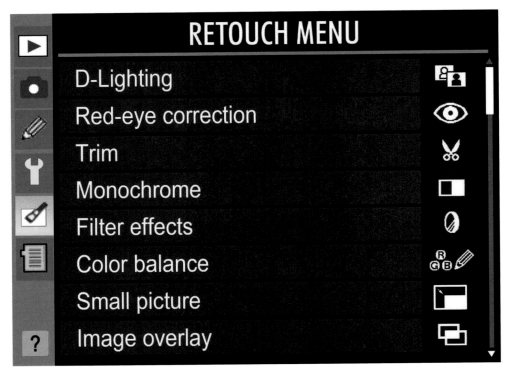

Figure 3.39
The Retouch menu allows simple in-camera editing.

This menu allows you to create a new copy of an existing image with trimmed or retouched characteristics. You can apply D-Lighting, remove red-eye, create a monochrome image, apply filter effects, rebalance color, overlay one image on another, and compare two images side-by-side. Just select a picture during Playback mode, press OK to produce the Retouch menu screen, and then scroll down to one of the retouching options. You can also go directly to the Retouch menu, select a retouching feature, and then choose a picture from the standard D90 picture selection screen shown multiple times in Chapter 2.

The Retouch menu is most useful when you want to create a modified copy of an image on the spot, for immediate printing or e-mailing without first importing into your computer for more extensive editing. You can also use it to create a JPEG version of an image in the camera when you are shooting RAW-only photos.

While you can retouch images that have already been processed by the Retouch menu, you may notice some quality loss. Some retouching options are mutually exclusive: you can't apply Quick Retouch to images that have had D-Lighting applied, and vice versa. Once you've applied a Filter effect, you can't apply a second filter effect to a copied image, except for those given the Cross Screen effect. Quick Retouch, D-Lighting, Red-Eye Correction, and Filter effects (except for Cross Screen) can't be applied to monochrome copies. Use of the Trim or Small Picture options create copies that cannot be further modified in the Retouch menu. There are quite a few additional conflicts that you may discover as you work with this menu. In real life, few of us do a lot of retouching to images in the camera; when things start to get complicated, it's a better idea to work on them in your image editor.

To create a retouched copy of an image:

1. While browsing among images in Playback mode, press OK when an image you want to retouch is displayed on the screen. The Retouch menu will pop up, and you can select a retouching option.

2. From the Retouch menu, select the option you want and press the multi-selector right button. The Nikon D90's standard image selection screen appears. Scroll among the images as usual with the left/right multi-selector buttons, press the Zoom button to examine a highlighted image more closely, and press OK to choose that image.

3. Work with the options available from that particular Retouch menu feature and press OK to create the modified copy, or Playback to cancel your changes.

4. The retouched image will bear a file name that reveals its origin. For example, if you make a Small Picture version of an image named DSC_0112.jpg, the reduced-size copy will be named SSC_0113.jpg. Copies incorporating other retouching features would be named CSC_0113.jpg instead.

D-Lighting

This option brightens the shadows of pictures that have already been taken, as shown in Figure 3.40. It is a useful tool for backlit photographs or any image with deep shadows with important detail. Once you've selected your photo for modification, you'll be shown side-by-side images with the unaltered version on the left, and your adjusted version on the right. Press the multi-selector's up/down buttons to choose from High, Normal, or Low corrections. Press the Zoom button to magnify the image. When you're happy with the corrected image on the right, compared to the original on the left, press OK to save the copy to your memory card (see Figure 3.41).

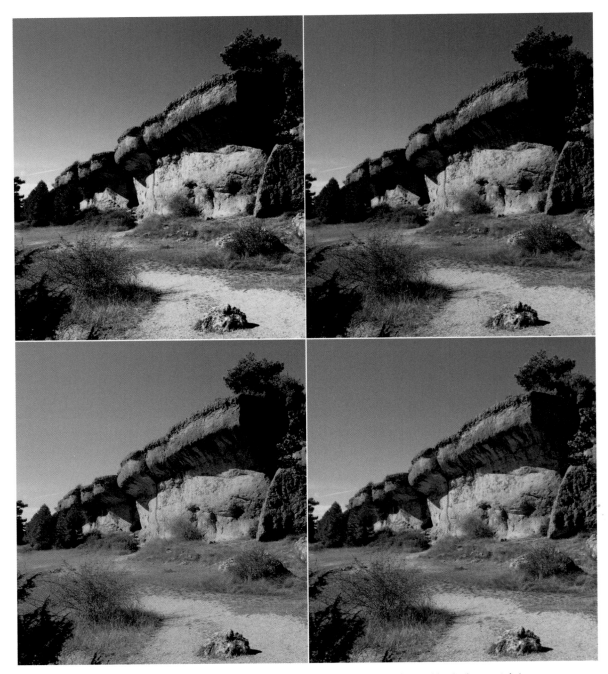

Figure 3.40 No D-Lighting (upper left); low (upper right); normal (lower left); and high (lower right).

Figure 3.41
Use the
D-Lighting
feature to
brighten dark
shadows while
producing min-
imal changes in
the highlights.

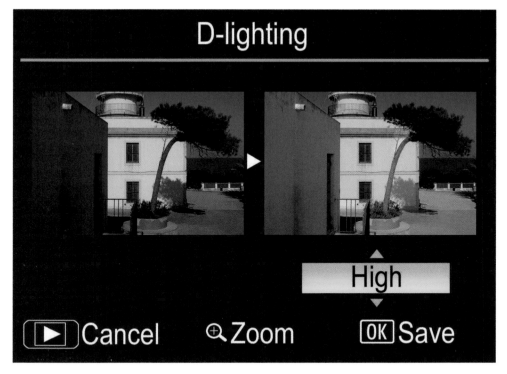

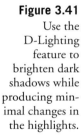

Red-Eye Correction

This Retouch menu tool can be used to remove the residual red-eye look that remains after applying the Nikon D90's other remedies, such as the red-eye reduction lamp. (You can use the red-eye tools found in most image editors, as well.)

Your Nikon D90 has a fairly effective red-eye reduction flash mode. Unfortunately, your camera is unable, on its own, to totally *eliminate* the red-eye effects that occur when an electronic flash (or, rarely, illumination from other sources) bounces off the retinas of the eye and into the camera lens. Animals seem to suffer from yellow or green glowing pupils, instead; the effect is equally undesirable. The effect is worst under low-light conditions (exactly when you might be using a flash) as the pupils expand to allow more light to reach the retinas. The best you can hope for is to *reduce* or minimize the red-eye effect.

The best way to truly eliminate red-eye is to raise the flash up off the camera so its illumination approaches the eye from an angle that won't reflect directly back to the retina and into the lens. The extra height of the built-in flash may not be sufficient, however. That alone is a good reason for using an external flash. If you're working with your D90's built-in flash, your only recourse may be to switch on the red-eye reduction flash mode.

That causes a lamp on the front of the camera to illuminate with a half-press of the shutter release button, which may result in your subjects' pupils contracting, decreasing the amount of the red-eye effect. (You may have to ask your subject to look at the lamp to gain maximum effect.)

If your image still displays red-eye effects, you can use the Retouch menu to make a copy with red-eye reduced further. First, select a picture that was taken with flash (non-flash pictures won't be available for selection). After you've selected the picture to process, press OK. The image will be displayed on the LCD. You can magnify the image with the Zoom button, scroll around the zoomed image with the multi-selector buttons, and zoom out with the Zoom Out button. While zoomed, you can cancel the zoom by pressing the OK button.

When you are finished examining the image, press OK again. The D90 will look for red-eye, and, if detected, it will create a copy that has been processed to reduce the effect. If no red-eye is found, a copy is not created. Figure 3.42 shows an original image (left) and its processed copy (right).

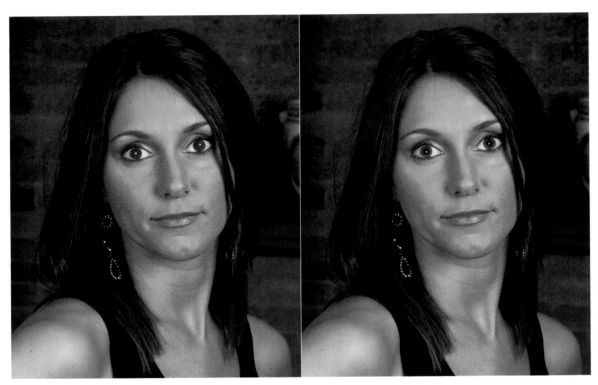

Figure 3.42 An image with red-eye (left) can be processed to produce a copy with no red-eye effects (right).

Trim

This option creates copies in specific sizes based on the final size you select, chosen from among 3:2, 4:3, and 5:4 aspect rations (proportions). You can use this feature to create smaller versions of a picture for e-mailing without the need to first transfer the image to your own computer. If you're traveling, create your smaller copy here, insert the memory card in a card reader at an Internet café, your library's public computers, or some other computer, and e-mail the reduced-size version. Just follow these steps:

1. **Select your photo.** Choose Trim from the Retouch menu. You'll be shown the standard Nikon D90 image selection screen. Scroll among the photos using the multi-selector left/right buttons, and press OK when the image you want to trim is highlighted. While selecting, you can temporarily enlarge the highlighted image by pressing the Zoom button.

2. **Choose your aspect ratio.** Rotate the main command dial to change from 3:2, 4:3, and 5:4 aspect ratios. These proportions happen to correspond to the proportions of common print sizes, including the two most popular sizes: 4×6-inches (3:2) and 8×10-inches (5:4).

3. **Crop in on your photo.** Press the Zoom button to crop in on your picture. The pixel dimensions of the cropped image at the selected proportions will be displayed in the upper-left corner (see Figure 3.43) as you zoom. The current framed size is outlined in yellow within an inset image in the lower-right corner.

4. **Move cropped area within the image.** Use the multi-selector left/right and up/down buttons to relocate the yellow cropping border within the frame.

5. **Save the cropped image.** Press OK to save a copy of the image using the current crop and size, or press the Playback button to exit without creating a copy. Copies created from JPEG Fine, Normal, or Standard have the same Image Quality setting as the original; copies made from RAW files or any RAW+JPEG setting will use JPEG Fine compression.

Table 3.1 Trim Sizes

Aspect Ratio	Sizes Available
3:2	3424×2280, 2560×1704, 1920×1280, 1280×856, 960×640, 640×424
4:3	3424×2568, 2560×1920, 1920×1440, 1280×960, 960×720, 640×480
5:4	3216×2568, 2400×1920, 1808×1440, 1200×960, 986×720, 608×480

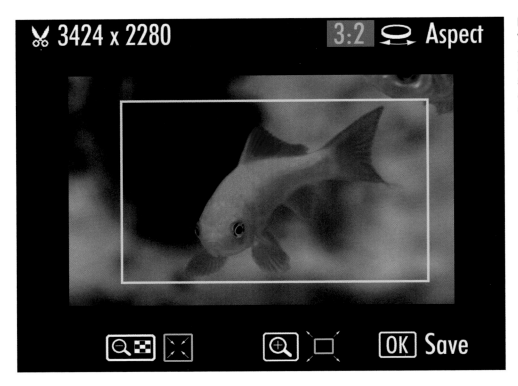

Figure 3.43
The Trim feature of the Retouch menu allows in-camera cropping.

Monochrome

This Retouch choice allows you to produce a copy of the selected photo as a black-and-white image, sepia-toned image, or cyanotype (blue-and-white). You can fine-tune the color saturation of the previewed Sepia or Cyanotype version by pressing the multi-selector up button to increase color richness, and the down button to decrease saturation. When satisfied, press OK to create the monochrome duplicate.

Filter Effects

Add effects somewhat similar to photographic filters with this tool. You can choose from among six different choices:

- **Skylight.** This option makes the image slightly less blue.

- **Warm.** Use this filter to add a rich warm cast to the duplicate.

- **Red, Green, Blue intensifiers.** These three options makes the red, green, and blue hues brighter, respectively. Use them to brighten a rose, intensify the greens of foliage, or deepen the blue of the sky.

- **Cross screen.** This option adds radiating star points to bright objects—such as the reflection of light sources on shiny surfaces. You can choose four different attributes of your stars:

  - **Number of points.** You can select from four, six, or eight points for each star added to your image.

  - **Filter amount.** Select from three different intensities, represented by two, three, and four stars in the menu (this doesn't reflect the actual number of stars in your image, which is determined by the number of bright areas in the photo).

  - **Filter angle.** Select from three different angles: steep, approximately 45 degrees, and a shallower angle.

  - **Length of points.** Three different lengths for the points can be chosen: short, medium, and long.

Color Balance

This option produces the screen shown in Figure 3.44, with a preview image of your photo. Use the multi-selector up/down (green/pink) and left/right buttons (blue/red) to bias the color of your image in the direction of the hues shown on the color square below the preview.

Figure 3.44
Press the multi-selector buttons to bias the color in the direction you prefer.

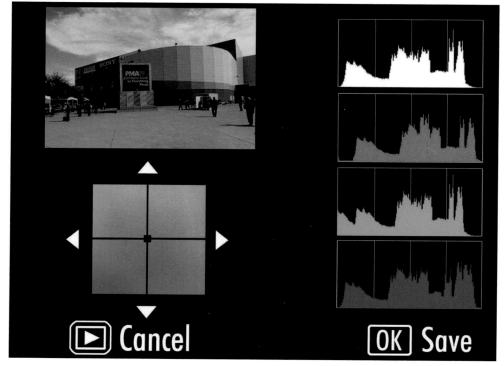

Small Picture

This Retouch menu option allows you to create small copies of full images (without cropping or trimming) at resolutions of 640×480, 320×240, or 160×120. All three of these optional small sizes may be useful for e-mailing, website display, or use in presentations on television screens.

To create a Small Picture copy:

1. Choose Small Picture from the Retouch menu.

2. Select Choose Size and specify your preference from among the three available sizes, 640×480, 320×240, or 160×120. Press OK.

3. Next, choose Select Picture and choose your image using the standard Nikon D90 image selection screen.

4. Press the up/down button to mark a highlighted image for reduction.

5. You can select more than one picture, marking each with the up/down button. Use the button to unmark any photos if you change your mind.

6. Press OK. You'll see a message: Create Small Picture? 2 Images. (Or whatever number of images you have marked.)

7. Press OK to create the small pictures.

Image Overlay

You'll have to scroll down to view the next few entries in the Retouch menu following this last one (see Figure 3.45). The Image Overlay tool allows you to combine two RAW photos (only NEF files can be used) in a composite image that Nikon claims is better than a "double exposure" created in an image-editing application because the overlays are made using RAW data. To produce this composite image, follow these steps:

1. Choose Image Overlay. The screen shown in Figure 3.46 will be displayed, with the Image 1 box highlighted.

2. Press OK and the Nikon D90's image selection screen appears. Choose the first image for the overlay and press OK.

3. Press the multi-selector right button to highlight the Image 2 box, and press OK to produce the image selection screen. Choose the second image for the overlay.

4. By highlighting either the Image 1 or Image 2 boxes and pressing the multi-selector up/down buttons, you can adjust the "gain," or how much of the final image will be "exposed" from the selected picture. You can choose from X0.5 (half-exposure) to X2.0 (twice the exposure) for each image. The default value is 1.0 for each, so that each image will contribute equally to the final exposure.

Figure 3.45
More entries in
the Retouch
menu.

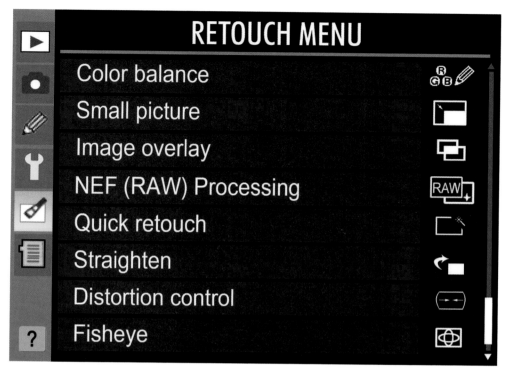

Figure 3.45
More entries in
the Retouch
menu.

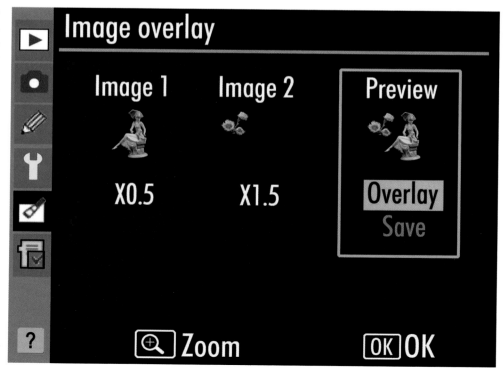

Figure 3.46
Overlay two
RAW images
to produce
a "double
exposure."

5. Use the multi-selector right button to highlight the Preview box and view the combined picture. Press the Zoom button to enlarge the view.

6. When you're ready to store your composite copy, press the multi-selector down button when the Preview box is highlighted to select Save, and press OK. The combined image is stored on the memory card.

NEF (RAW) Processing

Use this tool to create a JPEG version of any image saved in either straight RAW (with no JPEG version) or RAW+Basic (with a Basic JPEG version). You can select from among several parameters to "process" your new JPEG copy right in the camera.

1. Choose a RAW image. Select NEF (RAW) Processing from the Retouch menu. You'll be shown the standard Nikon D90 image selection screen. Use the left/right buttons to navigate among the RAW images displayed. Press OK to select the highlighted image.

2. In the NEF (RAW) processing screen, shown in Figure 3.47, you can use the multi-selector up/down keys to select from five different attributes of the RAW image information to apply to your JPEG copy. Choose Image quality (Fine, Normal, or Basic), Image size (Large, Medium, or Small), White balance, Exposure compensation, and Set Picture Control parameters.

Tip

The White Balance parameter cannot be selected for images created with the Image Overlay tool, and the Preset manual white balance setting can be fine-tuned only with images that were originally shot using the Preset white balance setting. Exposure compensation cannot be adjusted for images taken using Active D-Lighting, and both white balance and optimize image settings cannot be applied to pictures taken using any of the DVP/Scene modes.

3. Press the Zoom button to magnify the image temporarily while the button is held down.

4. Press the Playback button if you change your mind, to exit from the processing screen.

5. When all parameters are set, highlight EXE (for Execute) and press OK. The D90 will create a JPEG file with the settings you've specified, and show an Image saved message on the LCD when finished.

Figure 3.47
Adjust five
parameters and
then save your
JPEG copy
from a RAW
original file.

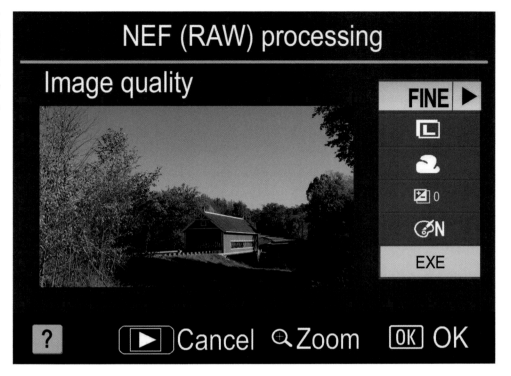

Quick Retouch

This option brightens the shadows of pictures that have already been taken. Once you've selected your photo for processing, use the multi-selector up/down keys in the screen that pops up (see Figure 3.48). The amount of correction that you select (High, Normal, or Low) will be applied to the version of the image shown at right. The left-hand version of the image shows the uncorrected version. While working on your image, you can press the Zoom image to temporarily magnify the original photo.

Quick Retouch brightens shadows, enhances contrast, and adds color richness (saturation) to the image. Press OK to create a copy on your memory card with the retouching applied.

Tip

Reminder: As I noted previously, with Quick Retouch and other Retouching menu tools, you can work with JPEG Fine, JPEG Normal, or JPEG Basic images to create a JPEG copy at the same quality level. However if you use a RAW or RAW+JPEG Basic original, the retouched copy is created at the JPEG Fine quality level.

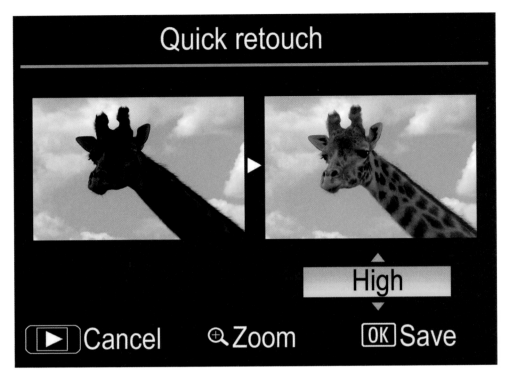

Figure 3.48
Quick Retouch applies D-Lighting, enhanced contrast, and added saturation to an image.

Straighten

This tool produces an aligned picture of the select image, rotated clockwise up to five degrees in 0.25-degree increments by pressing the right multi-selector button. To rotate counterclockwise, use the left multi-selector button. The D90 will trim the image slightly to create a square copy. A set of grid lines provides guidance as you straighten the picture.

When finished, press OK to create a copy on your memory card with the retouching applied, or press the Playback button to exit without creating a copy.

Distortion Control

This option creates a copy with reduced distortion at the edges of the image. It can correct for both barrel distortion (straight lines closest to the edge of the image appear to bow outwards) and pincushion distortion (straight lines closest to the edge appear to bend inwards).

You can choose Auto to let the camera evaluate your image and make the correction, or select Manual to specify the correction yourself. Use the right multi-selector button to reduce barrel distortion, and the left multi-selector button to minimize pincushion distortion. When finished, press OK to create a copy on your memory card with the correction applied, or press the Playback button to exit without creating a copy.

Fisheye

Use this tool to create a faux fisheye image, as shown in Figure 3.49. The right multi-selector button increases the effect and the amount of the original image that must be cropped out to give you a rectangular image. The left multi-selector button reduces the fisheye effect.

Figure 3.49
Create a distorted image with fisheye-like curves.

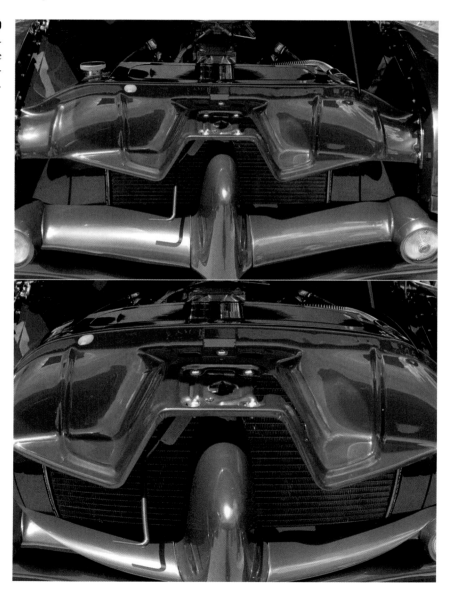

When finished, press OK to create a copy on your memory card with the fisheye effect applied, or press the Playback button to exit without creating a copy.

Side-by-Side

Use this option to compare a retouched photo side-by-side with the original from which it was derived. This option is shown on the pop-up menu that appears when you are viewing an image (or copy) full screen and press the OK button.

To use Side by Side comparisons:

1. Press the Playback button and review images in full-frame mode until you encounter a source image or retouched copy you want to compare. The retouched copy will have the retouching icon displayed in the upper-left corner. Press OK.

2. The Retouch menu with Trim, Monochrome, Filter effects, Small picture, and Side-by-Side comparison. (These are the only options that can be applied to an image that has already been retouched.) Scroll down to Before and After and press OK.

3. The original and retouched image will appear next to each other, with the retouching options you've used shown as a label above the images, as you can see in Figure 3.50.

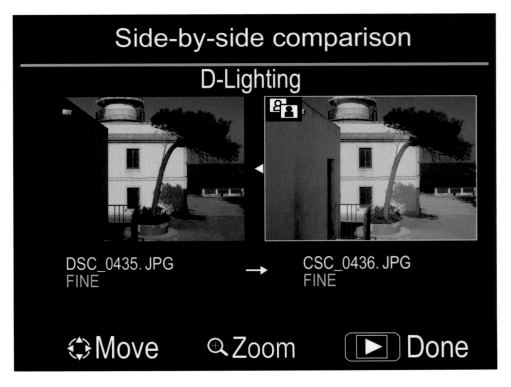

Figure 3.50
You can easily compare an original image and the retouched version side-by-side.

4. Highlight the original or the copy with the multi-selector left/right buttons, and press the Zoom button to magnify the image to examine it more closely.

5. If you have created more than one copy of an original image, select the retouched version shown, and press the multi-selector up/down buttons to view the other retouched copies. The up/down buttons will also let you view the other image used to create an Image overlay copy.

6. When done comparing, press the Playback button to exit.

Using My Menu

The last menu in the D90's main menu screen has two versions: Recent Settings and My Menu. The default mode is Recent Settings, which simply shows an ever-changing roster of the 20 menu items you used most recently. You'll probably find it more useful to activate the My Menu option instead, which contains only those menu items that you deposit there extracted from the Playback, Shooting, Custom Setting, Setup, and Retouch menus, based on your own decisions on which you use most. Remember that the D90 always returns to the last menu and menu entry accessed when you press the Menu button. So you can set up My Menu (see Figure 3.51) to include just the items access most frequently, and (as long as you haven't used another menu) jump to those items instantly by pressing the Menu button.

Figure 3.51
You can include your favorite menu items in the fast-access My Menu.

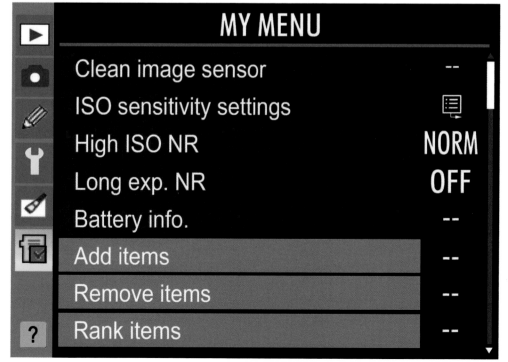

Switching back and forth is easy. The My Menu and Recent Settings menus each have a menu choice called Choose Tab. Highlight that entry and press the right multi-selector button to view a screen that allows you to activate either the My Menu or Recent Settings menu. Press OK to confirm.

I tend to include frequently used functions that aren't available using direct access buttons in My Menu. For example, I include High ISO NR and Long Exp. NR, and Battery info there, because I may want to turn noise reduction on or off, or check the status of my battery during shooting. I *don't* include ISO, QUAL, or WB changes in My Menu, even though they are available in the menu system, because I can quickly change those values by pressing their dedicated buttons and rotating the main and sub-command dials.

You can add or subtract entries on My Menu at any time, and re-order (or rank) the entries so the ones you access most often are shown at the top of the list. Here's all you need to know to work with My Menu. To add entries to My Menu:

1. Select My Menu and choose Add items.

2. A list of the available menus will appear (Playback, Shooting, Custom Setting, Setup, and Retouch menus). Highlight one and press the multi-selector's right button.

3. Within the selected menu, choose the menu item you want to add and press OK.

4. The label Choose Position appears at the top of the My Menu screen. Use the up/down buttons to select a rank among the entries, and press OK to confirm and add the new item.

5. Repeat steps 1-4 if you want to add more entries to My Menu.

To reorder the menu listings:

1. Within the My Menu screen, choose Rank Items.

2. Use the up/down buttons to select the item to be moved, and press OK.

3. Use the up/down buttons to relocate the selected item and press OK.

4. Repeat steps 2-3 to move additional entries.

To remove entries from the list you can simply press the Trash button while an item is highlighted in the My Menu screen. To remove multiple items, follow these steps:

1. Within the My Menu screen, choose Remove Items.

2. A list with checkboxes next to the menu items appears. Scroll down to an item you want to remove and press the multi-selector right button to mark its box. If you change your mind, highlight the item and press the right button again to unmark the box.

3. When finished, highlight Done and press the OK button.

4. Press OK to confirm the deletion.

4

Fine-Tuning Exposure

When you bought your Nikon D90, you probably thought your days of worrying about getting the correct exposure were over. To paraphrase an old Kodak tagline dating back to the 19th Century—the goal is, "you press the button, and the camera does the rest." For the most part, that's a realistic objective. The D90 is one of the smartest cameras available when it comes to calculating the right exposure for most situations. You can generally choose one of the Basic Zone modes, or spin the mode dial to Program (P), Aperture Priority (A), or Shutter Priority (S) and shoot away.

So, why am I including an entire chapter titled "Fine-Tuning Exposure"? As you learn to use your D90 creatively, you're going to find that the right settings—as determined by the camera's exposure meter and intelligence—need to be *adjusted* to account for your creative decisions or special situations.

For example, when you shoot with the main light source behind the subject, you end up with *backlighting*, which can result in an overexposed background and/or an underexposed subject. The Nikon D90 recognizes backlit situations nicely, and can properly base exposure on the main subject, producing a decent photo. Features like D-Lighting (discussed in Chapter 3) can fine-tune exposure to preserve detail in the highlights and shadows.

But, what if you *want* to underexpose the subject to produce a silhouette effect? Or, perhaps, you might want to flip up the D90's built-in flash unit to fill in the shadows on your subject. The more you know about how to use your D90, the more you'll run into situations where you want to creatively tweak the exposure to provide a different look than you'd get with a straight shot.

This chapter shows you the fundamentals of exposure, so you'll be better equipped to override the Nikon D90's default settings when you want to or need to. After all, correct exposure is one of the foundations of good photography, along with accurate focus and sharpness, appropriate color balance, freedom from unwanted noise and excessive contrast, as well as pleasing composition.

The Nikon D90 gives you a great deal of control over all of these, although composition is entirely up to you. You must still frame the photograph to create an interesting arrangement of subject matter, but all the other parameters are basic functions of the camera. You can let your D90 set them for you automatically, you can fine-tune how the camera applies its automatic settings, or you can make them yourself, manually. The amount of control you have over exposure, sensitivity (ISO settings), color balance, focus, and image parameters like sharpness and contrast make the D90 a versatile tool for creating images.

In the next few pages, I'm going to give you a grounding in one of those foundations, and explain the basics of exposure, either as an introduction or as a refresher course, depending on your current level of expertise. When you finish this chapter, you'll understand most of what you need to know to take well-exposed photographs creatively in a broad range of situations.

Getting a Handle on Exposure

In the most basic sense, exposure is all about light. Exposure can make or break your photo. Correct exposure brings out the detail in the areas you want to picture, providing the range of tones and colors you need to create the desired image. Poor exposure can cloak important details in shadow, or wash them out in glare-filled featureless expanses of white. However, getting the perfect exposure requires some intelligence—either that built into the camera or the smarts in your head—because digital sensors can't capture all the tones we are able to see. If the range of tones in an image is extensive, embracing both inky black shadows and bright highlights, we often must settle for an exposure that renders most of those tones—but not all—in a way that best suits the photo we want to produce.

For example, look at the two typical tourist snapshots presented side by side in Figure 4.1. For the image on the left, the camera, set for Spot metering, calculated exposure based on the scene in the background that is visible through the archway. While the background is reasonably well-exposed, the interior, the statues, and the ceiling overhead are quite underexposed. For the version at right, Spot metering was used to read the ceiling of the scene, producing a more detailed interior shot, but badly overexposing the exterior details. The camera's sensor simply can't capture detail in both dark areas and bright areas in a single shot.

The solution, in this particular case, was to resort to a technique called High Dynamic Range (HDR) photography, in which the two exposures from Figure 4.1 were combined in an image editor such as Photoshop, or a specialized HDR tool like Photomatix (available for both Windows and Mac OS for about $100 from www.hdrsoft.com). The resulting shot is shown in Figure 4.2. I'll explain more about HDR photography later in this chapter. For now, though, I'm going to concentrate on showing you how to get the best exposures possible without resorting to such tools, using only the features of your Nikon D90.

To understand exposure, you need to understand the six aspects of light that combine to produce an image. Start with a light source—the sun, an interior lamp, or a the glow from a campfire—and trace its path to your camera, through the lens, and finally to the sensor that captures the illumination. Here's a brief review of the things within our control that affect exposure.

■ **Light at its source.** Our eyes and our cameras—film or digital—are most sensitive to that portion of the electromagnetic spectrum we call *visible light*. That light has several important aspects that are relevant to photography, such as color, and harshness (which is determined primarily by the apparent size of the light source as it illuminates a subject). But, in terms of exposure, the important attribute of a light source is its *intensity*. We may have direct control over intensity, which might be the case with an interior light that can be brightened or dimmed. Or, we might have only indirect control over intensity, as with sunlight, which can be made to appear dimmer by introducing translucent light-absorbing or reflective materials in its path.

Figure 4.1
At left, the image is exposed for the background highlights, losing shadow detail. At right, the exposure captures detail in the shadows, but the background highlights are washed out.

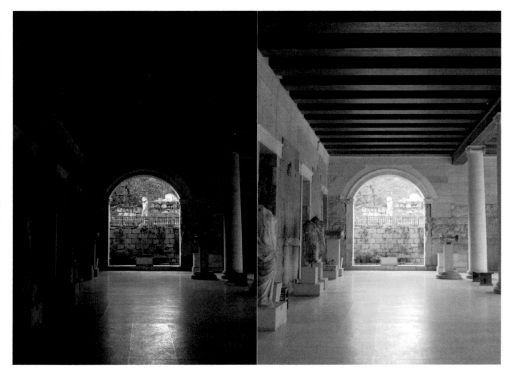

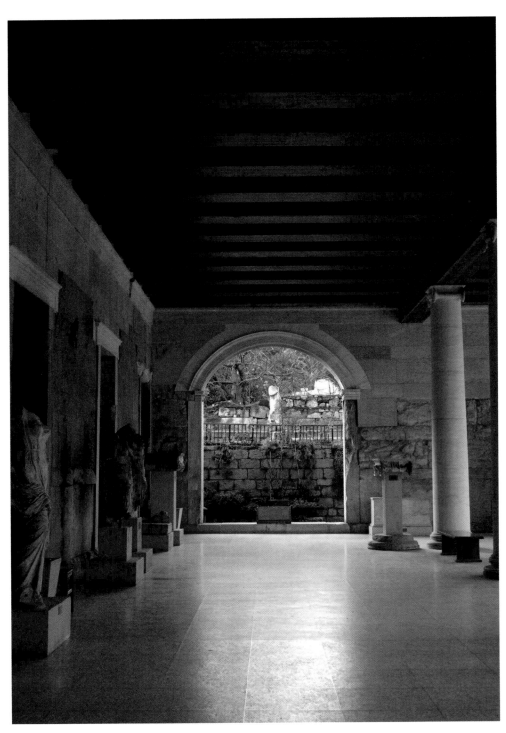

Figure 4.2
Combining the two exposures produces the best compromise image.

- **Light's duration.** We tend to think of most light sources as continuous. But, as you'll learn in Chapter 7, the duration of light can change quickly enough to modify the exposure, as when the main illumination in a photograph comes from an intermittent source, such as an electronic flash.

- **Light reflected, transmitted, or emitted.** Once light is produced by its source, either continuously or in a brief burst, we are able to see and photograph objects by the light that is reflected from our subjects towards the camera lens; transmitted (say, from translucent objects that are lit from behind), or emitted (by a candle or television screen). When more or less light reaches the lens from the subject, we need to adjust the exposure. This part of the equation is under our control to the extent we can increase the amount of light falling on or passing through the subject (by adding extra light sources or using reflectors), or by pumping up the light that's emitted (by increasing the brightness of the glowing object).

- **Light passed by the lens.** Not all the illumination that reaches the front of the lens makes it all the way through. Filters can remove some of the light before it enters the lens. Inside the lens barrel is a variable-sized diaphragm called an *aperture* that dilates and contracts to control the amount of light that enters the lens. You, or the D90's autoexposure system, can control exposure by varying the size of the aperture. The relative size of the aperture is called the *f/stop* (see Figure 4.3).

- **Light passing through the shutter.** Once light passes through the lens, the amount of time the sensor receives it is determined by the D90's shutter, which can remain open for as long as 30 seconds (or even longer if you use the Bulb setting) or as briefly as 1/4,000th second.

- **Light captured by the sensor.** Not all the light falling onto the sensor is captured. If the number of photons reaching a particular photosite doesn't pass a set threshold, no information is recorded. Similarly, if too much light illuminates a pixel in the sensor, then the excess isn't recorded or, worse, spills over to contaminate adjacent pixels. We can modify the minimum and maximum number of pixels that contribute to image detail by adjusting the ISO setting. At higher ISOs, the incoming light is amplified to boost the effective sensitivity of the sensor.

These factors—the quantity of light produced by the light source, the amount reflected or transmitted towards the camera, the light passed by the lens, the amount of time the shutter is open, and the sensitivity of the sensor—all work proportionately and reciprocally to produce an exposure. That is, if you double the amount of light that's available, increase the aperture by one stop, make the shutter speed twice as long, or boost the ISO setting 2X, you'll get twice as much exposure. Similarly, you can increase any of these factors while decreasing one of the others by a similar amount to keep the same exposure.

F/STOPS AND SHUTTER SPEEDS

If you're *really* new to more advanced cameras (and I realize that many soon-to-be-ambitious photographers do purchase the D90 as their first digital SLR), you might need to know that the lens aperture, or f/stop, is a ratio, much like a fraction, which is why f/2 is larger than f/4, just as 1/2 is larger than 1/4. However, f/2 is actually *four times* as large as f/4. (If you remember your high-school geometry, you'll know that to double the area of a circle, you multiply its diameter by the square root of two: 1.4.)

Lenses are usually marked with intermediate f/stops that represent a size that's twice as much/half as much as the previous aperture. So, a lens might be marked:

f/2, f/2.8, f/4, f/5.6, f/8, f/11, f/16, f/22, with each larger number representing an aperture that admits half as much light as the one before, as shown in Figure 4.3.

Shutter speeds are actual fractions (of a second), but the numerator is omitted, so that 60, 125, 250, 500, 1,000, and so forth represent 1/60th, 1/125th, 1/250th, 1/500th, and 1/1,000th second. To avoid confusion, Nikon uses quotation marks to signify longer exposures: 2", 2.5", 4", and so forth representing 2.0, 2.5, and 4.0-second exposures, respectively.

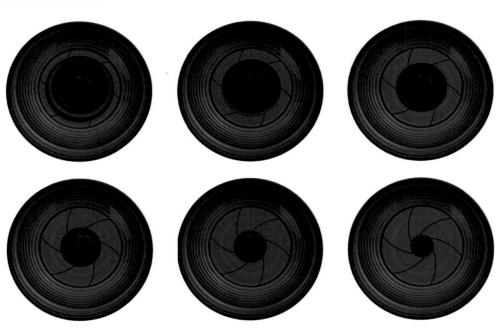

Figure 4.3
Top row (left to right): f/2, f/2.8, f/4; bottom row, f/5.6, f/8, f11.

Most commonly, exposure settings are made using the aperture and shutter speed, followed by adjusting the ISO sensitivity if it's not possible to get the preferred exposure; that is, the one that uses the "best" f/stop or shutter speed for the depth-of-field (range of sharp focus) or action stopping we want (produced by short shutter speeds, as I'll explain later). Table 4.1 shows equivalent exposure settings using various shutter speeds and f/stops.

Table 4.1 Equivalent Exposures

Shutter speed	f/stop	Shutter speed	f/stop
1/30th second	f/22	1/500th second	f/5.6
1/60th second	f/16	1/1,000th second	f/4
1/125th second	f/11	1/2,000th second	f/2.8
1/250th second	f/8	1/4,000th second	f/2

When the D90 is set for P (Program) mode, the metering system selects the correct exposure for you automatically, but you can change quickly to an equivalent exposure by holding down the shutter release button halfway ("locking" the current exposure), and then spinning the main command dial until the desired *equivalent* exposure combination is displayed. You can use this standard Flexible Program feature more easily if you remember that you need to rotate the dial toward the *left* when you want to increase the amount of depth-of-field or use a slower shutter speed; rotate to the *right* when you want to reduce the depth-of-field or use a faster shutter speed. (The reverse is true if you've swapped the dial functions as described in Chapter 3.) The need for more/less DOF and slower/faster shutter speed are the primary reasons you'd want to use Program Shift. I'll explain Program mode exposure shifting options in more detail later in this chapter.

In Aperture Priority (A) and Shutter Priority (S) modes, you can change to an equivalent exposure using a different combination of shutter speed and aperture, but only by either adjusting the aperture in Aperture Priority mode (the camera then chooses the shutter speed) or shutter speed in Shutter Priority mode (the camera then selects the aperture). I'll cover all these exposure modes and their differences later in the chapter.

How the D90 Calculates Exposure

Your Nikon D90 calculates exposure by measuring the light that passes through the lens and is bounced up by the mirror to a 420-segment RGB sensor located near the focusing surface, using a pattern you can select (more on that later) and based on the assumption that each area being measured reflects about the same amount of light as a neutral gray card with 18-percent reflectance. That assumption is necessary, because different subjects reflect different amounts of light. In a photo containing a white cat and a dark gray cat, the white cat might reflect five times as much light as the gray cat. An exposure based on the white cat will cause the gray cat to appear to be black, while an exposure based only on the gray cat will make the white cat washed out. Light-measuring devices handle this by assuming that the areas measured average a standard value of 18-percent gray, a figure that's been used as a rough standard (most vendors don't calibrate their metering for exactly 18-percent gray; the actual figure may be closer to 13 or 14 percent) for many years.

In most cases, your camera's light meter will do a good job of calculating the right exposure, especially if you use the exposure tips in the next section. But if you want to double-check, or feel that exposure is especially critical, take the light reading off an object of known reflectance. Photographers sometimes carry around an 18 percent gray card (available from any camera store) and, for critical exposures, actually use that card, placed in the subject area, to measure exposure (or to set a custom white balance if needed).

You could, in many cases, arrive at a reasonable exposure by pointing your D90 at an evenly lit object, such as an actual gray card or the palm of your hand (the backside of the hand is too variable). It's more practical though, to use your D90's system to meter the actual scene, using the options available to you when using one of the PASM modes. (In DVP/Scene modes, the metering decisions are handled by the camera's programming.)

Tip

Of course, if you use such a gray card, strictly speaking, you need to use about one-half stop *more* exposure than metered, because the D90 is calibrated for a lighter tone, rather than the 18-percent gray you just measured. If you're using a human palm instead, add one full stop more exposure.

To meter properly you'll want to choose both the *metering method* (how light is evaluated) and *exposure method* (how the appropriate shutter speeds and apertures are chosen). (See Figure 4.4.) I'll describe both in the following sections. But first, let's clear up that black cat/gray cat/white cat conundrum, without using any actual cats. Black, white, and gray cats have been a standard metaphor for many years, as well, so I'm going to explain this concept using a different, and more cooperative, life form: peppers.

Figure 4.5 shows three peppers. The yellow peppers at top represent an off-white cat, or any object that is very light but which contains detail that we want to see in the light areas. The red peppers in the center are a stand-in for a gray cat, because they have most

Figure 4.4
Exposure
modes.

DVP/Scene
modes

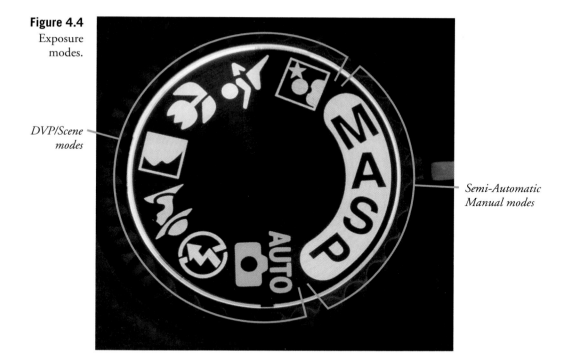

Semi-Automatic
Manual modes

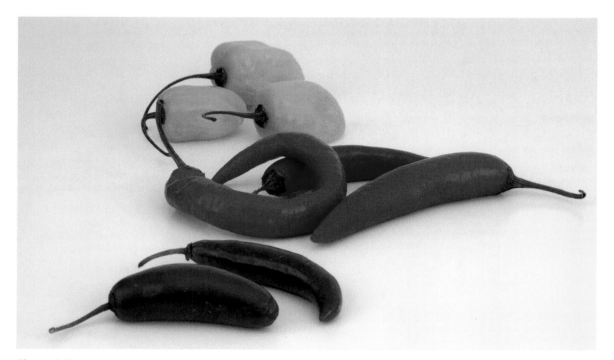

Figure 4.5 The yellow peppers, red peppers, and green peppers represent light, middle, and dark tones.

of their details in the middle tones. The green peppers serve as our black cat, because it is a dark object with detail in its shadows.

The colors confuse the issue, so I'm going to convert our color peppers to black-and-white. For the version shown in Figure 4.6, the exposure was optimized for the white (yellow) paper, changing its tonal value to a medium, 18-percent gray. The dark (green) and medium-toned (red) peppers are now *too* dark. For Figure 4.7, the exposure was optimized for the dark (green) pepper, making most of its surface, now, fall into the middle-tone, 18-percent gray range. The yellow (light) and midtone (red) peppers are now too light.

The solution, of course, is to measure exposure from the object with the middle tones that most closely correspond to the 18-percent gray "standard." Do that, and you wind up with a picture that more closely resembles the original tonality of the red, yellow, and green peppers, and which looks, in black-and-white, like Figure 4.8.

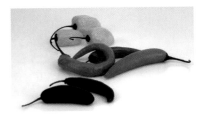
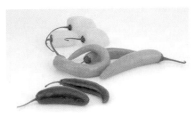
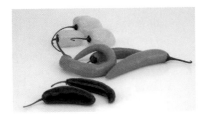

Figure 4.6 Exposing for the light-colored peppers at upper left renders the other two types excessively dark.

Figure 4.7 Exposing for the dark peppers (lower left) causes the vegetables in the upper two-thirds of the picture to become too light.

Figure 4.8 Exposing for the middle-toned red peppers in the center produces an image in which the tones of all three types appear accurately.

F/STOPS VERSUS STOPS

In photography parlance, *f/stop* always means the aperture or lens opening. However, for lack of a current commonly used word for one exposure increment, the term *stop* is often used. (In the past, EV served this purpose, but Exposure Value and its abbreviation has been inextricably intertwined with its use in describing Exposure Compensation.) In this book, when I say "stop" by itself (no f/), I mean one whole unit of exposure, and am not necessarily referring to an actual f/stop or lens aperture. So, adjusting the exposure by "one stop" can mean both changing to the next shutter speed increment (say, from 1/125th second to 1/250th second) or the next aperture (such as f/4 to f/5.6). Similarly, 1/3 stop or 1/2 stop increments can mean either shutter speed or aperture changes, depending on the context. Be forewarned.

To meter properly, you'll want to choose both the *metering method* (how light is evaluated) and *exposure method* (how the appropriate shutter speeds and apertures are chosen based on the metered information). I'll describe both in the following sections.

MODES, MODES, AND MORE MODES

Call them modes or methods, the Nikon D90 seems to have a lot of different sets of options that are described using similar terms. Here's how to sort them out:

- **Metering method.** These modes determine the *parts of the image* within the 420-sensor array that are examined in order to calculate exposure. The D90 may look at many different points within the image, segregating them by zone (Matrix metering), examine the same number of points, but give greater weight to those located in the middle of the frame (Center-Weighted metering), or evaluate only a limited number of points in a limited area (Spot metering).

- **Exposure method.** These modes determine *which* settings are used to expose the image. The D90 may adjust the shutter speed, the aperture, or both, depending on the method you choose.

Choosing a Metering Method

The D90 has three different schemes for evaluating the light received by its exposure sensors, Matrix (with several variations, depending on what lens you have attached); Center-Weighted; and Spot metering. Matrix metering is always used when you select one of the DVP/Scene modes; you can't change to Center-Weighted or Spot metering when using Auto, Auto/No Flash, Portrait, Landscape, Sports, Close-up, or Night Portrait modes. Exposure will generally be calculated well in one of these Scene modes, but the ability to choose an alternate metering method is one of the major reasons to select Program, Aperture Priority, Shutter Priority, or Manual exposure instead.

In P, A, S, and M exposure modes, select the metering mode you want to use (Matrix, Center-Weighted, or Spot) by rotating the main command dial while pressing the metering mode located just southwest of the shutter release. Here is what you need to know about each metering method:

Matrix Metering

For its Matrix metering mode, the D90 slices up the frame into 420 different zones, arrayed in 10 rows of 42 columns that cover most of the sensor area, shown in Figure 4.9. When Matrix metering is active, its icon (shown as an overlay at the upper-right corner of the figure) appears on the top-panel monochrome LCD/control panel.

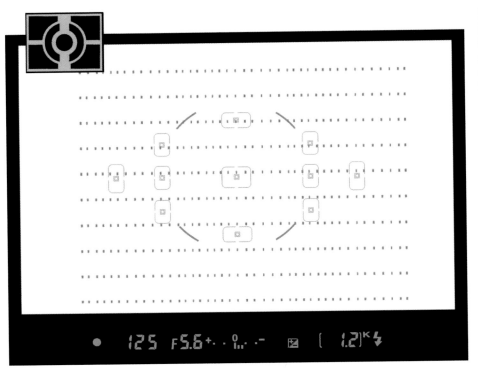

Figure 4.9
Matrix metering calculates exposure based on 420 points in the frame.

In all cases, the D90 evaluates the differences between the zones, and compares them with a built-in database of several hundred thousand images to make an educated guess about what kind of picture you're taking. For example, if the top sections of a picture are much lighter than the bottom portions, the algorithm can assume that the scene is a landscape photo with lots of sky. An image that includes most of the lighter portions in the center area may be a portrait. The Nikon D90 also uses information other than brightness to make its evaluation:

- **3D Color Matrix metering II.** This metering mode is used by default when the D90 is equipped with a lens that has a type G or type D designator in its name, such as the AF-S DX Nikkor 16-85mm f/3.5-5.6G ED VR lens. The G after the f/5.6 is the giveaway. (More on lens nomenclature in Chapter 6.) The camera calculates exposure based on brightness, colors of the subject matter (that is, blue pixels in the upper part of the image are probably sky; green pixels in the lower half probably foliage), focus point, and distance information. The D90 is able to use that additional distance data to better calculate what kind of scene you have framed. For example, if you're shooting a portrait with a longer focal-length lens focused to about 5 to 12 feet from the camera, and the upper half of the scene is very bright, the camera assumes you would prefer to meter for the rest of the image, and discount the bright area. However, if the camera has a wide-angle lens attached and is focused at infinity, the D90 can assume you're taking a landscape photo and take the bright upper area into account to produce better looking sky and clouds.

■ **Color Matrix metering II.** If you have a non-G or non-D lens equipped with a CPU chip (these are generally older lenses, although chips can be added to optics which lack them), the distance range is not used. Instead, only focus, brightness, and color information is taken into account to calculate an appropriate exposure.

Matrix metering is best for most general subjects, because it is able to intelligently analyze a scene and make an excellent guess of what kind of subject you're shooting a great deal of the time. The camera can tell the difference between low-contrast and high-contrast subjects by looking at the range of differences in brightness across the scene. Because the D90 has a fairly good idea about what kind of subject matter you are shooting, it can underexpose slightly when appropriate to preserve highlight detail when image contrast is high. (It's often possible to pull detail out of shadows that are too dark using an image editor, but once highlights are blown out to white pixels, they are gone forever.)

Center-Weighted Metering

In this mode, the exposure meter emphasizes a zone about 8mm in diameter in the center of the frame to calculate exposure, as shown in Figure 4.10. (You can change the size of the center area using CSM #b3, as described in Chapter 3.) About 75 percent of the

Figure 4.10
Center-Weighted metering calculates exposure based on the full frame, but gives 75 percent of the weight to the approximate center area shown; the remaining 25 percent of the exposure is determined by the rest of the image area.

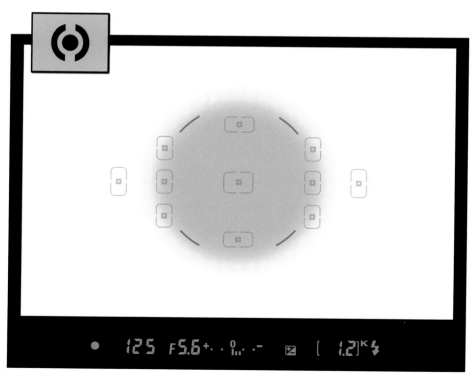

exposure is based on that central area, and the remaining exposure is based on the rest of the frame. The theory, here, is that, for most pictures, the main subject will be located in the center. So, if the D90 reads the center portion and determines that the exposure for that region should be f/8 at 1/250th second, while the outer area, which is a bit darker, calls for f/4 at 1/125th second, the camera will give the center portion the most weight and arrive at a final exposure of f/5.6 at 1/250th second.

Center-Weighting works best for portraits, architectural photos, backlit subjects with extra-bright backgrounds (such as snow or sand), and other pictures in which the most important subject is located in the middle of the frame. As the name suggests, the light reading is *weighted* towards the central portion, but information is also used from the rest of the frame. If your main subject is surrounded by very bright or very dark areas, the exposure might not be exactly right. However, this scheme works well in many situations if you don't want to use one of the other modes. This mode can be useful for close-ups of subjects like flowers, or for portraits.

Spot Metering

Spot metering is favored by those of us who used to work with a handheld light meter to measure exposure at various points (such as metering highlights and shadows separately). However, you can use Spot metering in any situation where you want to individually measure the light reflecting from light, midtone, or dark areas of your subject—or any combination of areas.

This mode confines the reading to a limited area in the center of the viewfinder, making up only 3.5 percent of the image, as shown in Figure 4.11. The circle is centered on the current focus point, unless you're using Auto-Area autofocus. (See Chapter 3 and Chapter 5 for descriptions.) In that case, the center focus zone is used. However, the metering circle *is larger than the focus zone*, so don't fall into the trap of believing that exposure is being measured only within the brackets that represent the active focus point. This is the only metering method you can use to tell the D90 exactly where to measure exposure.

You'll find Spot metering useful when you want to base exposure on a small area in the frame. If that area is in the center of the frame, so much the better. If not, you'll have to make your meter reading for an off-center subject and then lock exposure by pressing the shutter release halfway, or by pressing the AE Lock button. This mode is best for subjects where the background is significantly brighter or darker.

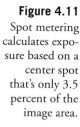

Figure 4.11
Spot metering calculates exposure based on a center spot that's only 3.5 percent of the image area.

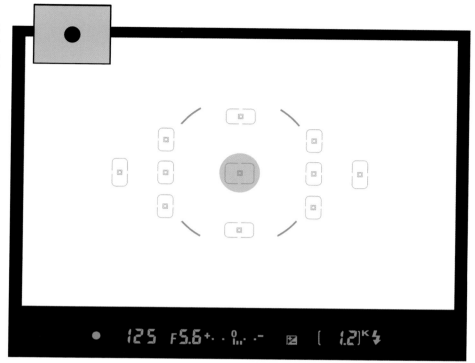

Choosing an Exposure Method

The Nikon D90's DVP/Scene modes choose an exposure method for you. But there are three semi-automated methods (plus manual) that you can use to choose the appropriate shutter speed and aperture. You can choose among them by rotating the mode dial until the one you want is selected. Your choice of which is best for a given shooting situation will depend on things like your need for lots of (or less) depth-of-field, a desire to freeze action or allow motion blur, or how much noise you find acceptable in an image. Each of the D90's exposure methods emphasizes one aspect of image capture or another. This section introduces you to all four.

Aperture Priority

In A mode (don't confuse this with Auto; some point-and-shoot cameras use the letter A to represent automatic mode), you specify the lens opening used, and the D90 selects the shutter speed. Aperture Priority is especially good when you want to use a particular lens opening to achieve a desired effect. Perhaps you'd like to use the smallest f/stop possible to maximize depth-of-field in a close-up picture. Or, you might want to use a large f/stop to throw everything except your main subject out of focus, as in Figure 4.12.

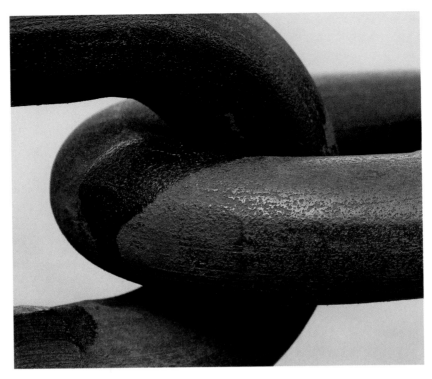

Figure 4.12
Use Aperture
Priority to
"lock in" a
large f/stop
when you want
to blur the
background.

Maybe you'd just like to "lock in" a particular f/stop because it's the sharpest available aperture with that lens. Or, you might prefer to use, say, f/2.8 on a lens with a maximum aperture of f/1.4, because you want the best compromise between speed and sharpness.

Aperture Priority can even be used to specify a *range* of shutter speeds you want to use under varying lighting conditions, which seems almost contradictory. But think about it. You're shooting a soccer game outdoors with a telephoto lens and want a relatively high shutter speed, but you don't care if the speed changes a little should the sun duck behind a cloud. Set your D90 to A, and adjust the aperture until a shutter speed of, say, 1/1,000th second is selected at your current ISO setting. (In bright sunlight at ISO 400, that aperture is likely to be around f/11.) Then, go ahead and shoot, knowing that your D90 will maintain that f/11 aperture (for sufficient depth-of-field as the soccer players move about the field), but will drop down to 1/750th or 1/500th second if necessary should the lighting change a little.

A Lo or HI indicator in the viewfinder, accompanied by a Subject Is Too Dark or Subject Is Too Bright warning on the LCD indicates that the D90 is unable to select an appropriate shutter speed at the selected aperture and that over- and underexposure will occur at the current ISO setting. That's the major pitfall of using A: you might select an f/stop that is too small or too large to allow an optimal exposure with the available shutter speeds. For example, if you choose f/2.8 as your aperture and the illumination is quite bright (say, at the beach or in snow), even your camera's fastest shutter speed might not be able to cut down the amount of light reaching the sensor to provide the right exposure. Or, if you select f/8 in a dimly lit room, you might find yourself shooting with a very slow shutter speed that can cause blurring from subject movement or camera shake. Aperture Priority is best used by those with a bit of experience in choosing settings. Many seasoned photographers leave their D90 set on A all the time.

Shutter Priority

Shutter Priority (S) is the inverse of Aperture Priority: you choose the shutter speed you'd like to use, and the camera's metering system selects the appropriate f/stop. Perhaps you're shooting action photos and you want to use the absolute fastest shutter speed available with your camera; in other cases, you might want to use a slow shutter speed to add some blur to a sports photo that would be mundane if the action were completely frozen (see Figure 4.13). Shutter Priority mode gives you some control over how much action-freezing capability your digital camera brings to bear in a particular situation.

You'll also encounter the same problem as with Aperture Priority when you select a shutter speed that's too long or too short for correct exposure under some conditions. I've shot outdoor soccer games on sunny Fall evenings and used Shutter Priority mode to lock in a 1/1,000th second shutter speed, only to find my D90 refused to shoot when the sun dipped behind some trees and there was no longer enough light to shoot at that speed, even with the lens wide open.

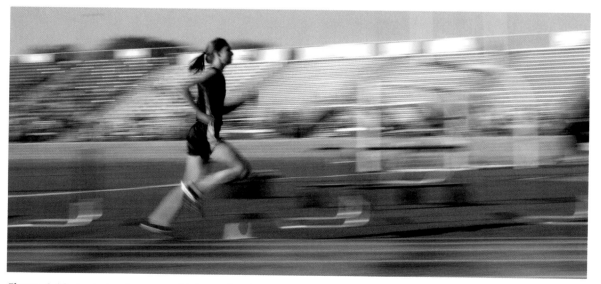

Figure 4.13 Lock the shutter at a high speed to freeze action—or use a slower speed to allow some interesting motion blur.

Like A mode, it's possible to choose an inappropriate shutter speed. If that's the case, the maximum aperture of your lens (to indicate underexposure) or the minimum aperture (to indicate overexposure) will blink.

Program Mode

Program mode (P) uses the D90's built-in smarts to select the correct f/stop and shutter speed using a database of picture information that tells it which combination of shutter speed and aperture will work best for a particular photo. If the correct exposure cannot be achieved at the current ISO setting, the Lo or HI indicator in the viewfinder and LCD will appear. You can then boost or reduce the ISO to increase or decrease sensitivity.

The D90's recommended exposure can be overridden if you want. Use the EV setting feature (described later, because it also applies to S and A modes) to add or subtract exposure from the metered value. And, as I mentioned earlier in this chapter, in Program mode you can rotate the command dial to change from the recommended setting to an equivalent setting (as shown in Table 4.1) that produces the same exposure, but using a different combination of f/stop and shutter speed.

This is called "Flexible Program" by Nikon. Rotate the command dial clockwise to reduce the size of the aperture (going from, say, f/4 to f/5.6), so that the D90 will automatically use a slower shutter speed (going from, say, 1/250 second to 1/125 second). Rotate the command dial counterclockwise to use a larger aperture, while automatically producing a shorter shutter speed that provides the same equivalent exposure as metered in P mode. An asterisk appears next to the P in the LCD and viewfinder so you'll know you've overridden the D90's default program setting. Your adjustment remains in force until you rotate the command dial until the asterisk disappears, or you switch to a different exposure mode, or turn the D90 off.

MAKING EV CHANGES

Sometimes you'll want more or less exposure than indicated by the D90's metering system. Perhaps you want to underexpose to create a silhouette effect, or overexpose to produce a high-key look. It's easy to use the D90's exposure compensation system to override the exposure recommendations. Press the EV button on the top of the camera (just southeast of the shutter release). Then rotate the command dial counterclockwise to add exposure, and clockwise to subtract exposure. The EV change you've made remains for the exposures that follow, until you manually zero out the EV setting. The EV plus/minus icon appears in the viewfinder and monochrome status panel to warn you that an exposure compensation change has been entered. You can increase or decrease exposure over a range of plus or minus five stops. (If you've activated Easy Exposure Compensation using CSM #b2, as described in Chapter 3, you don't have to hold down the EV button; rotating the main or subcommand dials alone changes the EV value when using Program, Aperture Priority, Shutter Priority, or Manual exposure modes.)

Manual Exposure

Part of being an experienced photographer comes from knowing when to rely on your D90's automation (with DVP/Scene modes or P mode), when to go semiautomatic (with S or A), and when to set exposure manually (using M). Some photographers actually prefer to set their exposure manually, as the D90 will be happy to provide an indication of when its metering system judges your manual settings provide the proper exposure, using the analog exposure scale at the bottom of the viewfinder and on the status LCD.

Manual exposure can come in handy in some situations. You might be taking a silhouette photo and find that none of the exposure modes or EV correction features give you exactly the effect you want. Set the exposure manually to use the exact shutter speed and f/stop you need. Or, you might be working in a studio environment using multiple flash units. The additional flash are triggered by slave devices (gadgets that set off the flash when they sense the light from another flash, or, perhaps from a radio or infrared remote control). Your camera's exposure meter doesn't compensate for the extra illumination, so you need to set the aperture manually.

Although, depending on your proclivities, you might not need to set exposure manually very often, you should still make sure you understand how it works. Fortunately, the D90 makes setting exposure manually very easy. Just rotate the mode dial to change to Manual mode, and then turn the command dial to set the shutter speed, and the sub-command dial to adjust the aperture. Press the shutter release halfway or press the AE Lock button, and the exposure scale in the viewfinder shows you how far your chosen setting diverges from the metered exposure.

Adjusting Exposure with ISO Settings

Another way of adjusting exposures is by changing the ISO sensitivity setting. Sometimes photographers forget about this option, because the common practice is to set the ISO once for a particular shooting session (say, at ISO 200 for bright sunlight outdoors, or ISO 800 when shooting indoors) and then forget about ISO. The reason for that is that ISOs higher than ISO 200 or 400 are seen as "bad" or "necessary evils." However, changing the ISO is a valid way of adjusting exposure settings, particularly with the Nikon D90, which produces good results at ISO settings that create grainy, unusable pictures with some other camera models.

Indeed, I find myself using ISO adjustment as a convenient alternate way of adding or subtracting exposure when shooting in Manual mode, and as a quick way of choosing equivalent exposures when in Program or Shutter Priority or Aperture Priority modes. For example, I've selected a Manual exposure with both f/stop and shutter speed suitable for my image using, say, ISO 200. I can change the exposure in one-third-stop increments by holding the ISO button on the left side of the back of the camera and spinning the main command dial to change the ISO to 400 (for one additional stop) or to 100 (for one less stop's worth of exposure). I keep my preferred f/stop and shutter speed in either case, but still adjust the exposure.

Or, perhaps, I am using S mode and the metered exposure at ISO 200 is 1/500th second at f/11. If I decide on the spur of the moment I'd rather use 1/500th second at f/8, I can change the ISO to 100. Of course, it's a good idea to monitor your ISO changes, so you don't end up at H1 (ISO 6,400) accidentally.

ISO settings can, of course, also be used to boost or reduce sensitivity in particular shooting situations. The D90 can use ISO settings from ISO 100 (Lo 1.0) up to H 1.0 (6,400 equivalent). The camera can also adjust the ISO automatically as appropriate for various lighting conditions. When you choose the Auto ISO setting in the Shooting menu, as described in Chapter 3, the D90 adjusts the sensitivity dynamically to suit the subject matter, based on minimum shutter speed and ISO limits you have prescribed. As I noted in Chapter 3, you should use Auto ISO cautiously if you don't want the D90 to use an ISO higher than you might otherwise have selected.

Dealing with Noise

Visual image noise is that random grainy effect that some like to use as a special effect, but which, most of the time, is objectionable because it robs your image of detail even as it adds that "interesting" texture. Noise is caused by two different phenomena: high ISO settings and long exposures.

High ISO noise commonly appears when you raise your camera's sensitivity setting above ISO 400. With the Nikon D90, noise may become visible at ISO 800, and is often fairly noticeable at ISO 1,600. At ISO 3,200 noise is usually quite bothersome. Nikon tips you off that ISO 6,400 may be a tool used in special circumstances only by labeling it H1.0; you can expect noise and an increase in contrast in any pictures taken at this lofty rating. High ISO noise appears as a result of the amplification needed to increase the sensitivity of the sensor. While higher ISOs do pull details out of dark areas, they also amplify non-signal information randomly, creating noise. You'll find a High ISO NR choice in the Shooting menu, where you can specify High, Norm, or Low noise reduction, or turn the feature off entirely. Because noise reduction tends to soften the grainy look while robbing an image of detail, you may want to disable the feature if you're willing to accept a little noise in exchange for more details.

A similar noisy phenomenon occurs during long time exposures, which allow more photons to reach the sensor, increasing your ability to capture a picture under low-light conditions. However, the longer exposures also increase the likelihood that some pixels will register random phantom photons, often because the longer an imager is "hot" the warmer it gets, and that heat can be mistaken for photons. There's also a special kind of noise that CMOS sensors like the one used in the D90 are potentially susceptible to. With a CCD, the entire signal is conveyed off the chip and funneled through a single amplifier and analog-to-digital conversion circuit. Any noise introduced there is, at least, consistent. CMOS imagers, on the other hand, contain millions of individual amplifiers and A/D converters, all working in unison. Because all these circuits don't necessarily all process in precisely the same way all the time, they can introduce something called fixed-pattern noise into the image data.

Fortunately, Nikon's electronics geniuses have done an exceptional job minimizing noise from all causes in the D90. Even so, you might still want to apply the optional long exposure noise reduction that can be activated using Long exp. NR in the Shooting menu, where the feature can be turned On or Off. This type of noise reduction involves the D90 taking a second, blank exposure, and comparing the random pixels in that image with the photograph you just took. Pixels that coincide in the two represent noise and can safely be suppressed. This noise reduction system, called *dark frame subtraction,* effectively doubles the amount of time required to take a picture, and is used only for exposures longer than one second. Noise reduction can reduce the amount of detail in your picture, as some image information may be removed along with the noise. So, you might want to use this feature with moderation.

You can also apply noise reduction to a lesser extent using Photoshop, and when converting RAW files to some other format, using your favorite RAW converter, or an industrial-strength product like Noise Ninja (www.picturecode.com) to wipe out noise after you've already taken the picture.

Bracketing

Bracketing is a method for shooting several consecutive exposures using different settings, as a way of improving the odds that one will be exactly right. Before digital cameras took over the universe, it was common to bracket exposures, shooting, say, a series of three photos at 1/125th second, but varying the f/stop from f/8 to f/11 to f/16. In practice, smaller than whole-stop increments were used for greater precision, and lenses with apertures that were set manually commonly had half-stop detents on their aperture rings, or could easily be set to a mid-way position between whole f/stops. It was just as common to keep the same aperture and vary the shutter speed, although in the days before electronic shutters, film cameras often had only whole increment shutter speeds available.

Today, cameras like the D90 can bracket exposures much more precisely, and bracket white balance as well. The D90 can also bracket Active D-Lighting (ADL) settings to change the way the camera preserves the details in highlights and shadows. While WB bracketing is sometimes used when getting color absolutely correct in the camera is important, auto exposure bracketing (for both flash and conventional exposures) is used much more often. When this feature is activated, the D90 takes up to three consecutive photos: usually one at the metered "correct" exposure, one with less exposure, and one with more exposure, using an increment of your choice up to +2/–2 stops.

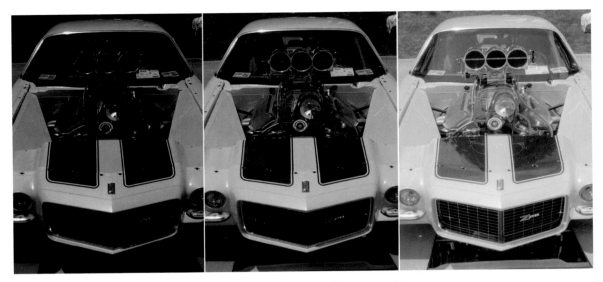

Figure 4.14 Bracketing can give you three different exposures of the same subject.

You can select from two or three shots in the bracket set, and change the order in which the exposures are made. The D90 uses the exposure increment selected under CSM #b1 (EV steps for exposure cntrl), so you can bracket either in 1/2 stop or 1/3 stop increments.

Nikon makes bracketing trickier than it needs to be, so I'm going to concentrate on autoexposure bracketing first. Once you understand that, ADL and white balance bracketing are a lot easier to comprehend. Just follow these steps:

1. **Choose type of bracketing.** First, select the type of bracketing you want to do, using CSM#e4, as explained in Chapter 4. You can select Autoexposure and Flash, Autoexposure Only, Flash Only, White Balance, and ADL Bracketing.

2. **Choose bracketing order.** Use CSM #e6 to select the order in which the bracketed exposures are made. You might prefer the "Normal" setting: Metered exposure>Underexposure>Overexposure. That will take one image at your camera's autoexposure setting, followed by one that is one increment less, and one that is one increment more. On the other hand, you might prefer to have your bracket set arrayed in the same order as the amount of exposure, with Underexposure>Metered exposure>Overexposure, as shown in Figure 4.14. With this choice, your images will range from darkest to lightest, which seems more natural to me.

3. **Press the BKT button.** It's located on the left side of the front of the camera, just below the Flash button.

4. **Select number and type of bracketed exposures.** With the BKT button held down, rotate the main command dial to choose the number of shots in the sequence and the type of sequence. Your choices include:

- **0.** This turns bracketing off. Use this to disable bracketing after you've finished. If you are taking pictures and notice some significant differences in consecutive exposures, you may have forgotten to turn off bracketing. It's easy to do this.

- **3.** Turn the main command dial counterclockwise one click to select 3 bracketed exposures. The D90 will take three shots, one at the metered exposure, one underexposed by one increment, and one overexposed by one increment. The order in which these shots are taken is determined by the bracket order setting you made in CSM #e6. Use this choice when you feel that the metered exposure is probably correct, but you'd like to see one shot over and one shot under to see if they might provide a different look.

- **–2.** One click of the main command dial clockwise tells the D90 to shoot just two bracketed shots, one at the metered exposure, and one that's one increment less. Use this setting when you think the metered exposure may overexposure your image a bit, or when you want a slightly darker image of, say, a silhouetted figure.

- **+2.** A second click of the main command dial clockwise produces a two-step bracket set at the metered exposure and one stop more. This kind of bracket will let you shoot, say, a backlighted subject at the metered exposure (which may produce a silhouette) and a second picture with more exposure, which will bring back detail in the shadowed area.

5. **Choose bracket increment.** With the BKT button still held down, rotate the sub-command dial to choose the exposure increment, either 0.3, 0.7, 1, 1.3, 1.7, or 2 EV. If you've redefined the exposure increment to half-stops in CSM #b1, your choices will be .5, 1.0, 1.5, and 2.0 stops.

6. **Frame and shoot.** As you take your photos the camera will vary the exposure based on the bracketing "program" you selected, and in the order you specified in CSM #e6. If you're using flash bracketing, white balance bracketing, then the flash level or white balance along the blue-amber axis will be varied instead. With ADL bracketing, one shot will be taken using Active D-Lighting, and a second shot taken with the ADL feature turned off.

In Single Shot mode, you'll need to press the shutter release button the number of times you specified for the exposures in your bracketed burst (2 or 3 shots). I've found it easy to forget that I am shooting bracketed pictures, stop taking my sequence, and then wondering why the remaining pictures in my defined burst are "incorrectly" exposed. To avoid that, I often set the D90 to one of the two Continuous Shooting modes, so that all my bracketed pictures are taken at once.

The D90 does provide indicators on the monochrome LCD (a BKT indicator as well as a bracketing progress indicator), but they may be overlooked.

7. **Turn bracketing off.** When you're finished bracketing shots, remember to press the BKT button and rotate the main command dial under the number of shots in the sequence is 0F, and the BKT indicator is no longer displayed.

Bracketing and Merge to HDR

While my goal in this book is to show you how to take great photos *in the camera* rather than how to fix your errors in Photoshop, the Merge to HDR (high dynamic range) feature in Adobe's flagship image editor is too cool to ignore. The ability to have a bracketed set of exposures that are identical except for exposure, is key to getting good results with this Photoshop feature, which allows you to produce images with a full, rich dynamic range that includes a level of detail in the highlights and shadows that is almost impossible to achieve with digital cameras. In contrasty lighting situations, even the Nikon D90 has a tendency to blow out highlights when you expose solely for the shadows or midtones.

Suppose you wanted to photograph a dimly lit room that had a bright window showing an outdoors scene. Proper exposure for the room might be on the order of 1/60th second at f/2.8 at ISO 200, while the outdoors scene probably would require f/11 at 1/400th second. That's almost a 7 EV step difference (approximately 7 f/stops) and well beyond the dynamic range of any digital camera, including the Nikon D90.

When you're using Merge to HDR, you'd take two to three pictures, one for the shadows, one for the highlights, and perhaps one for the midtones. Then, you'd use the Merge to HDR command to combine all of the images into one HDR image that integrates the well-exposed sections of each version. You can use the Nikon D90's bracketing feature to produce those images.

The images should be as identical as possible, except for exposure. So, it's a good idea to mount the D90 on a tripod, use a remote release like the Nikon ML-L3 infrared remote, and take all the exposures in one burst. Just follow these steps:

1. Mount the D90 on a tripod and activate remote mode by pressing the Drive button and rotating the main command dial until the Remote icon appears. (The tripod and remote release are optional, but you'll find it easier to merge your shots if the camera remains stationary.)

2. Press the BKT button and rotate the main command dial to choose the 3-shot bracket set. Rotate the subcommand dial to set the increment to 2EV. Merge to HDR works best with a significant difference in exposure between the bracketed shots; subtle changes are not better here.

3. Press the Drive Mode button and select Continuous High. This will ensure that all three bracketed shots are taken consecutively once you've triggered the shutter with the remote release.

4. Set the D90 to A (Aperture Priority). This forces the D90 to bracket the exposures by changing the shutter speed. You don't want the bracketed exposures to have different aperture settings, because the depth-of-field will change, perhaps enough to disturb a smooth merger of the final shots.

5. Hold down the QUAL button and choose RAW exposures. You'll need RAW files to give you the 16-bit high dynamic range images that the Merge to HDR feature processes best.

6. Manually focus or autofocus the D90.

7. Trigger the remote release to take all the exposures in the bracketed set. Repeat if you'd like to produce a second set.

8. Copy your images to your computer and continue with the Merge to HDR steps listed next.

The next steps show you how to combine the separate exposures into one merged high dynamic range image. The sample images shown in Figures 4.15, 4.16, and 4.18 show the results you can get from a two-shot bracketed sequence. I merged only two pictures for simplicity, because the differences between three or more bracketed exposures, even when taken at exposures that are one stop apart, can be too subtle to show up well on the printed page. My two examples were taken from a longer sequence, and actually have a two-stop difference.

1. If you use an application to transfer the files to your computer, make sure it does not make any adjustments to brightness, contrast, or exposure. You want the real raw information for Merge to HDR to work with. If you do everything correctly, you'll end up with at least two photos like the ones shown in Figures 4.15 and 4.16.

2. Load the images into Photoshop using your preferred RAW converter. Make sure the 16-bits-per-channel depth is retained (don't reduce them to 8-bit files). You can load them ahead of time and save as 16-bit Photoshop .PSD files, as I did for my example photos.

3. Activate Merge to HDR by choosing File>Automate>Merge to HDR.

4. Select the photos to be merged, as shown in Figure 4.17, where I have specified the two 16-bit PSD files. You'll note a check box that can be used to automatically align the images if they were not taken with the D90 mounted on a rock-steady support.

5. Once HDR merge has done its thing, you must save in .PSD, .PFM, .TIFF, or .EXR formats to retain the 16-bit file's floating-point data, in case you want to work with the HDR image later. Otherwise, you can convert to a normal 24-bit file and save in any compatible format.

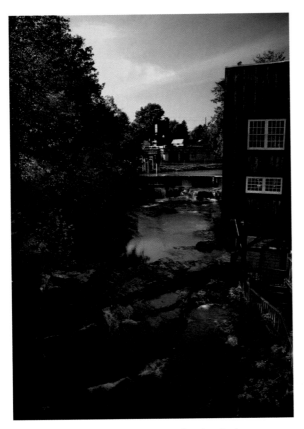

Figure 4.15 Make one exposure for the shadow areas.

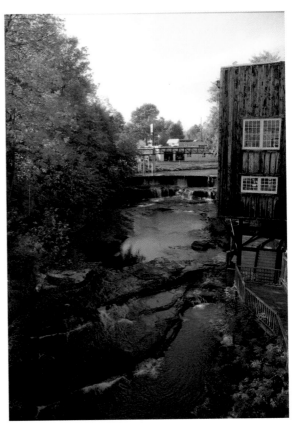

Figure 4.16 Make a second exposure for the highlights, such as the sky.

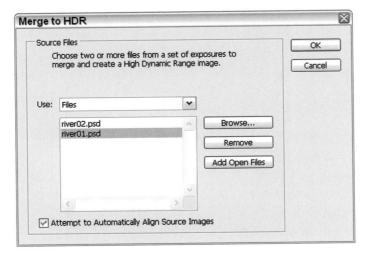

Figure 4.17
Use the Merge to HDR command to combine the two images.

If you do everything correctly, you'll end up with a photo like the one shown in Figure 4.18, which has the properly exposed foreground of the first shot, and the well-exposed sky of the second image. Note that, ideally, nothing should move between shots. In the example pictures, the river is moving, but the exposures were made so close together that, after the merger, you can't really tell.

Figure 4.18
You'll end up with an extended dynamic range photo like this one.

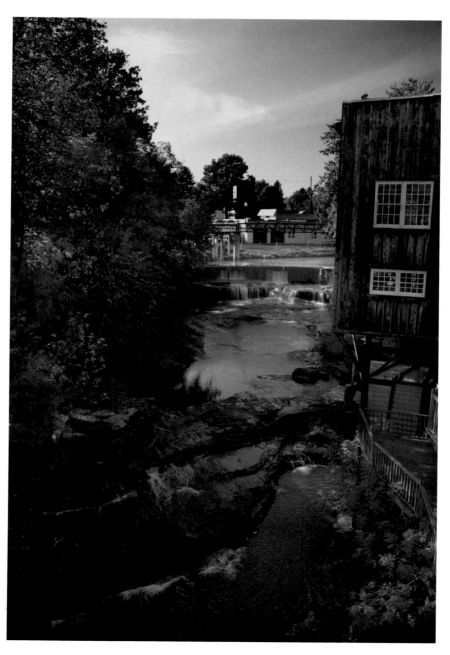

What if you don't have the opportunity, inclination, or skills to create several images at different exposures, as described? If you shoot in RAW format, you can still use Merge to HDR, working with a *single* original image file. What you do is import the image into Photoshop several times, using Adobe Camera Raw to create multiple copies of the file at different exposure levels.

For example, you'd create one copy that's too dark, so the shadows lose detail, but the highlights are preserved. Create another copy with the shadows intact and allow the highlights to wash out. Then, you can use Merge to HDR to combine the two and end up with a finished image that has the extended dynamic range you're looking for. (This concludes the image-editing portion of the chapter. We now return you to our alternate sponsor: photography.)

Fixing Exposures with Histograms

While you can often recover poorly exposed photos in your image editor, your best bet is to arrive at the correct exposure in the camera, minimizing the tweaks that you have to make in post-processing. However, you can't always judge exposure just by viewing the image on your D90's LCD after the shot is made. Instead, you can use a histogram, which is a chart displayed on the D90's LCD that shows the number of tones being captured at each brightness level. You can use the information to provide correction for the next shot you take.

You can view a histogram for an image displayed during playback by pressing the multi-selector up/down buttons to switch to either of the two histogram overlays described in Chapter 3. The RGB Histogram is shown in Figure 4.19.

The histogram at top, in white, is called a brightness or *luminance* histogram. It is a chart that includes a representation of up to 256 vertical lines on a horizontal axis that show the number of pixels in the image at each brightness level, from 0 (black) on the left side to 255 (white) on the right. (The LCD doesn't have enough pixels to show each and every one of the 256 lines, but, instead provides a representation of the shape of the curve formed.) The more pixels at a given level, the taller the bar at that position. If no bar appears at a particular position on the scale from left to right, there are no pixels at that particular brightness level. The three charts underneath it, in red, green, and blue, show the same tonal relationships in the red, green, and blue channels of your image, respectively.

As you can see, a typical histogram produces a mountain-like shape, with most of the pixels bunched in the middle tones, with fewer pixels at the dark and light ends of the scale. Ideally, though, there will be at least some pixels at either extreme, so that your image has both a true black and a true white representing some details. Learn to spot histograms that represent over- and underexposure, and add or subtract exposure using an EV modification to compensate.

Figure 4.19
A histogram shows the relationship of tones in an image

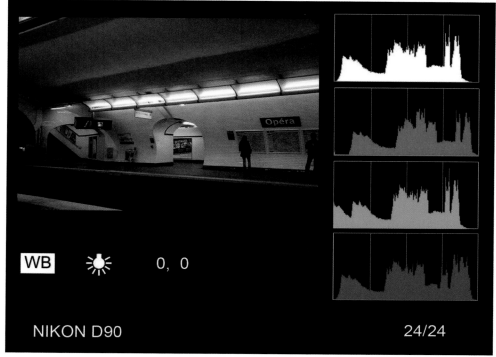

For example, Figure 4.20 shows the histogram for an image that is badly underexposed. You can guess from the shape of the histogram that many of the dark tones to the left of the graph have been clipped off. There's plenty of room on the right side for additional pixels to reside without having them become overexposed. Or, a histogram might look like Figure 4.21, which is overexposed. In either case, you can increase or decrease the exposure (either by changing the f/stop or shutter speed in Manual mode or by adding or subtracting an EV value in A or S modes) to produce the corrected histogram shown in Figure 4.22, earlier, in which the tones "hug" the right side of the histogram to produce as many highlight details as possible. See "Making EV Changes," in the sidebar on page 180 for information on dialing in exposure compensation.

The histogram can also be used to aid in fixing the contrast of an image, although gauging incorrect contrast is more difficult. For example, if the histogram shows all the tones bunched up in one place in the image, the photo will be low in contrast. If the tones are spread out more or less evenly, the image is probably high in contrast. In either case, your best bet may be to switch to RAW (if you're not already using that format) so you can adjust contrast in post processing. However, you can also change to a user-defined Picture Style setting with contrast set lower (–1 to –3) or higher (+1 to +3), and brightness adjusted to –1 or +1 as required. Active D-Lighting can also change the apparent brightness/contrast ratios, as discussed in Chapter 3.

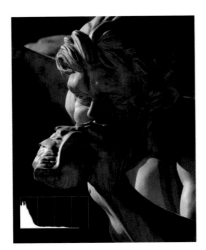

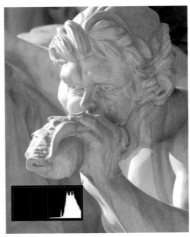

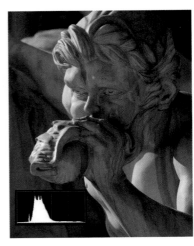

Figure 4.20 This histogram shows an underexposed image.

Figure 4.21 This histogram reveals that the image is overexposed.

Figure 4.22 This histogram reveals that the image is correctly exposed.

One useful, but often overlooked tool in evaluating histograms is the Highlight display (which can be activated under Display mode in the Playback menu), as described in Chapter 3. The Highlight display shows blown-out highlights in the image with a black blinking border. Highlights can give you a better picture of what information is being lost to overexposure.

In working with histograms, your goal should be to have all the tones in an image spread out between the edges, with none clipped off at the left and right sides. Underexposing (to preserve highlights) should be done only as a last resort, because retrieving the under-exposed shadows in your image editor will frequently increase the noise, even if you're working with RAW files. A better course of action is to expose for the highlights, but, when the subject matter makes it practical, fill in the shadows with additional light, using reflectors, fill flash, or other techniques rather than allowing them to be seriously underexposed.

5

Advanced Shooting Tips for Your Nikon D90

Getting the right exposure is one of the foundations of a great photograph, but a lot more goes into a compelling shot than good tonal values. A sharp image, proper white balance, good color, and other factors all can help elevate your image from good to exceptional. So, now that you've got a good understanding of exposure tucked away, you'll want to learn how to work with some additional exposure options, use the automatic and manual focusing controls available with the Nikon D90, and master some of the many ways you can fine-tune your images.

This chapter is a bit of a grab bag, because I'm including some specific advanced shooting techniques that didn't quite fit into the other chapters. If you master these concepts, you can be confident that you're well on your way towards mastering your Nikon D90. In fact, you'll be ready for the discussions of using lenses (Chapter 6) and working with light (Chapter 7).

How Focus Works

Although Nikon added autofocus capabilities to its cameras in the 1980s, back in the day of film, prior to that focusing was always done manually. Honest. Even though viewfinders were bigger and brighter than they are today, special focusing screens, magnifiers, and other gadgets were often used to help the photographer achieve correct focus. Imagine what it must have been like to focus manually under demanding, fast-moving conditions such as sports photography.

Focusing was problematic because our eyes and brains have poor memory for correct focus, which is why your eye doctor must shift back and forth between sets of lenses and ask, "Does that look sharper—or was it sharper before?" in determining your correct prescription. Similarly, manual focusing involves jogging the focus ring back and forth as you go from almost in focus, to sharp focus, to almost focused again. The little clockwise and counterclockwise arcs decrease in size until you've zeroed in on the point of correct focus. What you're looking for is the image with the most contrast between the edges of elements in the image.

The camera also looks for these contrast differences among pixels to determine relative sharpness. There are two ways that sharp focus is determined:

- **Phase Detection.** In this mode, used when focusing through the optical viewfinder, the selected autofocus sampling area is divided into two halves by a lens in the autofocus sensor. The two halves are compared, much like (actually, exactly like) a two-window rangefinder used in surveying, weaponry—and non-SLR cameras like the venerable Leica M film models. The contrast between the two images changes as focus is moved in or out, until sharp focus is achieved when the images are "in phase," or lined up. Phase Detection is the normal mode used by the D90. As with any rangefinder-like function, accuracy is better when the "base length" between the two images is larger. (Think back to your high-school trigonometry; you could calculate a distance more accurately when the separation between the two points where the angles were measured was greater.) For that reason, phase detection autofocus is more accurate with larger (wider) lens openings than with smaller lens openings, and may not work at all when the *maximum* f/stop available in a lens is smaller than f/5.6. The D90 is able to perform these comparisons very quickly. As shown in Figure 5.1, the D90 can automatically select any of the 11 focus points automatically, or allow you to choose one manually.

- **Contrast Detection.** This is a slower mode, suitable for static subjects, and used by the Nikon D90 with Live View modes. It's a bit easier to understand, and is illustrated by Figure 5.2. At left in the extreme enlargement of some foliage, the transitions between pixels are soft and blurred. Even the boundary between the bright leaves and darker leaves in the background is smudged. When the image is brought into focus (right), the transitions are sharp and clear. Although this example is a bit exaggerated so you can see the results on the printed page, it's easy to understand that when maximum contrast in a subject is achieved, it can be deemed to be in sharp focus. One advantage of contrast detection is that the focus point can be virtually anywhere on the screen, not at one of the 11 fixed focus points used with phase detection.

The D90's autofocus mechanism, like all such systems found in SLR cameras, evaluates the degree of focus, but, unlike the human eye, it is able to remember the progression perfectly, so that autofocus can lock in much more quickly and, with an image that has sufficient contrast, more precisely. Indeed, with the "lining up" process used during phase detection, the camera knows immediately whether correct focus is closer or

Figure 5.1
Any of the 11 autofocus points can be selected by the photographer manually or by the camera automatically.

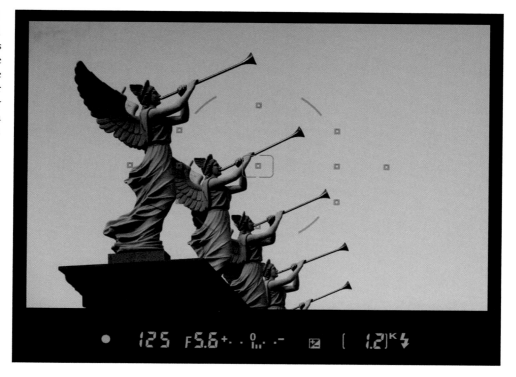

Figure 5.2
Focus in Contrast Detection mode evaluates the increase in contrast in the edges of subjects, starting with a blurry image (left) and producing a sharp, contrasty image (right).

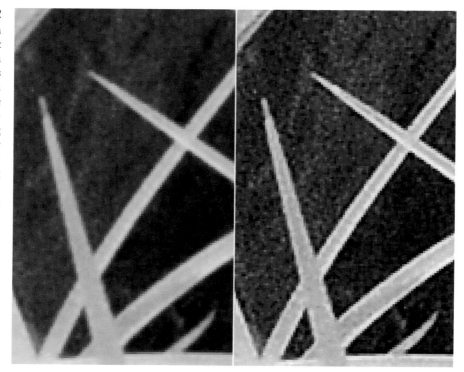

farther than the current focus setting, and how much correction needs to be made. So, autofocus is very fast.

Unfortunately, while the D90's focus system finds it easy to measure degrees of apparent focus at each of the focus points in the viewfinder, it doesn't really know with any certainty *which* object should be in sharpest focus. Is it the closest object? The subject in the center? Something lurking *behind* the closest subject? A person standing over at the side of the picture? Many of the techniques for using autofocus effectively involve telling the D90 exactly what it should be focusing on, by choosing a focus zone or by allowing the camera to choose a focus zone for you. I'll address that topic shortly.

Making Sense of Sensors

Learning to use the Nikon D90's autofocus system is easy, but you do need to fully understand how the system works to get the most benefit from it. Once you're comfortable with autofocus, you'll know when it's appropriate to use the manual focus option, too. The important thing to remember is that focus isn't absolute. For example, some things that look in sharp focus at a given viewing size and distance might not be in focus at a larger size and/or closer distance. In addition, the goal of optimum focus isn't always to make things look sharp. Not all of an image will be or should be sharp. Controlling exactly what is sharp and what is not is part of your creative palette. Use of depth-of-field characteristics to throw part of an image out of focus while other parts are sharply focused is one of the most valuable tools available to a photographer. But selective focus works only when the desired areas of an image are in focus properly. For the digital SLR photographer, correct focus can be one of the trickiest parts of the technical and creative process.

To make your job easier, the D90 has a precision 11-point autofocus system that uses a separate CMOS sensor in the viewing system and the process I earlier called *phase detection* to measure the amount of contrast of the image by "lining up" two halves of edges or lines in the image, much like a range-finding device. As I noted, phase detection tells the autofocus system when the image at the active autofocus point is in sharp focus. One of these points, in the center of the 11-point array, is of the advanced "cross" type (that is, it measures in both horizontal and vertical directions) and can be selected automatically by the camera, or manually by you, the photographer. All the focus zones available are represented by the 11 focus points visible in the viewfinder, and shown earlier in Figure 5.1.

As noted, your camera's autofocus sensors require a certain minimum aperture to operate, which, because the camera focuses using the largest f/stop, is why autofocus capabilities are possible only with lenses having an f/5.6 or larger maximum aperture. The system also must have enough light to clearly illuminate the area being focused on. If necessary, the AF assist beam built into the D90 and Nikon's dedicated flash units provide additional light that helps assure enough illumination for autofocus.

The number and type of autofocus sensors can affect how well the system operates. As I mentioned, the Nikon D90 has 11 AF points. Nikon's high-end cameras, like the D300, D700, D3, and D3x have a whopping 51 autofocus points. These focus sensors can consist of vertical or horizontal lines of pixels, cross-shapes, and often a mixture of these types within a single camera, although, as I mentioned, the D90 includes a single cross-type sensor in the center. The more AF points available, the more easily the camera can differentiate among areas of the frame, and the more precisely you can specify the area you want to be in focus if you're manually choosing a focus spot.

As the camera collects focus information from the sensors, it then evaluates it to determine whether the desired sharp focus has been achieved. The calculations may include whether the subject is moving, and whether the camera needs to "predict" where the subject will be when the shutter release button is fully depressed and the picture is taken. The speed with which the camera is able to evaluate focus and then move the lens elements into the proper position to achieve the sharpest focus determines how fast the autofocus mechanism is. Although your D90 will almost always focus more quickly than a human, there are types of shooting situations where that's not fast enough. For example, if you're having problems shooting sports because the D90's autofocus system manically follows each moving subject, a better choice might be to switch Autofocus modes or shift into Manual and prefocus on a spot where you anticipate the action will be, such as a goal line or soccer net. At night football games, for example, when I am shooting with a telephoto lens almost wide open, I sometimes focus manually on one of the referees who happens to be standing where I expect the action to be taking place (say, a halfback run or a pass reception).

Improved Cross-Type Focus Point

One improvement that Nikon D90 owners sometimes overlook is the upgrade to an improved cross-type focus point in the center position. Why is this important? It helps to review exactly how the D90 determines focus.

The value of a cross-type focus sensor in phase detection is that such sensors can line up edges and interpret image contrast in both horizontal and vertical directions, as can be seen in Figure 5.3. The two upper photos show a horizontal-type sensor evaluating a subject, which happens to be a piece of aged wood siding heavily creased with horizontal lines. At upper left, the sensor sees blurry lines, which become sharper when the wood is brought into focus. This type of subject is of average difficulty for a horizontal sensor: easier to interpret than an image with no pattern at all, and harder to focus than, say, vertical lines, which would stand out more clearly. You can see that a horizontal focus sensor does a good job but has some weaknesses. (A vertical-only focus sensor would have the same reduced performance with vertical lines and better focusing with horizontal lines.)

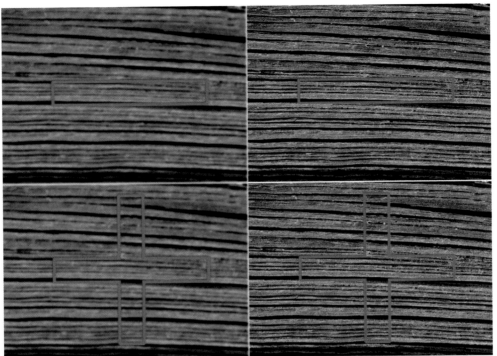

Horizontal (and vertical) focus sensors can interpret image contrast in only one direction (top), while cross-type sensors can evaluate contrast in both horizontal and vertical directions.

At the bottom of the figure you'll see the same subject being evaluated by a cross-type sensor. The horizontal lines are still more difficult to interpret with the horizontal arm of the cross, but they stand out in sharp contrast (even in the blurry version at lower left) and allow the camera to align the edges and snap the image into focus easily, as you can see at lower right. In this example, both the horizontal and cross-type sensors were able to produce an equally sharp focus (upper and lower right), but the cross-type sensor probably focused the image a tad faster. And, in lower light levels, with subjects that were moving, or with subjects that have no pattern and less contrast to begin with, the cross-type sensor not only works faster but can focus subjects that a horizontal- or vertical-only sensor can't handle at all.

So, you can see that having a cross-type focus sensor in the center of the viewing area is a definite advantage.

Focus Modes

The D90 has three AF modes: AF-S (also known as Single Autofocus or Single-Servo Autofocus), AF-C (Continuous Autofocus or Continuous-Servo Autofocus), and AF-A (which switches between the two as appropriate). I'll explain all of these in more detail later in this section. But first, some confusion…

MANUAL FOCUS

With manual focus activated by sliding the switch on the lens, or the AF/M switch on the body near the lens mount, your D90 lets you set the focus yourself. There are some advantages and disadvantages to this approach. While your batteries will last longer in Manual focus mode, it will take you longer to focus the camera for each photo, a process that can be difficult. Modern digital cameras, even dSLRs, depend so much on autofocus that the viewfinders of models that have less than full-frame-sized sensors are no longer designed for optimum manual focus. Pick up any film camera and you'll see a bigger, brighter viewfinder with a focusing screen that's a joy to focus on manually.

Adding Circles of Confusion

You know that increased depth-of-field brings more of your subject into focus. But more depth-of-field also makes autofocusing (or manual focusing) more difficult because the contrast is lower between objects at different distances. So, autofocus with a 200mm lens (or zoom setting) may be easier than at a 28mm focal length (or zoom setting) because the longer lens has less apparent depth-of-field. By the same token, a lens with a maximum aperture of f/1.8 will be easier to autofocus (or manually focus) than one of the same focal length with an f/4 maximum aperture, because the f/4 lens has more depth-of-field *and* a dimmer view. That's yet another reason why lenses with a maximum aperture smaller than f/5.6 can give your D90's autofocus system fits—increased depth-of-field joins forces with a dimmer image, and more difficulty in achieving phase detection.

To make things even more complicated, many subjects aren't polite enough to remain still. They move around in the frame, so that even if the D90 is sharply focused on your main subject, it may change position and require refocusing. An intervening subject may pop into the frame and pass between you and the subject you meant to photograph. You (or the D90) have to decide whether to lock focus on this new subject, or remain focused on the original subject. Finally, there are some kinds of subjects that are difficult to bring into sharp focus because they lack enough contrast to allow the D90's AF system (or our eyes) to lock in. Blank walls, a clear blue sky, or other subject matter may make focusing difficult.

If you find all these focus factors confusing, you're on the right track. Focus is, in fact, measured using something called a *circle of confusion*. An ideal image consists of zillions of tiny little points, which, like all points, theoretically have no height or width. There is perfect contrast between the point and its surroundings. You can think of each point as a pinpoint of light in a darkened room. When a given point is out of focus, its edges decrease in contrast and it changes from a perfect point to a tiny disc with blurry edges (remember, blur is the lack of contrast between boundaries in an image). (See Figure 5.4.)

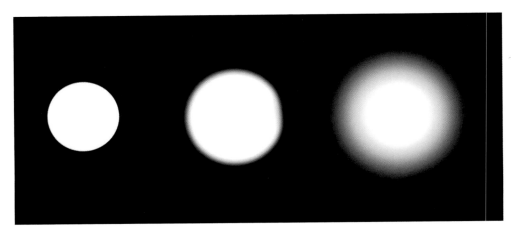

Figure 5.4

When a pin-point of light (left) goes out of focus, its blurry edges form a circle of confusion (center and right).

If this blurry disc—the circle of confusion—is small enough, our eye still perceives it as a point. It's only when the disc grows large enough that we can see it as a blur rather than a sharp point that a given point is viewed as out of focus. You can see, then, that enlarging an image, either by displaying it larger on your computer monitor or by making a large print, also enlarges the size of each circle of confusion. Moving closer to the image does the same thing. So, parts of an image that may look perfectly sharp in a 5 × 7-inch print viewed at arm's length, might appear blurry when blown up to 11 × 14 and examined at the same distance. Take a few steps back, however, and it may look sharp again.

To a lesser extent, the viewer also affects the apparent size of these circles of confusion. Some people see details better at a given distance and may perceive smaller circles of confusion than someone standing next to them. For the most part, however, such differences are small. Truly blurry images will look blurry to just about everyone under the same conditions.

Technically, there is just one plane within your picture area, parallel to the back of the camera (or sensor, in the case of a digital camera), that is in sharp focus. That's the plane in which the points of the image are rendered as precise points. At every other plane in front of or behind the focus plane, the points show up as discs that range from slightly blurry to extremely blurry until, as you can see in Figure 5.5, the out-of-focus areas become one large blur that, when coupled by reduced illumination, de-emphasizes an unattractive background.

In practice, the discs in many of these planes will still be so small that we see them as points, and that's where we get depth-of-field. Depth-of-field is just the range of planes that include discs that we perceive as points rather than blurred splotches. The size of this range increases as the aperture is reduced in size and is allocated roughly one-third in front of the plane of sharpest focus, and two-thirds behind it. The range of sharp focus is always greater behind your subject than in front of it.

Figure 5.5
The rough white brick background is almost totally blurred, thanks to reduced illumination and a wide f/stop.

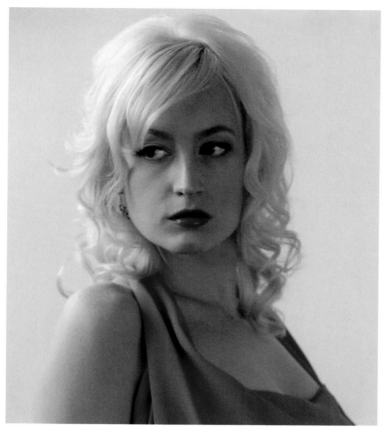

Using Autofocus with the Nikon D90

Autofocus can sometimes be frustrating for the new digital SLR photographer, especially those coming from the point-and-shoot world. That's because correct focus plays a greater role among your creative options with a dSLR, even when photographing the same subjects. Most non-dSLR digital cameras have sensors that are much tinier than the sensor in the D90. Those smaller sensors require shorter focal lengths, which (as you'll learn in Chapter 6) have, effectively, more depth-of-field.

The bottom line is that with the average point-and-shoot camera, *everything* is in focus from about one foot to infinity and at virtually every f/stop. Unless you're shooting close-up photos a few inches from the camera, the depth-of-field is prodigious, and autofocus is almost a non-factor. The D90, on the other hand, uses longer focal length lenses to achieve the same field of view with its larger sensor, so there is less depth-of-field. That's a *good* thing, creatively, because you have the choice to use selective focus to isolate subjects. But it does make the correct use of autofocus more critical.

To maintain the most creative control, you have to choose three attributes:

■ **How much is in focus.** Generally, by choosing the f/stop used, you'll determine the *range* of sharpness/amount of depth-of-field. The larger the DOF, the "easier" it is for the autofocus system's locked-in focus point to be appropriate (even though, strictly speaking, there is only one actual plane of sharp focus). With less depth-of-field, the accuracy of the focus point becomes more critical, because even a small error will result in an out-of-focus shot.

■ **What subject is in focus.** The portion of your subject that is zeroed in for autofocus is determined by the autofocus zone that is active, and which is chosen either by you or by the Nikon D90 (as described next). For example, when shooting portraits, it's actually okay for part of the subject—or even part of the subject's face—to be slightly out of focus as long as the eyes (or even just the *nearest* eye) appear sharp.

■ **When focus is applied.** For static shots of objects that aren't moving, *when* focus is applied doesn't matter much. But when you're shooting sports, or birds in flight (see Figure 5.6), or children, the subject may move within the viewfinder as you're framing the image. Whether that movement is across the frame or headed right towards you, timing the instant when autofocus is applied can be important.

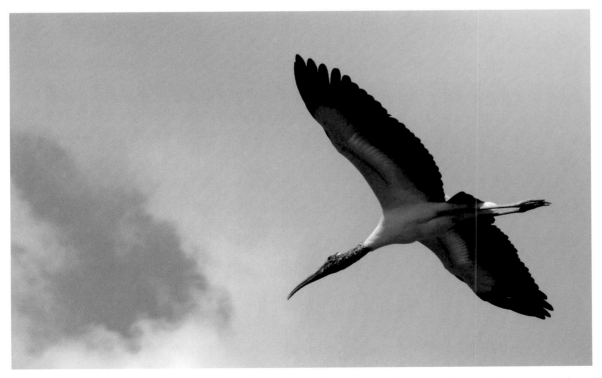

Figure 5.6 When capturing moving subjects, such as birds in flight, timing the instant when autofocus is applied can be important.

Your Autofocus Mode Options

Choosing the right Autofocus mode and the way in which focus points are selected is your key to success. Using the wrong mode for a particular type of photography can lead to a series of pictures that are all sharply focused—on the wrong subject. When I first started shooting sports with an autofocus SLR (back in the film camera days), I covered one game alternating between shots of base runners and outfielders with pictures of a promising young pitcher, all from a position next to the third base dugout. The base runner and outfielder photos were great, because their backgrounds didn't distract the autofocus mechanism. But all my photos of the pitcher had the focus tightly zeroed in on the fans in the stands behind him. Because I was shooting film instead of a digital camera, I didn't know about my gaffe until the film was developed. A simple change, such as locking in focus or focus zone manually, or even manually focusing, would have done the trick.

There are two main autofocus options you need to master to make sure you get the best possible automatic focus with your Nikon D90: Autofocus mode and Autofocus Area. I'll explain each of them separately.

Autofocus Mode

This choice determines *when* your D90 starts to autofocus, and what it does when focus is achieved. Automatic focus is not something that happens all the time when your camera is turned on. To save battery power, your D90 generally doesn't start to focus the lens until you partially depress the shutter release. (You can also use the AE/AL Lock button to start autofocus, as described in Chapter 3.) Autofocus isn't some mindless beast out there snapping your pictures in and out of focus with no feedback from you after you press that button. There are several settings you can modify that return at least a modicum of control to you.

Your first decision should be whether you set the D90 to AF-S, AF-C, AF-A, or Manual. To change to any of the Automatic modes, press the AF button on the top of the camera (to the right of the monochrome status LCD), and rotate the main command dial until the focus mode you want to use appears on the LCD. With the camera set for one of the DVP/Scene modes, AF-S will be used automatically, except when using the Sports/Action Scene mode. To switch to Manual mode, slide the AF/M switch on the body or the AF/M or M-A/M switch on the lens to M.

AF-S

In this mode, also called *Single Autofocus,* focus is set once and remains at that setting until the button is fully depressed, taking the picture, or until you release the shutter button without taking a shot. You can also use the AE-L/AF-L button, as described in Chapter 3, if you've set that button to lock focus when pressed. For non-action photography, this setting is usually your best choice, as it minimizes out-of-focus pictures (at the expense of spontaneity). The drawback here is that you might not be able to take a picture at all while the camera is seeking focus; you're locked out until the autofocus mechanism is happy with the current setting. AF-S/Single Autofocus is sometimes referred to as *Focus Priority* for that reason. Because of the small delay while the camera zeroes in on correct focus, you might experience slightly more shutter lag. This mode uses less battery power.

When sharp focus is achieved, the focus confirmation light at the lower left will remain green, without flashing. By keeping the shutter button depressed halfway, you'll find you can reframe the image while retaining the focus (and exposure) that's been set.

AF-C

This mode, also known as *Continuous Autofocus* is the mode to use for sports and other fast-moving subjects. In this mode, once the shutter release is partially depressed, the camera sets the focus but continues to monitor the subject, so that if it moves or you move, the lens will be refocused to suit. Focus and exposure aren't really locked until you press the shutter release down all the way to take the picture. You'll often see Continuous Autofocus referred to as *Release Priority.* If you press the shutter release down all the way while the system is refining focus, the camera will go ahead and take a picture, even if the image is slightly out of focus. You'll find that AF-C produces the least amount of shutter lag of any Autofocus mode: press the button and the camera fires. It also uses the most battery power, because the autofocus system operates as long as the shutter release button is partially depressed.

AF-C uses a technology called *predictive AF*, which allows the D90 to calculate the correct focus if the subject is moving toward or away from the camera at a constant rate. It uses either the automatically selected AF point or the point you select manually to set focus.

AF-A

This setting is actually a combination of the first two. When selected, the camera focuses using AF-S AF and locks in the focus setting. But, if the subject begins moving, it will switch automatically to AF-C and change the focus to keep the subject sharp. AF-A is a good choice when you're shooting a mixture of action pictures and less dynamic shots and want to use AF-S when possible. The camera will default to that mode, yet switch automatically to AF-C when it would be useful for subjects that might begin moving unexpectedly. However, as with AF-S, the shutter can be released only when the subject at the selected focus point is in focus.

Manual Focus

In this mode, or when you've set the lens autofocus switch to Manual (or when you're using a non AF-S lens), the D90 always focuses manually using the rotating focus ring on the lens barrel. However, if you are using a lens with a maximum aperture of at least f/5.6, the focus confirmation light in the viewfinder will glow a steady green when the image is correctly manually focused.

Autofocus Area

Where Autofocus mode chooses when to autofocus, the Autofocus Area parameter tells your Nikon D90 how to choose which of the 11 focus points in the viewfinder should be used to evaluate and lock in focus. Ordinarily, your camera would like to be able to choose among the available AF points itself. In fact, that's the default behavior, and when CSM #a1 is set to Auto-Area, the D90 chooses the focus point automatically in Auto, No-Flash, Portrait, Landscape, Night Portrait, and PASM (Program, Aperture Priority, Shutter Priority, Manual) exposure modes. Giving the D90 free rein in selecting a focus point works well much of the time, and you can use this default mode with confidence.

If you want to choose a focus point yourself, you must do two things. First, you must rotate the Focus Selector lever on the back of the camera (to the right of the LCD) from the L (locked) position to the * (unlocked) position. When the focus point is unlocked, you can use the multi-selector pad to shift the active point to any of the 11 focus points seen in the viewfinder.

The second thing to do is to switch CSM #a1 from Auto-Area (which *always* chooses the focus point automatically) to Single Point, Dynamic Area, or 3D Tracking (11 Points). These modes change the D90's behavior as follows:

■ **Single Point.** You choose which of the 11 points are used, and the Nikon D90 sticks with that focus bracket, no matter what. This mode is best for stationary subjects, and is used automatically in Close-up scene mode. In this mode, you always select the focus point manually, using the multi-selector button. The D90 evaluates focus based solely on the point you select, making this a good choice for subjects that don't move much.

■ **Dynamic Area.** You can select the focus point, but the D90 can use other focus points as well. You'd want to use this mode when photographing subjects that are moving unpredictably, but want the flexibility of being able to choose one of the 11 focus zones yourself. Once you've specified the focus bracket you want using the multi-selector's buttons, the D90 will use that area exclusively in Single-Servo Autofocus mode (AF-S, described next). If you've chosen Continuous Autofocus mode (AF-C) or Automatic Autofocus mode (AF-A), if the subject begins moving after autofocus is activated, the D90 will focus based on information from one of the other focus zones. Well suited for sports photography, this mode is applied automatically with the Sports scene setting, and can be used with other types of moving subjects, such as active children.

■ **Auto-Area.** This default mode chooses the focus point for you, and can use distance information when working with a G or D lens that supplies that data to the camera. (See Chapter 6 for more on the difference between G/D lenses and other kinds of lenses.)

■ **3D Tracking (11 points).** In this mode, you select the focus point using the multi-selector, but if you subsequently reframe the picture slightly, the D90 uses distance information when in AF-C or AF-A modes to refocus on the original subject if necessary. (When using AF-S, this mode functions the same as Single Point focus area mode.) This mode is useful if you need to reframe a relatively static subject from time to time. If your subject leaves the frame entirely, you'll need to release the shutter button and refocus.

CENTER FOCUS POINT SIZE

Use CSM #a2 to set the D90 center focus point to Normal Zone (for subjects that fit within the focus point bracket shown in the center of Figure 5.7) or for Wide Zone, to focus on subjects that are moving or larger than the default center focus point. This choice is disabled when using Auto-Area focus point selection. Wide, Normal, and, in addition, Face Priority focus point zones can be set separately for Live View mode using CSM #a7, as I'll describe later in this chapter.

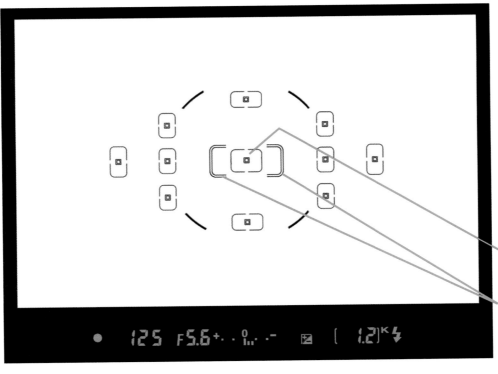

Figure 5.7
With Normal Zone focus, the center focus point is represented by the inner brackets; with Wide Zone focus, the center focus point is defined by the two double brackets surrounding the center.

Normal center focus zone

Wide center focus zone

Other Autofocus Parameters

As described in Chapter 3, there are several other autofocus parameters that can be set in the Custom Settings menu. You don't need to flip back; I'll recap them here.

■ **CSM #a4. AF Point Illumination.** Set to Auto to allow the D90 to decide whether to illuminate the selected focus point in red when the camera judges that there isn't sufficient contrast with the background. Choose On if you want the selected focus point always highlighted in red (not a good choice when shooting against a red background). Set to Off if you don't want the AF point highlighted.

■ **CSM #a5. Focus Point Wrap-Around.** Select Wrap if you want the multi-selector to wrap around from the left side to the right side, right side to the left side, or top to bottom as you choose a focus point manually. Set to No Wrap (the default), and the focus point display will stop at the left, right, top, and bottom edges of the screen.

■ **CSM #a6. AE-L/AF-L for MB-D80.** If you're using the MB-D80 battery pack/vertical grip, use this setting to define the behavior of the AE-L/AF-L button on the grip.

Working with Live View

Live View is one of those features that experienced SLR users (especially those dating from the film era) sometimes think they don't need—until they try it. While dSLR veterans didn't really miss what we've come to know as Live View, it was at least, in part, because, until the last several years they didn't have it and couldn't miss what they never had. After all, why would you eschew a big, bright, magnified through-the-lens optical view that showed depth-of-field fairly well, and which was easily visible under virtually all ambient light conditions? LCD displays, after all, were small, tended to wash out in bright light, and didn't really provide you with an accurate view of what your picture was going to look like.

There were technical problems, as well. Real-time previews disabled a dSLR's Phase Detect autofocus system, as focus is ordinarily achieved by measuring contrast through the optical viewfinder, which is blocked when the mirror is flipped up for a live view. Extensive previewing had the same effect on the sensor as long exposures: the sensor heated up, producing excess noise. Pointing the camera at a bright light source when using a real-time view could damage the sensor. The list of potential problems goes on and on.

That was then. This is now.

The Nikon D90 has a gorgeous three-inch LCD that can be viewed under a variety of lighting conditions and from wide-ranging angles, so you don't have to be exactly behind the display to see it clearly (see Figure 5.8). It offers a 100-percent view of the sensor's capture area (the optical viewfinder shows just 95 percent of the sensor's field of view). It's large enough to allow manual focusing—but if you want to use automatic focus with contrast detection, the D90 can do that, too. You still have to avoid pointing your D90 at bright light sources (especially the Sun) when using Live View, but the real-time preview can be used for fairly long periods without frying the sensor. (Image quality can degrade, but the camera issues a warning when the sensor starts to overheat.)

Unlike some of the previous attempts at a Live View-type mode by other vendors, the D90's Live View works. No beam-splitting prisms that divert some light to the sensor, no grainy black-and-white, real-time preview, no need for a spare sensor to provide a simulated Live View. Nikon's system works just like you'd want it to: the mirror flips up, the shutter opens, autofocus is achieved using contrast detection from the sensor image, and what the sensor sees is displayed in full color on the LCD on the back of the camera. You can expect every new camera introduced by Nikon and every other vendor to include Live View features from now on. And, expect Live View to get better.

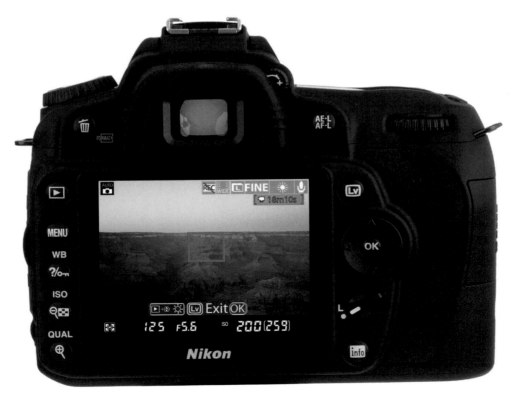

Figure 5.8
Live View really shines on the Nikon D90's large three-inch LCD.

What You Can/Cannot Do with Live View

You may not have considered just what you can do with Live View, because the capability is so novel. But once you've played with it, you'll discover dozens of applications for this capability, as well as a few things that you can't do. Here's a list of Live View Do's/Don'ts/Cans/Can'ts.

- **Shoot stills and movies.** You can take still pictures or movies using Live View.

- **Preview your images on a TV.** Connect your Nikon D90 to a television using the video cable, and you can preview your image on a large television or HDTV screen.

- **Preview remotely.** Extend the cable between the camera and TV screen, and you can preview your images some distance away from the camera.

- **Shoot from your computer.** Nikon offers optional Camera Control Pro software you need to control your camera from your computer, so you can preview images and take pictures without physically touching the Nikon D90.

- **Continuous shooting.** You can shoot bursts of images using Live View, but all shots will use the focus and exposure setting established for the first picture in the series.

- **Shoot from tripod or handheld.** Of course, holding the camera out at arm's length to preview an image is poor technique, and will introduce a lot of camera shake. If you want to use Live View for handheld images, use an image-stabilized lens and/or a high shutter speed. A tripod is a better choice if you can use one.

- **Watch your power.** Live View uses a lot of juice and will deplete your battery rapidly. The optional AC adapter is a useful accessory.

Enabling Live View

Before using Live View, you should double-check three settings that affect how your image or movie is taken. These settings include:

- **Metering mode.** Choose Matrix, Center-Weighted, or Spot metering by holding down the Metering button (located to the southwest of the shutter release) and rotating the main command dial. You must select the metering mode before activating Live View, as it cannot be changed once you've entered Live View mode.

- **Autofocus mode.** Hold down the AF button at the lower right of the top edge of the D90, and rotate the main command dial to choose Wide-Area (a large red box appears on the LCD), Normal Area (a smaller red box appears), or Face Priority modes (no box is shown). (I'll describe these later in this chapter.) You can change AF mode while Live View is activated, but it's usually better to make this setting now so you won't forget. Note that you can also specify a default Live View Autofocus mode using CSM #a7.

- **Movie settings.** Use the Shooting menu's Movie Settings entry, as described in Chapter 3, to select movie quality (1280 × 720, 640 × 424, or 320 × 216) and Sound (On/Off) prior to entering Live View.

To activate Live View, press the LV button, located to the upper right of the back-panel color LCD. A display like the one shown in Figure 5.9 appears. Not all of the information appears all the time. For example, the Time Remaining indicator shows only when there are 30 seconds or less remaining for Live View shooting. The indicators overlaid on the image can be displayed or suppressed by pressing the INFO button. As you press the INFO button repeatedly, the LCD cycles among overlaid shooting information on/overlaid shooting information off/shooting information off with alignment grid display. The overlaid indicators include:

■ **Shooting mode.** This indicator shows the mode dial position you've selected, including any of the PASM (Program, Aperture Priority, Shutter Priority, and Manual) modes, as well as one of the Scene modes. You can change modes while Live View is active. This indicator appears on the LCD even when Shooting Information is turned off.

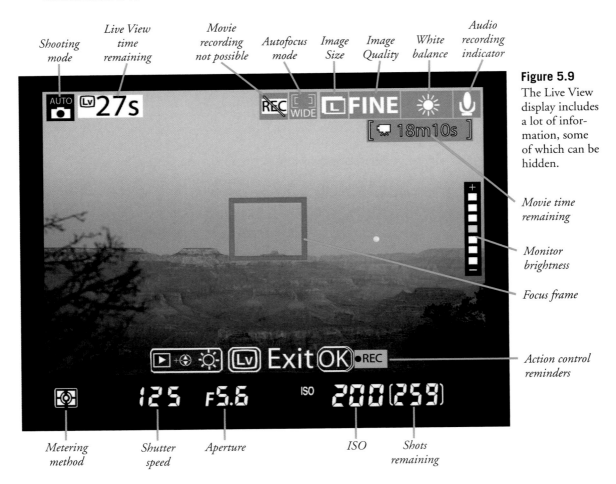

Figure 5.9
The Live View display includes a lot of information, some of which can be hidden.

- **Live View time remaining.** This is displayed when the amount of shooting time in Live View mode is 30 seconds or less. Although Live View is possible for 60 minutes, if the D90 overheats, this countdown display appears and the camera exits Live View before damage is done.

- **No Movies Possible.** This shows that it is not possible to shoot movies, because there is not enough space remaining on your memory card.

- **Current Autofocus mode.** Shows whether Wide Area, Normal Area, or Face Priority autofocus will be used. This indicator still appears when the alignment grid is displayed, even when other Shooting Information is turned off.

- **Image Size.** Displays the current resolution, L (Large), M (Medium), or S (Small).

- **Image Quality.** Shows JPEG Image Quality: Fine, Norm, or Basic.

- **White balance.** Displays the current white balance preset or WB Auto.

- **Audio recording indicator.** Shows when the monaural microphone is being used.

- **Movie time remaining.** Indicates the number of minutes and seconds remaining for movie shooting.

- **Monitor brightness.** Press the Playback button to display this indicator, then use the up/down buttons on the multi-selector to adjust LCD brightness up or down.

- **Action control reminders.** These three indicators just serve as a reminder for the key controls. From left to right they are: Monitor Brightness (Playback+up/down); LV button to Exit Live View; OK button to activate movie recording.

- **Alignment grid.** (Not shown in the figure.) This set of lines can be used to help line up horizontal or vertical lines.

Additional information is arrayed along the bottom of the LCD image, more or less duplicating much of the data in the LED display that is seen through the viewfinder. These indicators include:

- **Metering method.** Shows whether Matrix, Center-Weighted, or Spot metering is selected. Choose before entering Live View.

- **Shutter speed.** The currently selected shutter speed.

- **F/stop.** The current f/stop.

- **ISO value.** Shows the ISO sensitivity setting, or ISO Auto.

- **Shots remaining.** Indicates the number of images remaining on your memory card at the current Image Size and Image Quality settings.

Shooting in Live View

Shooting stills and movies in Live View is easy. Just follow these steps:

1. **Check your settings.** I described the settings you should consider before entering Live View earlier in this section.

2. **Press the LV button.** Activate Live View by pressing the button. The D90 can be handheld or mounted on a tripod. (Using a tripod mode makes it easier to obtain and keep sharp focus.) You can exit Live View at any time by pressing the LV button again.

3. **Zoom in/out.** Check your view by pressing the Zoom In button (located at the lower-left corner next to the color LCD). Five levels of magnification are available, up to 6.7X zoom. A navigation box appears in the lower right of the LCD with a yellow box representing the portion of the image zoomed. Use the multi-selector keys to change the zoomed area within the full frame. Press the Zoom Out button to zoom out again.

4. **Focus.** Use either autofocus or manual focus to focus the image. Note that the D90 will *not* refocus while shooting movies, even if you press the shutter release down again.

   - **When using Wide Area and Normal Area autofocus,** the focus zone will be outlined in red. Change the Focus Lock lever from L to * and you can move the focus zone around the screen with the multi-selector buttons. When sharp focus is achieved, the focus zone box will turn green. The D90 uses Single Autofocus (AF-S), so focus is locked when you hold the shutter release down or press the AE-L/AF-L button.

   - **When using Face Priority,** a double yellow border will be displayed when the camera detects a face. You don't need to press the shutter release to activate this behavior. (Up to five faces may be detected; the D90 focuses on the face that is closest to the camera.) When you press down the shutter release halfway, the camera attempts to focus the face. As sharp focus is achieved, the border turns green. (See Figure 5.10.) If the camera is unable to focus, the border blinks red. Single Autofocus (AF-S) is used.

   - **When using Manual focus,** use the multi-selector to choose a focus point and press the shutter release halfway. Turn the focus ring on the lens. When sharp focus is achieved, the focus confirmation indicator at the lower left of the LCD will turn a steady green.

5. **Make exposure adjustments.** While using an automatic exposure mode, you can add or subtract exposure using the EV settings, as described in Chapter 4. Hold down the EV button (just southeast of the shutter release) and rotate the main command dial to add or subtract exposure. The back-panel color LCD will brighten or darken to represent the exposure change you make.

6. **Shoot.** Press the shutter release all the way down to take a still picture, or press the OK button to start motion picture filming. Stop filming by pressing the OK button again. Movies up to 2GB in size can be taken (assuming there is sufficient room on your memory card), which limits you to 5 minutes for an HDTV clip, and up to 20 minutes for other sizes.

Figure 5.10
Face detection can locate and focus on any faces in your image.

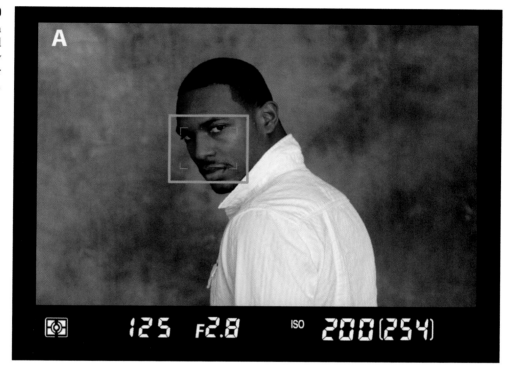

NOT MUCH OF A LIMITATION

Unless you are shooting an entire performance from a fixed position, such as a stage play, the five-minute limitation on HDTV movie duration won't put much of a crimp in your style. Good motion picture practice calls for each production to consist of a series of relatively *short* clips, with 10 to 20 seconds a good average. You can assemble and edit your D90 movies into one long, finished production using one of the many movie-editing software packages available. Andy Warhol might have been successful with his 1963 five-hour epic *Sleep*, but the rest of us will do better with short sequences of the type produced by the Nikon D90.

Continuous Shooting

The Nikon D90's 4.5 frames-per-second Continuous Shooting release mode reminds me how far digital photography has brought us. The first accessory I purchased when I worked as a newspaper sports photographer some years ago was a motor drive for my film SLR. It enabled me to snap off a series of shots in rapid succession, which came in very handy when a fullback broke through the line and headed for the end zone. Even a seasoned action photographer can miss the decisive instant when a crucial block is made, or a baseball superstar's bat shatters and pieces of cork fly out. Continuous shooting simplifies taking a series of pictures, either to ensure that one has more or less the exact moment you want to capture or to capture a sequence that is interesting as a collection of successive images. (Time Lapse photography is another kind of continuous shooting, and you'll find a discussion of special software packages, such as Nikon Camera Control Pro and Breeze Systems' NKRemote in Chapter 8.)

The D90's "motor drive" capabilities are, in many ways, much superior to what you get with a film camera. For one thing, a motor-driven film camera can eat up film at an incredible pace, which is why many of them were used with cassettes that held hundreds of feet of film stock. At three frames per second (typical of film cameras), a short burst of a few seconds can burn up as much as half of an ordinary 36 exposure roll of film. The Nikon D90, which fires off bursts at a faster frame rate (up to 4.5 frames per second), has reusable "film," so if you waste a few dozen shots on non-decisive moments, you can erase them and shoot more.

The increased capacity of digital film cards gives you a prodigious number of frames to work with. At a basketball game I covered earlier this year, I took more than 1,000 images in a couple hours. Yet, even shooting JPEG Fine, I could fit more than 560 images on a single 4GB memory card. Given an average burst of about six frames per sequence (nobody really takes 15-20 shots or more at one stretch in a basketball game), I was able to capture almost 100 different sequences before I needed to swap cards.

To use the D90's continuous shooting modes, press Drive mode button to the immediate right of the top-panel monochrome status LCD, and rotate the main command dial until the Continuous H or Continuous L icons appear. At Continuous H, the D90 fires at up to 4.5 frames per second; at Continuous L, the frame rate can be as high as the value selected in CSM #d6 (from 1 to 4 frames per second). When you partially depress the shutter button, the viewfinder will display at the right side a number representing the maximum number of shots you can take at the current quality settings. As a practical matter, the buffer in the Nikon D90 will generally allow you to take up to a dozen JPEG shots in a single burst, but only a few RAW photos.

To get the maximum number of shots, reduce the image-quality setting by switching to JPEG only (from RAW+Basic), to a lower JPEG quality setting, or by reducing the D90's resolution from L to M or S. The reason the size of your bursts is limited is that

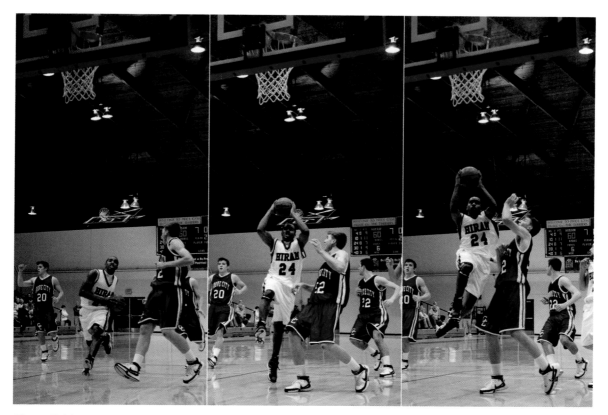

Figure 5.11 Continuous shooting allows you to capture an entire sequence of exciting moments as they unfold.

continuous images are first shuttled into the D90's internal memory buffer, then doled out to the memory card as quickly as they can be written to the card. Technically, the D90 takes the RAW data received from the digital image processor and converts it to the output format you've selected—either JPG or NEF (RAW)—and deposits it in the buffer ready to store on the card.

This internal "smart" buffer can suck up photos much more quickly than the memory card and, indeed, some memory cards are significantly faster or slower than others. When the buffer fills, you can't take any more continuous shots until the D90 has written some of them to the card, making more room in the buffer. (You should keep in mind that faster memory cards write images more quickly, freeing up buffer space faster.)

The frame rate you select will depend on the kind of shooting you want to do. Here are some guidelines:

- **4.5 fps.** The max rate of 4.5 fps is available when using Continuous High mode. Use this for sports and other subjects where you want to optimize your chances of capturing the decisive moment. Perhaps you're shooting some active kids and want to grab their most appealing expressions. This fast frame rate can improve the odds.

However, there is no guarantee that even at 4.5 fps the crucial instant won't occur *between* frames. For example, when shooting major league baseball games, if I want to shoot a batter I keep both eyes open, and keep one of them on the pitcher. Then, I start taking my sequence just as the pitcher releases the ball. My goal is to capture the batter making contact with the ball. But even at 4.5 fps, I find that a hitter connects between frames. I usually must take pictures of a couple dozen at-bats to get a shot of bat and ball connecting.

- **4.0-3.0 fps.** When using Continuous L, you can choose the frame rate. A slower rate can be useful for activities that aren't quite so fast moving. But, there's another benefit. Using the fastest frame rate means that your camera may fill up its buffer and won't be ready for the next sequence. If you don't want to miss any sequences, using a slightly slower frame rate can help prevent buffer overload.

- **2.0-1.0 fps.** You can set Continuous L mode to use a relatively pokey frame rate, too. Use these rates when you just want to be able to take pictures quickly, and aren't interested in filling up your memory card with mostly duplicated images. At 1 fps you can hold down the shutter release and fire away, or ease up when you want to pause. At higher frame rates, by the time you've decided to stop shooting, you may have taken an extra three or four shots that you really don't want. Slow frame rates are good for bracketing, too. Set the D90 to take a three-frame bracket burst, and you can take all three with one press of the shutter release. You'll find that slower frame rates also come in handy for subjects that are moving around in interesting ways (photographic models come to mind) but don't change their looks or poses quickly enough to merit a 4.5 fps burst.

A Tiny Slice of Time

Exposures that seem impossibly brief can reveal a world we didn't know existed. In the 1930s, Dr. Harold Edgerton, a professor of electrical engineering at MIT, pioneered high-speed photography using a repeating electronic flash unit he patented called the *stroboscope*. As the inventor of the electronic flash, he popularized its use to freeze objects in motion, and you've probably seen his photographs of bullets piercing balloons and drops of milk forming a coronet-shaped splash.

Electronic flash freezes action by virtue of its extremely short duration—as brief as 1/50,000th second or less. Although the D90's built-in flash unit can give you these ultra-quick glimpses of moving subjects, an external flash, such as one of the Nikon Speedlights, offers even more versatility. You can read more about using electronic flash to stop action in Chapter 7.

Of course, the D90 is fully capable of immobilizing all but the fastest movement using only its shutter speeds, which range all the way up to a respectably quick 1/4,000th second. Indeed, you'll rarely have need for such a brief shutter speed in ordinary shooting.

If you wanted to use an aperture of f/1.8 at ISO 200 outdoors in bright sunlight, for some reason, a shutter speed of 1/4,000th second would more than do the job. You'd need a faster shutter speed only if you moved the ISO setting to a higher sensitivity, say, to compensate for a polarizing filter you attached to your lens. Under less than full sunlight, 1/4,000th second is more than fast enough for any conditions you're likely to encounter.

Most sports action can be frozen at 1/2,000th second or slower, and for many sports a slower shutter speed is actually preferable—for example, to allow the wheels of a racing automobile or motorcycle, or the propeller on a classic aircraft to blur realistically. Other times, freezing a moment in time concentrates the focus of the picture on the interaction of the subjects. Figure 5.12 is an example. The 1/1000th second shutter speed effectively stopped the soccer players in mid-stride, creating a tableau in which each athlete pictured had a role.

If you want to do some exotic action-freezing photography, you can use the Nikon D90's faster shutter speeds, or resort to an electronic flash (internal or external), which, as you'll learn in Chapter 7, provides the effect of a high shutter speed because of its short duration.

Of course, you'll need a lot of light. High shutter speeds cut very fine slices of time and sharply reduce the amount of illumination that reaches your sensor. To use 1/4,000th

Figure 5.12
An action-stopping shutter speed froze these players in place.

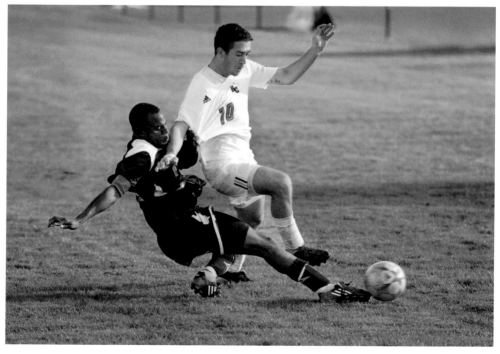

second at an aperture of f/6.3, you'd need an ISO setting of 800—even in full daylight. To use an f/stop smaller than f/6.3 or an ISO setting lower than 1,600, you'd need more light than full daylight provides. (That's why electronic flash units work so well for high-speed photography when used as the sole illumination; they provide both the effect of a brief shutter speed and the high levels of illumination needed.)

High shutter speeds with electronic flash comes with a penalty: you have to use a shutter speed slower than 1/200th second. Perhaps you want to stop some action in daylight with a brief shutter speed and use electronic flash only as supplemental illumination to fill in the shadows. Unfortunately, under most conditions you can't use flash with your D90 at any shutter speed faster than 1/200th second. That's the fastest speed at which the camera's focal plane shutter is fully open: at shorter speeds, the "slit" (described in more detail in Chapter 7) comes into play, so that the flash will expose only the small portion of the sensor exposed by the slit during its duration.

Working with Short Exposures

You can have a lot of fun exploring the kinds of pictures you can take using very brief exposure times, whether you decide to take advantage of the action-stopping capabilities of your built-in or external electronic flash or work with the Nikon D90's faster shutter speeds. Here are a few ideas to get you started:

- **Take revealing images.** Fast shutter speeds can help you reveal the real subject behind the façade, by freezing constant motion to capture an enlightening moment in time. Legendary fashion/portrait photographer Philippe Halsman used leaping photos of famous people, such as the Duke and Duchess of Windsor, Richard Nixon, and Salvador Dali to illuminate their real selves. Halsman said, "*When you ask a person to jump, his attention is mostly directed toward the act of jumping and the mask falls so that the real person appears.*" Try some high-speed portraits of people you know in motion to see how they appear when concentrating on something other than the portrait.

- **Create unreal images.** High-speed photography can also produce photographs that show your subjects in ways that are quite unreal. A helicopter in mid-air with its rotors frozen or a motocross cyclist leaping over a ramp, but with all motion stopped so that the rider and machine look as if they were frozen in mid-air, make for an unusual picture. When we're accustomed to seeing subjects in motion, seeing them stopped in time can verge on the surreal.

- **Capture unseen perspectives.** Some things are *never* seen in real life, except when viewed in a stop-action photograph. M.I.T's Dr. Harold Edgerton captured a series of famed balloon burst images back in the 1930s that were only a starting point. Freeze a hummingbird in flight for a view of wings that never seem to stop. Or, capture the splashes as liquid falls into a bowl, as shown in Figure 5.13. No electronic flash was required for this image (and wouldn't have illuminated the water in the bowl as evenly). Instead, a clutch of high-intensity lamps and an ISO setting of 1,600 allowed the D90 to capture this image at 1/2,000th second.

■ **Vanquish camera shake and gain new angles.** Here's an idea that's so obvious it isn't always explored to its fullest extent. A high enough shutter speed can free you from the tyranny of a tripod, making it easier to capture new angles, or to shoot quickly while moving around, especially with longer lenses. I tend to use a monopod or tripod for almost everything when I'm not using an image-stabilized lens, and I end up missing some shots because of a reluctance to adjust my camera support to get a higher, lower, or different angle. If you have enough light and can use an f/stop wide enough to permit a high shutter speed, you'll find a new freedom to choose your shots (see Figure 5.3). I have a favored 170mm-500mm lens that I use for sports and wildlife photography, almost invariably with a tripod, as I don't find the "reciprocal of the focal length" rule particularly helpful in most cases. I would *not* handhold this hefty lens at its 500mm setting with a 1/500th second shutter speed under most circumstances. Nor, if you want to account for the crop factor, would I use 1/750th second. However, at 1/2,000th second or faster, it's entirely possible for a steady hand to use this lens without a tripod or monopod's extra support, and I've found that my whole approach to shooting animals and other elusive subjects changes in High-Speed mode. Selective focus allows dramatically isolating my prey wide open at f/6.3, too.

Figure 5.13
A large amount of artificial illumination and an ISO 1600 sensitivity setting allowed capturing this shot at 1/2,000th second without use of an electronic flash.

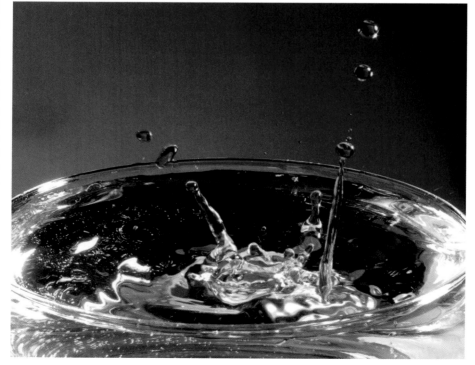

Long Exposures

Longer exposures are a doorway into another world, showing us how even familiar scenes can look much different when photographed over periods measured in seconds. At night, long exposures produce streaks of light from moving, illuminated subjects like automobiles or amusement park rides. Extra-long exposures of seemingly pitch-dark subjects can reveal interesting views using light levels barely bright enough to see by. At any time of day, including daytime (in which case you'll often need the help of neutral density filters to make the long exposure practical), long exposures can cause moving objects to vanish entirely, because they don't remain stationary long enough to register in a photograph.

Three Ways to Take Long Exposures

There are actually three common types of lengthy exposures: *timed exposures, bulb exposures*, and *time exposures*. The Nikon D90 offers only the first two. Because of the length of the exposure, all shots with very slow shutter speeds should be taken with a tripod to hold the camera steady.

- **Timed exposures.** These are long exposures from 1 second to 30 seconds, measured by the camera itself. To take a picture in this range, simply use Manual or S modes and use the main command dial to set the shutter speed to the length of time you want, choosing from preset speeds of 1.0, 1.3, 1.6, 2.0, 2.5, 3.2, 4.0, 5.0, 6.0, 8.0, 10.0, 13.0, 15.0, 20.0, 25.0, and 30.0 seconds (because the D90 uses 1/3 stop increments). The advantage of timed exposures is that the camera does all the calculating for you. There's no need for a stop-watch. If you review your image on the LCD and decide to try again with the exposure doubled or halved, you can dial in the correct exposure with precision. The disadvantage of timed exposures is that you can't take a photo for longer than 30 seconds.

- **Bulb exposures.** This type of exposure is so-called because in the olden days the photographer squeezed and held an air bulb attached to a tube that provided the force necessary to keep the shutter open. Traditionally, a bulb exposure is one that lasts as long as the shutter release button is pressed; when you release the button, the exposure ends. To make a bulb exposure with the D90, set the camera on Manual mode, set the f/stop, and then use the main command dial to select the shutter speed immediately after 30 seconds—Bulb. Then, press the shutter to start the exposure, and release it again to close the shutter.

- **Time exposures.** This is a setting found on some cameras to produce longer exposures. With cameras that implement this option, the shutter opens when you press the shutter release button, and remains open until you press the button again. With the Nikon D90, you can't get this exact effect; the best you can do is use a Bulb exposure.

Working with Long Exposures

Because the D90 produces such good images at longer exposures, and there are so many creative things you can do with long-exposure techniques, you'll want to do some experimenting. Get yourself a tripod or another firm support and take some test shots with long exposure noise reduction both enabled and disabled (to see whether you prefer low noise or high detail) and get started. Here are some things to try:

■ **Make people invisible.** One very cool thing about long exposures is that objects that move rapidly enough won't register at all in a photograph, while the subjects that remain stationary are portrayed in the normal way. That makes it easy to produce people-free landscape photos and architectural photos at night or, even, in full daylight if you use a plain gray neutral density filter (or two or three) to allow an exposure of at least a few seconds. At ISO 100, f/22, and a pair of ND8 neutral density filters (which each remove three stops' worth of light—giving you, in effect, the equivalent of ISO 1.5!) you can use exposures of nearly two seconds; overcast days and/or even more neutral density filtration would work even better if daylight people-vanishing is your goal. They'll have to be walking *very* briskly and across the field of view (rather than directly toward the camera) for this to work. At night, it's much easier to achieve this effect with the 20- to 30-second exposures that are possible, as you can see in Figures 5.14 and 5.15

■ **Create streaks.** If you aren't shooting for total invisibility, long exposures with the camera on a tripod can produce some interesting streaky effects. Even a single ND8 filter will let you shoot at f/22 and 1/6th second in daylight. Figure 5.16 shows one kind of effect you can get.

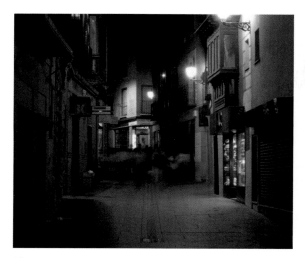

Figure 5.14 This alleyway is thronged with people, as you can see in this two-second exposure using only the available illumination.

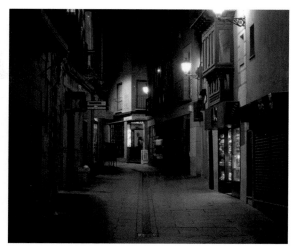

Figure 5.15 With the camera still on a tripod, a 30-second exposure rendered the passersby almost invisible.

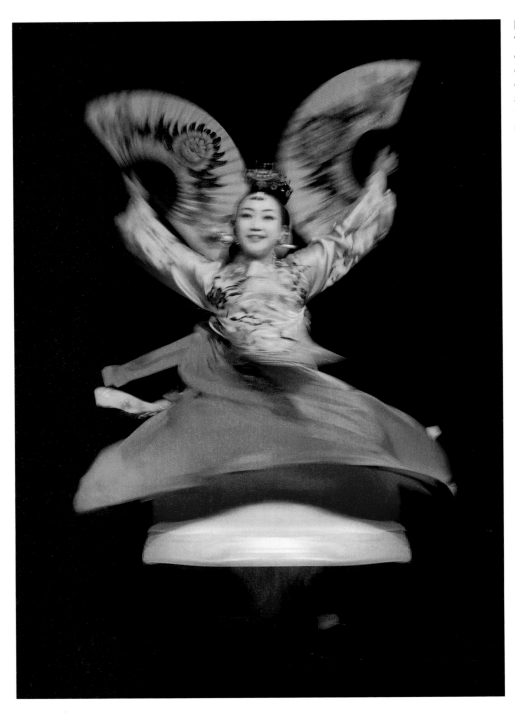

Figure 5.16
This Korean dancer produced a swirl of color as she spun during the 1/4 second exposure.

- **Produce light trails.** At night, car headlights and taillights and other moving sources of illumination can generate interesting light trails. If the lights aren't moving, you can make them move by zooming or jiggling the camera during a long exposure. Your camera doesn't even need to be mounted on a tripod; handholding the D90 for longer exposures adds movement and patterns to your trails. If you're shooting fireworks, a longer exposure may allow you to combine several bursts into one picture (see Figure 5.17).

- **Blur waterfalls, etc.** You'll find that waterfalls and other sources of moving liquid produce a special type of long-exposure blur, because the water merges into a fantasy-like veil that looks different at different exposure times, and with different waterfalls. Cascades with turbulent flow produce a rougher look at a given longer exposure than falls that flow smoothly. Although blurred waterfalls have become almost a cliché, there are still plenty of variations for a creative photographer to explore.

- **Show total darkness in new ways.** Even on the darkest, moonless nights, there is enough starlight or glow from distant illumination sources to see by, and, if you use a long exposure, there is enough light to take a picture, too.

Figure 5.17
A long exposure allows capturing several bursts of fireworks in one image.

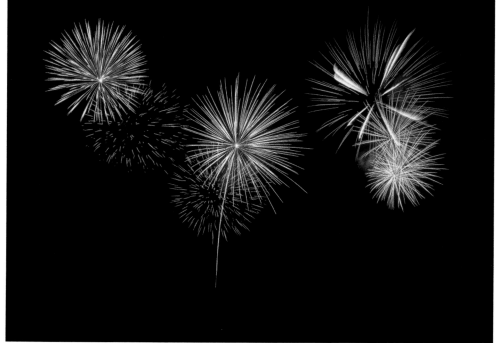

Geotagging with the Nikon GP-1

The Nikon D90 gained a lot of credibility as a tool for serious photographers when it debuted with a GPS port that accepts the new Nikon GP-1 Global Positioning System device. The unit makes it easy to tag your images with the same kind of longitude, latitude, altitude, and time stamp information that is supplied by the GPS unit you use in your car. (Don't have a GPS? Photographers who get lost in the boonies as easily as I do *must* have one of these!) The geotagging information is stored in the metadata space within your image files, and can be accessed by Nikon View NX, or by online photo services such as mypicturetown.com and Flickr. Having this information available makes it easier to track where your pictures are taken. That can be essential, as I learned from a trip out West this Spring, where I found that the red rocks, canyons, and arroyos of Nevada, Utah, Arizona, and Colorado all pretty much look alike to my untrained eye.

Like all GPS units, the Nikon GP-1 obtains its data by triangulating signals from satellites orbiting the Earth. It works with the Nikon D90, as well as more upscale Nikon cameras, such as the D200, D300, D700, D3, and D3x. It also works with the older Nikon D2x/D2xs and D2H/D2Hs. At about $225, it's not cheap, but those who need geotagging—especially for professional mapping or location applications—will find it to be a bargain.

The GP-1 (see Figure 5.18) slips onto the accessory shoe on top of the Nikon D90. It connects to the GPS port on the camera using the Nikon GP1-CA90 cable, which plugs

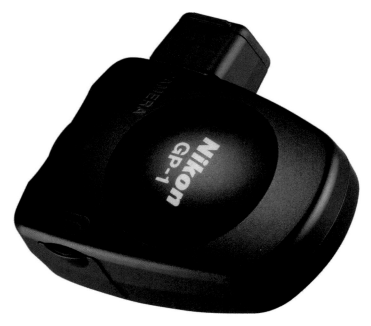

Figure 5.18
Nikon GP-1 geotagging unit.

into the connector marked CAMERA on the GP-1 and into the separate port marked GPS (and described in Chapter 2). If you want to use the unit with one of the other supported cameras, you'll need to buy the GP1-CA10 cable as well—it attaches to the 10-pin port on the front of the D200/D300/D700/D3/D3x. The device also has a port labeled with a remote control icon, so you can plug in the Nikon MC-DC2 remote cable release, which would otherwise attach to the GPS port when you're not using the geotagging unit.

A third connector connects the GP-1 to your computer using a USB cable. Once attached, the device is very easy to use. You need to activate the Nikon D90's GPS capabilities in the GPS choice within the Setup menu.

The first step is to allow the GP-1 to acquire signals from at least three satellites. If you've used a GPS in your car, you'll know that satellite acquisition works best outdoors under a clear sky and out of the "shadow" of tall buildings, and the Nikon unit is no exception. It takes about 40-60 seconds for the GP-1 to "connect." A red blinking LED means that GPS data is not being recorded; a green blinking LED signifies that the unit has acquired three satellites and is recording data. When the LED is solid green, the unit has connected to four or more satellites, and is recording data with optimum accuracy.

Next, set up the camera by selecting the GPS option found under the Setup menu on the Nikon D90. Then, select Auto Meter Off to disable automatic shutoff of the D90's exposure meters. That will assure that the camera doesn't go to sleep while you're using the GPS unit. Of course, in this mode the camera will use more power (the meters never go off, and the GPS draws power constantly), but you don't want to go through the 40-60-second satellite acquisition step each time you take a picture. Next, use the Position option in the GPS menu to activate the unit.

You're all set. Once the unit is up and running, you can view GPS information using photo information screens available on the color LCD (and described in Chapter 2). The GPS screen, which appears only when a photo has been taken using the GPS unit, looks like Figure 5.19.

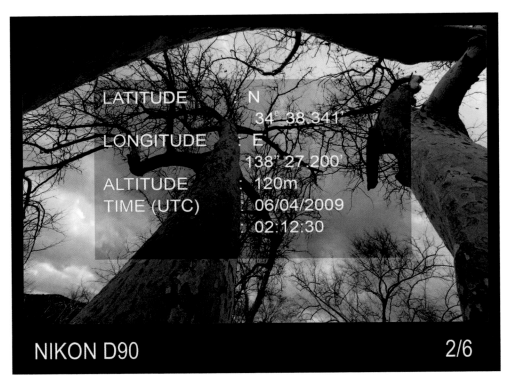

6

Working with Lenses

There's no disputing the fact that there is a key reason why many digital SLR buyers choose Nikon cameras: Nikon lenses. Some favor Nikon cameras because of the broad selection of quality lenses. Others already possess a large collection of Nikon optics (perhaps dating from the owner's photography during the film era), and the ability to use those lenses on the latest digital cameras is a big plus. A few may be attracted to the Nikon brand because there are many inexpensive lenses (including a few in the $100-$200 price range) that make it possible to assemble a basic kit for cameras like the D90 without spending a lot of cash.

It's true that there is a mind-bending assortment of high-quality lenses available to enhance the capabilities of Nikon cameras. You can use thousands of current and older lenses introduced by Nikon and third-party vendors since 1959, although lenses made before 1977 may need an inexpensive modification for use with the D90 and cameras *other* than the Nikon D60, D40, and D40x. (More on this later.) These lenses can give you a wider view, bring distant subjects closer, let you focus closer, shoot under lower light conditions, or provide a more detailed, sharper image for critical work. Other than the sensor itself, the lens you choose for your dSLR is the most important component in determining image quality and perspective of your images.

This chapter explains how to select the best lenses for the kinds of photography you want to do.

Sensor Sensibilities

From time to time, you've heard the term *crop factor*, and you've probably also heard the term *lens multiplier factor*. Both are misleading and inaccurate terms used to describe the same phenomenon: the fact that cameras like the D90 (and most other affordable digital SLRs) provide a field of view that's smaller and narrower than that produced by certain other (usually much more expensive) cameras, when fitted with exactly the same lens.

Figure 6.1 quite clearly shows the phenomenon at work. The outer rectangle, marked 1X, shows the field of view you might expect with a 28mm lens mounted on one of Nikon's "full-frame" (non-cropped) cameras, like the Nikon D700, D3, or D3x. The area marked 1.5X shows the field of view you'd get with that 28mm lens installed on a D90. It's easy to see from the illustration that the 1X rendition provides a wider, more expansive view, while the inner field of view is, in comparison, *cropped*.

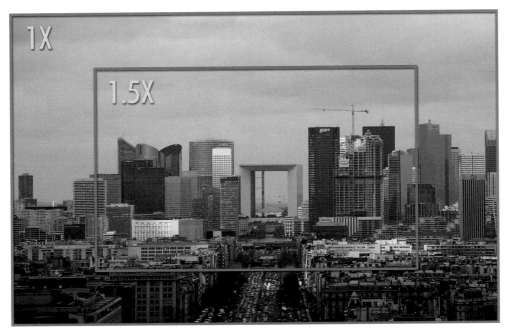

Figure 6.1
Nikon offers digital SLRs with full-frame (1X) crops, as well as 1.5X crops.

The cropping effect is produced because the sensors of DX cameras like the Nikon D90 are smaller than the sensors of the D700, D3, or D3x. The "full-frame" camera has a sensor that's the size of the standard 35mm film frame, 24mm × 36mm. Your D90's sensor does *not* measure 24mm × 36mm; instead, it specs out at 23.6 × 15.8 mm, or about 66.7 percent of the area of a full-frame sensor, as shown by the red boxes in the figure. You can calculate the relative field of view by dividing the focal length of the lens by .667. Thus, a 100mm lens mounted on a D90 has the same field of view as a 150mm lens on the Nikon D700. We humans tend to perform multiplication operations in our heads more easily than division, so such field of view comparisons are usually calculated using the reciprocal of .667—1.5—so we can multiply instead (100 / .667=150; 100 × 1.5=150).

This translation is generally useful only if you're accustomed to using full-frame cameras (usually of the film variety) and want to know how a familiar lens will perform on a digital camera. I strongly prefer *crop factor* over *lens multiplier*, because nothing is being multiplied; a 100mm lens doesn't "become" a 150mm lens—the depth-of-field and lens aperture remain the same. (I'll explain more about these later in this chapter.) Only the field of view is cropped. But *crop factor* isn't much better, as it implies that the 24 × 36mm frame is "full" and anything else is "less." I get e-mails all the time from photographers who point out that they own full-frame cameras with 36mm × 48mm sensors (like the Mamiya 645ZD or Hasselblad H3D-39 medium format digitals). By their reckoning, the "half-size" sensors found in cameras like the Nikon D700 and D3/D3xare "cropped."

If you're accustomed to using full-frame film cameras, you might find it helpful to use the crop factor "multiplier" to translate a lens's real focal length into the full-frame equivalent, even though, as I said, nothing is actually being multiplied. Throughout most of this book, I've been using actual focal lengths and not equivalents, except when referring to specific wide-angle or telephoto focal length ranges and their fields of view.

Crop or Not?

There's a lot of debate over the "advantages" and "disadvantages" of using a camera with a "cropped" sensor, versus one with a "full-frame" sensor. The arguments go like these:

- **"Free" 1.5X teleconverter.** The Nikon D90 (and other cameras with the 1.5X crop factor) magically transforms any telephoto lens you have into a longer lens, which can be useful for sports, wildlife photography, and other endeavors that benefit from more reach. Yet, your f/stop remains the same (that is, a 300mm f/4 becomes a very fast 450mm f/4 lens). Some discount this advantage, pointing out that the exact same field of view can be had by taking a full-frame image, and trimming it to the 1.5X equivalent. While that is strictly true, it doesn't take into account a factor called *pixel density*. While both the Nikon D90 and the full-frame D700 have sensors with 12 megapixels of resolution, the D90 packs all those pixels together much more tightly, into that 23.6 × 15.8mm area. So, your 300mm f/4 lens delivers the same field-of-view as a 450mm optic at the D90's full 12MP resolution. When you crop the D700 image to get the same FOV, you're using only five megapixels worth of resolution. So, while both images will be framed the same, the D90 version, with its higher pixel density, will be sharper.

- **Dense pixels = more noise.** The other side of the pixel density coin is that the denser packing of pixels in the D90 sensor means that each pixel must be smaller, and will have less light-gathering capabilities. Larger pixels capture light more efficiently, reducing the need to amplify the signal when boosting ISO sensitivity, and, therefore, producing less noise. In an absolute sense, this is true, and cameras like the D700 and D3 *do* have sensational high-ISO performance. However, the D90's sensor is improved over earlier cameras (for one thing, it is a high-sensitivity CMOS sensor, rather than a noisier CCD sensor like that found in the predecessor Nikon D80), so you'll find it performs very well at higher ISOs. Indeed, its ISO sensitivity is more or less comparable to that of the Nikon D3x, which also relies on high-density pixel-packing to achieve its 24.5MP resolution. You needn't hesitate to use ISO 1600 (or even higher) with the Nikon D90: just don't expect the same results at H1.0 (ISO 6400 equivalent) as D700 owners get from their cameras.

- **Lack of wide-angle perspective.** Of course, the 1.5X "crop" factor applies to wide-angle lenses, too, so your 20mm ultrawide lens becomes a hum-drum 30mm near-wide-angle, and a 35mm focal length is transformed into what photographers call a "normal" lens. Zoom lenses, like the 18-105mm lens that is often purchased with the D90 in a kit, have less wide-angle perspective at their minimum focal length. The 18-105mm optic, for example, is the equivalent of a 27mm moderate wide angle when zoomed to its widest setting. Nikon has "fixed" this problem by providing several different extra-wide zooms specifically for the DX format, including the (relatively) affordable 12-24mm f/4 and 10-24mm f/3.5-4.5G DX Nikkors. You'll never really lack for wide-angle lenses, but some of us will need to buy wider optics to regain the expansive view we're looking for.

- **Mixed body mix-up.** The relatively small number of Nikon D90 owners who also have a Nikon full-frame camera like the D700 can't ignore the focal-length mix-up factor. If you own both FX and DX-format cameras (some D90 owners use them as a backup to a D700, for example), it's vexing to have to adjust to the different fields of view that the cameras provide. If you remove a given lens from one camera and put it on the other, the effective focal length/field of view changes. That 17-35mm f/2.8 zoom works as an ultrawide to wide angle on a D700, but functions more as a moderate wide-angle to normal lens on a D90. To get the "look" on both cameras, you'd need to use a 12-24mm zoom on the D90, and the 17-35mm zoom on the D700. It's possible to become accustomed to this FOV shake-up and, indeed, some photographers put it to work by mounting their longest telephoto lens on the D90 and their wide-angle lenses on their full-frame camera. But, if you've never owned both an FX and DX camera, you should be aware of the possible confusion.

Your First Lens

Some Nikon dSLRs are almost always purchased with a lens. The entry- and mid-level Nikon dSLRs, including the Nikon D90, are often bought by those new to digital photography, frequently by first-time SLR or dSLR owners who find the AF-S DX Nikkor 18-105mm f/3.5-5.6G ED VR or AF-S DX Zoom-Nikkor 18-55mm f/3.5-5.6G ED II, both with vibration reduction, irresistible bargains. Other Nikon models, including the Nikon D300, D700, and D3/D3x, are generally purchased without a lens by veteran Nikon photographers who already have a complement of optics to use with their cameras.

I bought my D90 with the 18-105mm VR lens, even though I already had a (large) collection of lenses, because the VR was an attractive feature, and the lens is perfect to mount on the camera when I loan it to family members who have little photographic experience. Depending on which category of photographer you fall into, you'll need to make a decision about what kit lens to buy, or decide what other kind of lenses you need to fill out your complement of Nikon optics. This section will cover "first lens" concerns, while later in the chapter we'll look at "add-on lens" considerations.

When deciding on a first lens, there are several factors you'll want to consider:

- **Cost.** You might have stretched your budget a bit to purchase your Nikon D90, so the 18-105mm VR kit lens helps you keep the cost of your first lens fairly low. In addition, there are excellent moderately priced lenses available that will add from $100 to $300 to the price of your camera if purchased at the same time.

- **Zoom range.** If you have only one lens, you'll want a fairly long zoom range to provide as much flexibility as possible. Fortunately, the several popular basic lenses for the D90 have 3X to 5.8X zoom ranges (I'll list some of them next), extending from moderate wide-angle/normal out to medium telephoto. Either is fine for everyday shooting, portraits, and some types of sports.

- **Adequate maximum aperture.** You'll want an f/stop of at least f/3.5 to f/4 for shooting under fairly low light conditions. The thing to watch for is the maximum aperture when the lens is zoomed to its telephoto end. You may end up with no better than an f/5.6 maximum aperture. That's not great, but you can often live with it, particularly with a lens having vibration reduction (VR) capabilities, because you can often shoot at lower shutter speeds to compensate for the limited maximum aperture.

- **Image quality.** Your starter lens should have good image quality, because that's one of the primary factors that will be used to judge your photos. Even at a low price, several of the different lenses that can be used with the D90 kit include extra-low dispersion glass and aspherical elements that minimize distortion and chromatic aberration; they are sharp enough for most applications. If you read the user evaluations in the online photography forums, you know that owners of the kit lenses have been very pleased with its image quality.

- **Size matters.** A good walking-around lens is compact in size and light in weight.

- **Fast/close focusing.** Your first lens should have a speedy autofocus system (which is where the Silent Wave motor found in all but the bargain basement lenses [older, non-AF-S models] is an advantage). Close focusing (to 12 inches or closer) will let you use your basic lens for some types of macro photography.

You can find comparisons of the lenses discussed in the next section, as well as third-party lenses from Sigma, Tokina, Tamron, and other vendors, in online groups and websites. I'll provide my recommendations, but more information is always helpful.

Buy Now, Expand Later

When the Nikon D90 was introduced, it was available only in kit form with the 18-105mm VR lens. By the time this book is published, I expect to see it offered packaged with other lenses—all good, basic lenses that can serve you well as a "walk-around" lens (one you keep on the camera most of the time, especially when you're out and about without your camera bag). The number of options available to you is actually quite amazing, even if your budget is limited to about $100-$350 for your first lens. One other vendor, for example, offers only 18mm-70mm and 18mm-55mm kit lenses in that price range, plus a 24mm-85mm zoom. Here's a list of Nikon's best-bet "first" lenses. Don't worry about sorting out the alphabet soup right now; I provide a complete list of Nikon lens "codes" later in the chapter.

- **AF-S DX Nikkor 18-105mm f/3.5-5.6G ED VR.** This new lens, introduced at the same time as the D90, is my choice as a "walking-around" lens for this camera. I much prefer it over the 18-200mm VR (described later), even though it has a more limited zoom range. Its focal length range is quite sufficient for most general photography, and at around $300 with the camera (or slightly more when purchased separately), it's a real bargain (see Figure 6.2).

- **AF-S DX Nikkor 18-55mm f/3.5-5.6G VR.** This new VR version of the 18-55 is a better choice than the basic 18-55 optic, which remains available from many stores. That's because the vibration reduction ("anti-shake") feature of this lens partially offsets the relatively slow maximum aperture of the lens at the telephoto position. It can be mated with Nikon's AF-S DX VR Zoom-Nikkor 55-200mm f/4-5.6G IF-ED to give you a two-lens VR pair that will handle everything from 18mm to 200mm, at a relatively low price (see Figure 6.3).

- **AF-S DX Zoom-Nikkor 18-55mm f/3.5-5.6G ED II.** This is the least expensive basic zoom Nikon offers, and suitable for the D90 if you're really pinching pennies. You can always upgrade to better lenses in the near future. This one may be hard to find, because once the VR version was introduced, demand for this model dropped off significantly.

- **AF-S DX Nikkor 16-85mm f/3.5-5.6G ED VR.** The 16-85mm VR lens is the zoom that would make a lot of sense as a kit lens for the D90 if price were no object. It costs a significant fraction of the price of the D90 itself! If you really want to use just a single lens with your camera, this one provides an excellent combination of focal lengths, image quality, and features. Its zoom range extends from a true wide-angle (equivalent to a 24mm lens on a full-frame camera) to useful medium tele-photo (about 128mm equivalent), and so can be used for everything from

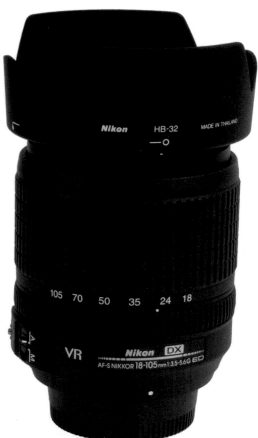

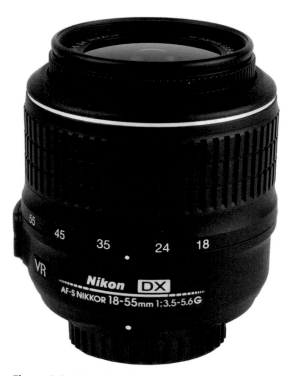

Figure 6.2 AF-S DX Nikkor 18-105mm f/3.5-5.6G ED VR was anointed as the basic kit lens when the D90 was introduced.

Figure 6.3 The AF-S DX Nikkor 18-55mm f/3.5-5.6G VR is a low-cost basic lens option for the Nikon D90.

architecture to portraiture to sports. If you think vibration reduction is useful only with longer telephoto lenses, you may be surprised at how much it helps you hand-hold your D90 even at the widest focal lengths. The only disadvantage to this lens is its relatively slow speed (f/5.6) when you crank it out to the telephoto end.

■ **AF-S DX Zoom-Nikkor 18-70mm f/3.5-4.5G IF-ED.** If you don't plan on getting a longer zoom-range basic lens and can't afford the 16-85 zoom, I highly recommend this aging, but impressive lens, if you can find one in stock. Originally introduced as the kit lens for the venerable Nikon D70, the 18-70mm zoom quickly gained a reputation as a very sharp lens at a bargain price. It doesn't provide a view that's as long or as wide as the 16-85, but it's a half-stop faster at its maximum zoom position. You may have to hunt around to find one of these, but they are available for $250-$300 and well worth it. I own one to this day, and use it regularly, although it spends most of its time installed on my D70, which has been converted to infrared-only photography.

■ **AF-S DX Zoom-Nikkor 18-135mm f/3.5-5.6G IF-ED.** This lens has been sold as a kit lens for intermediate amateur-level Nikons, and some retailers with stock on hand are packaging it with the D90 body as well. While decent, it's really best suited for the crowd who buy one do-everything lens and then never purchase another. Available for less than $300, you won't tie up a lot of money in this lens. There's no VR, so, for most, the 18-105mm VR lens is a better choice.

■ **AF-S DX VR Zoom-Nikkor 18-200mm f/3.5-5.6G IF-ED.** I owned this lens for about three months, and decided it really didn't meet my needs. It was introduced as an ideal "kit" lens for the Nikon D200 a few years back, and, at the time had almost everything you might want. It's a holdover, more upscale kit lens for the D90. Its stunning 11X zoom range covers everything from the equivalent of 27mm to 300mm when the 1.5X crop factor is figured in, and its VR capabilities plus light weight let you use it without a tripod most of the time. However, I found the image quality to be good, but not outstanding, and the slow maximum aperture at 200mm to be limiting when a fast shutter speed is required to stop action. The "zoom creep" (a tendency for the lens to zoom when the camera is tilted up or down) found in many examples will drive you nuts after awhile (see Figure 6.4).

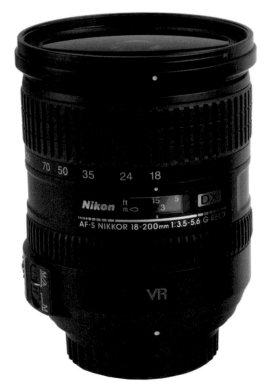

Figure 6.4
The AF-S DX VR Zoom-Nikkor 18-200mm f/3.5-5.6G IF-ED (right) is a lightweight "walking-around" lens.

■ **AF-S VR Zoom-Nikkor 24-120mm f/3.5-5.6G IF-ED.** I felt I had to mention this lens because I see a large number of them available used at low prices. There are two versions, an older non-VR lens, and this model, which added vibration reduction, internal focusing, and some extra low dispersion (ED) elements to improve image quality. Unfortunately, while image quality is very good at the maximum 120mm, the lens softens quite a bit at shorter focal lengths and at larger apertures, making it less suitable as an all-around tool.

What Lenses Can You Use?

The previous section helped you sort out what basic lens you need to buy with your Nikon D90. Now, you're probably wondering what lenses can be added to your growing collection (trust me, it will grow). You need to know which lenses are suitable and, most importantly, which lenses are fully compatible with your Nikon D90.

With the Nikon D90, the compatibility issue is a simple one: It can use any modern-era Nikon lens with the AF-S or AF designation, with full availability of all autofocus, auto aperture, autoexposure, and image-stabilization features (if present). You can also use any Nikon AI, AI-S, or AI-P lens, which are manual focus lenses produced starting in 1977 and effectively through the present day, because Nikon continues to offer a limited number of manual focus lenses for those who need them.

Nikon lenses produced prior to 1977 must have a minor conversion done to be used safely, because cameras other than certain Nikon entry-level models (such as the D40, D40x, and D60) have a pin on the lens mount that can be damaged by an older, unmodified lens. John White at www.aiconversions.com will do the work for about $35 to allow these older lenses to be safely used on any Nikon digital camera.

As far as third-party (non-Nikon) lenses go, your D90 will accept virtually all modern lenses produced by Tokina, Tamron, Sigma, and other vendors. They will autofocus just fine on a Nikon D90, but if you also own a D40/D40x/D60, they will autofocus only with those lenses that contain an internal focusing motor. Vendors have different designators to indicate these lenses, such as HSM (for hyper-sonic motor). You'll have to check with the manufacturer of non-Nikon lenses to see if they are compatible with the D90, particularly since some vendors have been gradually introducing revamped versions of their existing lenses with the addition of an internal motor.

Today, in addition to its traditional full-frame lenses, Nikon offers lenses with the DX designation, which is intended for use only on DX-format cameras. While the lens mounting system is the same, DX lenses have a coverage area that fills only the smaller frame, allowing the design of more compact, less-expensive lenses especially for non-full-frame cameras.

Ingredients of Nikon's Alphanumeric Soup

Nikon has always been fond of appending cryptic letters and descriptors onto the names of its lenses. Here's an alphabetical list of lens terms you're likely to encounter, either as part of the lens name or in reference to the lens's capabilities. Not all of these are used as parts of a lens's name; but you may come across some of these terms in discussions of particular Nikon optics:

- **AF, AF-D, AF-I, AF-S.** In all cases, AF stands for *autofocus* when appended to the name of a Nikon lens. An extra letter is added to provide additional information. A plain-old AF lens is an autofocus lens that uses a slot-drive motor in the camera body to provide autofocus functions (and so cannot be used in AF mode on the Nikon D40, D40x, or D60, which lack the camera body motor). The D means that it's a D-type lens (described later in this listing); the I indicates that focus is through a motor inside the lens; and the S means that a super-special (Silent Wave) motor in the lens provides focusing. (Don't confuse a Nikon AF-S lens with the AF-S [Single-Servo Autofocus mode]). Nikon is currently upgrading its older AF lenses with AF-S versions, but it's not safe to assume that all newer Nikkors are AF-S, or even offer autofocus. For example, the brand-new PC-E Nikkor 24mm f/3.5D ED perspective control lens must be focused manually, and Nikon offers a surprising collection of other manual focus lenses to meet specialized needs.

- **AI, AI-S.** All Nikkor lenses produced after 1977 have either automatic aperture indexing (AI) or automatic indexing-shutter (AI-S) features that eliminate the previous requirement to manually align the aperture ring on the camera when mounting a lens. Within a few years, all Nikkors had this automatic aperture indexing feature (except for G-type lenses, which have no aperture ring at all), including Nikon's budget-priced Series E lenses, so the designation was dropped at the time the first autofocus (AF) lenses were introduced.

- **E.** The E designation was used for Nikon's budget-priced E Series optics, five prime and three zoom manual focus lenses built using aluminum or plastic parts rather than the preferred brass parts of that era, so they were considered less rugged. All are effectively AI-S lenses. They do have good image quality, which makes them a bargain for those who treat their lenses gently and don't need the latest autofocus features. They were available in 28mm f/2.8, 35mm f/2.5, 50mm f/1.8, 100mm f/2.8, and 135mm f/2.8 focal lengths, plus 36-72mm f/3.5, 75mm-150mm f/3.5, and 70-210mm f/4 zooms. (All these would be considered fairly "fast" today.)

- **D.** Appended to the maximum f/stop of the lens (as in f/2.8D), a D-Series lens is able to send focus distance data to the camera, which uses the information for flash exposure calculation and 3D Color Matrix II matrix metering.

- **DC.** The DC stands for defocus control, which allows managing the out-of-focus parts of an image to produce better-looking portraits and close-ups.

- **DX.** The DX lenses are designed for use with digital cameras using the APS-C–sized sensor having the 1.5X crop factor. The image circle they produce isn't large enough to fill up a full 35mm frame at all focal lengths, but they can be used on Nikon's full-frame models using the automatic/manual DX crop mode.

- **ED (or LD/UD).** The ED (extra low dispersion) designation indicates that some lens elements are made of a special hard and scratch-resistant glass that minimizes the divergence of the different colors of light as they pass through, thus reducing chromatic aberration (color "fringing") and other image defects. A gold band around the front of the lens indicates an optic with ED elements. You sometimes find LD (low dispersion) or UD (ultra-low dispersion) designations.

- **FX.** When Nikon introduced the Nikon D3 as its first full-frame camera, it coined the term "FX," representing the 23.9 × 36mm sensor format as a counterpart to "DX," which was used for its 15.8 × 23.6mm APS-C-sized sensors. Although FX hasn't been officially applied to any Nikon lenses so far, expect to see the designation used more often to differentiate between lenses that are compatible with any Nikon digital SLR (FX) and those that operate only on DX-format cameras, or in DX mode when used on an FX camera like the D700, D3, and D3x.

- **G.** G-type lenses have no aperture ring, and you can use them at other than the maximum aperture only with electronic cameras like the D90 that set the aperture automatically or by using the command dial while the Exposure Compensation/ Aperture button is depressed. This includes all Nikon digital dSLRs.

- **IF.** Nikon's *internal focusing* lenses change focus by shifting only small internal lens groups with no change required in the lens's physical length, unlike conventional double helicoid focusing systems that move all lens groups toward the front or rear during focusing. IF lenses are more compact and lighter in weight, provide better balance, focus more closely, and can be focused more quickly.

- **IX.** These lenses were produced for Nikon's long-discontinued Pronea 6i and S APS film cameras. While the Pronea could use many standard Nikon lenses, IX lenses cannot be mounted on any Nikon digital SLR.

- **Micro.** Nikon uses the term *micro* to designate its close-up lenses. Most other vendors use *macro* instead.

- **PC (Perspective Control).** A PC lens is capable of shifting the lens from side to side (and up/down) to provide a more realistic perspective when photographing architecture and other subjects that otherwise require tilting the camera so that the sensor plane is not parallel to the subject. Older Nikkor PC lenses offered shifting only, but more modern models, such as the PC-E Nikkor 24mm f/3.5D ED lens introduced early in 2008. allow both shifting and tilting.

- **UV.** This term is applied to special (and expensive) lenses designed to pass ultra-violet light.

- **UW.** Lenses with this designation are designed for underwater photography with Nikonos camera bodies, and cannot be used with Nikon digital SLRs.

- **VR.** Nikon has an expanding line of vibration reduction (VR) lenses, including several very affordable models and the AF-S DX Nikkor 16-85mm f/3.5-5.6G ED VR lens, which shifts lens elements internally to counteract camera shake. The VR feature allows using a shutter speed up to four stops slower than would be possible without vibration reduction.

What Lenses Can Do for You

No one can afford to buy even a percentage of the lenses available. The sanest approach to expanding your lens collection is to consider what each of your options can do for you and then choose the type of lens and specific model that will really boost your creative opportunities. So, in the sections that follow, I'm going to provide a general guide to the sort of capabilities you can gain for your D90 by adding a lens to your repertoire.

- **Wider perspective.** Your 18-105mm f/3.5-5.6, 18-55mm f/3.5-5.6, or 16-85mm f/4-5.6 lens has served you well for moderate wide-angle shots. Now you find your back is up against a wall and you *can't* take a step backwards to take in more subject matter. Perhaps you're standing on the rim of the Grand Canyon, and you want to take in as much of the breathtaking view as you can. You might find yourself just behind the baseline at a high-school basketball game and want an interesting shot with a little perspective distortion tossed in the mix.

- **Bring objects closer.** A long lens brings distant subjects closer to you, offers better control over depth-of-field, and avoids the perspective distortion that wide-angle lenses provide. They compress the apparent distance between objects in your frame. Don't forget that the Nikon D90's crop factor narrows the field of view of all these lenses, so your 70-300mm lens looks more like a 105mm-450mm zoom through the viewfinder. The image shown in Figure 6.5 was taken using a wide 16mm lens, while the image in Figures 6.6 and 6.7 were taken from the same position as Figure 6.4, but with focal lengths of 40mm and 85mm, respectively.

- **Bring your camera closer.** Macro lenses allow you to focus to within an inch or two of your subject. Nikon's best close-up lenses are all fixed focal length optics in the 60mm to 200mm range, but you'll find good macro zooms available from Sigma and others. They don't tend to focus quite as close, but they provide a bit of flexibility when you want to vary your subject distance (say, to avoid spooking a skittish creature).

- **Look sharp.** Many lenses are prized for their sharpness and overall image quality. While your run-of-the-mill lens is likely to be plenty sharp for most applications,

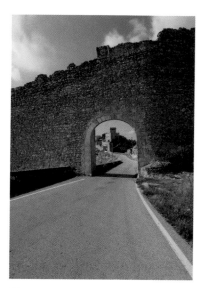

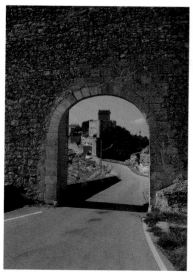

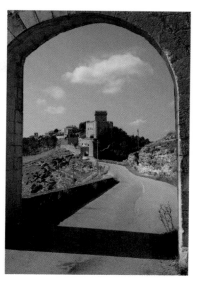

Figure 6.5 An ultrawide-angle lens provided this view of an 8th Century castle.

Figure 6.6 This photo, taken from roughly the same distance shows the view using a "normal" lens.

Figure 6.7 A medium telephoto lens captured this close-up view of the castle from approximately the same shooting position.

the very best optics are even better over their entire field of view (which means no fuzzy corners), are sharper at a wider range of focal lengths (in the case of zooms), and have better correction for various types of distortion. Of course, these lenses cost a great deal more (sometimes $1,000 or more each).

■ **More speed.** Your Nikon 70-300mm f/4.5-5.6 telephoto zoom lens might have the perfect focal length and sharpness for sports photography, but the maximum aperture won't cut it for night baseball or football games, or, even, any sports shooting in daylight if the weather is cloudy or you need to use some ungodly fast shutter speed, such as 1/4,000th second. You might be happier to gain a full f/stop with a AF-S Nikkor 300mm f/4D IF-ED for a little more than $1,000, mated to a 1.4x teleconverter (giving you a 420mm f/5.6 lens). Or, maybe you just need the speed and can benefit from an f/1.8 or f/1.4 prime lens. They're all available in Nikon mounts (there's even an 85mm f/1.4 and 50mm f/1.4 for the real speed demons). With any of these lenses you can continue photographing under the dimmest of lighting conditions without the need for a tripod or flash.

■ **Special features.** Accessory lenses give you special features, such as tilt/shift capabilities to correct for perspective distortion in architectural shots. You'll also find macro lenses, including the new AF-S Micro-Nikkor 60mm f/2.8G ED. Fisheye lenses like the AF DX Fisheye-Nikkor 10.5mm f/2.8G ED, and all other VR (vibration reduction) lenses also count as special-feature optics.

Zoom or Prime?

Zoom lenses have changed the way serious photographers take pictures. One of the reasons that I own 12 SLR film bodies dating back to the pre-zoom days is that in ancient times it was common to mount a different fixed focal length prime lens on various cameras and take pictures with two or three cameras around your neck (or tucked in a camera case) so you'd be ready to take a long shot or an intimate close-up or wide-angle view on a moment's notice, without the need to switch lenses. It made sense (at the time) to have a half-dozen or so bodies (two to use, one in the shop, one in transit, and a couple backups). Zoom lenses of the time had a limited zoom range, were heavy, and not very sharp (especially when you tried to wield one of those monsters handheld). That's all changed today. Smaller, longer, sharper zoom lenses, many with VR features, are available.

When selecting between zoom and prime lenses, there are several considerations to ponder. Here's a checklist of the most important factors. I already mentioned image quality and maximum aperture earlier, but those aspects take on additional meaning when comparing zooms and primes.

- **Logistics.** As prime lenses offer just a single focal length, you'll need more of them to encompass the full range offered by a single zoom. More lenses mean additional slots in your camera bag, and extra weight to carry. Just within Nikon's line alone you can choose from a good selection of general purpose (if you can count lenses that won't autofocus with the D90 as "general purpose") prime lenses in 28mm, 35mm, 50mm, 85mm, 100mm, 135mm, and 200mm focal lengths, all of which are overlapped by the 18-200mm zoom I mentioned earlier. Even so, you might be willing to carry an extra prime lens or two in order to gain the speed or image quality that lens offers.

- **Image quality.** Prime lenses usually produce better image quality at their focal length than even the most sophisticated zoom lenses at the same magnification. Zoom lenses, with their shifting elements and f/stops that can vary from zoom position to zoom position, are in general more complex to design than fixed focal length lenses. That's not to say that the very best prime lenses can't be complicated as well. However, the exotic designs, aspheric elements, and low-dispersion glass can be applied to improving the quality of the lens, rather than wasting a lot of it on compensating for problems caused by the zoom process itself.

- **Maximum aperture.** Because of the same design constraints, zoom lenses usually have smaller maximum apertures than prime lenses, and the most affordable zooms have a lens opening that grows effectively smaller as you zoom in. The difference in lens speed verges on the ridiculous at some focal lengths. For example, the 18mm-55mm basic zoom gives you a 55mm f/5.6 lens when zoomed all the way out, while prime lenses in that focal length commonly have f/1.8 or faster maximum apertures. Indeed, the fastest f/2, f/1.8, f1/4, and f/1.2 lenses are all manual focus primes (at least on the D90), and if you require speed, a fixed focal length lens is what you should rely on. Figure 6.8 shows an image taken with a Nikon 85mm f /1.8 lens.

■ **Speed.** Using prime lenses takes time and slows you down. It takes a few seconds to remove your current lens and mount a new one, and the more often you need to do that, the more time is wasted. If you choose not to swap lenses when using a fixed focal length lens you'll still have to move closer or farther away from your subject to get the field of view you want. A zoom lens allows you to change magnifications and focal lengths with the twist of a ring and generally saves a great deal of time.

Figure 6.8
An 85mm f/1.8 lens was perfect for this hand-held photo at a concert.

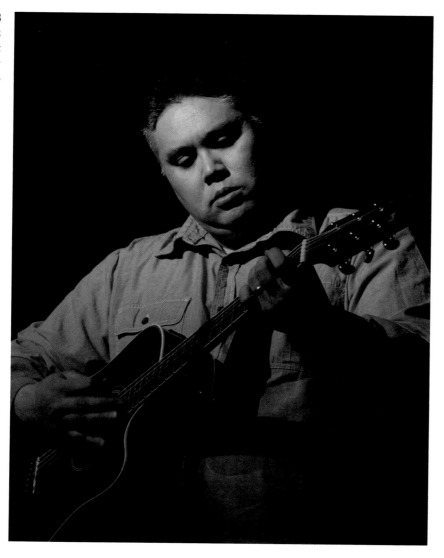

Categories of Lenses

Lenses can be categorized by their intended purpose—general photography, macro photography, and so forth—or by their focal length. The range of available focal lengths is usually divided into three main groups: wide-angle, normal, and telephoto. Prime lenses fall neatly into one of these classifications. Zooms can overlap designations, with a significant number falling into the catch-all wide-to-telephoto zoom range. This section provides more information about focal length ranges, and how they are used.

When the 1.5X crop factor (mentioned at the beginning of this chapter) is figured in, any lens with an equivalent focal length of 10mm to 16mm is said to be an *ultrawide-angle lens*; from about 16mm to 30mm is said to be a *wide-angle lens*. *Normal lenses* have a focal length roughly equivalent to the diagonal of the film or sensor, in millimeters, and so fall into the range of about 30mm to 40 on a D90. *Short telephoto lenses* start at about 40mm to 70mm, with anything from 70mm to 250 mm qualifying as a conventional *telephoto*. For the Nikon D90, anything from about 300mm-400mm or longer can be considered a *super-telephoto*.

Using Wide-Angle and Wide-Zoom Lenses

To use wide-angle prime lenses and wide zooms, you need to understand how they affect your photography. Here's a quick summary of the things you need to know.

- **More depth-of-field.** Practically speaking, wide-angle lenses offer more depth-of-field at a particular subject distance and aperture. (But see the sidebar below for an important note.) You'll find that helpful when you want to maximize sharpness of a large zone, but not very useful when you'd rather isolate your subject using selective focus (telephoto lenses are better for that).

- **Stepping back.** Wide-angle lenses have the effect of making it seem that you are standing farther from your subject than you really are. They're helpful when you don't want to back up, or can't because there are impediments in your way.

- **Wider field of view.** While making your subject seem farther away, as implied above, a wide-angle lens also provides a larger field of view, including more of the subject in your photos.

- **More foreground.** As background objects retreat, more of the foreground is brought into view by a wide-angle lens. That gives you extra emphasis on the area that's closest to the camera. Photograph your home with a normal lens/normal zoom setting, and the front yard probably looks fairly conventional in your photo (that's why they're called "normal" lenses). Switch to a wider lens and you'll discover that your lawn now makes up much more of the photo. So, wide-angle lenses are great when you want to emphasize that lake in the foreground, but problematic when your intended subject is located farther in the distance.

- **Super-sized subjects.** The tendency of a wide-angle lens to emphasize objects in the foreground, while de-emphasizing objects in the background can lead to a kind of size distortion that may be more objectionable for some types of subjects than others. Shoot a bed of flowers up close with a wide angle, and you might like the distorted effect of the larger blossoms nearer the lens. Take a photo of a family member with the same lens from the same distance, and you're likely to get some complaints about that gigantic nose in the foreground.

- **Perspective distortion.** When you tilt the camera so the plane of the sensor is no longer perpendicular to the vertical plane of your subject, some parts of the subject are now closer to the sensor than they were before, while other parts are farther away. So, buildings, flagpoles, or NBA players appear to be falling backwards, as you can see in Figure 6.9. While this kind of apparent distortion (it's not caused by a defect in the lens) can happen with any lens, it's most apparent when a wide angle is used.

Figure 6.9
Tilting the camera back produces this "falling back" look in architectural photos.

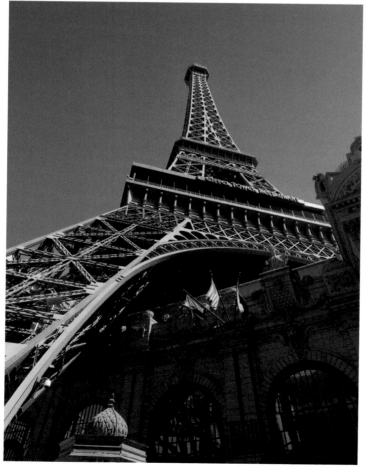

- **Steady cam.** You'll find that you can handhold a wide-angle lens at slower shutter speeds, without need for vibration reduction, than you can with a telephoto lens. The reduced magnification of the wide-lens or wide-zoom setting doesn't emphasize camera shake like a telephoto lens does.

- **Interesting angles.** Many of the factors already listed combine to produce more interesting angles when shooting with wide-angle lenses. Raising or lowering a telephoto lens a few feet probably will have little effect on the appearance of the distant subjects you're shooting. The same change in elevation can produce a dramatic effect for the much-closer subjects typically captured with a wide-angle lens or wide-zoom setting.

DOF IN DEPTH

The DOF advantage of wide-angle lenses is diminished when you enlarge your picture; believe it or not, a wide-angle image enlarged and cropped to provide the same subject size as a telephoto shot would have the *same* depth-of-field. Try it: take a wide-angle photo of a friend from a fair distance, and then zoom in to duplicate the picture in a telephoto image. Then, enlarge the wide shot so your friend is the same size in both. The wide photo will have the same depth-of-field (and will have much less detail, too).

Avoiding Potential Wide-Angle Problems

Wide-angle lenses have a few quirks that you'll want to keep in mind when shooting so you can avoid falling into some common traps. Here's a checklist of tips for avoiding common problems:

- **Symptom: converging lines.** Unless you want to use wildly diverging lines as a creative effect, it's a good idea to keep horizontal and vertical lines in landscapes, architecture, and other subjects carefully aligned with the sides, top, and bottom of the frame. That will help you avoid undesired perspective distortion. Sometimes it helps to shoot from a slightly elevated position so you don't have to tilt the camera up or down.

- **Symptom: color fringes around objects.** Lenses are often plagued with fringes of color around backlit objects, produced by *chromatic aberration*, which is produced when all the colors of light don't focus in the same plane or same lateral position (that is, the colors are offset to one side). This phenomenon is more common in wide-angle lenses and in photos of subjects with contrasty edges. Some kinds of chromatic aberration can be reduced by stopping down the lens, while all sorts can be reduced by using lenses with low diffraction index glass (or ED elements, in Nikon nomenclature) and by incorporating elements that cancel the chromatic aberration of other glass in the lens.

- **Symptom: lines that bow outward.** Some wide-angle lenses cause straight lines to bow outwards, with the strongest effect at the edges. In fisheye (or *curvilinear*) lenses, this defect is a feature, as you can see in Figure 6.10. When distortion is not desired, you'll need to use a lens that has corrected barrel distortion. Manufacturers like Nikon do their best to minimize or eliminate it (producing a *rectilinear* lens), often using *aspherical* lens elements (which are not cross-sections of a sphere). You can also minimize barrel distortion simply by framing your photo with some extra space all around, so the edges where the defect is most obvious can be cropped out of the picture. Some image editors, including Photoshop and Photoshop Elements and Nikon Capture NX, have a lens distortion correction feature.

- **Symptom: dark corners and shadows in flash photos.** The Nikon D90's built-in electronic flash is designed to provide even coverage for lenses as wide as 17mm. If you use a wider lens, you can expect darkening, or *vignetting*, in the corners of the frame. At wider focal lengths, the lens hood of some lenses (my 18mm-70mm lens is a prime offender) can cast a semi-circular shadow in the lower portion of the frame when using the built-in flash. Sometimes removing the lens hood or zooming in a bit can eliminate the shadow. Mounting an external flash unit, such as the mighty Nikon SB-900 can solve both problems, as this high-end flash unit (it costs almost half as much as the D90 camera) has zoomable coverage up to as wide as the field of view of a 14mm lens when used with the included adapter. Its higher vantage point eliminates the problem of lens-hood shadow, too.

Figure 6.10
Many wide-angle lenses cause lines to bow outwards toward the edges of the image; with a fisheye lens, this tendency is considered an interesting feature.

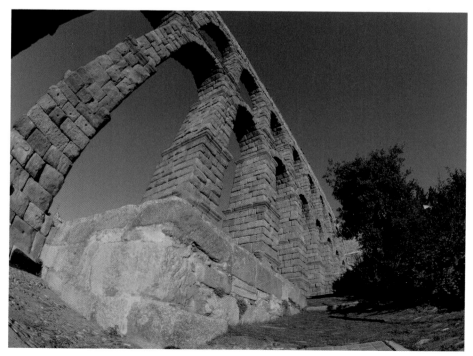

Using Telephoto and Tele-Zoom Lenses

Telephoto lenses also can have a dramatic effect on your photography, and Nikon is especially strong in the long-lens arena, with lots of choices in many focal lengths and zoom ranges. You should be able to find an affordable telephoto or tele-zoom to enhance your photography in several different ways. Here are the most important things you need to know. In the next section, I'll concentrate on telephoto considerations that can be problematic—and how to avoid those problems.

- **Selective focus.** Long lenses have reduced depth-of-field within the frame, allowing you to use selective focus to isolate your subject. You can open the lens up wide to create shallow depth-of-field, or close it down a bit to allow more to be in focus. The flip side of the coin is that when you *want* to make a range of objects sharp, you'll need to use a smaller f/stop to get the depth-of-field you need. Like fire, the depth-of-field of a telephoto lens can be friend or foe. Figure 6.11 shows a photo of a statue shot with a 200mm lens and a wider f/2.8 f/stop to de-emphasize the distracting background.

- **Getting closer.** Telephoto lenses bring you closer to wildlife, sports action, and candid subjects. No one wants to get a reputation as a surreptitious or "sneaky" photographer (except for paparazzi), but when applied to candids in an open and honest way, a long lens can help you capture memorable moments while retaining enough distance to stay out of the way of events as they transpire.

- **Reduced foreground/increased compression.** Telephoto lenses have the opposite effect of wide angles: they reduce the importance of things in the foreground by squeezing everything together. This compression even makes distant objects appear to be closer to subjects in the foreground and middle ranges. You can use this effect as a creative tool to squeeze subjects together.

- **Accentuates camera shakiness.** Telephoto focal lengths hit you with a double-whammy in terms of camera/photographer shake. The lenses themselves are bulkier, more difficult to hold steady, and may even produce a barely perceptible see-saw rocking effect when you support them with one hand halfway down the lens barrel. Telephotos also magnify any camera shake. It's no wonder that vibration reduction is popular in longer lenses.

- **Interesting angles require creativity.** Telephoto lenses require more imagination in selecting interesting angles, because the "angle" you do get on your subjects is so narrow. Moving from side to side or a bit higher or lower can make a dramatic difference in a wide-angle shot, but raising or lowering a telephoto lens a few feet probably will have little effect on the appearance of the distant subjects you're shooting.

Figure 6.11
A wide f/stop
helped isolate
the statue while
allowing the
background to
go out of focus.

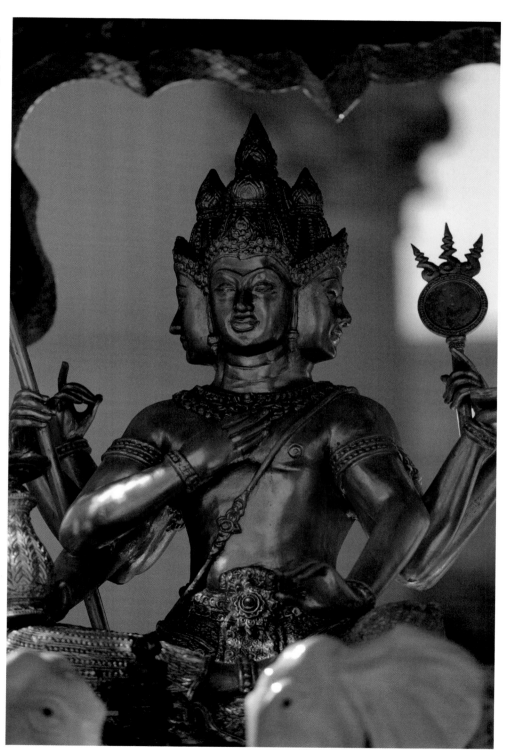

Avoiding Telephoto Lens Problems

Many of the "problems" that telephoto lenses pose are really just challenges and are not that difficult to overcome. Here is a list of the seven most common picture maladies and suggested solutions.

- **Symptom: flat faces in portraits.** Head-and-shoulders portraits of humans tend to be more flattering when a focal length of 50mm to 85mm is used. Longer focal lengths compress the distance between features like noses and ears, making the face look wider and flat. A wide angle might make noses look huge and ears tiny when you fill the frame with a face. So stick with 50mm to 85mm focal lengths, going longer only when you're forced to shoot from a greater distance, and wider only when shooting three-quarters/full-length portraits, or group shots.

- **Symptom: blur due to camera shake.** Use a higher shutter speed (boosting ISO if necessary), consider an image-stabilized lens, or mount your camera on a tripod, monopod, or brace it with some other support. Of those three solutions, only the first will reduce blur caused by *subject* motion; a VR lens or tripod won't help you freeze a racecar in mid-lap.

- **Symptom: color fringes.** Chromatic aberration is the most pernicious optical problem found in telephoto lenses. There are others, including spherical aberration, astigmatism, coma, curvature of field, and similarly scary-sounding phenomena. The best solution for any of these is to use a better lens that offers the proper degree of correction, or stop down the lens to minimize the problem. But that's not always possible. Your second-best choice may be to correct the fringing in your favorite RAW conversion tool or image editor. Photoshop's Lens Correction filter (found in the Filter menu's Distort submenu) offers sliders that minimize both red/cyan and blue/yellow fringing.

- **Symptom: lines that curve inwards.** Pincushion distortion is found in many telephoto lenses. You might find after a bit of testing that it is worse at certain focal lengths with your particular zoom lens. Like chromatic aberration, it can be partially corrected using tools like the correction tools built into Photoshop and Photoshop Elements. You can see an exaggerated example in Figure 6.12, especially at the upper-left edges where the walls and roof bend noticeably; pincushion distortion isn't always this obvious.

- **Symptom: low contrast from haze or fog.** When you're photographing distant objects, a long lens shoots through a lot more atmosphere, which generally is muddied up with extra haze and fog. That dirt or moisture in the atmosphere can reduce contrast and mute colors. Some feel that a skylight or UV filter can help, but this practice is mostly a holdover from the film days. Digital sensors are not sensitive enough to UV light for a UV filter to have much effect. So you should be prepared to boost contrast and color saturation in your Picture Controls menu or image editor if necessary.

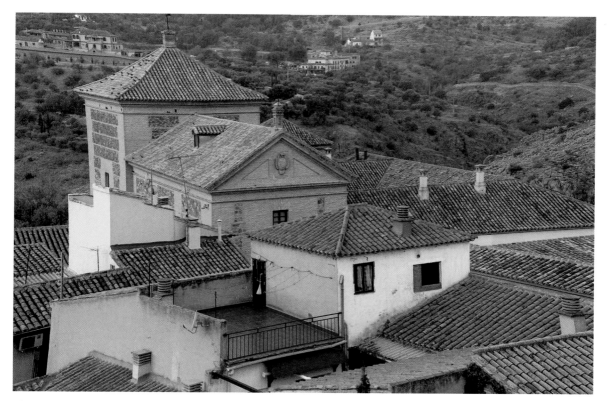

Figure 6.12 Pincushion distortion in telephoto lenses causes lines to bow inwards from the edges.

- **Symptom: low contrast from flare.** Lenses are furnished with lens hoods for a good reason: to reduce flare from bright light sources at the periphery of the picture area, or completely outside it. Because telephoto lenses often create images that are lower in contrast in the first place, you'll want to be especially careful to use a lens hood to prevent further effects on your image (or shade the front of the lens with your hand).

- **Symptom: dark flash photos.** Edge-to-edge flash coverage isn't a problem with telephoto lenses as it is with wide angles. The shooting distance is. A long lens might make a subject that's 50 feet away look as if it's right next to you, but your camera's flash isn't fooled. You'll need extra power for distant flash shots, and probably more power than your D90's built-in flash provides. The Nikon SB-900 speedlight, for example, can automatically zoom its coverage to illuminate the area captured by a 200mm telephoto lens, with three light distribution patterns (Standard, Center-Weighted, and Even). (Try *that* with the built-in flash!)

Telephotos and Bokeh

Bokeh describes the aesthetic qualities of the out-of-focus parts of an image and whether out-of-focus points of light—circles of confusion—are rendered as distracting fuzzy discs or smoothly fade into the background. *Boke* is a Japanese word for "blur," and the h was added to keep English speakers from rendering it monosyllabically to rhyme with *broke.* Although bokeh is visible in blurry portions of any image, it's of particular concern with telephoto lenses, which, thanks to the magic of reduced depth-of-field, produce more obviously out-of-focus areas.

Bokeh can vary from lens to lens, or even within a given lens depending on the f/stop in use. Bokeh becomes objectionable when the circles of confusion are evenly illuminated, making them stand out as distinct discs, or, worse, when these circles are darker in the center, producing an ugly "doughnut" effect. A lens defect called spherical aberration may produce out-of-focus discs that are brighter on the edges and darker in the center, because the lens doesn't focus light passing through the edges of the lens exactly as it does light going through the center. (Mirror or *catadioptric* lenses also produce this effect.)

Other kinds of spherical aberration generate circles of confusion that are brightest in the center and fade out at the edges, producing a smooth blending effect, as you can see at bottom in Figure 6.13. Ironically, when no spherical aberration is present at all, the discs are a uniform shade, which, while better than the doughnut effect, is not as pleasing as the bright center/dark edge rendition. The shape of the disc also comes into play, with round smooth circles considered the best, and nonagonal or some other polygon (determined by the shape of the lens diaphragm) considered less desirable.

If you plan to use selective focus a lot, you should investigate the bokeh characteristics of a particular lens before you buy. Nikon user groups and forums will usually be full of comments and questions about bokeh, so the research is fairly easy.

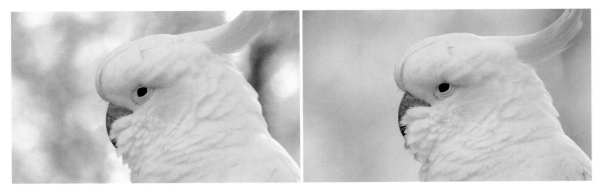

Figure 6.13 Bokeh is less pleasing when the discs are prominent left), and less obtrusive when they blend into the background (right).

Add-ons and Special Features

Once you've purchased your telephoto lens, you'll want to think about some appropriate accessories for it. There are some handy add-ons available that can be valuable. Here are a couple of them to think about.

Lens Hoods

Lens hoods are an important accessory for all lenses, but they're especially valuable with telephotos. As I mentioned earlier, lens hoods do a good job of preserving image contrast by keeping bright light sources outside the field of view from striking the lens and, potentially, bouncing around inside that long tube to generate flare that, when coupled with atmospheric haze, can rob your image of detail and snap. In addition, lens hoods serve as valuable protection for that large, vulnerable, front lens element. It's easy to forget that you've got that long tube sticking out in front of your camera and accidentally whack the front of your lens into something. It's cheaper to replace a lens hood than it is to have a lens repaired, so you might find that a good hood is valuable protection for your prized optics.

When choosing a lens hood, it's important to have the right hood for the lens, usually the one offered for that lens by Nikon or the third-party manufacturer. You want a hood that blocks precisely the right amount of light: neither too much light nor too little. A hood with a front diameter that is too small can show up in your pictures as vignetting. A hood that has a front diameter that's too large isn't stopping all the light it should. Generic lens hoods may not do the job.

When your telephoto is a zoom lens, it's even more important to get the right hood, because you need one that does what it is supposed to at both the wide-angle and telephoto ends of the zoom range. Lens hoods may be cylindrical, rectangular (shaped like the image frame), or petal shaped (that is, cylindrical, but with cut-out areas at the corners that correspond to the actual image area). Lens hoods should be mounted in the correct orientation (a bayonet mount for the hood usually takes care of this).

Telephoto Converters

Teleconverters (often called telephoto extenders outside the Nikon world), multiply the actual focal length of your lens, giving you a longer telephoto for much less than the price of a lens with that actual focal length. These converters fit between the lens and your camera and contain optical elements that magnify the image produced by the lens. Available in 1.4X, 1.7X, and 2.0X configurations from Nikon, a teleconverter transforms, say, a 200mm lens into a 280mm, 340mm, or 400mm optic, respectively. Given the D90's crop factor, your 200mm lens now has the same field of view as a 420mm, 510mm, or 600mm lens on a full-frame camera. At around $300-$400 each, converters are quite a bargain, aren't they?

The only drawback is that Nikon's TC II teleconverters can be used only with a limited number of Nikkor AF-S lenses. The compatible models include the 200mm f/2G ED-IF AF-S VR Nikkor, 300mm f/2.8G ED-IF AF-S VR Nikkor, 400mm f/2.8D ED-IF AF-S II Nikkor, 80-200mm f/2.8D ED-IF AF-S ,70-200mm f/2.8G ED-IF AF-S VR Zoom-Nikkor, 200-400mm f/4G ED-IF AF-S VR Zoom-Nikkor, 300mm f/4D ED-IF AF-S Nikkor, 500mm f/4D ED-IF AF-S II Nikkor, and 600mm f/4D ED-IF AF-S II Nikkor. These tend to be pricey (or ultra-pricey lenses). Teleconverters from Sigma, Kenko, Tamron, and others cost less, and may be compatible with a broader range of lenses. (They work especially well with lenses from the same vendor that produces the teleconverter.)

There are other downsides. While extenders retain the closest focusing distance of your original lens, autofocus is maintained only if the lens's original maximum aperture is f/4 or larger (for the 1.4X extender) or f/2.8 or larger (for the 2X extender). The components reduce the effective aperture of any lens they are used with, by one f/stop with the 1.4X converter, 1.5 f/stops with the 1.7X converter, and two f/stops with the 2X extender. So, your 200mm f/2.8 lens becomes a 280mm f/4 or 400mm f/5.6 lens. Although Nikon converters are precision optical devices, they do cost you a little sharpness, but that improves when you reduce the aperture by a stop or two. Each of the converters is compatible only with a particular set of lenses greater, so you'll want to check Nikon's compatibility chart to see if the component can be used with the lens you want to attach to it.

If your lenses are compatible and you're shooting under bright lighting conditions, the Nikon extenders make handy accessories. I recommend the 1.4X version because it robs you of very little sharpness and only one f/stop. The 1.7X version also works well, too, but I've found the 2X teleconverter to exact too much of a sharpness and speed penalty to be of much use.

Macro Focusing

Some telephotos and telephoto zooms available for the Nikon D90 have particularly close focusing capabilities, making them *macro* lenses. Of course, the object is not necessarily to get close (get too close and you'll find it difficult to light your subject). What you're really looking for in a macro lens is to magnify the apparent size of the subject in the final image. Camera-to-subject distance is most important when you want to back up farther from your subject (say, to avoid spooking skittish insects or small animals). In that case, you'll want a macro lens with a longer focal length to allow that distance while retaining the desired magnification.

Nikon makes five lenses that are officially designated as macro lenses. They include:

- **AF-S Micro-Nikkor 60mm f/2.8G ED.** This new type-G lens supposedly replaces the type-D lens listed next, adding an internal Silent Wave autofocus motor that should operate faster, and which is also compatible with cameras lacking a body motor, such as the Nikon D40/D40x, D60, D5000, and D3000. It also has ED lens elements for improved image quality. However, because it lacks an aperture ring, you can control the f/stop only when the lens is mounted directly on the camera or used with automatic extension tubes. Should you want to reverse a macro lens using a special adapter (the Nikon BR2-A ring) to improve image quality or mount it on a bellows, you're better off with a lens having an aperture ring.

■ **AF Micro-Nikkor 60mm f/2.8D.** This non-AF-S lens won't autofocus on the Nikon D90, but, then, you might be manually focusing most of the time when shooting close-ups, and may appreciate the lower cost of an "obsolete" lens.

■ **AF-S VR Micro-Nikkor 105mm f/2.8G IF-ED.** This G-series lens did replace a similar D-type, non-AF-S version that also lacked VR. I own the older lens, too, and am keeping it because I find VR a rather specialized tool for macro work. Some 99 percent of the time, I shoot close-ups with my D90 mounted on a tripod or, at the very least, on a monopod, so camera vibration is not much of a concern. Indeed, *subject* movement is a more serious problem, especially when shooting plant life outdoors on days plagued with even slight breezes. Because my outdoor subjects are likely to move while I am composing my photo, I find both VR and autofocus not very useful. I end up focusing manually most of the time, too. This lens provides a little extra camera-to-subject distance, so you'll find it very useful, but consider the older non-G, non-VR version, too, if you're in the market and don't mind losing autofocus features.

■ **AF Micro-Nikkor 200mm f/4D IF-ED.** With a price tag of about $1,300, you'd probably want this lens only if you planned a great deal of close-up shooting at greater distances. It focuses down to 1.6 feet, and is manual-focus only with the D90, but provides enough magnification to allow interesting close-ups of subjects that are farther away. A specialized tool for specialized shooting.

■ **PC Micro-Nikkor 85mm f/2.8D.** Priced about the same as the 200mm Micro-Nikkor, this is a manual focus lens (on *any* camera; it doesn't offer autofocus features) that has both tilt and shift capabilities, so you can adjust the perspective of the subject as you shoot. The tilt feature lets you "tilt" the plane of focus, providing the illusion of greater depth-of-field, while the shift capabilities make it possible to shoot down on a subject from an angle and still maintain its correct proportions. If you need one of these for perspective control, you already know it; if you're still wondering how you'd use one, you probably have no need for these specialized capabilities. However, I have recently watched some very creative fashion and wedding photographers use this lens for portraits, applying the tilting features to throw parts of the image wildly out of focus to concentrate interest on faces, and so forth. None of these are likely pursuits of the average Nikon D90 photographer, but I couldn't resist mentioning this interesting lens.

You'll also find macro lenses, macro zooms, and other close-focusing lenses available from Sigma, Tamron, and Tokina. If you want to focus closer with a macro lens, or any other lens, you can add an accessory called an *extension tube*, like the one shown in Figure 6.14, or a *bellows extension*. These add-ons move the lens farther from the focal plane, allowing it to focus more closely. Nikon also sells add-on close-up lenses, which look like filters, and allow lenses to focus more closely.

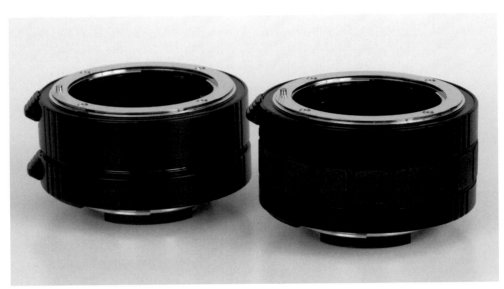

Figure 6.14
Extension tubes enable any lens to focus more closely to the subject.

Vibration Reduction

Nikon has a burgeoning line of more than 15 lenses with built-in vibration reduction (VR) capabilities. I probably shouldn't have mentioned a specific number, because I expect another half dozen or so new VR lenses to be introduced rather early in the life of this book.

The VR feature uses lens elements that are shifted internally in response to vertical or horizontal motion of the lens, which compensates for any camera shake in those directions. Vibration reduction is particularly effective when used with telephoto lenses, which magnify the effects of camera and photographer motion. However, VR can be useful for lenses of shorter focal lengths, such as Nikon's 16-85mm, 18-105mm, and 18-55mm VR lenses. Other Nikon VR lenses provide stabilization with zooms that are as wide as 24mm.

VIBRATION REDUCTION: IN THE CAMERA OR IN THE LENS?

The adoption of image stabilization/anti-shake technology into the camera bodies of models from Sony, Olympus, Pentax, and Samsung has revived an old debate about whether VR belongs in the camera or in the lens. Perhaps it's my Nikon bias showing, but I am quite happy not to have vibration reduction available in the body itself. Here are some reasons:

- Should in-camera VR fail, you have to send the whole camera in for repair, and camera repairs are generally more expensive than lens repairs. I like being able to simply switch to another lens if I have a VR problem.

- VR in the camera doesn't steady your view in the viewfinder, whereas a VR lens shows you a steadied image as you shoot.

- You're stuck with the VR system built in to your camera. If an improved system is incorporated into a lens and the improvements are important to you, just trade in your old lens for the new one.

- When building VR in the camera, a compromise system that works with all lenses must be designed. VR in the lens, however, can be custom-tailored to each specific lens's needs.

Vibration reduction offers two to three shutter speed increments' worth of shake reduction. (Nikon claims a four-stop gain, which I feel may be optimistic.) This extra margin can be invaluable when you're shooting under dim lighting conditions or handholding a lens for, say, wildlife photography. Perhaps that shot of a foraging deer would require a shutter speed of 1/2,000th second at f/5.6 with your AF-S VR Zoom-Nikkor 200-400mm f/4G IF-ED lens. Relax. You can shoot at 1/250th second at f/11 and get a photo that is just as sharp, as long as the deer doesn't decide to bound off. Or, perhaps you're shooting indoors and would prefer to shoot at 1/15th second at f/4. Your 16mm-85mm VR lens can grab the shot for you at its wide-angle position. However, consider these facts:

- **VR doesn't freeze subject motion.** Vibration reduction won't freeze moving subjects in their tracks, because it is effective only at compensating for *camera* motion. It's best used in reduced illumination, to steady the up-down swaying of telephoto lenses, and to improve close-up photography. If your subject is in motion, you'll still need a shutter speed that's fast enough to stop the action.

- **VR adds to shutter lag.** The process of adjusting the lens elements, like autofocus, takes time, so vibration reduction may contribute to a slight increase in shutter lag. If you're shooting sports, that delay may be annoying, but I still use my VR lenses for sports all the time!

- **Use when appropriate.** You may find that your results are worse when using VR while panning, although newer Nikon VR lenses work fine when the camera is deliberately moved from side to side during exposure. Older lenses can confuse the panning motion with camera wobble and provide too much compensation. You might want to switch off VR when panning or when your camera is mounted on a tripod.

- **Do you need VR at all?** Remember that an inexpensive monopod might be able to provide the same additional steadiness as a VR lens, at a much lower cost. If you're out in the field shooting wild animals or flowers and think a tripod isn't practical, try a monopod first.

The AF-S VR Zoom-Nikkor 70-200mm f/2.8G IF-ED, though atypical for the average D90 owner, is typical of the VR lenses Nikon offers, so I'll use it as an example. It has the basic controls shown in Figure 6.15, to adjust focus range (full, or limited to infinity down to 2.5 meters); VR On/Off, and Normal VR/Active VR (the latter an aggressive mode used in extreme situations, such as a moving car). Not visible (it's over the horizon, so to speak) is the M/A-M focus mode switch, which allows changing from autofocus (with manual override) to manual focus.

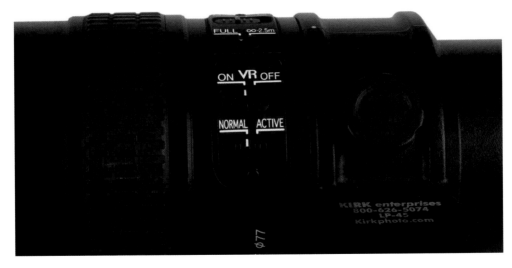

Figure 6.15
On the Nikon 70-200mm VR zoom you'll find (top to bottom): the focus limit switch, VR on/off switch, and Normal/Active VR adjustment.

7

Making Light Work for You

Successful photographers and artists have an intimate understanding of the importance of light in shaping an image. Rembrandt was a master of using light to create moods and reveal the character of his subjects. Artist Thomas Kinkade's official tagline is "Painter of Light." The late Dean Collins, co-founder of Finelight Studios, revolutionized how a whole generation of photographers learned and used lighting. While writing this book, I attended a seminar called "Captivated by the Light," run by photo guru Ed Pierce. It's impossible to underestimate how the use of light adds to—and how misuse can detract from—your photographs.

All forms of visual art use light to shape the finished product. Sculptors don't have control over the light used to illuminate their finished work, so they must create shapes using planes and curved surfaces so that the form envisioned by the artist comes to life from a variety of viewing and lighting angles. Painters, in contrast, have absolute control over both shape and light in their work, as well as the viewing angle, so they can use both the contours of their two-dimensional subjects and the qualities of the "light" they use to illuminate those subjects to evoke the image they want to produce.

Photography is a third form of art. The photographer may have little or no control over the subject (other than posing human subjects) but can often adjust both viewing angle *and* the nature of the light source to create a particular compelling image. The direction and intensity of the light sources create the shapes and textures that we see. The distribution and proportions determine the contrast and tonal values: whether the image is stark or high key, or muted and low in contrast. The colors of the light (because even "white" light has a color balance that the sensor can detect), and how much of those colors the subject reflects or absorbs, paint the hues visible in the image.

As a Nikon D90 photographer, you must learn to be a painter and sculptor of light if you want to move from *taking* a picture to *making* a photograph. This chapter provides an introduction to using the two main types of illumination: *continuous* lighting (such as daylight, incandescent, or fluorescent sources) and the brief, but brilliant snippets of light we call *electronic flash.*

Continuous Illumination versus Electronic Flash

Continuous lighting is exactly what you might think: uninterrupted illumination that is available all the time during a shooting session. Daylight, moonlight, and the artificial lighting encountered both indoors and outdoors count as continuous light sources (although all of them can be "interrupted" by passing clouds, solar eclipses, a blown fuse, or simply by switching off a lamp). Indoor continuous illumination includes both the lights that are there already (such as incandescent lamps or overhead fluorescent lights indoors) and fixtures you supply yourself, including photoflood lamps or reflectors used to bounce existing light onto your subject.

The surge of light we call electronic flash are produced by a burst of photons generated by an electrical charge that is accumulated in a component called a *capacitor* and then directed through a glass tube containing xenon gas, which absorbs the energy and emits the brief flash. Electronic flash is notable because it can be much more intense than continuous lighting, lasts only a brief moment, and can be much more portable than supplementary incandescent sources. It's a light source you can carry with you and use anywhere.

Indeed, your D90 has a flip-up electronic flash unit built in, as shown in Figure 7.1. But you can also use an external flash, either mounted on the D90's accessory shoe or used off-camera and linked with a cable or triggered by a slave light (which sets off a flash when it senses the firing of another unit). Studio flash units are electronic flash, too, and aren't limited to "professional" shooters, as there are economical "monolight" (one-piece flash/power supply) units available in the $200 price range. Anyone can buy a couple to store in a closet and use to set up a home studio, or use as supplementary lighting when traveling away from home. You'll need a remote trigger mounted on the D90's accessory/hot shoe, or an accessory/hot shoe-to-PC connector adapter to use studio flash with your camera.

Figure 7.1
One form of
light that's
always available
is the flip-up
flash on your
D90.

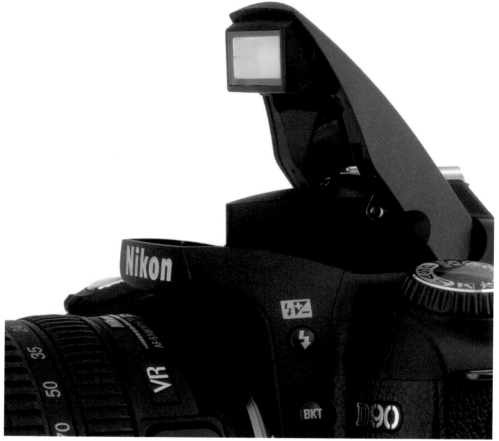

There are advantages and disadvantages to each type of illumination. Here's a quick checklist of pros and cons:

- **Lighting preview—Pro: continuous lighting.** With continuous lighting, you always know exactly what kind of lighting effect you're going to get and, if multiple lights are used, how they will interact with each other, as shown in Figure 7.2. With electronic flash, the general effect you're going to see may be a mystery until you've built some experience, and you may need to review a shot on the LCD, make some adjustments, and then reshoot to get the look you want. (In this sense, a digital camera's review capabilities replace the Polaroid test shots pro photographers relied on in decades past.)

- **Exposure calculation—Pro: continuous lighting.** Your D90 has no problem calculating exposure for continuous lighting, because it remains constant and can be measured through a sensor that interprets the light reaching the viewfinder. The amount of light available just before the exposure will, in almost all cases, be the

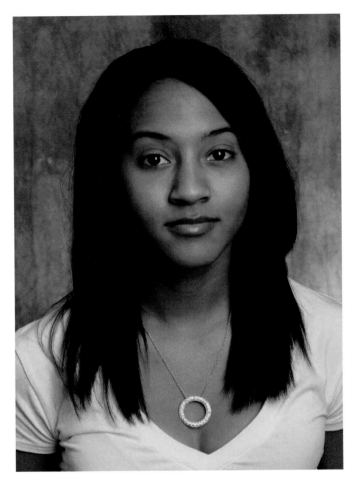

Figure 7.2
You always know how the lighting will look when using continuous illumination.

same amount of light present when the shutter is released. The D90's Spot metering mode can be used to measure and compare the proportions of light in the highlights and shadows, so you can make an adjustment (such as using more or less fill light) if necessary. You can even use a handheld light meter to measure the light yourself.

■ **Exposure calculation—Con: electronic flash.** Electronic flash illumination doesn't exist until the flash fires, and so it can't be measured by the D90's exposure sensor when the mirror is flipped up during the exposure. Instead, the light must be measured by metering the intensity of a preflash that is triggered an instant before the main flash, as it is reflected back to the camera and through the lens. An alternative is to use a sensor built into the flash itself and measure reflected light that has not traveled through the lens. If you have a do-it-yourself bent, there are handheld flash meters, too, including models that measure both flash and continuous light.

- **Evenness of illumination—Pro/con: continuous lighting.** Of continuous light sources, daylight, in particular, provides illumination that tends to fill an image completely, lighting up the foreground, background, and your subject almost equally. Shadows do come into play, of course, so you might need to use reflectors or fill-in light sources to even out the illumination further, but barring objects that block large sections of your image from daylight, the light is spread fairly evenly. Indoors, however, continuous lighting is commonly less evenly distributed. The average living room, for example, has hot spots and dark corners. But on the plus side, you can *see* this uneven illumination and compensate with additional lamps:

- **Evenness of illumination—Con: electronic flash.** Electronic flash units (like continuous light sources such as lamps that don't have the advantage of being located 93 million miles from the subject) suffer from the effects of their proximity. The *inverse square law*, first applied to both gravity and light by Sir Isaac Newton, dictates that as a light source's distance increases from the subject, the amount of light reaching the subject falls off proportionately to the square of the distance. In plain English, that means that a flash or lamp that's eight feet away from a subject provides only one-quarter as much illumination as a source that's four feet away (rather than half as much). (See Figure 7.3.) This translates into relatively shallow "depth-of-light."

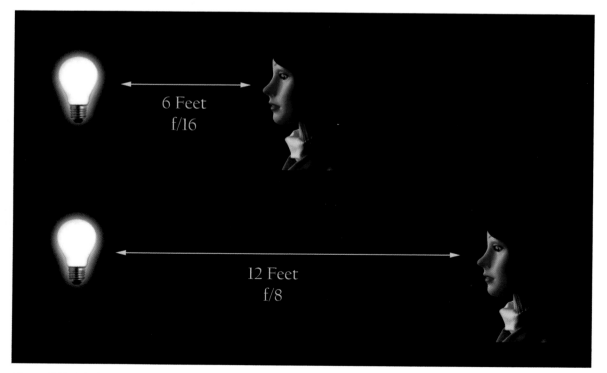

Figure 7.3 A light source that is twice as far away provides only one-quarter as much illumination.

- **Action stopping—Con: continuous lighting.** Action stopping with continuous light sources is completely dependent on the shutter speed you've dialed in on the camera. And the speeds available are dependent on the amount of light available and your ISO sensitivity setting. Outdoors in daylight, there will probably be enough sunlight to let you shoot at 1/2,000th second and f/6.3 with a non-grainy sensitivity setting of ISO 400. That's a fairly useful combination of settings if you're not using a super-telephoto with a small maximum aperture. But inside, the reduced illumination quickly has you pushing your D90 to its limits. For example, if you're shooting indoor sports, there probably won't be enough available light to allow you to use a 1/2,000th second shutter speed (although I routinely shoot indoor basketball with my D90 at ISO 1600 and 1/500 second at f/4). In many indoor sports situations, you may find yourself limited to 1/500 second or slower.

- **Action stopping—Pro: electronic flash.** When it comes to the ability to freeze moving objects in their tracks, the advantage goes to electronic flash. The brief duration of electronic flash serves as a very high "shutter speed" when the flash is the main or only source of illumination for the photo. Your D90's shutter speed may be set for 1/200th second during a flash exposure, but if the flash illumination predominates, the *effective* exposure time will be the 1/1,000 to 1/50,000 second or less duration of the flash, as you can see in Figure 7.4, because the flash unit reduces

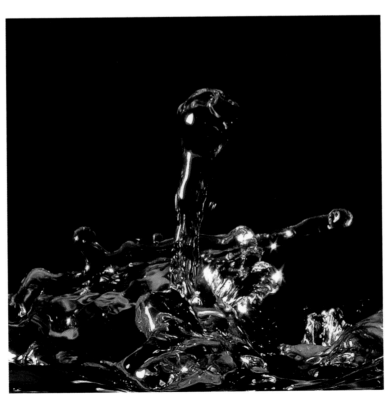

Figure 7.4
Electronic flash can freeze almost any action.

the amount of light released by cutting short the duration of the flash. The only fly in the ointment is that, if the ambient light is strong enough, it may produce a secondary, "ghost" exposure, as I'll explain later in this chapter.

- **Cost—Pro: continuous lighting.** Incandescent or fluorescent lamps are generally much less expensive than electronic flash units, which can easily cost several hundred dollars. I've used everything from desktop hi-intensity lamps to reflector flood lights for continuous illumination at very little cost. There are lamps made especially for photographic purposes, too, priced up to $50 or so. Maintenance is economical, too: many incandescent or fluorescents use bulbs that cost only a few dollars.

- **Cost—Con: electronic flash.** Electronic flash units aren't particularly cheap. The lowest-cost dedicated flash designed specifically for the Nikon dSLRs is about $110. Such units are limited in features, however, and intended for those with entry-level cameras. Plan on spending some money to get the features that a sophisticated electronic flash offers.

- **Flexibility—Con: continuous lighting.** Because incandescent and fluorescent lamps are not as bright as electronic flash, the slower shutter speeds required (see Action stopping, on the previous page) mean that you may have to use a tripod more often, especially when shooting portraits. The incandescent variety of continuous lighting gets hot, especially in the studio, and the side effects range from discomfort (for your human models) to disintegration (if you happen to be shooting perishable foods like ice cream). The heat also makes it more difficult to add filtration to incandescent sources.

- **Flexibility—Pro: electronic flash.** Electronic flash's action-freezing power allows you to work without a tripod in the studio (and elsewhere), adding flexibility and speed when choosing angles and positions. Flash units can be easily filtered, and, because the filtration is placed over the light source rather than the lens, you don't need to use high-quality filter material. For example, a couple sheets of unexposed, processed Ektachrome film can make a dandy infrared-pass filter for your flash unit. Roscoe or Lee lighting gels, which may be too flimsy to use in front of the lens, can be mounted or taped in front of your flash with ease.

Continuous Lighting Basics

While continuous lighting and its effects are generally much easier to visualize and use than electronic flash, there are some factors you need to take into account, particularly the color temperature of the light. (Color temperature concerns aren't exclusive to continuous light sources, of course, but the variations tend to be more extreme and less predictable than those of electronic flash, which output relatively consistent daylight-like illumination.)

Color temperature, in practical terms, is how "bluish" or how "reddish" the light appears to be to the digital camera's sensor. Indoor illumination is quite warm, comparatively, and appears reddish to the sensor. Daylight, in contrast, seems much bluer to the sensor. Our eyes (our brains, actually) are quite adaptable to these variations, so white objects don't appear to have an orange tinge when viewed indoors, nor do they seem excessively blue outdoors in full daylight. Yet, these color temperature variations are real and the sensor is not fooled. To capture the most accurate colors, we need to take the color temperature into account in setting the color balance (or *white balance*) of the D90—either automatically using the camera's smarts or manually using our own knowledge and experience.

When using the Nikon D90, you don't need to think in terms of actual color temperature (although you can measure existing color temperature using the Preset feature described later), because the camera won't let you set white balance using color temperature values, which are measured in *degrees Kelvin.* But it is useful to know that warmer (more reddish) color temperatures (measured in degrees Kelvin) are the *lower* numbers, while cooler (bluer) color temperatures are *higher* numbers. It might not make sense to say that 3,400K is warmer than 6,000K, but that's the way it is. If it helps, think of a glowing red ember contrasted with a white-hot welder's torch, rather than fire and ice.

You can set white balance by type of illumination, and then fine-tune it in the D90 using the Shooting menu's White Balance option, as described in Chapter 3. In most cases, however, the Nikon D90 will do an acceptable job of calculating white balance for you, so Auto can be used as your choice most of the time. Use the preset values or set a custom white balance that matches the current shooting conditions when you need to. The only really problematic light sources are likely to be fluorescents. Vendors, such as GE and Sylvania, may actually provide a figure known as the *color rendering index* (or CRI), which is a measure of how accurately a particular light source represents standard colors, using a scale of 0 (some sodium-vapor lamps) to 100 (daylight and most incandescent lamps). Daylight fluorescents and deluxe cool white fluorescents might have a CRI of about 79 to 95, which is perfectly acceptable for most photographic applications. Warm white fluorescents might have a CRI of 55. White deluxe mercury vapor lights are less suitable with a CRI of 45, while low-pressure sodium lamps can vary from CRI 0-18.

Remember that if you shoot RAW, you can specify the white balance of your image when you import it into Photoshop, Photoshop Elements, or another image editor using Nikon Capture NX, Adobe Camera Raw, or your preferred RAW converter. While color-balancing filters that fit on the front of the lens exist, they are primarily useful for film cameras, because film's color balance can't be tweaked as extensively as that of a sensor.

Daylight

Daylight is produced by the sun, and so is moonlight (which is just reflected sunlight). Daylight is present, of course, even when you can't see the sun. When sunlight is direct, it can be bright and harsh. If daylight is diffused by clouds, softened by bouncing off objects such as walls or your photo reflectors, or filtered by shade, it can be much dimmer and less contrasty.

Daylight's color temperature can vary quite widely. It is highest in temperature (most blue) at noon when the sun is directly overhead, because the light is traveling through a minimum amount of the filtering layer we call the atmosphere. The color temperature at high noon may be 6,000K. At other times of day, the sun is lower in the sky and the particles in the air provide a filtering effect that warms the illumination to about 5,500K for most of the day. Starting an hour before dusk and for an hour after sunrise, the warm appearance of the sunlight is even visible to our eyes when the color temperature may dip to 5,000-4,500K, as shown in Figure 7.5.

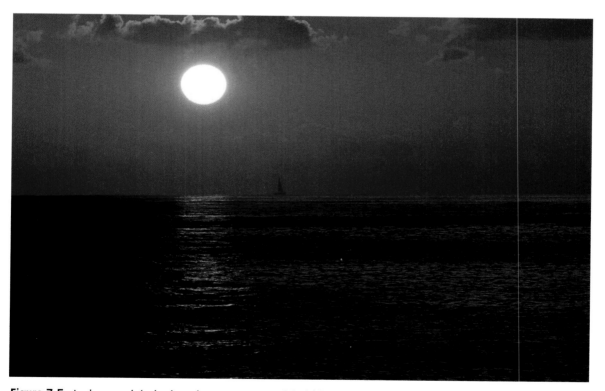

Figure 7.5 At dawn and dusk, the color temperature of daylight may dip as low as 4,500K, and at sunset can go even lower.

Incandescent/Tungsten Light

The term incandescent or tungsten illumination is usually applied to the direct descendents of Thomas Edison's original electric lamp. Such lights consist of a glass bulb that contains a vacuum, or is filled with a halogen gas, and contains a tungsten filament that is heated by an electrical current, producing photons and heat. Tungsten-halogen lamps are a variation on the basic light bulb, using a more rugged (and longer-lasting) filament that can be heated to a higher temperature, housed in a thicker glass or quartz envelope, and filled with iodine or bromine ("halogen") gases. The higher temperature allows tungsten-halogen (or quartz-halogen/quartz-iodine, depending on their construction) lamps to burn "hotter" and whiter. Although popular for automobile headlamps today, they've also been used for photographic illumination.

The other qualities of this type of lighting, such as contrast, are dependent on the distance of the lamp from the subject, type of reflectors used, and other factors that I'll explain later in this chapter.

Fluorescent Light/Other Light Sources

Fluorescent light has some advantages in terms of illumination, but some disadvantages from a photographic standpoint. This type of lamp generates light through an electrochemical reaction that emits most of its energy as visible light, rather than heat, which is why the bulbs don't get as hot. The type of light produced varies depending on the phosphor coatings and type of gas in the tube. So, the illumination fluorescent bulbs produce can vary widely in its characteristics.

That's not great news for photographers. Different types of lamps have different "color temperatures" that can't be precisely measured in degrees Kelvin, because the light isn't produced by heating. Worse, fluorescent lamps have a discontinuous spectrum of light that can have some colors missing entirely. A particular type of tube can lack certain shades of red or other colors (see Figure 7.6), which is why fluorescent lamps and other alternative technologies such as sodium-vapor illumination can produce ghastly looking human skin tones if the white balance isn't set correctly. Their spectra can lack the reddish tones we associate with healthy skin and emphasize the blues and greens popular in horror movies.

There *is* good news, however. There are special fluorescent lamps compatible with the Spiderlites sold through dealers affiliated with the F. J. Westcott Company (www.fjwestcott.com), designed especially for photography, with the color balance and other properties required. They can be used for direct light, placed in softboxes (described later), and used in other ways.

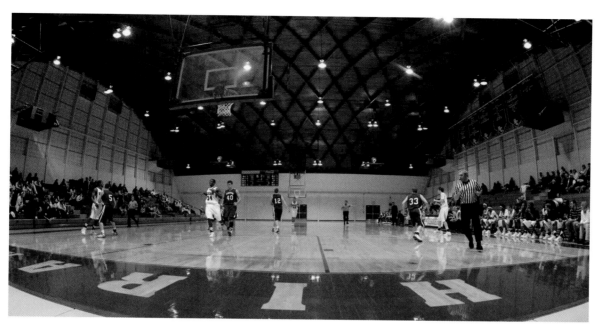

Figure 7.6 The uncorrected lighting in the gym added a distinct greenish cast to this image when exposed with a daylight white balance setting.

Adjusting White Balance

I showed you how to adjust white balance in Chapter 3, using the D90's built-in presets, white balance shift capabilities, and white balance bracketing (there's more on bracketing in Chapter 4, too).

In most cases, however, the D90 will do a good job of calculating white balance for you, so Auto can be used as your choice most of the time. Use the preset values or set a custom white balance that matches the current shooting conditions when you need to. The only really problematic light sources are likely to be fluorescents. Vendors, such as GE and Sylvania, may actually provide a figure known as the *color rendering index* (or CRI), which is a measure of how accurately a particular light source represents standard colors, using a scale of 0 (some sodium-vapor lamps) to 100 (daylight and most incandescent lamps). Daylight fluorescents and deluxe cool white fluorescents might have a CRI of about 79 to 95, which is perfectly acceptable for most photographic applications. Warm white fluorescents might have a CRI of 55. White deluxe mercury vapor lights are less suitable with a CRI of 45, while low-pressure sodium lamps can vary from CRI 0-18.

Remember that if you shoot RAW, you can specify the white balance of your image when you import it into Photoshop, Photoshop Elements, or another image editor using your preferred RAW converter. While color-balancing filters that fit on the front of the lens exist, they are primarily useful for film cameras, because film's color balance can't be tweaked as extensively as that of a sensor.

Electronic Flash Basics

Until you delve into the situation deeply enough, it might appear that serious photographers have a love/hate relationship with electronic flash. You'll often hear that flash photography is less natural looking, and that the built-in flash in most cameras should never be used as the primary source of illumination because it provides a harsh, garish look. Indeed, most "pro" cameras like the Nikon D3/D3x don't have a built-in flash at all. Available ("continuous") lighting is praised, and built-in flash photography seems to be roundly denounced.

In truth, however, the bias is against *bad* flash photography. Indeed, flash has become the studio light source of choice for pro photographers, because it's more intense (and its intensity can be varied to order by the photographer), freezes action, frees you from using a tripod (unless you want to use one to lock down a composition), and has a snappy, consistent light quality that matches daylight. (While color balance changes as the flash duration shortens, some Nikon flash units can communicate to the camera the exact white balance provided for that shot.) And even pros will cede that the built-in flash of the Nikon D90 has some important uses as an adjunct to existing light, particularly to illuminate dark shadows using a technique called *fill flash*.

But electronic flash isn't as inherently easy to use as continuous lighting. As I noted earlier, electronic flash units are more expensive, don't show you exactly what the lighting effect will be (unless you use a second source called a *modeling light* for a preview), and the exposure of electronic flash units is more difficult to calculate accurately.

How Electronic Flash Works

The bursts of light we call electronic flash are produced by a flash of photons generated by an electrical charge that is accumulated in a component called a *capacitor* and then directed through a glass tube containing xenon gas, which absorbs the energy and emits the brief flash. For the pop-up flash built into the D90, the full burst of light lasts about 1/1,000th second and provides enough illumination to shoot a subject 10 feet away at f/4 using the ISO 100 setting. In a more typical situation, you'd use ISO 200, f/5.6 to f/8 and photograph something 8 to 10 feet away. As you can see, the built-in flash is somewhat limited in range; you'll see why external flash units are often a good idea later in this chapter.

An electronic flash (whether built in or connected to the D90 through a cable plugged into a hot shoe adapter) is triggered at the instant of exposure, during a period when the sensor is fully exposed by the shutter. As I mentioned earlier in this book, the D90 has a vertically traveling shutter that consists of two curtains. The first curtain opens and moves to the opposite side of the frame, at which point the shutter is completely open. The flash can be triggered at this point (so-called *first-curtain sync*), making the flash exposure. Then, after a delay that can vary from 30 seconds to 1/200th second (with the D90; other cameras may sync at a faster or slower speed), a second curtain begins moving across the sensor plane, covering up the sensor again. If the flash is triggered just before the second curtain starts to close, then *second-curtain sync* is used. In both cases, though, a shutter speed of 1/200th second is the maximum that can be used to take a photo.

Figure 7.7 illustrates how this works, with a fanciful illustration of a generic shutter (your D90's shutter does *not* look like this, and some vertically traveling shutters move bottom to top rather than the top-to-bottom motion shown). Both curtains are tightly closed at upper left. At upper right, the first curtain begins to move downwards, starting to expose a narrow slit that reveals the sensor behind the shutter. At lower left, the first curtain moves downwards farther until, as you can see at lower right in the figure, the sensor is fully exposed.

When first-curtain sync is used, the flash is triggered at the instant that the sensor is completely exposed. The shutter then remains open for an additional length of time (from 30 seconds to 1/200th second), and the second curtain begins to move downward, covering the sensor once more. When second-curtain sync is activated, the flash is triggered *after* the main exposure is over, just before the second curtain begins to move downward.

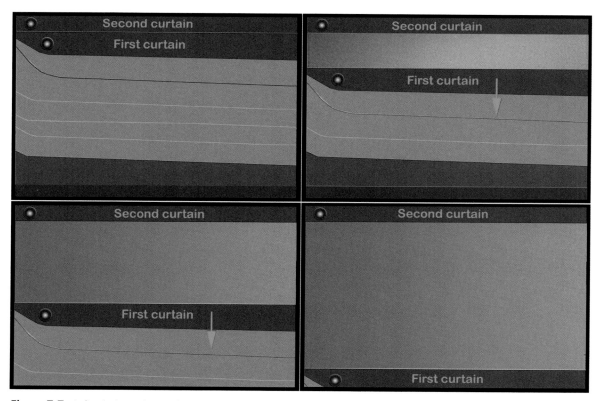

Figure 7.7 A focal plane shutter has two curtains, the lower, or front curtain, and an upper, second curtain.

Ghost Images

The difference between triggering the flash when the shutter just opens, or just when it begins to close might not seem like much. But whether you use first-curtain sync (the default setting) or second-curtain sync (an optional setting) can make a significant difference to your photograph *if the ambient light in your scene also contributes to the image.*

At faster shutter speeds, particularly 1/200th second, there isn't much time for the ambient light to register, unless it is very bright. It's likely that the electronic flash will provide almost all the illumination, so first-curtain sync or second-curtain sync isn't very important. However, at slower shutter speeds, or with very bright ambient light levels, there is a significant difference, particularly if your subject is moving, or the camera isn't steady.

In any of those situations, the ambient light will register as a second image accompanying the flash exposure, and if there is movement (camera or subject), that additional image will not be in the same place as the flash exposure. It will show as a ghost image and, if the movement is significant enough, as a blurred ghost image trailing in front of or behind your subject in the direction of the movement.

As I noted, when you're using first-curtain sync, the flash's main burst goes off the instant the shutter opens fully (a pre-flash used to measure exposure in auto flash modes fires *before* the shutter opens). This produces an image of the subject on the sensor. Then, the shutter remains open for an additional period (30 seconds to 1/200th second, as I said). If your subject is moving, say, towards the right side of the frame, the ghost image produced by the ambient light will produce a blur on the right side of the original subject image, making it look as if your sharp (flash-produced) image is chasing the ghost. For those of us who grew up with lightning-fast superheroes who always left a ghost trail *behind them,* that looks unnatural (see Figure 7.8).

So, Nikon uses second-curtain sync to remedy the situation. In that mode, the shutter opens, as before. The shutter remains open for its designated duration, and the ghost image forms. If your subject moves from the left side of the frame to the right side, the ghost will move from left to right, too. *Then,* about 1.5 milliseconds before the second shutter curtain closes, the flash is triggered, producing a nice, sharp flash image *ahead* of the ghost image. Voilà! We have monsieur *Speed Racer* outdriving his own trailing image.

Avoiding Sync Speed Problems

Using a shutter speed faster than 1/200th second can cause problems. Triggering the electronic flash only when the shutter is completely open makes a lot of sense if you think about what's going on. To obtain shutter speeds faster than 1/200th second, the D90 exposes only part of the sensor at one time, by starting the second curtain on its journey before the first curtain has completely opened, as shown in Figure 7.9. That effectively provides a briefer exposure as a slit that's narrower than the full height of the

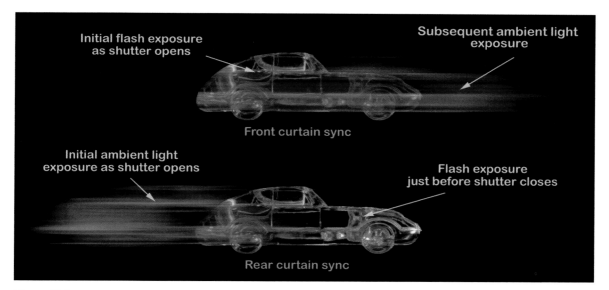

Figure 7.8 First-curtain sync produces an image that trails in front of the flash exposure (top), while second-curtain sync creates a more "natural looking" trail behind the flash image.

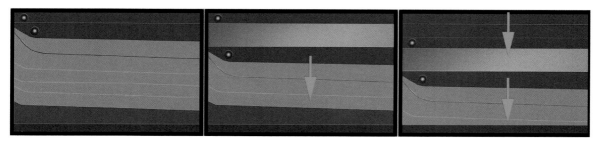

Figure 7.9 A closed shutter (left); partially open shutter as the first curtain begins to move downwards (middle); only part of the sensor is exposed as the slit moves (right).

sensor passes over the surface of the sensor. If the flash were to fire during the time when the first and second curtains partially obscured the sensor, only the slit that was actually open would be exposed.

You'd end up with only a narrow band, representing the portion of the sensor that was exposed when the picture is taken. For shutter speeds *faster* than 1/200th second, the second curtain begins moving *before* the first curtain reaches the top of the frame. As a result, a moving slit, the distance between the first and second curtains, exposes one portion of the sensor at a time as it moves from the bottom to the top. Figure 7.9 shows three views of our typical (but imaginary) focal plane shutter. At left is pictured the closed shutter; in the middle version you can see the first curtain has moved up about 1/4 of the distance to the top, and in the right-hand version, the second curtain has started to "chase" the first curtain across the frame towards the top.

If the flash is triggered while this slit is moving, only the exposed portion of the sensor will receive any illumination. You end up with a photo like the one shown in Figure 7.10. Note that a band across the top of the image is black. That's a shadow of the second shutter curtain, which had started to move when the flash was triggered. Sharp-eyed readers will wonder why the black band is at the *bottom* of the frame rather than at the top, where the second curtain begins its journey. The answer is simple: your lens flips the image upside down and forms it on the sensor in a reversed position. You never notice that, because the camera is smart enough to show you the pixels that make up your photo in their proper orientation during picture review. But this image flip is why, if your sensor gets dirty and you detect a spot of dust in the upper half of a test photo, if cleaning manually, you need to look for the speck in the *bottom* half of the sensor.

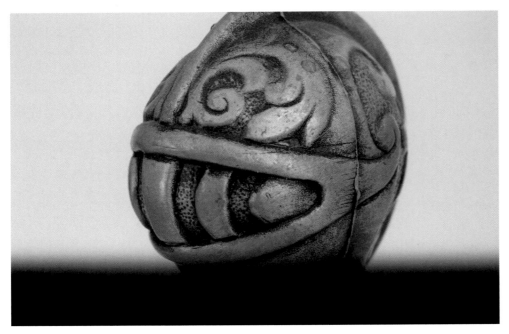

Figure 7.10
If a shutter speed faster than 1/200th second is used, you can end up photographing only a portion of the image.

I generally end up with sync speed problems only when shooting in the studio, using studio flash units rather than my D90's built-in flash or a Nikon dedicated Speedlight. That's because if you're using either type of "smart" flash, the camera knows that a strobe is attached, and remedies any unintentional goof in shutter speed settings. If you happen to set the D90's shutter to a faster speed in S or M mode, the camera will automatically adjust the shutter speed down to 1/200th second. In A, P, or any of the Scene modes, where the D90 selects the shutter speed, it will never choose a shutter speed higher than 1/200th second when using flash. In P mode, shutter speed is automatically set between 1/60th to 1/200th second when using flash.

But when using a non-dedicated flash, such as a studio unit plugged into the D90's hot shoe connector, the camera has no way of knowing that a flash is connected, so shutter speeds faster than 1/200th second can be set inadvertently. Note that the D90 can use a feature called *high-speed sync* that allows shutter speeds faster than 1/200th second with certain external dedicated Nikon flash units. When using high-speed sync, the flash fires a continuous serious of bursts at reduced power for the entire duration of the exposure, so that the illumination is able to expose the sensor as the slit moves. High-speed sync, which works only in PSAM modes, is set using the controls that adjust the compatible external flash.

Determining Exposure

Calculating the proper exposure for an electronic flash photograph is a bit more complicated than determining the settings for continuous light. The right exposure isn't simply a function of how far away your subject is (which the D90 can figure out based on the autofocus distance that's locked in just prior to taking the picture). Various objects reflect more or less light at the same distance so, obviously, the camera needs to measure the amount of light reflected back and through the lens. Yet, as the flash itself isn't available for measuring until it's triggered, the D90 has nothing to measure.

The solution is to fire the flash twice. The initial shot is a *monitor preflash* that can be analyzed, then followed virtually instantaneously by a main flash (to the eye the bursts appear to be a single flash) that's given exactly the calculated intensity needed to provide a correct exposure. As a result, the primary flash may be longer in duration for distant objects and shorter in duration for closer subjects, depending on the required intensity for exposure. This through-the-lens evaluative flash exposure system is called i-TTL (intelligent Through The Lens), and it operates whenever the pop-up internal flash is used, or you have attached a Nikon dedicated flash unit to the D90.

Guide Numbers

Guide numbers, usually abbreviated GN, are a way of specifying the power of an electronic flash in a way that can be used to determine the right f/stop to use at a particular shooting distance and ISO setting. In fact, before automatic flash units became prevalent, the GN was actually used to do just that. A GN is usually given as a pair of numbers for both feet and meters that represent the range at ISO 100. For example, the Nikon D90's built-in flash has a GN in i-TTL mode of 12/39 (meters/feet) at ISO 100 (Lo 1). In Manual mode, the true guide number is a fraction higher: 13/43 meters/feet. To calculate the right exposure at that ISO setting, you'd divide the guide number by the distance to arrive at the appropriate f/stop.

Using the D90's built-in flash as an example, at ISO 100 (Lo 1) with its GN of 43 in Manual mode, if you wanted to shoot a subject at a distance of 10 feet, you'd use f/4.3. (43 divided by 10), or, in practice, f/4.0. At 5 feet, an f/stop of f/8 would be used. Some quick mental calculations with the GN will give you any particular electronic flash's range. You can easily see that the built-in flash would begin to peter out at about 13 feet if you stuck to the lowest ISO of 100, because you'd need an aperture of f/2.8. Of course, in the real world you'd probably bump the sensitivity up to a setting of ISO 800 so you could use a more practical f/8 at 13 feet, and the flash would be effective all the way out to 20 feet or more at wider f/stops.

Today, guide numbers are most useful for comparing the power of various flash units, rather than actually calculating what exposure to use. You don't need to be a math genius to see that an electronic flash with a GN in feet of, say, 131 at ISO 100 (like the SB-900) would be *a lot* more powerful than your built-in flash. At ISO 100, you could use f/5.6 to shoot as far as 22 feet.

Flash Metering Mode

The built-in flash in the Nikon D90, as well as external flash units attached to the camera, use the same three metering modes that are available for continuous light sources: Matrix, Center-Weighted, and Spot. You can choose a metering mode based on the same subject factors as those explained in Chapter 4 (for example, use Spot metering to measure exposure from an isolated subject within the frame). Choice of a metering mode determines how the flash reacts to balance the existing light with the light from the electronic unit:

- **iTTL Balanced Fill-in flash.** This flash mode is used when you choose Matrix or Center-Weighted exposure metering. The Nikon D90 measures the available light and then adjusts the flash output to produce a natural balance between main subject and background. This setting is useful for most photographic situations.

- **Standard i-TTL Fill-flash.** This mode is activated when you use Spot metering or choose the standard mode with an external flash unit's controls. The flash output adjusted only for the main subject of your photograph, and the brightness of the background is not factored in. Use this mode when you want to emphasize the main subject at the expense of proper exposure for the background.

Choosing a Flash Sync Mode

The Nikon D90 has five flash sync modes, with icons resembling those shown in Figure 7.11, which determine when and how the flash is fired (as I'll explain shortly). They are selected from the Quick Settings screen, or by holding down the Flash button on the front of the camera lens housing while rotating the command dial. In both cases, the mode chosen appears in the Quick Settings Screen as the selection is made.

Not all sync modes are available with all exposure modes. Depending on whether you're using DVP/Scene modes, or Program, Aperture Priority, Shutter Priority, or Manual exposure modes, one or more of the following sync modes may not be available. I'm

Figure 7.11

The icons representing the sync modes found in the D90 include (top row, left to right), Front-curtain sync/Auto, Rear-curtain sync, Red-eye reduction, and (bottom row, left to right), Slow sync, and Slow sync with red-eye reduction.

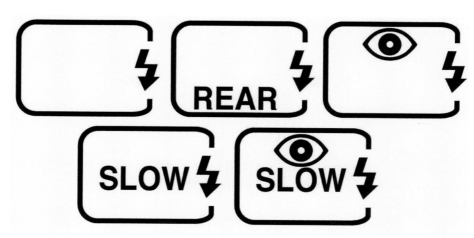

going to list the sync options available for each exposure mode separately, although that produces a little duplication among the options that are available with several exposure modes. However, this approach should reduce the confusion over which sync method is available with which exposure mode.

In Program and Aperture Priority modes you can select these flash modes:

■ **Front-curtain sync/fill flash.** In this mode, represented by a lightning bolt symbol, the flash fires as soon as the front curtain opens completely. The shutter then remains open for the duration of the exposure, until the rear curtain closes. If the subject is moving and ambient light levels are high enough, the movement will cause a secondary "ghost" exposure that appears to be a stream of light advancing ahead of the flash exposure of the same subject. You'll find more on "ghost" exposures next.

■ **Rear-curtain sync.** With this setting, the front curtain opens completely and remains open for the duration of the exposure. Then, the flash is fired and the rear curtain closes. If the subject is moving and ambient light levels are high enough, the movement will cause a secondary "ghost" exposure that appears to stream *behind* the flash exposure. In Program and Aperture Priority modes, the D90 will combine rear-curtain sync with slow shutter speeds (just like slow sync, discussed below) to balance ambient light with flash illumination. (It's best to use a tripod to avoid blur at these slow shutter speeds.)

■ **Red-eye reduction.** In this mode, there is a one-second lag after pressing the shutter release before the picture is actually taken, during which the D90's red-eye reduction lamp lights, causing the subject's pupils to contract (assuming they are looking at the camera), and thus reducing potential red-eye effects. Don't use with moving subjects or when you can't abide the delay.

■ **Slow sync.** This setting allows the D90 in Program and Aperture Priority modes to use shutter speeds as slow as 30 seconds with the flash to help balance a background illuminated with ambient light with your main subject, which will be lit by the electronic flash. You'll want to use a tripod at slower shutter speeds, of course. As shown in Figure 7.6, it's common that the ambient light will be much warmer than the electronic flash's "daylight" balance, so, if you want the two sources to match, you may want to use a warming filter on the flash. That can be done with a gel if you're using an external flash like the SB-900, or by taping an appropriate warm filter over the D90's built-in flash. (That's not a convenient approach, and many find the warm/cool mismatch objectionable and don't bother with filtration.)

■ **Red-eye reduction with slow sync.** This mode combines slow sync with the D90's red-eye reduction behavior when using Program or Aperture Priority modes.

In Shutter Priority and Manual exposure modes, you can select the following three flash synchronization settings:

■ **Front-curtain sync/fill flash.** This setting should be your default setting. This mode is also available in Program and Aperture Priority mode, as described above, and, with high ambient light levels, can produce ghost images, discussed below.

■ **Red-eye reduction.** In this mode, with its one-second lag and red-eye lamp flash, is described above.

■ **Rear-curtain sync.** As noted previously, in this sync mode, the front curtain opens completely and remains open for the duration of the exposure. Then, the flash is fired and the rear curtain closes. If the subject is moving and ambient light levels are high enough, the movement will cause that "ghost" exposure that appears to be trailing the flash exposure.

In Auto, Portrait, and Close-Up DVP/Scene modes, the following flash sync options are available:

■ **Auto.** This setting is the same as front-curtain sync, but the flash pops up automatically in dim lighting conditions.

■ **Red-eye reduction auto.** In this mode, there is a one-second lag after pressing the shutter release before the picture is actually taken, during which the D90's red-eye reduction lamp lights, causing the subject's pupils to contract (assuming they are looking at the camera), and thus reducing potential red-eye effects. Don't use with moving subjects or when you can't abide the delay.

■ **Flash off.** This is not really a sync setting, although it is available from the same selection screen. It disables the flash for those situations in which you absolutely do not want it to pop up and fire.

In Night Portrait mode, only slow synchronization flash and flash off modes are available:

■ **Slow sync.** This setting allows the D90 to select shutter speeds as slow as 30 seconds with the flash to help balance a background illuminated with ambient light with your main subject, which will be lit by the electronic flash. Best for shooting pictures at night when the subjects in the foreground are important, and you want to avoid a pitch-black background. I recommend using a tripod in this mode.

■ **Red-eye reduction with slow sync.** Another mode that calls for a tripod, this sync setting mode combines slow sync with the D90's red-eye reduction preflash. This is the one to use when your subjects are people who will be facing the camera.

■ **Flash off.** Disables the flash in museums, concerts, religious ceremonies, and other situations in which you absolutely do not want it to pop up and fire.

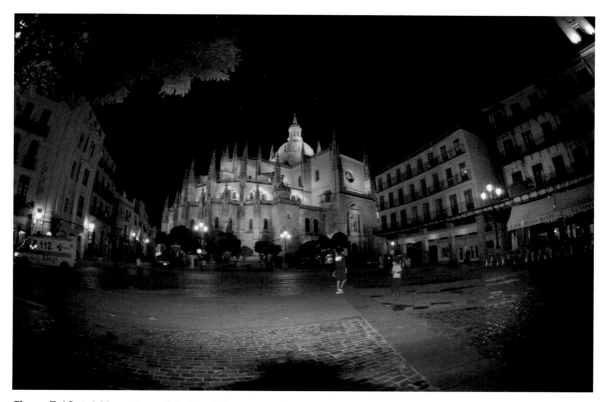

Figure 7.12 I deliberately used flash and slow sync with a scene otherwise illuminated by tungsten light to create this unconventional mixed-lighting image.

A Typical Electronic Flash Sequence

Here's what happens when you take a photo using electronic flash, either the unit built into the Nikon D90, or an external flash like the Nikon SB-900:

1. **Sync mode.** Choose the flash sync mode by holding down the Flash button and rotating the main command dial until the icon representing the choice you want is displayed in the top-panel monochrome LCD (see Figure 7.11).

2. **Metering method.** Choose the metering method you want, from Matrix, Center-Weighted, or Spot metering.

3. **Activate flash.** Press the flash pop-up button to flip up the built-in flash, or mount (or connect with a cable) an external flash and turn it on. A ready light appears in the viewfinder or on the back of the flash when the unit is ready to take a picture.

4. **Check exposure.** Select a shutter speed when using Manual, Program, or Shutter Priority modes; select an aperture when using Aperture Priority and Manual exposure modes.

5. **Preview lighting.** If you want to preview the lighting effect, press the depth-of-field button to produce a modeling flash burst (if it's been activated in CSM e3 in the Custom Setting Menu as described in Chapter 3).

6. **Lock flash setting (if desired).** Optionally, if the main subject is located significantly off-center, you can frame so the subject is centered, lock the flash at the exposure needed to illuminate that subject, and then reframe using the composition you want. Lock the flash level using the Flash Value Lock button, which can be assigned to the Fn or AE-L/AF-L buttons in CSM #f3, CSM #f4. Press the FV lock button, and the flash will emit a preflash to determine the correct flash level, and then the D90 will lock the flash at that level until you press the FV lock button again to release it. FV lock icons appear in the monochrome LCD status panel and the viewfinder.

7. **Take photo.** Press the shutter release down all the way.

8. **D90 receives distance data.** A D- or G-series lens now supplies focus distance to the D90.

9. **Preflash emitted.** The internal flash, if used, or external flash sends out one or two preflash bursts. One burst can be used to control additional wireless flash units in Commander mode, while one burst is used to determine exposure.

10. **Exposure calculated.** The preflash bounces back and is measured by the 420-pixel RGB sensor in the viewfinder. It measures brightness and contrast of the image to calculate exposure. If you're using Matrix metering, the D90 evaluates the scene to determine whether the subject may be backlit (for fill flash), or a subject that requires extra ambient light exposure to balance the scene with the flash exposure,

or classifies the scene in some other way. The camera to subject information as well as the degree of sharp focus of the subject matter is used to locate the subject within the frame. If you've selected Spot metering, only standard i-TTL (without balanced fill-flash) is used.

11. **Mirror up.** The mirror flips up. At this point exposure and focus are locked in.

12. **Flash fired.** At the correct triggering moment (depending on whether front or rear sync is used), camera sends a signal to one or more flashes to start flash discharge. The flash is quenched as soon as the correct exposure has been achieved.

13. **Shutter closes.** The shutter closes and mirror flips down. You're ready to take another picture. Remember to press the FV lock button again to release the flash exposure if your next shot will use a different composition.

14. **Exposure confirmed.** Ordinarily, the full charge in the flash may not be required. If the flash indicator in the viewfinder blinks for about three seconds after the exposure, that means that the entire flash charge was required, and it *could* mean that the full charge wasn't enough for a proper exposure. Be sure to review your image on the LCD to make sure it's not underexposed, and, if it is, make adjustments (such as increasing the ISO setting of the D90) to remedy the situation.

High-Speed (FP) Sync

Triggering the electronic flash only when the shutter is completely open makes a lot of sense if you think about what's going on. To obtain shutter speeds faster than 1/200th second, the D90 exposes only part of the sensor at one time, by starting the second curtain on its journey before the first curtain has completely opened. That effectively provides a briefer exposure as a slit that's narrower than the height of the sensor passes over the surface of the sensor. If the flash were to fire during the time when the first and second curtains partially obscured the sensor, only the slit that was actually open would be exposed.

However, the D90 and certain Nikon external flashes provide a partial solution, called *high-speed sync* or *FP sync* (focal plane sync). Those flash units can fire a series of flashes consecutively in rapid succession, producing the illusion of a longer continuous flash, although at reduced intensity. These multiple flashes have a duration long enough to allow exposing the area of the sensor revealed by the traveling slit as it makes its full pass. However, the reduced intensity means that your flash's range is greatly reduced.

This technique is most useful outdoors when you need fill-in flash, but find that 1/200th second is way too slow for the f/stop you want to use. For example, at ISO 200, an outdoors exposure is likely to be 1/200th second at, say, f/14, which is perfectly fine for an ambient/balanced fill-flash exposure if you don't mind the extreme depth-of-field offered by the small f/stop. But, what if you'd rather shoot at 1/1600th second at f/5.6? High-speed sync will let you do that, and you probably won't mind the reduced flash power, because you're looking for fill flash, anyway. This sync mode offers more flexibility than, say, dropping down to L 1.0 (ISO 100 equivalent).

To use auto FP sync with units like the Nikon SB-900, SB-800, SB-600, and SB-R200 units, there is no setting to make on the flash itself. You need to use CSM #e5 to turn the feature on. When that setting is activated and a compatible external flash is attached, higher shutter speeds can be used with full synchronization, at reduced flash output. High-speed sync cannot be used with the built-in flash.

Working with Nikon Flash Units

If you want to work with dedicated Nikon flash units, at this time you have five choices: the D90's built-in flash, the Nikon SB-900, SB-600, SB-400 on-camera flash units, and the SB-R200 wireless remote flash. These share certain features, which I'll discuss while pointing out differences among them. Nikon may introduce additional flash units during the life of this book, but the current batch and the Nikon Creative Lighting System ushered in with them were significant steps forward.

Nikon D90 Built-in Flash

In automatic mode, the built-in flash has a guide number of 12/39 (meters/feet) at ISO 100 (Lo 1), and must be activated by manually flipping it up when not using one of the DVP/Scene modes that feature automatic pop-up. This flash is powerful enough to provide primary direct flash illumination when required, but can't be angled up for diffuse bounce flash off the ceiling. It's useful for balanced fill flash, and can operate in Commander mode, which allows the built-in flash to trigger one or more off-camera flash units. You can use Manual flash mode and CSM #e2 to dial down the intensity of the built-in flash to 1/128 power.

Because the built-in flash draws its power from the D90's battery, extensive use will reduce the power available to take pictures. For that reason alone, use of an external flash unit can be a good idea when you plan to take a lot of flash pictures.

Nikon SB-900

The Nikon SB-900 (see Figure 7.13) is currently the flagship of the Nikon flash line up, and has a guide number of 34/111.5 (meters/feet) when the "zooming" flash head (which can be set to adjust the coverage angle of the lens) is set to the 35mm position. It has all the features of the D90's flash unit, including Commander mode, repeating flash, modeling light, and selectable power output, along with some extra capabilities.

For example, you can angle the flash and rotate it to provide bounce flash. It includes additional, non-through-the-lens exposure modes, thanks to its built-in light sensor, and can "zoom" and diffuse its coverage angle to illuminate the field of view of lenses from 8mm (with the wide angle/diffusion dome attached) to 120mm on a D90. The

SB-900 also has its own powerful focus assist lamp to aid autofocus in dim lighting, and has reduced red-eye effects simply because the unit, when attached to the D90, is mounted in a higher position that tends to eliminate reflections from the eye back to the camera lens.

Nikon SB-600

This lower-cost unit (see Figure 7.14) has a guide number of 30/98 (meters/feet) when set to the 35mm zoom position. It has many of the SB-900's features, including zoomable flash coverage equal to the field of view of a 16-56mm lens on the D90 (24-85mm settings with a full-frame camera), and 14mm with a built-in diffuser panel. It has a built-in modeling flash feature, but lacks repeating flash, accessory filters, and an included flash diffuser dome, which can be purchased separately.

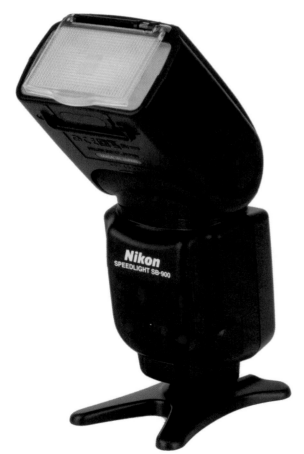

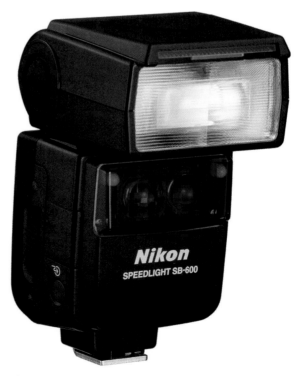

Figure 7.13 The Nikon SB-900 is currently the flagship of the Nikon electronic flash line up.

Figure 7.14 The Nikon SB-600 is a popular medium-priced electronic flash with most of the features of the SB-900, except for Commander mode to control remote units.

Nikon SB-400

The entry-level SB-400 (see Figure 7.15) is a good choice for most Nikon D90 applications. It's built specifically for entry-level Nikon cameras like the D40 or D90, and has a limited, easy-to-use feature set. It has a limited ISO 100 guide number of 21/68 at the 18mm zoom-head position. It tilts up for bounce flash to 90 degrees, with click detents at the 0, 60, 75, and 90 degree marks. Unless you feel the need for an emergency flash or fill-flash unit that's only slightly more powerful than the D90's built-in flash, for the most flexibility, you might want to consider the SB-600.

Nikon SB-R200

This is a specialized wireless-only flash (see Figure 7.16) that's especially useful for close-up photography, and is often purchased in pairs for use with the Nikon R1 and R1C1 Wireless Close-Up Speedlight systems. Its output power is low at 10/33 (meters/feet) for ISO 100 as you might expect for a unit used to photograph subjects that are often inches from the camera. It has a fixed coverage angle of 78 degrees horizontal and 60 degrees vertical, but the flash head tilts down to 60 degrees and up to 45 degrees (with detents every 15 degrees in both directions). In this case, "up" and "down" has a different meaning, because the SB-R200 can be mounted on the SX-1 Attachment Ring mounted around the lens, so the pair of flash units are on the sides and titled toward or away from the optical axis. It supports i-TTL, D-TTL, TTL (for film cameras), and Manual modes.

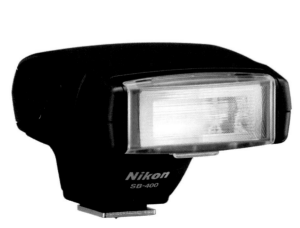

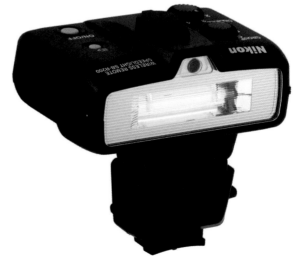

Figure 7.15 The Nikon SB-400 is an entry-level flash best suited for Nikon's entry-level dSLRs.

Figure 7.16 The Nikon SB-R200 is a wireless macro-only flash supplied with the Nikon R1 and R1C1 Wireless Close-Up Speedlight systems.

Flash Techniques

This next section will discuss using specific features of the Nikon D90's built-in flash, as well as those of the Nikon dedicated external flash units. It's not possible to discuss every feature and setting of the external flash units in this chapter (entire books have been written to do that), so I'll simply provide an overview here.

Using the Zoom Head

External flash zoom heads can adjust themselves automatically to match lens focal lengths in use reported by the D90 to the flash unit, or you can adjust the zoom head position manually. With flash units prior to the SB-900, automatic zoom adjustment wasted some of your flash's power, because the flash unit assumed that the focal length reported comes from a full-frame camera. Because of the 1.5X crop factor, the flash coverage when the flash is set to a particular focal length was wider than is required by the D90's cropped image. The SB-900, on the other hand, automatically determines whether your camera is an FX-format, full-frame model, or is a DX "cropped sensor" model like the Nikon D90, and adjusts coverage angle to suit.

You can manually adjust the zoom position yourself, if you want the flash coverage to correspond to something other than the focal length in use. Just press the Zoom button on the SB-900, and turn the selector dial clockwise to increase the zoom value, or counterclockwise to decrease the zoom value. You can also adjust the zoom position by repeatedly pressing the zoom button.

Flash Modes

The external flash units have various flash modes included, which are available or not available with different camera models (both film and digital types, dating back many years). They are categorized by Nikon into nine different groups, which may be confusing to new digital camera owners who probably haven't heard of most of these cameras. While a table showing most of the groups is included in the manuals for the external flash units, the table is irrelevant for D90 users (unless you happen to own an older digital or film SLR, as well). For digital cameras, there are only two main groups: digital cameras *not* compatible with the Nikon Creative Lighting System (Nikon D1-series cameras, and the Nikon D100), and digital cameras that *are* compatible with CLS (including the D90). Groups I through VII, which support various combinations of features, consist of various film SLRs. You can ignore those options, unless you're using your external flash with an older film camera.

The TTL automatic flash modes available for the SB-900 are as follows:

■ **AA.** Auto Aperture flash. The SB-900 uses a built-in light sensor to measure the amount of flash illumination reflected back from the subject, and adjusts the output to produce an appropriate exposure based on the ISO, aperture, focal length, and flash compensation values set on the D90. This setting on the flash can be used with the D90 in Program or Aperture Priority modes.

- **A.** Non-TTL auto flash. The SB-900's sensor measures the flash illumination reflected back from the subject, and adjusts the output to provide an appropriate exposure. This setting on the flash can be used when the D90 is set to Aperture Priority or Manual modes. You can use this setting to manually "bracket" exposures, as adjusting the aperture value of the lens will produce more or less exposure.

- **GN.** Distance priority manual. You enter a distance value, and the SB-800 adjusts light output based on distance, ISO, and aperture to produce the right exposure in either Aperture Priority or Manual exposure modes. Press the Mode button on the flash until the GN indicator appears, then press the SEL button to highlight the distance display, using the plus and minus buttons to enter the distance value you want (from 1 to 65.6 feet, or 0.3 to 20 meters). The SB-800 will indicate a recommended aperture, which you then set on the lens mounted on the D90.

- **M.** Manual flash. The flash fires at a fixed output level. Press the MODE button until M appears on the SB-800's LCD panel. Press the SEL button and the plus or minus buttons to increase or decrease the output value of the flash. Use the table in the flash manual to determine a suggested aperture setting for a given distance. Then, set that aperture on the D90 in either Aperture Priority or Manual exposure modes. (You can also use manual flash with the D90's built-in unit by choosing a flash level in CSM #e3, as described in Chapter 4, and calculating the appropriate aperture.) (Good luck. I use test shots to calculate the f/stop, myself.)

- **RPT.** Repeating flash. The flash fires repeatedly to produce a multiple flash strobing effect. To use this mode, set the D90's exposure mode to Manual. Then set up the number of repeating flashes per frame, frequency, and flash output level, as described in Chapter 4. When using the D90's built-in flash, use CSM #e3; with the SB-900, press the MODE button, and rotate the selector dial to display RPT. Set flash output level with Function button 1 and the selector dial, and choose the number of flashes with the Function button 2 and the selector dial. Finally, press Function button 3 and rotate the selector dial to choose the frequency.

BURN OUT

When using repeating flash with the built-in flash or the SB-900, or *any* large number of consecutive flashes in any mode (more than about 15 shots at full power), allow the flash to cool off (Nikon recommends a 10-minute time out) to avoid overheating the flash. The SB-900 will signal you with a warning chime that rings twice when it's time for a cooling-off period. The flash will actually disable itself, if necessary, to prevent damage.

Working with Wireless Commander Mode

The D90's built-in flash can be set to Commander mode (as described in Chapter 4) and used to control other compatible flash units. The Nikon SB-900 can also be a flash "Commander" to communicate with and trigger other flash units. Nikon offers a unit called the SU-800, which is a commander unit that has no built-in visible flash, and which controls other units using infrared signals.

The SU-800 has several advantages. It's useful for cameras like the D3 and D2xs, which have no built-in flash to function in Commander mode, and could also be used with the D90 to function as a commander that doesn't have any effect on the exposure. However, you can achieve much the same effect by dialing down the D90's built-in flash to 1/128 power, or by setting the built-in flash to - - (flash cancelled) in Commander mode to turn off the built-in flash during exposure. The real advantage the SU-800 has over the D90's built-in flash is its "reach." Because it uses IR illumination rather than visible light to communicate with remote flashes, the infrared burst can be much stronger, doubling its effective control range to 66 feet.

To use the D90 to control other flash units in Advanced Wireless Lighting mode, if you want the built-in flash as the commander, you need to set it to that mode using CSM #e2, as described next. Once you have set either the D90's built-in flash or the SB-900 as the Master/Commander, you can specify a shooting mode, either Manual with a power output setting you determine from 1/1 to 1/128, or for TTL automatic exposure. When using TTL, you can dial in from −1.0 to +3.0 flash exposure compensation for the master flash. You can also specify a channel (1, 2, 3, or 4) that all flashes will use to communicate among themselves. (If other Nikon photographers are present, choosing a different channel prevents your flash from triggering their remotes, and vice versa.)

Each remote flash unit can also be set to one of three groups (A, B, or C), so you can set the exposure compensation and exposure mode of each group separately. For example, one or more flashes in one group can be reduced in output compared to the flashes in the other group, to produce a particular lighting ratio of effect. You'll find instructions for setting exposure mode, channel, and compensation next (for the built-in flash).

Setting Commander Mode for the D90's Built-in Flash

Setting Commander mode for the built-in flash unit may seem complicated, but it's fairly easy once you've gone through it a few times. Here are the instructions you need.

1. Navigate to CSM #e2, and choose Commander Mode (see Figure 7.17).

2. Use the multi-selector left/right buttons to highlight Mode in the Built-in flash row, then press the up/down buttons to choose TTL, M, or - - (flash disabled). Then use the multi-selector right button to highlight the Comp. parameter in the third column. If you chose TTL, you can select exposure compensation from −1 to +3.0;

choose M, and you can set flash output from 1/1 to 1/128; choose - - and the pre-flashes will still be used to control any remote units in use, but the built-in flash will not fire to contribute to the exposure.

3. Use the multi-selector right button to move down to Group A to select TTL, Manual, AA, or - - exposure (to deactivate that group), then highlight the Comp. column to set the exposure compensation/output power as above. Repeat for any additional groups you want to set up.

4. Use the multi-selector right button to highlight the Channel setting, and use the up/down buttons to select the channel that all the flash units will use to communicate.

5. Press OK when finished.

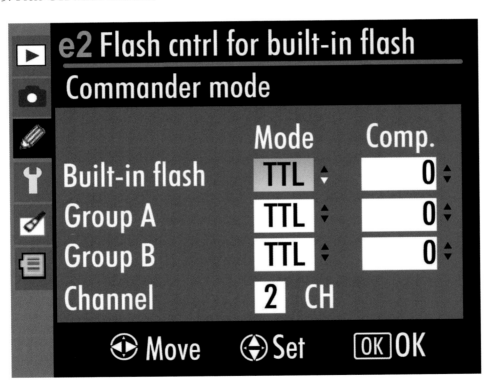

Figure 7.17
Commander mode for the built-in flash can be set in the Custom Setting menu.

Connecting External Flash

You have three basic choices for linking an external flash unit to your Nikon D90. They are as follows:

■ **Mount on the accessory shoe.** Sliding a compatible flash unit into the Nikon D90's accessory shoe provides a direct connection. With a Nikon dedicated flash, all functions of the flash are supported.

- **Connect to the accessory shoe with a cable or adapter.** The Nikon SC-28 and SC-29 TTL coiled remote cords have an accessory shoe on one end of a nine-foot cable to accept a flash, and a foot that slides into the camera accessory shoe on the other end, providing a link that is the same as when the flash is mounted directly on the camera. The SC-29 version also includes a focus assist lamp, like that on the camera and SB-900. You can also use an adapter in the accessory shoe that accepts a standard flash cable. In all cases, you should make sure that the external flash doesn't use a triggering voltage high enough to "fry" your camera's circuitry. You'll find more information on this, and recommendations for a voltage isolator to prevent problems, later in this chapter.

- **Wireless link.** An external Nikon electronic flash can be triggered by another Master flash such as the Nikon SB-900 in Commander mode or by the SU-800 infrared unit.

Using Flash Exposure Compensation

If you are using Program, Shutter Priority, Aperture Priority, or Manual exposure modes, you can manually add or subtract exposure to the flash exposure calculated by the D90. Just hold down the Flash button on the camera at the same time as the Exposure Compensation button (just southeast of the shutter release) and rotate the subcommand dial until the amount of exposure compensation you want appears on the top-panel monochrome LCD.

You can make adjustments from –3EV to +1EV in 1/3 EV increments. As with ordinary exposure compensation, the adjustment you make remains in effect until you zero it out by pressing the Flash button and rotating the subcommand dial until 0 appears on the monochrome control panel and in the viewfinder.

More Advanced Lighting Techniques

As you advance in your Nikon D90 photography, you'll want to learn more sophisticated lighting techniques, using more than just straight-on flash, or using just a single flash unit. Entire books have been written on lighting techniques (check out *David Busch's Quick Snap Guide to Lighting*). I'm going to provide a quick introduction to some of the techniques you should be considering.

Diffusing and Softening the Light

Direct light can be harsh and glaring, especially if you're using the flash built in to your camera, or an auxiliary flash mounted in the hot shoe and pointed directly at your subject. The first thing you should do is stop using direct light (unless you're looking for a stark, contrasty appearance as a creative effect).

There are a number of simple things you can do with both continuous and flash illumination.

■ **Use window light.** Light coming in a window can be soft and flattering, and a good choice for human subjects. Move your subject close enough to the window that its light provides the primary source of illumination. You might want to turn off other lights in the room, particularly to avoid mixing daylight and incandescent light (see Figure 7.18).

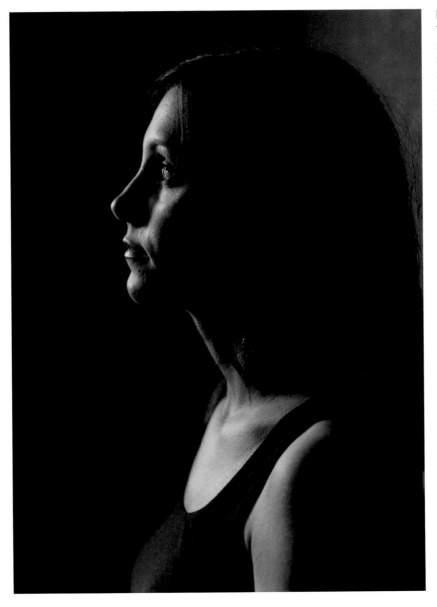

Figure 7.18
Window light makes the perfect diffuse illumination for informal soft-focus portraits like this one.

- **Use fill light.** Your D90's built-in flash makes a perfect fill-in light for the shadows, brightening inky depths with a kicker of illumination (see Figure 7.19).

- **Bounce the light.** External electronic flash units mounted on the D90 usually have a swivel that allows them to be pointed up at a ceiling for a bounce light effect. You can also bounce the light off a wall. You'll want the ceiling or wall to be white or have a neutral gray color to avoid a color cast.

Figure 7.19
Fill flash illuminated the shadows for this candid portrait.

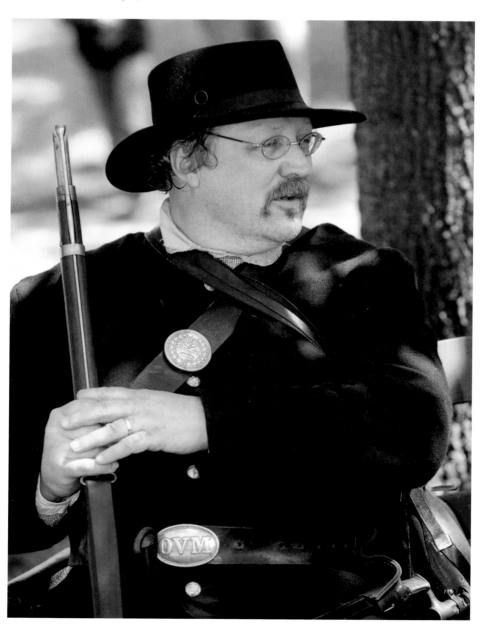

■ **Use reflectors.** Another way to bounce the light is to use reflectors or umbrellas that you can position yourself to provide a greater degree of control over the quantity and direction of the bounced light. Good reflectors can be pieces of foamboard, Mylar, or a reflective disk held in place by a clamp and stand. Although some expensive umbrellas and reflectors are available, spending a lot isn't necessary. A simple piece of white foamboard does the job beautifully. Umbrellas have the advantage of being compact and foldable, while providing a soft, even kind of light. They're relatively cheap, too, with a good 40-inch umbrella available for as little as $20.

■ **Use diffusers.** Nikon supplies a Sto-Fen-style diffuser dome with the SB-900 flash. You can purchase a similar diffuser for the SB-600 from Nikon, Sto-Fen, and some other vendors that offer clip-on diffusers. The two examples shown in Figures 7.20 and 7.21 fit over your electronic flash head and provide a soft, flattering light. These add-ons are more portable than umbrellas and other reflectors, yet provide a nice diffuse lighting effect.

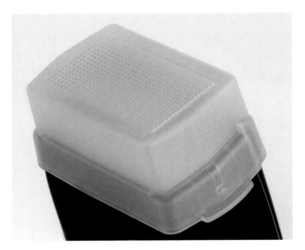

Figure 7.20 This diffuser dome is provided by Nikon with the SB-900, and softens the light of an external flash unit.

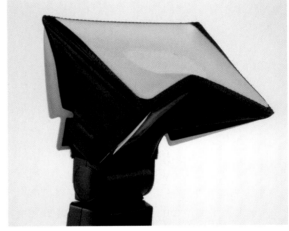

Figure 7.21 Softboxes use Velcro strips to attach them to just about any shoe-mount flash unit.

Using Multiple Light Sources

Once you gain control over the qualities and effects you get with a single light source, you'll want to graduate to using multiple light sources. Using several lights allows you to shape and mold the illumination of your subjects to provide a variety of effects, from backlighting to side lighting to more formal portrait lighting. You can start simply with several incandescent light sources, bounced off umbrellas or reflectors that you construct. Or you can use more flexible multiple electronic flash setups.

Effective lighting is the one element that differentiates great photography from candid or snapshot shooting. Lighting can make a mundane subject look a little more glamorous. Make subjects appear to be soft when you want a soft look, or bright and sparkly when you want a vivid look, or strong and dramatic if that's what you desire. As you might guess, having control over your lighting means that you probably can't use the lights that are already in the room. You'll need separate, discrete lighting fixtures that can be moved, aimed, brightened, and dimmed on command.

Selecting your lighting gear will depend on the type of photography you do, and the budget you have to support it. It's entirely possible for a beginning D90 photographer to create a basic, inexpensive lighting system capable of delivering high-quality results for a few hundred dollars, just as you can spend megabucks ($1,000 and up) for a sophisticated lighting system.

Basic Flash Setups

If you want to use multiple electronic flash units, the Nikon Speedlights described earlier will serve admirably. The higher-end models can be used with Nikon's wireless i-TTL features, which allow you to set up to three separate groups of flash units (several flashes can be included in each group) and trigger them using a master flash and the camera. Just set up one master unit, and arrange the compatible slave units around your subject. You can set the relative power of each unit separately, thereby controlling how much of the scene's illumination comes from the main flash, and how much from the auxiliary flash units, which can be used as fill flash, background lights, or, if you're careful, to illuminate the hair of portrait subjects.

Studio Flash

If you're serious about using multiple flash units, a studio flash setup might be more practical. The traditional studio flash is a multi-part unit, consisting of a flash head that mounts on your light stand, and is tethered to an AC (or sometimes battery) power supply. A single power supply can feed two or more flash heads at a time, with separate control over the output of each head.

When they are operating off AC power, studio flash don't have to be frugal with the juice, and are often powerful enough to illuminate very large subjects or to supply lots and lots of light to smaller subjects. The output of such units is measured in watt seconds (ws), so you could purchase a 200ws, 400ws, or 800ws unit, and a power pack to match.

Their advantages include greater power output, much faster recycling, built-in modeling lamps, multiple power levels, and ruggedness that can stand up to transport, because many photographers pack up these kits and tote them around as location lighting rigs. Studio lighting kits can range in price from a few hundred dollars for a set of lights, stands, and reflectors, to thousands for a high-end lighting system complete with all the necessary accessories.

A more practical choice these days are *monolights* (see Figure 7.22), which are "all-in-one" studio lights that sell for about $200-$400. They have the flash tube, modeling light, and power supply built into a single unit that can be mounted on a light stand. Monolights are available in AC-only and battery-pack versions, although an external battery eliminates some of the advantages of having a flash with everything in one unit. They are very portable, because all you need is a case for the monolight itself, plus the stands and other accessories you want to carry along. Because these units are so popular with photographers who are not full-time professionals, the lower-cost monolights are often designed more for lighter duty than professional studio flash. That doesn't mean they aren't rugged; you'll just need to handle them with a little more care, and, perhaps, not expect them to be used eight hours a day for weeks on end. In most other respects, however, monolights are the equal of traditional studio flash units in terms of fast recycling, built-in modeling lamps, adjustable power, and so forth.

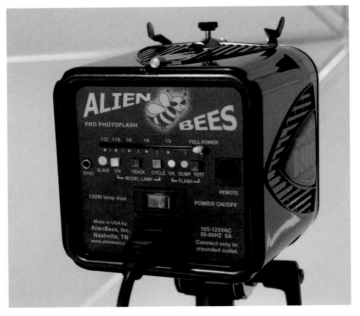

Figure 7.22
All-in-one "monolights" contain flash, power supply, and a modeling light in one compact package (umbrella not included).

Connecting Multiple Non-Dedicated Units to Your Nikon D90

Non-dedicated electronic flash units can't use the automated i-TTL features of your Nikon D90; you'll need to calculate exposure manually, through test shots evaluated on your camera's LCD, or by using an electronic flash meter. Moreover, you don't have to connect them to the accessory shoe on top of the camera. Instead, you can remove them from the camera and plug in an adaptor like the Nikon AS-15 onto the accessory shoe to provide a PC/X connector for use with an old-style camera sync cord.

You should be aware that older electronic flash units sometimes use a triggering voltage that is too much for your D90 to handle. You can actually damage the camera's electronics if the voltage is too high. You won't need to worry about this if you purchase brand-new units from Alien Bees, Adorama, or other vendors. But if you must connect an external flash with an unknown triggering voltage, I recommend using a Wein Safe Sync (see Figure 7.23), which isolates the flash's voltage from the camera triggering circuit.

Finally, some flash units have an optical slave trigger built in, or can be fitted with one, so that they fire automatically when another flash, including your camera's built-in unit, fires. Or, you can use radio control devices like the ones shown in Figure 7.24.

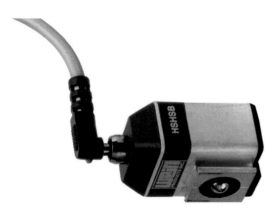

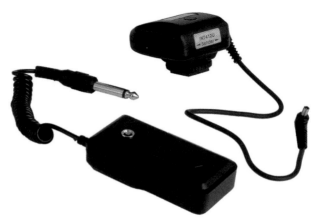

Figure 7.23 A voltage isolator can prevent frying your D90's flash circuits if you use an older electronic flash.

Figure 7.24 A radio-control device frees you from a sync cord tether between your flash and camera.

Other Lighting Accessories

Once you start working with light, you'll find there are plenty of useful accessories that can help you. Here are some of the most popular that you might want to consider.

Softboxes

Softboxes are large square or rectangular devices that may resemble a square umbrella with a front cover, and produce a similar lighting effect. They can extend from a few feet square to massive boxes that stand five or six feet tall—virtually a wall of light. With a flash unit or two inside a softbox, you have a very large, semi-directional light source that's very diffuse and very flattering for portraiture and other people photography.

Softboxes are also handy for photographing shiny objects. They not only provide a soft light, but if the box itself happens to reflect in the subject (say you're photographing a chromium toaster), the box will provide an interesting highlight that's indistinct and not distracting.

You can buy softboxes (like the one shown in Figure 7.25) or make your own. Some lengths of friction-fit plastic pipe and a lot of muslin cut and sewed just so may be all that you need.

Light Stands

Both electronic flash and incandescent lamps can benefit from light stands. These are lightweight, tripod-like devices (but without a swiveling or tilting head) that can be set on the floor, tabletops, or other elevated surfaces and positioned as needed. Light stands should be strong enough to support an external lighting unit, up to and including a relatively heavy flash with a softbox or umbrella reflectors. You want the supports to be capable of raising the lights high enough to be effective. Look for light stands capable of extending six to seven feet high. The nine-foot units usually have larger, steadier bases, and extend high enough that you can use them as background supports. You'll be using these stands for a lifetime, so invest in good ones. I bought the light stand shown in Figure 7.26 when I was in college, and I have been using it for decades.

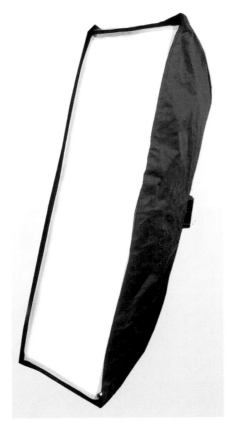

Figure 7.25 Softboxes provide an even, diffuse light source.

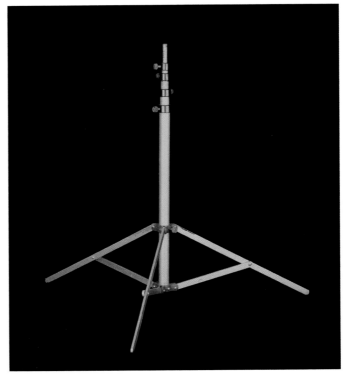

Figure 7.26 Light stands can hold lights, umbrellas, backdrops, and other equipment.

Backgrounds

Backgrounds can be backdrops of cloth, sheets of muslin you've painted yourself using a sponge dipped in paint, rolls of seamless paper, or any other suitable surface your mind can dream up. Backgrounds provide a complementary and non-distracting area behind subjects (especially portraits) and can be lit separately to provide contrast and separation that outlines the subject, or which helps set a mood.

I like to use plain-colored backgrounds for portraits, and white seamless backgrounds for product photography. You can usually construct these yourself from cheap materials and tape them up on the wall behind your subject, or mount them on a pole stretched between a pair of light stands.

Snoots and Barn Doors

These fit over the flash unit and direct the light at your subject. Snoots are excellent for converting a flash unit into a hair light, while barn doors give you enough control over the illumination by opening and closing their flaps that you can use another flash as a background light, with the capability of feathering the light exactly where you want it on the background. A barn door unit is shown in Figure 7.27.

Figure 7.27
Snoots and barn doors allow you to modulate the light from a flash or lamp, and they are especially useful for hair lights and background lights.

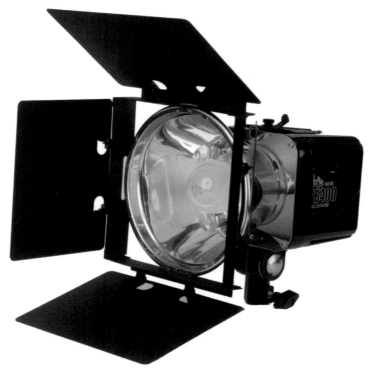

8

Useful Software for the Nikon D90

Unless you only take pictures and then immediately print them directly to a PictBridge-compatible printer, somewhere along the line you're going to need to make use of the broad array of software available for the Nikon D90. The picture-fixing options in the Retouch menu let you make only modest modifications to your carefully crafted photos. If your needs involve more than fixing red-eye, cropping and trimming, and maybe adjusting tonal values with D-Lighting, you're definitely going to want to use a utility or editor of some sort to perfect your images. After you've captured some great images and have them safely stored on your Nikon D90's memory card, you'll need to transfer them from your camera and Secure Digital card to your computer, where they can be organized, fine-tuned in an image editor, and prepared for web display, printing, or some other final destination.

Fortunately, there are lots of software utilities and applications to help you do all these things. This chapter will introduce you to a few of them. Please note that this is *not* a "how-to-do-it" software chapter. I'm going to use every available page in this book to offer advice on how to get the most from your D90. There's no space to explain how to use all the features of Nikon Capture NX, nor how to tweak RAW file settings in Adobe Camera Raw. Entire books have been written about both products. This chapter is intended solely to help you get your bearings among the large number of utilities and applications available, to help you better understand what each does, and how you might want to use them. At the very end of the chapter, however, I'm going to make an exception and provide some simple instructions for using Adobe Camera Raw, to help those who have been using Nikon's software exclusively get a feel for what you can do with the Adobe product.

The basic functions found in most of the programs discussed in this chapter include image transfer and management, camera control, and image editing. You'll find that many of the programs overlap several of these capabilities, so it's not always possible to categorize the discussions that follow by function. In fact, I'm going to start off by describing a few of the offerings available from Nikon.

Nikon's Applications and Utilities

If nothing else, Nikon has made sorting through the software for its digital cameras an interesting pursuit. Through the years, we've had various incarnations of programs with names like PictureProject, NikonView, and Nikon Capture. Some have been compatible with both the Nikon dSLR and amateur Coolpix product lines. Many of them have been furnished on disk with the cameras. Others, most notoriously Nikon Capture, have been an extra-cost option, which particularly infuriated those of us who had paid a lot for a Nikon dSLR, and found that we'd need to pay even more to get the software needed for the camera.

Recently, Nikon has begun splitting their software offerings into separate programs that are sort of stand-alone products, but which integrate with the others. For example, if you bought Nikon Capture NX you found that the program didn't really capture anything, as the previous Nikon Capture 4 did. If you wanted to operate the camera remotely, you needed to buy the off-shoot program, Nikon Camera Control Pro, which costs even *more* money.

If Nikon software wasn't interesting enough already, some years back Nikon began *encrypting* the white balance information in image files, so that third-party utility programmers needed to use Nikon's software development kit or reverse-engineer the encryption to make their utilities work with Nikon NEF files. Even today, each time a new Nikon dSLR is introduced, you must upgrade your copy of most Nikon software products, as well as third-party products like Adobe Camera Raw, to ensure compatibility with the new camera's files. The fact that these upgrades often are not available until months after the camera is introduced is nothing short of frustrating. For example, Version 4.6 of Adobe Camera Raw, the first compatible with the D90, wasn't available until October 10, 2008, almost two full weeks after I had begun shooting NEF photos with my D90. And, in this case, the Camera Raw update came relatively soon after the camera's availability: I've waited three weeks or more for compatible software from Adobe after I purchased a Nikon camera. As we used to say back in the days of film cameras, "Bummer!"

The next few sections provide some descriptions of the Nikon software you'll want to use with your D90.

Nikon ViewNX

This latest incarnation of Nikon's basic file viewer was introduced in March 2009 (Version 1.3.0 at this writing) and is better than ever, making it easy to browse through images, convert RAW files to JPEG or TIFF, and make corrections to white balance and exposure, either on individual files, or on batches of files. It works in tandem with Nikon Transfer and Nikon Capture NX, as you can open files inspected in ViewNX in one of the other programs—or within a third-party application you "register."

First and foremost, Nikon ViewNX is a great file viewer. There are three modes for looking at images: a Thumbnail Grid mode for checking out small previews of your images; an Image Viewer mode (see Figure 8.1) that shows a group of thumbnails along with an enlarged version of a selected image; and Full Screen mode, which allows you to examine an image in maximum detail.

If you like to shoot RAW+JPEG Basic, you can review image pairs as if they were a single image (rather than view the RAW and JPEG versions separately), and work with whichever version you need. The active focus area can be displayed in the image, and there are histogram, highlight, and shadow displays to help you evaluate an image.

Figure 8.1
NikonView NX is a great file viewer.

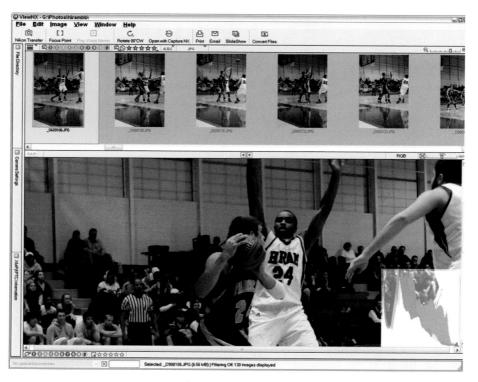

Should you want to organize your images, there are 10 labels available to classify images by criteria such as images printed, images copied, or images sent as e-mail, and you can mark your best shots for easier retrieval with a rating system of one to five stars. ViewNX also allows you to edit embedded XMP/IPTC Information in fields such as Creator, Origin, Image Title, and suitable keywords. The utility can be downloaded from the support/download pages of the Nikon website at www.nikonusa.com.

Nikon Transfer

It seems like everyone offers some sort of image transfer system that automatically recognizes when a memory card is inserted in a reader, or a digital camera like the Nikon D90 is attached to a computer using a USB cable. The most popular operating systems, from Mac OS X to Windows XP and Vista have their own built-in transfer programs, and Adobe Photoshop Elements 6.0 includes one in its suite of utilities.

Nikon Transfer, also updated in March 2009 (to Version 1.4.0) is particularly well-suited for D90 owners, because it integrates easily with other Nikon software products, including ViewNX and Nikon Capture NX. You can download photos to your computer, and then continue to work on them in the Nikon application (or third-party utility) of your choice.

When a memory card is inserted into a card reader, or when the D90 is connected to your computer through a USB cable, Nikon Transfer recognizes the device, searches it for thumbnails, and provides a display like the one shown in Figure 8.2. You can preview the images and mark the ones you want to transfer with checks to create a Transfer Queue.

Then, click on the Primary Destination tab (see Figure 8.3) and choose a location for the photos that will be transferred. Nikon Transfer can create a new folder for each transfer based on a naming convention you set up (click the Edit button next to the box at top center in the figure), or copy to a folder named after the current folder in the D90's memory card. You can keep the current file name as the files are transferred, or assign a new name with a prefix you designate, such as Spain07_ . The program will add a number from 001 to 999 to the file name prefix you specify.

One neat feature is the ability to name a Backup Destination location, so that all transferred pictures can also be copied to a second folder, which can be located on a different hard disk drive or other media. You can embed information such as copyright data, star ratings, and labels in the images as they are transferred. When the file transfer is complete, Nikon Transfer can launch an application of your choice, set with a few clicks in the Preferences tab (see Figure 8.4).

Figure 8.2
After Nikon Transfer displays thumbnails of the images on your memory card or camera, mark the ones you want to transfer.

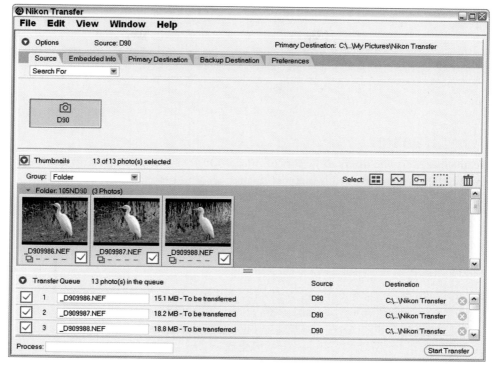

Figure 8.3
Copy files to a destination you specify using an optional file name template you can define.

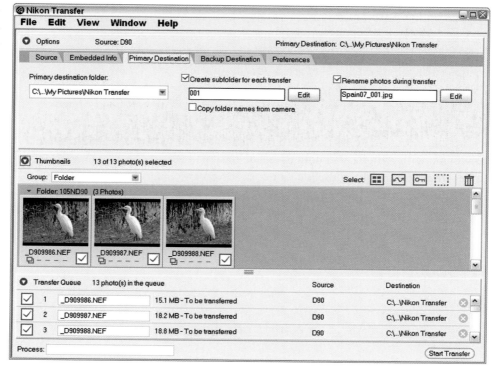

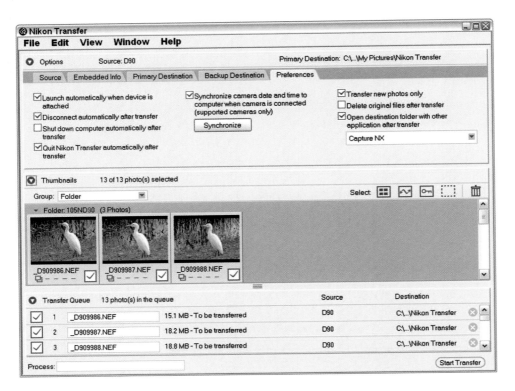

Figure 8.4
You can tell Nikon Transfer what to do after images are transferred in the Preferences tab.

Nikon Capture NX

Capture NX is a pretty hefty chunk of software for the typical entry-level Nikon D90 owner to tackle (and somewhat expensive at about $150), but if you're ambitious and willing to plant your pitons for a steep climb up the learning curve, the program is indeed a powerful image-editing utility. It's designed specifically to process Nikon's NEF-format RAW files (although this new edition has added the ability to manipulate JPEG and TIFF images as well). It includes an image browser (with labeling, sorting, and editing) that can be used to make many adjustments directly through the thumbnails. It also has advanced color management tools, impressive noise reduction capabilities, and batch processing features that allow you to apply sets of changes to collections of images. All the tools are arranged in dockable/expandable/collapsible palettes (see Figure 8.5) that tell you everything you need to know about an image, and provide the capabilities to push every pixel in interesting ways.

Photographers tend to love Capture NX or hate it, and it's easy to separate the fans from the furious. Those who are enamored of the program have invested a great deal of time in learning its quirky paradigm and now appreciate just how powerful Capture NX is. The detractors are usually those who are comfortable with another program, such as

Figure 8.5
Capture NX's tools are arranged in dockable palettes.

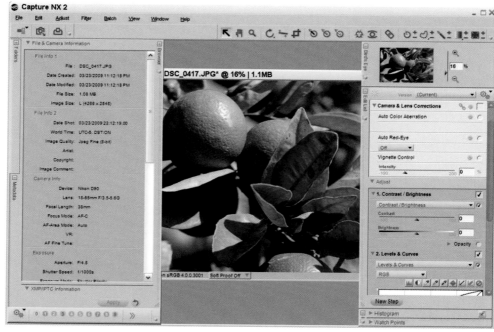

Photoshop or even Capture 4, this program's predecessor, and are upset that even the simplest functions can be confoundingly difficult for a new user to figure out. Capture NX's murky Help system isn't a lot of help; there's room for a huge book (or two) to explain how to use this program.

For example, instead of masks, Capture NX uses Nik Software's U Point technology, which applies Control Points to select and isolate parts of an image for manipulation. There are Color Control Points, with up to nine different sliders for each selected area (see Figure 8.6). There are also Black-and-White Control Points for setting dynamic range, Neutral Control Points for correcting color casts, and a Red-Eye Reduction Control Point that removes crimson glows from pupils.

The workflow revolves around an Edit List, which contains a list of enhancements, including Camera Adjustments, RAW Adjustments, Light & Color Adjustments, Detail Adjustments, and Lens Adjustments, which can each be controlled separately. You can add steps of your own, cancel adjustments individually, and store steps in the Edit List as Settings that can be applied to individual images or batches.

There are also Color Aberration Controls, D-Lighting, Image Dust Off, Vignette Control, Fisheye-to-Rectilinear Image Transformation ("de-fishing"), and a Distortion Control to reduce pincushion and barrel distortion.

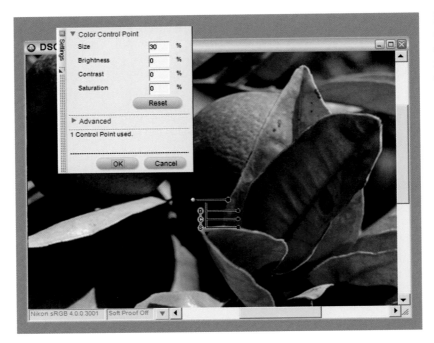

Figure 8.6
Control Points
are used to
make common
adjustments.

Nikon Camera Control Pro

Nikon's Camera Control Pro is a versatile extra-cost utility (priced at about $180) that allows you to communicate directly with your camera from your computer through a USB cable. Once the two are linked, you can perform a variety of functions:

■ **Shoot remotely.** Just about any shooting function you can adjust on the camera can be performed remotely, as you can see from the cluster of tabbed dialog boxes shown at the top and right of Figure 8.7. Set exposure mode, adjust the aperture, add or subtract exposure compensation, choose a focus area, change ISO sensitivity or white balance, all are at your command through the software. You can even change quality and size settings, turn on auto bracketing, and change image optimization settings. You can optionally disable the controls on the camera, to prevent having settings you made at the computer changed accidentally.

■ **Download directly to your computer.** When doing time-lapse photography, you can use Camera Control Pro to transfer the images you take directly to the computer.

■ **Upload comments.** Frustrated by the Nikon D90's text entry screen? Edit your Image Comment and upload it directly to the camera from your computer keyboard (lower left in Figure 8.7).

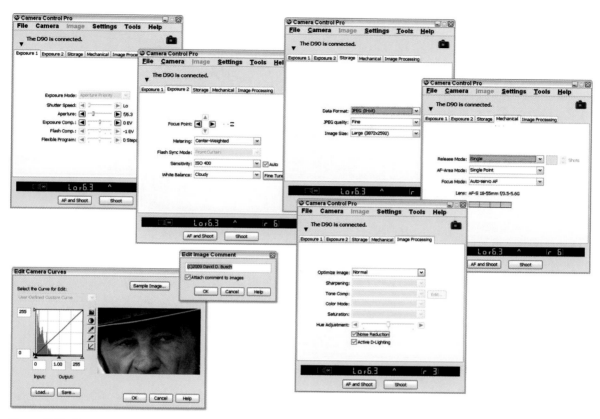

Figure 8.7 You can operate the D90 from your computer using Camera Control Pro.

■ **Create and save custom curves.** You can load a sample image and create a special tone compensation custom curve for that image using tools similar to those found in Photoshop.

■ **View and change Custom Settings.** This is one of my favorite features. While changing the Custom Settings for any of the Custom Setting options using the D90's menus isn't difficult (particularly after you've absorbed the information in Chapter 3), Camera Control Pro makes playing with these options a joy.

Other Software

Other useful software for your Nikon D90 falls into several categories. You might want to fine-tune your images, retouch them, change color balance, composite several images together, and perform other tasks we know as image editing, with a program like Adobe Photoshop, Photoshop Elements, or Corel Photo Paint.

You might want to play with the settings in RAW files, too, as you import them into an image editor. There are specialized tools expressly for tweaking RAW files, ranging from Adobe Camera Raw to PhaseOne's Capture One Pro (C1 Pro). A third type of manipulation is the specialized task of noise reduction, which can be performed within Photoshop, Adobe Camera Raw, or tools like Bibble Professional. There are also specialized tools just for noise reduction, such as Noise Ninja (also included with Bibble) and Neat Image. Some programs, like the incomparable DxO Optics Pro perform magical transformations that you can't achieve any other way.

Each of these utilities and applications deserves a chapter of its own, so I'm simply going to enumerate some of the most popular applications and utilities and tell you a little about what they do.

DxO Optics Pro

DxO Labs (www.DxO.com) offers an incredibly useful program called Optics Pro for both Windows and Mac OS ($170-$300) that is unique in the range of functions it provides. Ostensibly an image quality enhancement utility that "cures" some of the ails that plague even the best lenses, the latest v5 release also features a new RAW conversion engine that uses a new demosaicing algorithm to translate your NEF files into images with more detail, less noise, and fewer artifacts. These features meld well with the program's original mission: fixing the optical "geometry" of images, using settings custom-tailored for each individual lens. (I'm not kidding: when you "assemble" the program, you specify each and every camera body you want to use with Optics Pro, and designate exactly which lenses are included in your repertoire.)

Once an image has been imported into Optics Pro, it can be manipulated within one of four main sections: Light, Color, Geometry, and Details. It's especially useful for correcting optical flaws, color, exposure, and dynamic range, while adjusting perspective, distortion, and tilting. If you own a fisheye lens, Optics Pro will "de-fish" your images to produce a passable rectilinear photo from your curved image. A new Dust/Blemish Removal tool operates something like a manual version of the D90's Dust Off Reference Photo. The user creates a dust/blemish template, and the program removes dust from the marked area in multiple images. Figure 8.8 shows you DxO Optics Pro's clean user interface.

Phase One Capture One Pro (C1 Pro)

If there is a Cadillac of RAW converters for Nikon and Canon digital SLR cameras, C1 Pro has to be it. This premium-priced program from Phase One (www.phaseone.com) does everything, does it well, and does it quickly. If you can't justify the price tag of this professional-level software (as much as $500 for the top-of-the-line edition), there are "lite" versions for serious amateurs and cash-challenged professionals for as little as $130.

Figure 8.8
DxO Optics
Pro fixes lens
flaws, and
functions as a
high-tech RAW
converter and
noise reduction
utility, too.

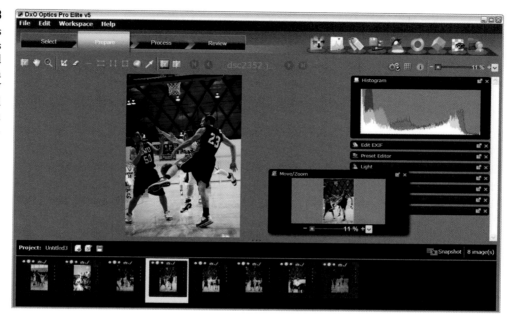

Aimed at photographers with high-volume needs (that would include school and portrait photographers, as well as busy commercial photographers), C1 Pro is available for both Windows and Mac OS X, and supports a broad range of digital cameras. Phase One is a leading supplier of megabucks digital camera backs for medium and larger format cameras, so they really understand the needs of photographers.

The latest features include individual noise reduction controls for each image, automatic levels adjustment, a "quick develop" option that allows speedy conversion from RAW to TIFF or JPEG formats, dual-image side-by-side views for comparison purposes, and helpful grids and guides that can be superimposed over an image. Photographers concerned about copyright protection will appreciate the ability to add watermarks to the output images.

Bibble Pro

One of my personal favorites among third-party RAW converters is Bibble Pro. It supports one of the broadest ranges of RAW file formats available (which can be handy if you find yourself with the need to convert a file from a friend or colleague's non-Nikon camera), including NEF files from Nikon cameras dating as far back as the Nikon D1, D1x/h, D2H, and D100. The utility supports lots of different platforms, too. It's available for Windows, Mac OS X, and, believe it or not, Linux.

Bibble (www.bibblelabs.com) works fast, which is important when you have to convert many images in a short time (event photographers will know what I am talking about!). Bibble's batch-processing capabilities also let you convert large numbers of files using settings you specify without further intervention. Its customizable interface lets you organize and edit images quickly and then output them in a variety of formats, including 16-bit TIFF and PNG. You can even create a web gallery from within Bibble. I often find myself disliking the generic file names applied to digital images by cameras, so I really like Bibble's ability to rename batches of files using new names that you specify.

Bibble is fully color managed, which means it can support all the popular color spaces (Adobe sRGB and so forth) and use custom profiles generated by third-party color-management software. There are two editions of Bibble, a Pro version and a Lite version. Because the Pro version is reasonably priced at $129, I don't really see the need to save $60 with the Lite edition, which lacks the top-line's options for tethered shooting, embedding IPTC-compatible captions in images, and can also be used as a Photoshop plug-in (if you prefer not to work with the application in its standalone mode). Bibble Pro now incorporates Noise Ninja technology, so you can get double-duty from this valuable application.

BreezeBrowser Pro

A versatile program you want to consider is BreezeBrowser Pro (Windows only), from Breeze Systems (www.breezesys.com) which performs several useful functions in addition to RAW file conversion and image browsing. It can produce contact sheets and proof images, generate nifty web pages with only a little input on your part, and, importantly in this GPS-crazy age, link geo-tagged images with Google Earth and online maps. Now that the Nikon D90 provides the compact Nikon GP-1 geo-tagging unit, which clips onto the camera's accessory shoe, software like BreezeBrowser provides an actual real-world application for this kind of data.

A real bargain at $69.95, BreezeBrowser Pro offers all the basic conversion, sharpening, resizing, and adjustments for your RAW images. You can create captioned web pages from within the program, and, if you want to sell your pictures, it will protect them with watermarking and provide a system for online ordering of images/prints. Batch rename features let you change the file name applied in the camera to something more useful, and edit the date/time stamps of your files. The Windows-only program is shown in Figure 8.9.

BreezeSystems NKRemote

If you find Nikon Camera Control Pro too pricey, you may find BreezeSystems' NKRemote (for Windows only) an attractive $95 alternative. It links to your camera through the USB cable, and offers direct control of virtually every camera control through a well-designed user interface, shown in Figure 8.10. It has a couple quirks—for example, you can discern the original Canon-oriented underpinnings of the program by the use of the label Tv (Time Value) for Shutter Priority. But the features are solid.

Figure 8.9
BreezeBrowser
Pro offers geo-
tagging and
support for
web image sales
among its
innovative fea-
tures.

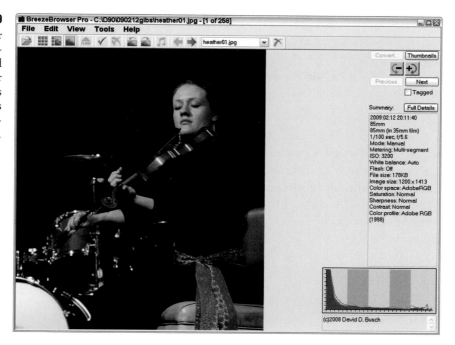

Figure 8.10
BreezeSystems
NKRemote
offers an eco-
nomical way to
control your
camera for
direct shooting
and time-lapse
photography,
especially in
Live View
mode (lower
right).

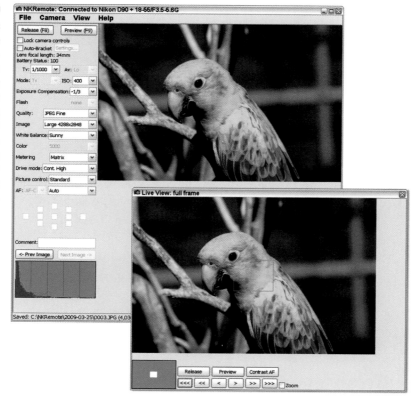

The program works not only with the Nikon D90, but with the D300, D700, D3/D3x, and earlier D200 cameras, so if you add another model to your kit you won't have to buy new software. NKRemote allows focusing automatically and manually from your PC (you can choose the focus point by checking one of 11 boxes in the AF interface), thanks to its support for the Live View feature available in all the cameras mentioned except the D200. You'll enjoy setting up your D90 on a long USB tether, and relaxing while you wait for that elusive plaid-bellied sapgrabber to perch within view of your lens.

You can shoot time-lapse photos to capture flowers blooming, construction sites constructing, or dawns breaking. It's easy to adjust Picture Controls from your PC, too. One of my favorite features is the Photo Booth capability, which you can set up to operate like one of those three-shots-for-a-dollar photo booths at the County Fair. In this mode, the software automatically takes a series of photos in sequence, and then immediately prints them out. If you're a professional (or aspiring pro), you can set up your photo booth at an event; otherwise, the feature is great fun to use at home. The Photobooth options are shown in Figure 8.11.

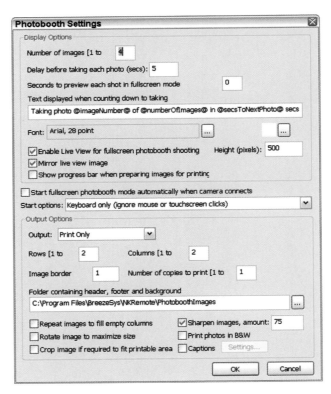

Figure 8.11
Set up your own automatic photo booth at an event, or at home, using NKRemote's options.

Photoshop/Photoshop Elements

Photoshop is the high-end choice for image editing, and Photoshop Elements is a great alternative for those who need some of the features of Photoshop, but can do without the most sophisticated capabilities, including editing CMYK files. Both editors use the latest version of Adobe's Camera Raw plug-in, which makes it easy to adjust things like image resolution, white balance, exposure, shadows, brightness, sharpness, luminance, and noise reduction. One plus with the Adobe products is that they are available in identical versions for both Windows and Macs (eventually!).

The latest version of Photoshop includes a built-in RAW plug-in that is compatible with the proprietary formats of a growing number of digital cameras, both new and old, and which can perform a limited number of manipulations on JPEG and TIFF files, too. This plug-in also works with Photoshop Elements, but with fewer features. Here's how easy it is to manipulate a RAW file using the Adobe converter:

1. Transfer the RAW images from your camera to your computer's hard drive.

2. In Photoshop, choose Open from the File menu, or use Bridge.

3. Select a RAW image file. The Adobe Camera Raw plug-in will pop up, showing a preview of the image, like the one shown in Figure 8.12.

Figure 8.12
The basic ACR dialog box looks like this when processing a single image.

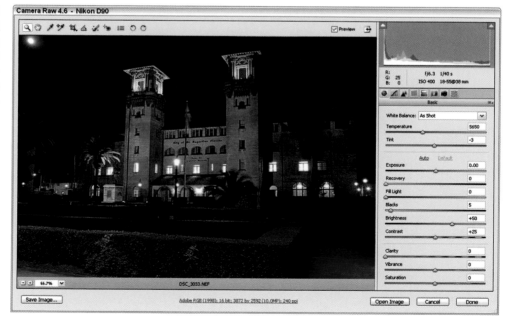

4. If you like, use one of the tools found in the toolbar at the top left of the dialog box. From left to right, they are as follows:

- **Zoom.** Operates just like the Zoom tool in Photoshop.

- **Hand.** Use like the Hand tool in Photoshop.

- **White Balance.** Click an area in the image that should be neutral gray or white to set the white balance quickly.

- **Color Sampler.** Use to determine the RGB values of areas you click with this eyedropper.

- **Crop.** Pre-crops the image so that only the portion you specify is imported into Photoshop. This option saves time when you want to work on a section of a large image, and you don't need the entire file.

- **Straighten.** Drag in the preview image to define what should be a horizontal or vertical line, and ACR will realign the image to straighten it.

- **Retouch.** Use to heal or clone areas you define.

- **Red-Eye Removal.** Quickly zap red pupils in your human subjects.

- **ACR Preferences.** Produces a dialog box of Adobe Camera Raw preferences.

- **Rotate Counterclockwise.** Rotates counterclockwise in 90-degree increments with a click.

- **Rotate Clockwise.** Rotates clockwise in 90-degree increments with a click.

5. Using the Basic tab, you can have ACR show you red and blue highlights in the preview that indicate shadow areas that are clipped (too dark to show detail) and light areas that are blown out (too bright). Click the triangles in the upper-left corner of the histogram display (shadow clipping) and upper-right corner (highlight clipping) to toggle these indicators on or off.

6. Also in the Basic tab you can choose white balance, either from the drop-down list or by setting a color temperature and green/magenta color bias (tint) using the sliders.

7. Other sliders are available to control exposure, recovery, fill light, blacks, brightness, contrast, vibrance, and saturation. A check box can be marked to convert the image to grayscale.

8. Make other adjustments (described in more detail below).

9. ACR makes automatic adjustments for you. You can click Default and make the changes for yourself, or click the Auto link (located just above the Exposure slider) to reapply the automatic adjustments after you've made your own modifications.

10. If you've marked more than one image to be opened, the additional images appear in a "filmstrip" at the left side of the screen. You can click on each thumbnail in the filmstrip in turn and apply different settings to each.

11. Click Open Image/Open image(s) into Photoshop using the settings you've made.

The Basic tab is displayed by default when the ACR dialog box opens, and it includes most of the sliders and controls you'll need to fine-tune your image as you import it into Photoshop. These include:

- **White Balance.** Leave it As Shot or change to a value such as Daylight, Cloudy, Shade, Tungsten, Fluorescent, or Flash. If you like, you can set a custom white balance using the Temperature and Tint sliders.

- **Exposure.** This slider adjusts the overall brightness and darkness of the image.

- **Recovery.** Restores detail in the red, green, and blue color channels.

- **Fill Light.** Reconstructs detail in shadows.

- **Blacks.** Increases the number of tones represented as black in the final image, emphasizing tones in the shadow areas of the image.

- **Brightness.** This slider adjusts the brightness and darkness of an image.

- **Contrast.** Manipulates the contrast of the midtones of your image.

- **Convert to Grayscale.** Mark this box to convert the image to black-and-white.

- **Vibrance.** Prevents over-saturation when enriching the colors of an image.

- **Saturation.** Manipulates the richness of all colors equally, from zero saturation (gray/black, no color) at the −100 setting to double the usual saturation at the +100 setting.

Additional controls are available on the Tone Curve, Detail, HSL/Grayscale, Split Toning, Lens Corrections, Camera Calibration, and Presets tabs, shown in Figure 8.13. The Tone Curve tab can change the tonal values of your image. The Detail tab lets you adjust sharpness, luminance smoothing, and apply color noise reduction. The HSL/Grayscale tab offers controls for adjusting hue, saturation, and lightness and converting an image to black and white. Split Toning helps you colorize an image with sepia or cyanotype (blue) shades. The Lens Corrections tab has sliders to adjust for chromatic aberrations and vignetting. The Camera Calibration tab provides a way for calibrating the color corrections made in the Camera Raw plug-in. The Presets tab (not shown) is used to load settings you've stored for reuse.

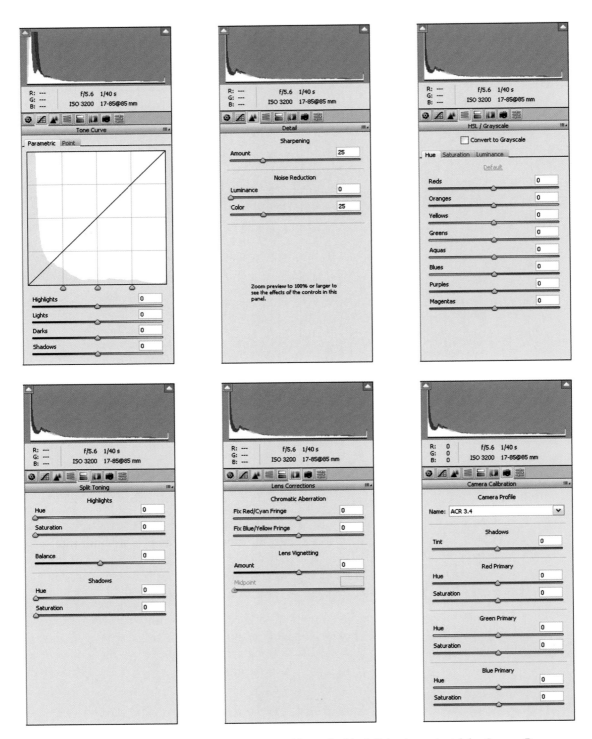

Figure 8.13 More controls are available within the additional tabbed dialog boxes in Adobe Camera Raw.

9

Nikon D90: Troubleshooting and Prevention

You won't expend a lot of effort keeping your Nikon D90 humming and operating smoothly. There's not a lot that can go wrong, and many problems can be fixed simply by resetting your camera by pressing the green-marked "reset" buttons (the "aperture" and "autofocus" buttons located at right on top of the camera) at the same time for a few seconds. An electronically-controlled camera like the Nikon D90 has fewer mechanical moving parts to fail, so they are less likely to "wear out." There is no film transport mechanism, no wind lever or motor drive, and, when using lenses with the AF-S designation (as described in Chapter 6), no complicated mechanical linkages from camera to lens to adjust the automatic focus. Instead, tiny, reliable motors are built into each lens (and you lose the use of only that lens should something fail), and one of the few major moving parts in the camera itself is a lightweight mirror (its small size is one of the advantages of the D90's 1.5X crop factor) that flips up and down with each shot.

Of course, the camera also has a moving shutter that can fail, but the shutter is built rugged enough that, even though Nikon doesn't provide an official toughness "rating," you can reasonably expect it to last 100,000 shutter cycles or more. Unless you're shooting sports in Continuous mode day in and day out, the shutter on your D90 is likely to last as long as you expect to use the camera.

The only other things on the camera that move are switches, dials, buttons, the flip-up electronic flash, and the door that slides open to allow you to remove and insert the Secure Digital card. Unless you're extraordinarily clumsy or unlucky and manage to give your built-in flash a good whack while it is in use, there's not a lot that can go wrong mechanically with your Nikon D90.

There are numerous electrical and electronic connections in the camera (many connected to those mechanical switches and dials), and components like the color LCD and top-panel status LCD that can potentially fail or suffer damage. You must contend with dust lodging itself on your sensor, and, from time to time, with the need to periodically update your camera's internal software, called *firmware*. This chapter will show you how to diagnose problems, fix some common ills, and, importantly, learn how to avoid them in the future.

Battery Powered

One of the chief liabilities of modern electronic cameras is that they are modern *electronic* cameras. Your D90 is fully dependent on two different batteries. Without them, the camera can't be used. Photographers from both the film and digital eras have grown used to this limitation, and I've grown to live with the need for batteries even though I shot for years using all-mechanical Nikon cameras that had no batteries (or even a built-in light meter!). The need for electrical power is the price we pay for modern conveniences like autofocus, autoexposure, LCD image display, backlit menus, and, of course, digital images.

One of the batteries you rely on is the EN-EL3e battery installed in the grip. It's rechargeable, can last for as long as 1,000 shots, and is user-replaceable if you have a spare. It's a time-tested battery, used, not only in the D90, but in its predecessor, the D80 and in the Nikon D200, D300, and even semi-pro Nikon D700 full-frame camera. This same battery (and charger) are also compatible with earlier models, like the Nikon D50 and D70/70s, which were furnished with a slightly different battery.

The second power cell in your camera is a so-called *clock battery*, which is also rechargeable, but is tucked away within the innards of the camera and can't be replaced by the user. The clock battery retains the settings of the camera when it's powered down, and, even, when the main battery is removed for charging. If you remove the EN-EL3e for long periods, the clock battery may discharge; but it will be quickly rejuvenated when you replace the main battery. (It's recharged by juice supplied by the EN-EL3e.) Although you can't replace this battery yourself, you can expect it to last for the useful life of the camera.

So, your main concern will be to provide a continuous, reliable source of power for your D90. As I noted in Chapter 1, you should always have a spare battery or two so you won't need to stop shooting when your internal battery dies. I recommend buying Nikon-brand batteries: saving $20 or so for an after-market battery may seem like a good deal, but it can cost you much more than that if the battery malfunctions and damages your camera.

A good use for those extra batteries is in the Nikon MB-D80 Multi-Power Battery Pack (about $160), which holds two EN-EL3e batteries, effectively doubling your total shooting time. The MB-D80 can also be used with the included AA Battery Holder, allowing you to use six AA batteries in a pinch (included) so users can use AA batteries as a power backup. This type of battery pack is sometimes called a *vertical grip*, because they include a supplemental AF-On button, a vertically oriented shutter release button with lock and front and rear command dials. The control combo makes it more convenient to shoot vertically oriented photos with the camera rotated 90 degrees. Although the MB-D80 was designed for the Nikon D80, it fits and works fine with the D90, which shares battery/electrical connections and a baseplate configuration with the earlier camera.

KEEPING TRACK OF YOUR BATTERIES AND MEMORY CARDS

Here's a trick I use to keep track of which batteries are fresh/discharged, and which memory cards are blank/exposed. I cut up some small slips of paper and fold them in half, forming a tiny "booklet." Then I write EXPOSED in red on the "inside" pages of the booklet and UNEXPOSED in green on the outside pages. Folded one way, the slips read EXPOSED; folded the other way, the slips read UNEXPOSED. I slip them inside the plastic battery cover, which you should *always* use when the batteries are not in the camera (to avoid shorting out the contacts), folded so the appropriate "state" of the batteries is visible. The same slips are used in the translucent plastic cases I use for my memory cards (see Figure 9.1). For my purposes, EXPOSED means the same as DISCHARGED, and UNEXPOSED is the equivalent of CHARGED. The color-coding is an additional clue as to which batteries/memory cards are good to go, or not ready for use.

Figure 9.1
Mark your batteries—or memory cards—so you'll know which are ready for use.

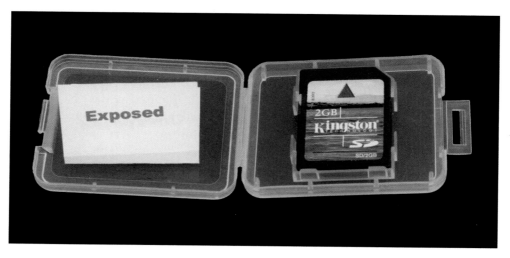

There are several techniques you can use to stretch the longevity of your D90's battery. To get the most from each charge, consider these steps:

- **Playback Menu: Image Review.** Turn off automatic image review after each shot using this menu option. You can still review your images by pressing the Playback button. Or, leave image review on, but set the display for the minimum four seconds as described next.

- **Monitor off Delay.** In CSM #c4, set for the minimum, four seconds, for playback, menus, shooting info display, and image review. That three-inch LCD uses a lot of juice, so reducing the amount of time it is active when you don't turn it off manually can boost the effectiveness of your battery.

- **Auto meter-off-delay.** Set to four seconds in CSM #c2 if you can tolerate such a brief active time.

- **Reduce LCD brightness.** In the Setup menu's LCD Brightness option, select the lowest of the seven brightness settings that work for you under most conditions. If you're willing to shade the LCD with your hand, you can often get away with lower brightness settings outdoors, which will further increase the useful life of your battery.

- **Turn off the Shooting Information Display.** Turn it on or off manually as needed by pressing the INFO button.

- **Reduce internal flash use.** No flash at all or fill flash use less power than a full blast.

- **Don't let the remote keep your D90 hanging.** Use CSM #c5 and select one minute to reduce the amount of time the D90 will remain awake waiting for an IR remote control signal.

- **Cancel VR.** Turn off vibration reduction if your lens (such as the 18-105mm VR kit lens) has that feature and you feel you don't need it.

- **Use a card reader.** When transferring pictures from your D90 to your computer, use a card reader instead of the USB cable. Linking your camera to your computer and transferring images using the cable takes longer and uses a lot more power.

Update Your Firmware

The camera relies on its "operating system," or *firmware*, which should be updated in a reasonable fashion as new releases become available. The firmware in your Nikon D90 handles everything from menu display (including fonts, colors, and the actual entries themselves), what languages are available, and even support for specific devices and features. Upgrading the firmware to a new version makes it possible to add or fine-tune features while fixing some of the bugs that sneak in.

Firmware upgrades are used most frequently to fix bugs in the software, and much less frequently to add or enhance features. The exact changes made to the firmware are generally spelled out in the firmware release announcement. You can examine the remedies provided and decide if a given firmware patch is important to you. If not, you can usually safely wait a while before going through the bother of upgrading your firmware—at least long enough for the early adopters (such as those who haunt the Digital Photography Review forums at www.dpreview.com) to report whether the bug fixes have introduced new bugs of their own. Each new firmware release incorporates the changes from previous releases, so if you skip a minor upgrade you should have no problems.

WHEN TO UPGRADE YOUR FIRMWARE

I *always* recommend waiting at least two weeks after a firmware upgrade is announced before changing the software in your camera. This is often in direct contradiction to the online Nikon "gurus" who breathlessly announce each new firmware release on their web pages, usually with links to where you can download the latest software. *Don't do it!* Yet. Nikon has, in the past, introduced firmware upgrades that were buggy and added problems of their own. If you own a camera affected by a new round of firmware upgrades, I urge you to wait and let a few million over-eager fellow users "beta test" this upgrade for you. Within a few weeks, any problems (although I don't expect there will be any) will surface and you'll know whether the update is safe. Your camera is working fine right now, so why take the chance?

How It Works

If you're computer savvy, you might wonder how your Nikon D90 is able to overwrite its own operating system—that is, how can the existing firmware be used to load the new version on top of itself? It's a little like lifting yourself by reaching down and pulling up on your bootstraps. Not ironically, that's almost exactly what happens: At your command (when you start the upgrade process), the D90 shifts into a special mode in which it is no longer operating from its firmware but, rather, from a small piece of software called a *bootstrap loader*, a separate, protected software program that functions only at startup or when upgrading firmware. The loader's function is to look for firmware to launch or, when directed, to copy new firmware from a Secure Digital card to the internal memory space where the old firmware is located. The loader software isn't set up to go hunting through your Secure Digital card for the firmware file. It looks only in the top or root directory of your card, so that's where you must copy the firmware you download. Once you've determined that a new firmware update is available for your camera and that you want to install it, just follow these steps. (If you chicken out, any Nikon Service Center can install the firmware upgrade for you.)

Why Three Firmware Modules?

Your Nikon D90's firmware is divided into three parts; all earlier Nikon models had the firmware in just two sections. Why chop the firmware up in the first place? And what's that third module for, anyway?

Previous Nikon cameras had an A and B firmware listing, located in the Firmware Version entry in the Setup menu. There's a good reason why the firmware was previously divided in twain. Each of the two modules was "in charge" of particular parts of the camera's operating system. So, when a bug was found, or a new feature added, it was possible, in many cases, to offer only an upgrade for either Firmware A or Firmware B, depending on which module was affected. Although mistakes in upgrading firmware are rare, you cut the opportunities for user errors in half when only one of the modules needs to be replaced.

But there's a more important reason for having at least two firmware modules. If your camera had just one, and you had the misfortune to munge that firmware during an ill-fated upgrade, it's very likely your camera would be magically transformed into a digital doorstop. Part of the firmware is needed simply to install (or re-install firmware) in the first place. With all Nikon cameras, Firmware A and Firmware B each has the capability of locating and installing replacement firmware. So, if A is ruined, you can use the routines in B to re-install a new copy of A. And vice versa. We can all agree that this is a wise move on Nikon's part.

So, what's Firmware L, currently found only in the Nikon D90 and D5000, used for? Some have speculated that the L firmware was a Language database, so that support for the camera could be expanded to include other languages without the need to mess with the A and B entries. I suspected that the L represented a lens database, perhaps to allow the EXPEED processor to compensate for vignetting or aberrations.

The L firmware is so mysterious that the first few Nikon representatives I asked didn't know exactly what it was for, either, but I managed to track down a techie who filled me in, while providing some additional insight into the workings of all three firmware modules. He confirmed that the Nikon D90 was the first Nikon camera to include this third firmware module, and that it was, indeed, a lens database that could be updated from time to time with information about new lenses as they were introduced. The function, he said, was to allow more sophisticated distance integration of information provided by Nikon D and G lenses. It's not too difficult to read between the lines and see what this minor, but significant breakthrough means for we Nikon shooters. Here's what we can look forward to:

- **Better metering.** The L firmware will provide improved and more accurate metering with Color Matrix II for the Nikon D90, D5000, and other Nikon models that are upgraded to include this new, third firmware module. This is only the most obvious benefit.

■ **New features.** With better information about the distance from the camera to the subject, based on improved lens databases, new features like Scene Selection and Face Recognition (and, in the Nikon D5000, subject focus tracking) will be more accurate and available in any shooting mode. Look for your Nikon to be dead-on accurate in evaluating scene types. At the same time, Face Recognition, which some see as a consumer-level gimmick, will become much more useful in more advanced cameras as your Nikon does a better job of picking out one, two, or even more human faces out of a scene, and then focusing and exposing for those faces more precisely.

■ **Better Focus Area Selection.** Various Nikon cameras have a large number of features that do nothing more than select which area to focus on—or to help us select an area. We've got Wide Area, Narrow Area, Auto Area, Dynamic Area, 3D, non-3D, and, depending on your camera and how old it is, you may have 11-point, 21-point, 51-point, Nearest Subject, and other modes.   Distance integration should help present and future Nikon cameras do a better job of selecting focus points, whether using normal modes, Subject Tracking or Face Selection.   I'm hoping that autofocus will be perfected to the point that we have to choose from a couple *fewer* focus options than we have right now.

■ **Better Live View.** Look for more distance integration in Live View. Currently, Live View in the D90 differs from that offered in cameras like the D300, D3, and D3x. These models use both phase detection when calculating focus using the conventional AF sensor (just as the D90 does when not using Live View) and contrast detection when autofocusing using the sensor image (as the D90 does when using Live View). While the D90 has only contrast detection, it's optimized to allow Face Detection, Wide Area, and Normal Area autofocus thanks, in part, to the distance integration information made available by the L firmware. Expect some changes in future Nikon cameras to allow distance integration in both Phase Detect and Contrast Detect modes.

■ **We are not alone.** All future cameras after the D90 and D5000 will include the L firmware. The Nikon tech I spoke to was not an official company spokesman, and obviously not permitted to pre-announce anything. But the fact that he was comfortable expressing his personal opinion that L firmware can be expected in future cameras could mean that all future cameras will have it.

■ **Non-D90 cameras can be upgraded.** Assuming that the solid-state memory used to store firmware has enough space, it should be possible to upgrade existing camera models to include the third, L-type, firmware. You may not have to send in your camera for the upgrade. It should be fairly simple to reprogram the A and B firmware modules to make provisions for using the L firmware, including a routine to load the new L firmware into memory the first time it is installed in an empty region of the firmware chip. I'm assuming that only upper-end cameras, such as the

D300, D3, and D3x will accommodate this, because, presumably, they were designed when the L firmware was already under development, and will have the extra firmware space. If not, you'll have to send your non-D90 camera in to Nikon for the firmware upgrade.

- **Better electronic flash.** You wanna bet that the SB-900 and later flash units won't work better with improved distance integration information, if not with the D90, with Nikon models set for introduction very soon? Don't bet the farm against this idea.

- **Lenses with flashable firmware?** Once Nikon gets on the firmware kick, we may even see lenses with flashable firmware so that as improvements in distance integration come along, the lens can communicate better data to the camera.

- **Significant new lenses on the way.** This is a no-brainer, as we're all expecting a variety of new primes and zooms, anyway. The new Nikon 10-20mm DX zoom lens was introduced while I was writing this book, in fact. But the mere existence of the L firmware strongly confirms that we can expect some new lenses that will take the 1.000 version to additional upgrades.

WARNING

Use a fully charged EN-EL3e charged battery or a Nikon AC adapter to ensure that you'll have enough power to operate the camera for the entire upgrade. Moreover, you should not turn off the camera while your old firmware is being overwritten. Don't open the Secure Digital card door or do anything else that might disrupt operation of the D90 while the firmware is being installed.

Getting Ready

Before you get started, I have to emphasize that at the time this book was written, no new firmware upgrades were available for the Nikon D90, so that I, personally, have never performed this task on my D90. However, I have upgraded the firmware for most of my other Nikon dSLRs, including the very similar D80 model. So, the procedure I am going to describe is the recommended process Nikon has traditionally used. But when it comes time to do an actual firmware upgrade for your D90, you should double check the instructions below against the recommended procedure that Nikon implements at that time. It should be very close to the steps I outline, but there may be some small differences.

The first thing to do is determine whether you need the current firmware update. First, confirm the version number of your Nikon D90's current firmware:

1. Turn on the D90.

2. Press the Menu button and select Firmware Version from the Setup menu. The camera's firmware version will be displayed, as in Figure 9.2.

3. Write down the version number for Parts A, B, and L.

4. Turn off the D90.

Figure 9.2
View your current firmware versions before upgrading.

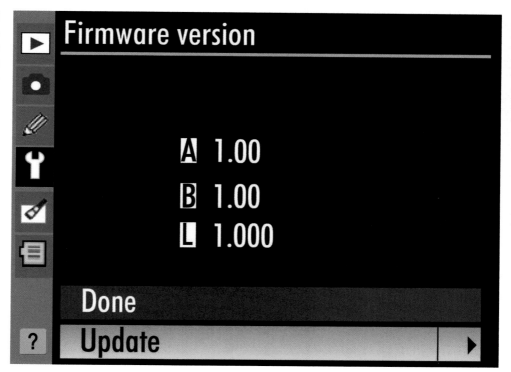

Next, go to the Nikon support site, locate, and download the firmware update. In the USA, the place to go is http://support.nikontech.com/, which will offer a list of choices, including one that says Current Firmware Downloads available for Nikon Products. Click that link, then click the DSLR link on the page displayed next. Scroll down to the D90 row in the table, and review the version number for the current update.

If the version is later than the one you noted in your camera, click the firmware link in either the Windows or Macintosh columns (depending on your computer) to download the file. It will have a name like D90Update.zip (Windows) or D90update.sitx (Macintosh). Extract the file to a folder on your computer using the unzipping or unstuffing software of your choice.

The D90's firmware comes in three parts, A, B and L, which can be updated individually. The actual update files will be named something like:

A9000101.bin

B9000101.bin

L9000101.bin

The final preparation you need to make is to decide whether you'd like to upgrade your firmware using a memory card reader, or by transferring the software to the D90 using the UC-E4 USB cable. In either case, you'll need to format a memory card in the D90. Then, perform one of the sets of steps in the sections that follow.

Updating from a Card Reader

To update from a card reader, use a reader connected to your computer with a USB cable. Then, follow these steps:

1. Insert a formatted memory card into the card reader. If you have been using Nikon Transfer or the "autoplay" features of your operating system to transfer images from your memory card to the computer, the automated transfer dialog box may appear. Close it.

2. The memory card will appear on your Macintosh desktop, or in the Computer/My Computer folders under Windows Vista/Windows XP.

3. Drag one of the firmware files to the memory card. You can install "A," "B," or "L" first (if all three are provided); it doesn't matter. If your particular upgrade consists of only one of the three files, drag that to the memory card. Remember to copy the firmware to the *root* (top) directory of the memory card. The D90 will be unable to find it if you place it in a folder.

Updating with a USB Connection

You can also copy the firmware to the D90's memory card using a USB connection. Just follow these steps:

1. With the camera turned off, insert the formatted memory card. Then, turn the camera back on.

2. Press the Menu button and navigate to the Setup menu.

3. Choose USB and set the option to Mass Storage, as described in Chapter 3.

4. Turn off the D90 and connect it to your computer using the UC-E4 USB cable.

5. Turn the camera back on. If you have been using Nikon Transfer or the "autoplay" features of your operating system to transfer images from your memory card to the computer, the automated transfer dialog box may appear. Close it.

6. The camera will appear on the Macintosh desktop, or in the Computer/My Computer folders under Windows Vista/Windows XP.

7. Drag one of the firmware files to the memory card. It doesn't matter whether you install "A," "B," or "L" first. If your particular upgrade consists of only one .bin file, drag that to the memory card. Remember to copy the firmware to the *root* (top) directory of the memory card. The D90 will be unable to find it if you place it in a folder.

8. Disconnect the camera from the computer.

Starting the Update

To perform the actual update, follow these steps:

1. With the memory card containing the firmware update software in the camera, turn on the camera.

2. Press the Menu button and select Firmware Version in the Setup menu.

3. Select Version Up and press the multi-selector button to the right.

4. When the firmware update screen appears, highlight Yes and press OK to begin the update.

5. The actual process may take a few minutes (from two to five). Be sure not to turn off the camera or perform any other operations while it is underway.

6. When the update is completed, the warning message will no longer be displayed on the screen. You can turn off the camera when the message disappears.

7. Remove the memory card.

8. Turn the D90 back on to load the updated firmware.

9. Press the Menu button and select Firmware Version in the Setup menu to view the current firmware number. If it matches the update, you've successfully upgraded that portion of the firmware.

10. Reformat the memory card.

11. If there is a second or third part to your firmware upgrade ("A," "B," or "L"), then repeat all the steps for the additional firmware software.

12. If you transferred the firmware files to the memory card using USB transfer, then go back to the Setup menu, choose USB, and set the option to MTP/PTP, as described in Chapter 3.

Protect Your LCD

The large three-inch color LCD on the back of your Nikon D90 almost seems like a target for banging, scratching, and other abuse. The LCD itself is quite rugged, and a few errant knocks are unlikely to shatter the protective cover over the LCD, and scratches won't easily mar its surface. However, if you want to be on the safe side, there are a number of protective products you can purchase to keep your LCD safe—and, in some cases, make it a little easier to view. Here's a quick overview of your options.

- **Plastic overlays.** The simplest solution (although not always the cheapest) is to apply a plastic overlay sheet or "skin" cut to fit your LCD. These adhere either by static electricity or through a light adhesive coating that's even less clingy than stick-it notes. You can cut down overlays made for PDAs (although these can be pricey at up to $19.95 for a set of several sheets), or purchase overlays sold specifically for digital cameras. Vendors such as Hoodman (www.hoodmanusa.com) offer overlays of this type. These products will do a good job of shielding your D90's LCD screen from scratches and minor impacts, but will not offer much protection from a good whack.

- **Acrylic shields.** These scratch-resistant acrylic panels, laser cut to fit your camera perfectly, are my choice as the best protection solution, and what I use on my own D90. At about $6 each, they also happen to be the least expensive option as well. I get mine, shown in Figure 9.3, from a company called 'da Products (www.daproducts.com). They attach using strips of sticky adhesive that hold the panel flush and tight, but which allow the acrylic to be pried off and the adhesive removed easily if you want to remove or replace the shield. They don't attenuate your view of the LCD and are non-reflective enough for use under a variety of lighting conditions

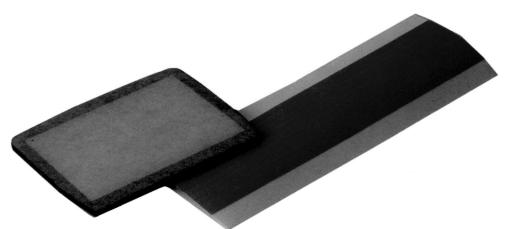

Figure 9.3
A tough acrylic shield, here shown with a piece of plastic containing a set of peel-off sticky strips to help it adhere to the camera, can protect your LCD from scratches.

- **Flip-up hoods.** These protectors slip on using the flanges around your D90's eye-piece, and provide a cover that completely shields the LCD, but unfolds to provide a three-sided hood that allows viewing the LCD while minimizing the extraneous light falling on it and reducing contrast. They're sold for about $40 by Delkin and Hoodman. If you want to completely protect your LCD from hard knocks and need to view the screen outdoors in bright sunlight, there is nothing better. However, I have a couple problems with these devices. First, with the cover closed, you can't peek down after taking a shot to see what your image looks like during picture review. You must open the cap each time you want to look at the LCD. Moreover, with the hood unfolded, it's difficult to look through the viewfinder: Don't count on being able to use the viewfinder *and* the LCD at the same time with one of these hoods in place.

- **Magnifiers.** If you look hard enough, you should be able to find an LCD magnifier that fits over the monitor panel and provides a 2X magnification. These often strap on clumsily, and serve better as a way to get an enlarged view of the LCD than as protection. Hoodman, Photodon (www.photodon.com), and other suppliers offer these specialized devices.

Troubleshooting Memory Cards

Sometimes good memory cards go bad. Sometimes good photographers can treat their memory cards badly. It's possible that a memory card that works fine in one camera won't be recognized when inserted into another. In the worst case, you can have a card full of important photos and find that the card seems to be corrupted and you can't access any of them. Don't panic! If these scenarios sound horrific to you, there are lots of things you can do to prevent them from happening, and a variety of remedies available if they do occur. You'll want to take some time—before disaster strikes—to consider your options.

All Your Eggs in One Basket?

The debate about whether it's better to use one large memory card or several smaller ones has been going on since even before there were memory cards. I can remember when computer users wondered whether it was smarter to install a pair of 200MB (not *gigabyte*) hard drives in their computer, or if they should go for one of those new-fangled 500MB models. By the same token, a few years ago the user groups were full of proponents who insisted that you ought to use 128MB memory cards rather than the huge 512MB versions. Today, most of the arguments involve 8GB cards versus 4GB cards, and I expect that as prices for 16GB SD cards continue to drop, they'll find their way into the debate as well.

Why all the fuss? Are 8GB memory cards more likely to fail than 4GB cards? Are you risking all your photos if you trust your images to a larger card? Isn't it better to use several smaller cards, so that if one fails you lose only half as many photos? Or, isn't it wiser to put all your photos onto one larger card, because the more cards you use, the better your odds of misplacing or damaging one and losing at least some pictures?

In the end, the "eggs in one basket" argument boils down to statistics, and how you happen to use your D90. The rationales can go both ways. If you have multiple smaller cards, you do increase your chances of something happening to one of them, so, arguably, you might be boosting the odds of losing some pictures. If all your images are important, the fact that you've lost 100 rather than 200 pictures isn't very comforting.

Also consider that the eggs/basket scenario assumes that the cards that are lost or damaged are always full. It's actually likely that your 8GB card might suffer a mishap when it's less than half full (indeed, it's more likely that a large card won't be completely filled before it's offloaded to a computer), so you really might not lose any more shots with a single 8GB card than with multiple 4GB or 2GB cards.

If you shoot photojournalist-type pictures, you probably change memory cards when they're less than completely full in order to avoid the need to do so at a crucial moment. (When I shoot sports, my cards rarely reach 80 to 90 percent of capacity before I change them.) Using multiple smaller cards means you have to change them that more often, which can be a real pain when you're taking a lot of photos. As an example, if you use 1GB memory cards with a Nikon D90 and shoot RAW+JPEG Basic, you may get only a few dozen pictures on the card. That's not even twice the capacity of a 36-exposure roll of film (remember those?). In my book, I prefer keeping all my eggs in one basket, and then making very sure that nothing happens to that basket.

The other reason comes into play when every single picture is precious to you and the loss of any of them would be a disaster. If you were a wedding photographer, for example, and unlikely to be able to restage the nuptials if a memory card goes bad, you'll probably want to shoot no more pictures than you can afford to lose on a single card, and have an assistant ready to copy each card removed from the camera onto a backup hard drive or DVD onsite.

If none of these options are available to you, consider *interleaving* your shots. Say you don't shoot weddings with a Nikon D90, but you do go on vacation from time to time. Take 50 or so pictures on one card, or whatever number of images might fill about 25 percent of its capacity. Then, replace it with a different card and shoot about 25 percent of that card's available space. Repeat these steps with diligence (you'd have to be determined to go through this inconvenience), and, if you use four or more memory cards you'll find your pictures from each location scattered among the different Secure Digital cards. If you lose or damage one, you'll still have *some* pictures from all the various stops on your trip on the other cards. That's more work than I like to do (I usually tote around a portable hard disk and copy the files to the drive as I go), but it's an option.

Another option is to transmit your images, as they are shot, over a network to your laptop, assuming a network and a laptop are available. A company called Eye-Fi (www.eye.fi [no .com]) markets a clever SD card with wireless capabilities built-in. They currently offer four models, including the basic Eye-Fi Home (about $50) which can be used to transmit your photos from the D90 to a computer on your home network (or any other network you set up somewhere, say, at a family reunion. Eye-Fi Share and Eye-Fi Share Video (about $60 and $80, respectively), which are basically exactly the same (Share Video is 4GB instead of 2GB in capacity), but includes software to allow you to upload your images from your camera through your computer network directly to websites such as Flickr, Facebook, Shutterfly, Nikon's own My Picturetown, and digital printing services that include Walmart Digital Photo Center. The most sophisticated option is Eye-Fi Explore, a 4GB SDHC card that adds geographic location labels to your photo (so you'll know where you took it), and frees you from your own computer network by allowing uploads from more than 10,000 WiFi hotspots around the USA. Very cool, and the ultimate in picture backup.

What Can Go Wrong?

There are lots of things that can go wrong with your memory card, but the ones that aren't caused by human stupidity are statistically very rare. Yes, a Secure Digital card's internal bit bin or controller can suddenly fail due to a manufacturing error or some inexplicable event caused by old age. However, if your SD card works for the first week or two that you own it, it should work forever. There's really not a lot that can wear out.

The typical Secure Digital card is rated for a Mean Time Between Failures of 1,000,000 hours of use. That's constant use 24/7 for more than 100 years! According to the manufacturers, they are good for 10,000 insertions in your camera, and should be able to retain their data (and that's without an external power source) for something on the order of 11 years. Of course, with the millions of SD cards in use, there are bound to be a few lemons here or there.

Given the reliability of solid-state memory compared to magnetic memory, though, it's more likely that your Secure Digital problems will stem from something that you do. SD cards are small and easy to misplace if you're not careful. For that reason, it's a good idea to keep them in their original cases or a "card safe" offered by Gepe (www.gepe.com), Pelican (www.pelican.com), and others. Always placing your memory card in a case can provide protection from the second-most common mishap that befalls Secure Digital cards: the common household laundry. If you slip a memory card in a pocket, rather than a case or your camera bag often enough, sooner or later it's going to end up in the washing machine and probably the clothes dryer, too. There are plenty of reports of relieved digital camera owners who've laundered their memory cards and found they still worked fine, but it's not uncommon for such mistreatment to do some damage.

Memory cards can also be stomped on, accidentally bent, dropped into the ocean, chewed by pets, and otherwise rendered unusable in myriad ways. Or, if the card is formatted in your computer with a memory card reader, your D90 may fail to recognize it. Occasionally, I've found that a memory card used in one camera would fail if used in a different camera (until I reformatted it in Windows, and then again in the camera). Every once in awhile, a card goes completely bad and—seemingly—can't be salvaged.

Another way to lose images is to do commonplace things with your SD card at an inopportune time. If you remove the card from the D90 while the camera is writing images to the card, you'll lose any photos in the buffer and may damage the file structure of the card, making it difficult or impossible to retrieve the other pictures you've taken. The same thing can happen if you remove the SD card from your computer's card reader while the computer is writing to the card (say, to erase files you've already moved to your computer). You can avoid this by *not* using your computer to erase files on a Secure Digital card but, instead, always reformatting the card in your D90 before you use it again.

What Can You Do?

Pay attention: If you're having problems, the *first* thing you should do is *stop* using that memory card. Don't take any more pictures. Don't do anything with the card until you've figured out what's wrong. Your second line of defense (your first line is to be sufficiently careful with your cards that you avoid problems in the first place) is to *do no harm* that hasn't already been done. Read the rest of this section and then, if necessary, decide on a course of action (such as using a data recovery service or software, described later) before you risk damaging the data on your card further.

Now that you've calmed down, the first thing to check is whether you've actually inserted a card in the camera. If you've set the camera in the Custom Setting so that the No Memory Card? option has been set to allow taking pictures without a card, it's entirely possible (although not particularly plausible) that you've been snapping away with no memory card to store the pictures to, which can lead to massive disappointment later on. You can avoid all this by setting the No Memory Card? (CSM #f6) feature to Release Locked, and leaving it there.

Things get more exciting when the card itself is put in jeopardy. If you lose a card, there's not a lot you can do other than take a picture of a similar card and print up some Have You Seen This Lost Flash Memory? flyers to post on utility poles all around town.

If all you care about is reusing the card, and have resigned yourself to losing the pictures, try reformatting the card in your camera. You may find that reformatting removes the corrupted data and restores your card to health. Sometimes I've had success reformatting a card in my computer using a memory card reader (this is normally a no-no because your operating system doesn't understand the needs of your D90), and *then* reformatting again in the camera.

If your Secure Digital card is not behaving properly, and you *do* want to recover your images, things get a little more complicated. If your pictures are very valuable, either to you or to others (for example, a wedding), you can always turn to professional data recovery firms. Be prepared to pay hundreds of dollars to get your pictures back, but these pros often do an amazing job. You wouldn't want them working on your memory card on behalf of the police if you'd tried to erase some incriminating pictures. There are many firms of this type, and I've never used them myself, so I can't offer a recommendation. Use a Google search to turn up a ton of them.

THE ULTIMATE IRONY

I recently purchased an 8GB Kingston memory card that was furnished with some nifty OnTrack data recovery software. The first thing I did was format the card to make sure it was OK. Then I hunted around for the free software, only to discover it was preloaded onto the memory card. I was supposed to copy the software to my computer before using the memory card for the first time. Fortunately, I had the OnTrack software that would reverse my dumb move, so I could retrieve the software. No, wait. I *didn't* have the software I needed to recover the software I erased. I'd reformatted it to oblivion. Chalk this one up as either the ultimate irony or Stupid Photographer Trick #523.

A more reasonable approach is to try special data recovery software you can install on your computer and use to attempt to resurrect your "lost" images yourself. They may not actually be gone completely. Perhaps your SD card's "table of contents" is jumbled, or only a few pictures are damaged in such a way that your camera and computer can't read some or any of the pictures on the card. Some of the available software was written specifically to reconstruct lost pictures, while other utilities are more general-purpose applications that can be used with any media, including floppy disks and hard disk drives. They have names like OnTrack, Photo Rescue 2, Digital Image Recovery, MediaRecover, Image Recall, and the aptly named Recover My Photos. You'll find a comprehensive list and links, as well as some picture-recovery tips at www.ultimateslr.com/memory-card-recovery.php. I like the RescuePRO software that SanDisk supplies (see Figure 9.4), especially since it came on a mini-CD that was totally unable to erase by mistake.

DIMINISHING RETURNS

Usually, once you've recovered any images on a Secure Digital card, reformatted it, and returned it to service, it will function reliably for the rest of its useful life. However, if you find a particular card going bad more than once, you'll almost certainly want to stop using it forever. See if you can get it replaced by the manufacturer if you can, but, in the case of SD card failures, the third time is never the charm.

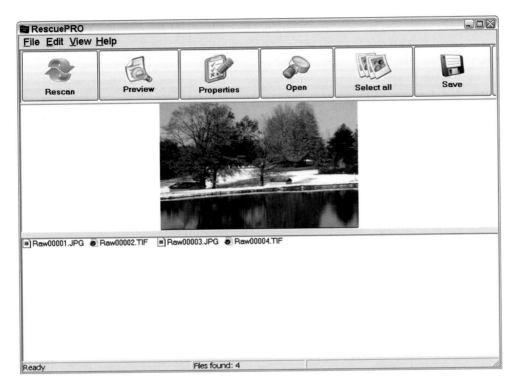

Figure 9.4
SanDisk
supplies
RescuePRO
recovery soft-
ware with some
of its memory
cards.

Clean Your Sensor

Yes, the Nikon D90 has a two-pronged sensor dust prevention scheme: an innovative air control system that keeps dust away from the sensor in the first place, and a sensor-shaking cleaning mechanism. But no dust-busting technology is 100-percent effective.

Indeed, there's no avoiding dust. No matter how careful you are, some of it is going to settle on your camera and on the mounts of your lenses, eventually making its way inside your camera to settle in the mirror chamber. As you take photos, the mirror flipping up and down causes the dust to become airborne and eventually make its way past the shutter curtain to come to rest on the anti-aliasing filter atop your sensor. There, dust and particles can show up in every single picture you take at a small enough aperture to bring the foreign matter into sharp focus. No matter how careful you are and how cleanly you work, eventually you will get some of this dust on your camera's sensor.

But as I mentioned, one of the Nikon D90's most useful new features is the automatic sensor cleaning system that reduces or eliminates the need to clean your camera's sensor manually. The sensor vibrates ultrasonically each time the D90 is powered either on or off (or both, at your option), shaking loose any dust.

Although the automatic sensor cleaning feature operates when you power the camera up or turn it off, (depending on the behavior you specify in the Setup menu), you can activate it manually at any time. Choose Clean Image Sensor from the Setup menu, and select Clean Now. If you'd rather specify when automatic cleaning occurs, choose On (clean at power up), Off (clean when the camera is switched off), On/Off (clean at both power up and power down), or Cleaning Off (no automatic sensor cleaning will take place).

If some dust does collect on your sensor, you can often map it out of your images (making it invisible) using software techniques with the Dust Off Ref Photo feature in the Setup menu. Operation of this feature is described in Chapter 3.

Of course, even with the Nikon D90's automatic sensor cleaning/dust resistance features, you may still be required to manually clean your sensor from time to time. This section explains the phenomenon and provides some tips on minimizing dust and eliminating it when it begins to affect your shots. I also cover this subject in my book, *Digital SLR Pro Secrets*, with complete instructions for constructing your own sensor cleaning tools. However, I'll provide a condensed version here of some of the information in that book, because sensor dust and sensor cleaning are two of the most contentious subjects Nikon D90 owners have to deal with.

Dust the FAQs, Ma'am

Here are some of the most frequently asked questions about sensor dust issues.

Q. I see tiny specks in my viewfinder. Do I have dust on my sensor?
A. If you see sharp, well-defined specks, they are clinging to the underside of your focus screen and not on your sensor. They have absolutely no effect on your photographs, and are merely annoying or distracting.

Q. I can see dust on my mirror. How can I remove it?
A. Like focus-screen dust, any artifacts that have settled on your mirror won't affect your photos. You can often remove dust on the mirror or focus screen with a bulb air blower, which will loosen it and whisk it away. Stubborn dust on the focus screen can sometimes be gently flicked away with a soft brush designed for cleaning lenses. I don't recommend brushing the mirror or touching it in any way. The mirror is a special front-surface-silvered optical device (unlike conventional mirrors, which are silvered on the back side of a piece of glass or plastic) and can be easily scratched. If you can't blow mirror dust off, it's best to just forget about it. You can't see it in the viewfinder, anyway.

Q. I see a bright spot in the same place in all of my photos. Is that sensor dust?
A. You've probably got either a "hot" pixel or one that is permanently "stuck" due to a defect in the sensor. A hot pixel is one that shows up as a bright spot only during long exposures as the sensor warms. A pixel stuck in the "on" position always appears in the image. Both show up as bright red, green, or blue pixels, usually surrounded by a small cluster of other improperly illuminated pixels, caused by the camera's

interpolating the hot or stuck pixel into its surroundings, as shown in Figure 9.5. A stuck pixel can also be permanently dark. Either kind is likely to show up when they contrast with plain, evenly colored areas of your image.

Finding one or two hot or stuck pixels in your sensor is unfortunately fairly common. They can be "removed" by telling the D90 to ignore them through a simple process called *pixel mapping*. If the bad pixels become bothersome, Nikon can remap your sensor's pixels with a quick trip to a service center.

Bad pixels can also show up on your camera's color LCD panel, but, unless they are abundant, the wisest course is to just ignore them.

Q. I see an irregular out-of-focus blob in the same place in my photos. Is that sensor dust?

A. Yes. Sensor contaminants can take the form of tiny spots, larger blobs, or even curvy lines if they are caused by minuscule fibers that have settled on the sensor. They'll appear out of focus because they aren't actually on the sensor surface but, rather, a fraction of a millimeter above it on the filter that covers the sensor. The smaller the f/stop used, the more in-focus the dust becomes. At large apertures, it may not be visible at all.

Q. I never see any dust on my sensor. What's all the fuss about?

A. Those who never have dust problems with their Nikon D90 fall into one of four categories: those for whom the camera's automatic dust removal features are working well; those who seldom change their lenses and have clean working habits that minimize the amount of dust that invades their cameras in the first place; those who simply don't notice the dust (often because they don't shoot many macro photos or other pictures using the small f/stops that makes dust evident in their images); and those who are very, very lucky.

Figure 9.5
A stuck pixel is surrounded by improperly interpolated pixels created by the D90's demosaicing algorithm.

Identifying and Dealing with Dust

Sensor dust is less of a problem than it might be because it shows up only under certain circumstances. Indeed, you might have dust on your sensor right now and not be aware of it. The dust doesn't actually settle on the sensor itself, but, rather, on a protective filter a very tiny distance above the sensor, subjecting it to the phenomenon of *depth-of-focus*. Depth-of-focus is the distance the focal plane can be moved and still render an object in sharp focus. At f/2.8 to f/5.6 or even smaller, sensor dust, particularly if small, is likely to be outside the range of depth-of-focus and blur into an unnoticeable dot.

However, if you're shooting at f/16 to f/22 or smaller, those dust motes suddenly pop into focus. Forget about trying to spot them by peering directly at your sensor with the shutter open and the lens removed. The period at the end of this sentence, about .33mm in diameter, could block a group of pixels measuring 40 × 40 pixels (160 pixels in all!). Dust spots that are even smaller than that can easily show up in your images if you're shooting large, empty areas that are light colored. Dust motes are most likely to show up in the sky, as in Figure 9.6, or in white backgrounds of your seamless product shots and are less likely to be a problem in images that contain lots of dark areas and detail.

To see if you have dust on your sensor, take a few test shots of a plain, blank surface (such as a piece of paper or a cloudless sky) at small f/stops, such as f/22, and a few wide

Figure 9.6
Only the dust spots in the sky are apparent in this shot.

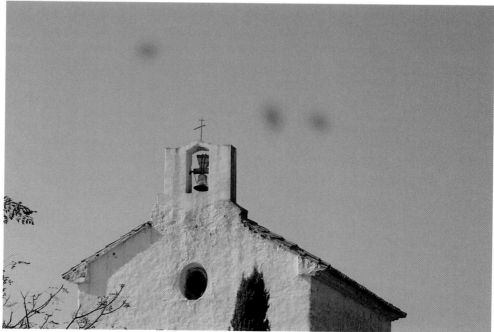

open. Open Photoshop or another image editor, copy several shots into a single document in separate layers, then flip back and forth between layers to see if any spots you see are present in all layers. You may have to boost contrast and sharpness to make the dust easier to spot.

Avoiding Dust

Of course, the easiest way to protect your sensor from dust is to prevent it from settling on the sensor in the first place. Here are my stock tips for eliminating the problem before it begins.

- **Clean environment.** Avoid working in dusty areas if you can do so. Hah! Serious photographers will take this one with a grain of salt, because it usually makes sense to go where the pictures are. Only a few of us are so paranoid about sensor dust (considering that it is so easily removed) that we'll avoid moderately grimy locations just to protect something that is, when you get down to it, just a tool. If you find a great picture opportunity at a raging fire, during a sandstorm, or while surrounded by dust clouds, you might hesitate to take the picture, but, with a little caution (don't remove your lens in these situations, and clean the camera afterwards!) you can still shoot. However, it still makes sense to store your camera in a clean environment. One place cameras and lenses pick up a lot of dust is inside a camera bag. Clean your bag from time to time, and you can avoid problems.

- **Clean lenses.** There are a few paranoid types that avoid swapping lenses in order to minimize the chance of dust getting inside their cameras. It makes more sense just to use a blower or brush to dust off the rear lens mount of the replacement lens first, so you won't be introducing dust into your camera simply by attaching a new, dusty lens. Do this before you remove the current lens from your camera, and then avoid stirring up dust before making the exchange.

- **Work fast.** Minimize the time your camera is lens-less and exposed to dust. That means having your replacement lens ready and dusted off, and a place to set down the old lens as soon as it is removed, so you can quickly attach the new lens.

- **Let gravity help you.** Face the camera downward when the lens is detached so any dust in the mirror box will tend to fall away from the sensor. Turn your back to any breezes, indoor forced air vents, fans, or other sources of dust to minimize infiltration.

- **Protect the lens you just removed.** Once you've attached the new lens, quickly put the end cap on the one you just removed to reduce the dust that might fall on it.

- **Clean out the vestibule.** From time to time, remove the lens while in a relatively dust-free environment and use a blower bulb like the one shown in Figure 9.7 (*not* compressed air or a vacuum hose) to clean out the mirror box area. A blower bulb is generally safer than a can of compressed air or a strong positive/negative airflow, which can tend to drive dust further into nooks and crannies.

- **Be prepared.** If you're embarking on an important shooting session, it's a good idea to clean your sensor *now*, rather than come home with hundreds or thousands of images with dust spots caused by flecks that were sitting on your sensor before you even started. Before I left on my recent trip to Spain, I put both cameras I was taking through a rigid cleaning regimen, figuring they could remain dust-free for a measly 10 days. I even left my bulky blower bulb at home, and took along a new, smaller version for emergencies.

- **Clone out existing spots in your image editor.** Photoshop and other editors have a clone tool or healing brush you can use to copy pixels from surrounding areas over the dust spot or dead pixel. This process can be tedious, especially if you have lots of dust spots and/or lots of images to be corrected. The advantage is that this sort of manual fix-it probably will do the least damage to the rest of your photo. Only the damaged pixels will be affected.

- **Use filtration in your image editor.** A semi-smart filter like Photoshop's Dust & Scratches filter can remove dust and other artifacts by selectively blurring areas that the plug-in decides represent dust spots. This method can work well if you have many dust spots, because you won't need to patch them manually. However, any automated method like this has the possibility of blurring areas of your image that you didn't intend to soften.

Figure 9.7
Use a robust air bulb like the Giottos Rocket for cleaning your sensor.

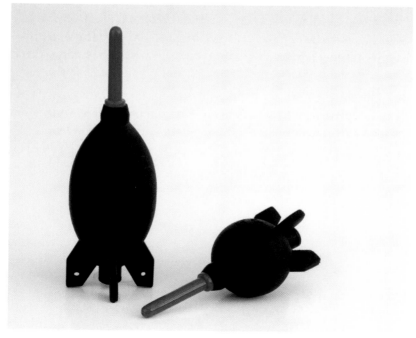

Sensor Cleaning

Those new to the concept of sensor dust actually hesitate before deciding to clean their camera themselves. Isn't it a better idea to pack up your D90 and send it to a Nikon service center so their crack technical staff can do the job for you? Or, at the very least, shouldn't you let the friendly folks at your local camera store do it?

Of course, if you choose to let someone else clean your sensor, they will be using methods that are more or less identical to the techniques you would use yourself. None of these techniques are difficult, and the only difference between their cleaning and your cleaning is that they might have done it dozens or hundreds of times. If you're careful, you can do just as good a job.

Of course vendors like Nikon won't tell you this, but it's not because they don't trust you. It's not that difficult for a real goofball to mess up his camera by hurrying or taking a shortcut. Perhaps the person uses the "bulb" method of holding the shutter open and a finger slips, allowing the shutter curtain to close on top of a sensor cleaning brush. Or, someone tries to clean the sensor using masking tape, and ends up with goo all over its surface. If Nikon recommended *any* method that's mildly risky, someone would do it wrong, and then the company would face lawsuits from those who'd contend they did it exactly in the way the vendor suggested, so the ruined camera is not their fault.

You can see that vendors like Nikon tend to be conservative in their recommendations, and, in doing so, make it seem as if sensor cleaning is more daunting and dangerous than it really is. Some vendors recommend only dust-off cleaning, through the use of reasonably gentle blasts of air, while condemning more serious scrubbing with swabs and cleaning fluids. However, these cleaning kits for the exact types of cleaning they recommended against are for sale in Japan only, where, apparently, your average photographer is more dexterous than those of us in the rest of the world. These kits are similar to those used by official repair staff to clean your sensor if you decide to send your camera in for a dust-up.

As I noted, sensors can be affected by dust particles that are much smaller than you might be able to spot visually on the surface of your lens. The filters that cover sensors tend to be fairly hard compared to optical glass. Cleaning the sensor in your Nikon D90 within the tight confines of the mirror box can call for a steady hand and careful touch. If your sensor's filter becomes scratched through inept cleaning, you can't simply remove it yourself and replace it with a new one.

There are four basic kinds of cleaning processes that can be used to remove dusty and sticky stuff that settles on your dSLR's sensor. All of these must be performed with the shutter locked open. I'll describe these methods and provide instructions for locking the shutter later in this section.

- **Air cleaning.** This process involves squirting blasts of air inside your camera with the shutter locked open. This works well for dust that's not clinging stubbornly to your sensor.

- **Brushing.** A soft, very fine brush is passed across the surface of the sensor's filter, dislodging mildly persistent dust particles and sweeping them off the imager.

- **Liquid cleaning.** A soft swab dipped in a cleaning solution such as ethanol is used to wipe the sensor filter, removing more obstinate particles.

- **Tape cleaning.** There are some who get good results by applying a special form of tape to the surface of their sensor. When the tape is peeled off, all the dust goes with it. Supposedly. I'd be remiss if I didn't point out right now that this form of cleaning is somewhat controversial; the other three methods are much more widely accepted.

Placing the Mirror/Shutter in the Locked and Fully Upright Position for Landing

Make sure you're using a fully charged battery or a Nikon AC adapter. Fortunately, the Nikon D90 is smart enough that it won't let you try to clean the sensor manually unless the battery has a sufficient charge.

1. Remove the lens from the camera and then turn on the camera.

2. You'll find the Lock Mirror Up for Cleaning menu choice in the Setup menu. Select it.

3. Choose Start. The mirror will flip up when you press the shutter release button, and the shutter will open.

4. Remove the lens from the camera.

5. Use one of the methods described below to remove dust and grime from your sensor. Be careful not to accidentally switch the power off or open the Secure Digital card or battery compartment doors as you work. If that happens, the shutter may be damaged if it closes onto your cleaning tool.

6. When you're finished, turn the power off, replace your lens, and switch your camera back on.

Air Cleaning

Your first attempts at cleaning your sensor should always involve gentle blasts of air. Many times, you'll be able to dislodge dust spots, which will fall off the sensor and, with luck, out of the mirror box. Attempt one of the other methods only when you've already tried air cleaning and it didn't remove all the dust.

Here are some tips for doing air cleaning:

- **Use a clean, powerful air bulb.** Your best bet is bulb cleaners designed for the job, like the Giottos Rocket shown in Figure 9.7. Smaller bulbs, like those air bulbs with a brush attached sometimes sold for lens cleaning or weak nasal aspirators may not provide sufficient air or a strong enough blast to do much good.

- **Hold the Nikon D90 upside down.** Then look up into the mirror box as you squirt your air blasts, increasing the odds that gravity will help pull the expelled dust downward, away from the sensor. You may have to use some imagination in positioning yourself.

- **Never use air canisters.** The propellant inside these cans can permanently coat your sensor if you tilt the can while spraying. It's not worth taking a chance.

- **Avoid air compressors.** Super-strong blasts of air are likely to force dust under the sensor filter and possibly damage some internal parts.

Brush Cleaning

If your dust is a little more stubborn and can't be dislodged by air alone, you may want to try a brush, charged with static electricity, which can pick off dust spots by electrical attraction. One good, but expensive, option is the Sensor Brush sold at www.visible-dust.com. A cheaper version can be purchased at www.copperhillimages.com. You need a 16mm version, like the one shown in Figure 9.8, which can be stroked across the short dimension of your D90's sensor.

Ordinary artist's brushes are much too coarse and stiff and have fibers that are tangled or can come loose and settle on your sensor. A good sensor brush's fibers are resilient and described as "thinner than a human hair." Moreover, the brush has a wooden handle that reduces the risk of static sparks. Check out my *Digital SLR Pro Secrets* book if you want to make a sensor brush (or sensor swabs) yourself.

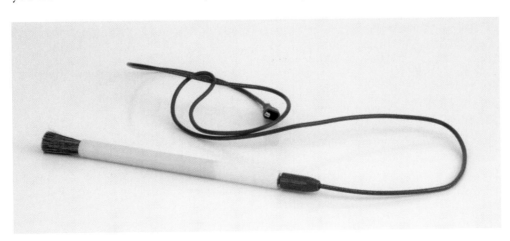

Figure 9.8
A proper brush, such as this model with a grounding strap, is required for dusting off your sensor.

Brush cleaning is done with a dry brush by gently swiping the surface of the sensor filter with the tip. The dust particles are attracted to the brush particles and cling to them. You should clean the brush with compressed air before and after each use, and store it in an appropriate air-tight container between applications to keep it clean and dust-free. Although these special brushes are expensive, one should last you a long time.

Liquid Cleaning

Unfortunately, you'll often encounter really stubborn dust spots that can't be removed with a blast of air or flick of a brush. These spots may be combined with some grease or a liquid that causes them to stick to the sensor filter's surface. In such cases, liquid cleaning with a swab may be necessary. During my first clumsy attempts to clean my own sensor, I accidentally got my blower bulb tip too close to the sensor, and some sort of deposit from the tip of the bulb ended up on the sensor. I panicked until I discovered that liquid cleaning did a good job of removing whatever it was that took up residence on my sensor.

You can make your own swabs out of pieces of plastic (some use fast food restaurant knives, with the tip cut at an angle to the proper size) covered with a soft cloth or Pec-Pad, as shown in Figures 9.9 and 9.10. However, if you've got the bucks to spend, you can't go wrong with good-quality commercial sensor cleaning swabs, such as those sold by Photographic Solutions, Inc. (www.photosol.com/swabproduct.htm).

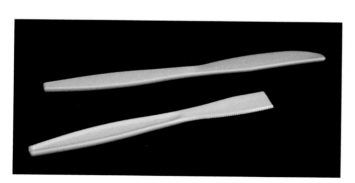

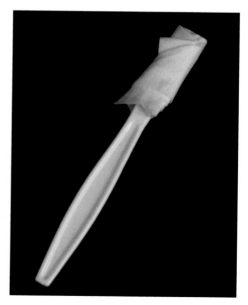

Figure 9.9 You can make your own sensor swab from a plastic knife that's been truncated.

Figure 9.10 Carefully wrap a Pec-Pad around the swab.

You want a sturdy swab that won't bend or break so you can apply gentle pressure to the swab as you wipe the sensor surface. Use the swab with methanol (as pure as you can get it, particularly medical grade; other ingredients can leave a residue), or the Eclipse 2 solution also sold by Photographic Solutions. Eclipse 2 (see Figure 9.11) is actually quite a bit purer than even medical-grade methanol. A couple drops of solution should be enough, unless you have a spot that's extremely difficult to remove. In that case, you may need to use extra solution on the swab to help "soak" the dirt off. Note: the E2 version of Eclipse is now recommended for cleaning what are termed "tin oxide" sensors, similar to the Nikon D90. If you have some of the older Eclipse solution, it's great for cleaning lenses! Buy the new stuff to be safe.

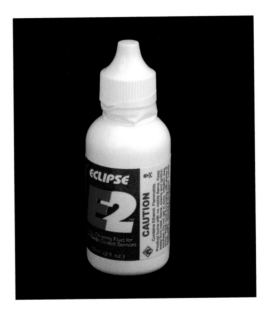

Figure 9.11
Pure Eclipse solution makes the best sensor cleaning liquid.

Once you overcome your nervousness at touching your D90's sensor, the process is easy. You'll wipe continuously with the swab in one direction, then flip it over and wipe in the other direction. You need to completely wipe the entire surface; otherwise, you may end up depositing the dust you collect at the far end of your stroke. Wipe; don't rub.

If you want a close-up look at your sensor to make sure the dust has been removed, you can pay $50-$100 for a special sensor "microscope" with an illuminator. Or, you can do like I do and work with a plain old Carson MiniBrite PO-25 illuminated 3X magnifier, as seen in Figure 9.12. (Older packaging and ads may call this a 2X magnifier, but it's actually a 3X unit.) It has a built-in LED and, held a few inches from the lens mount with the lens removed from your D90, provides a sharp, close-up view of the sensor, with enough contrast to reveal any dust that remains.

Figure 9.12
An illuminated magnifier like this Carson MiniBrite PO-25 can be used as a 'scope to view your sensor.

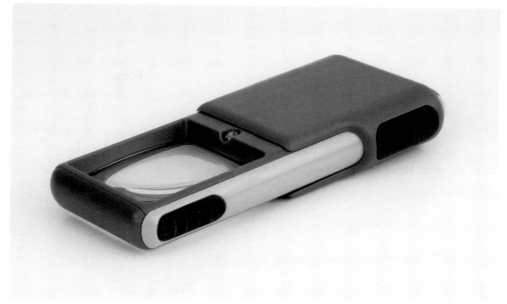

Tape Cleaning

There are people who absolutely swear by the tape method of sensor cleaning. The concept seems totally wacky, and I have never tried it personally, so I can't say with certainty that it either does or does not work. In the interest of completeness, I'm including it here. I can't give you a recommendation, so if you have problems, please don't blame me. The Nikon D90 is still too new to have generated any reports of users accidentally damaging the anti-dust coating on the sensor filter using this method.

Tape cleaning works by applying a layer of Scotch Brand Magic Tape to the sensor. This is a minimally sticky tape that some of the tape-cleaning proponents claim contains no adhesive. I did check this out with 3M, and can say that Magic Tape certainly *does* contain an adhesive. The question is whether the adhesive comes off when you peel back the tape, taking any dust spots on your sensor with it. The folks who love this method claim there is no residue. There have been reports from those who don't like the method that residue is left behind. This is all anecdotal evidence, so you're pretty much on your own in making the decision whether to try out the tape cleaning method.

Glossary

It's always handy to have a single resource where you can look up various terms you'll encounter while working with your digital camera. Here is the latest update of a glossary I've compiled over the years, with some new additions specifically for the Nikon D90.

AE-L/AF-L A button on the D90 that allows locking exposure and/or focus point prior to taking a photo.

ambient lighting Diffuse, non-directional lighting that doesn't appear to come from a specific source but, rather, bounces off walls, ceilings, and other objects in the scene when a picture is taken.

analog/digital converter The module in a camera that electronically converts the analog information captured by the D90's sensor into digital bits that can be stored as an image.

angle of view The area of a scene that a lens can capture, determined by the focal length of the lens. Lenses with a shorter focal length have a wider angle of view than lenses with a longer focal length.

anti-alias A process that smoothes the look of rough edges in images (called *jaggies* or *staircasing*) by adding partially transparent pixels along the boundaries of diagonal lines that are merged into a smoother line by our eyes. *See also* jaggies.

aperture The size of the opening in the iris or diaphragm of a lens, relative to the lens's focal length. Also called an *f/stop*. For example, with a lens having a focal length of 100mm, an f/stop with a diameter of 12.5mm would produce an aperture value of f/8.

Aperture Priority A camera setting that allows you to specify the lens opening or f/stop that you want to use, with the camera selecting the required shutter speed automatically based on its light-meter reading. *See also* Shutter Priority.

artifact A type of noise in an image, or an unintentional image component produced in error by a digital camera during processing, usually caused by the JPEG compression process in digital cameras, or, in some cases, by dust settling on the sensor.

aspect ratio The proportions of an image as printed, displayed on a monitor, or captured by a digital camera.

Autofocus A camera setting that allows the Nikon D90 to choose the correct focus distance for you, based on the contrast of an image (the image will be at maximum contrast when in sharp focus). The camera can be set for *Single-Servo Autofocus (AF-S)*, in which the lens is not focused until the shutter release is partially depressed, *Continuous-Servo Autofocus (AF-C)*, in which the lens refocuses constantly as you frame and reframe the image, and *Automatic Autofocus (AF-A)*, in which the D90 focuses using AF-S mode, but switches to AF-C mode if the subject starts to move. The D90 can also be set for Manual focus.

backlighting A lighting effect produced when the main light source is located behind the subject. Backlighting can be used to create a silhouette effect, or to illuminate translucent objects. *See also* front lighting and side lighting.

barrel distortion A lens defect that causes straight lines at the top or side edges of an image to bow outward into a barrel shape. *See also* pincushion distortion.

blooming An image distortion caused when a photosite in an image sensor has absorbed all the photons it can handle so that additional photons reaching that pixel overflow to affect surrounding pixels, producing unwanted brightness and overexposure around the edges of objects.

blur To soften an image or part of an image by throwing it out of focus, or by allowing it to become soft due to subject or camera motion. Blur can also be applied creatively in an image-editing program.

bokeh A term derived from the Japanese word for blur, which describes the aesthetic qualities of the out-of-focus parts of an image. Some lenses produce "good" bokeh and others offer "bad" bokeh. Some lenses produce uniformly illuminated out-of-focus discs. Others produce a disc that has a bright edge and a dark center, producing a "doughnut" effect, which is the worst from a bokeh standpoint. Lenses that generate a bright center that fades to a darker edge are favored, because their bokeh allows the circle of confusion to blend more smoothly with the surroundings. The bokeh characteristics of a lens are most important when you're using selective focus (say, when shooting a portrait) to deemphasize the background, or when shallow depth-of-field is a given because you're working with a macro lens, with a long telephoto, or with a wide-open aperture. *See also* circle of confusion.

bounce lighting Light bounced off a reflector, including ceiling and walls, to provide a soft, natural-looking light.

buffer The digital camera's internal memory where an image is stored immediately after it is taken until it can be written to the camera's non-volatile (semi-permanent) memory card.

burst mode The digital camera's equivalent of the film camera's motor drive, used to take multiple shots within a short period of time, each stored in a memory buffer temporarily before writing them to the media.

calibration A process used to correct for the differences in the output of a printer or monitor when compared to the original image. Once you've calibrated your scanner, monitor, and/or your image editor, the images you see on the screen more closely represent what you'll get from your printer, even though calibration is never perfect.

Camera Raw A plug-in included with Photoshop and Photoshop Elements that can manipulate the unprocessed images captured by digital cameras, such as the Nikon D90's NEF files. The latest versions of this module can also work with JPEG and TIFF images.

camera shake Movement of the camera, aggravated by slower shutter speeds, which produces a blurred image.

center-weighted meter A light-measuring device that emphasizes the area in the middle of the frame when calculating the correct exposure for an image. *See also* spot meter.

channel In an electronic flash, a channel is a protocol used to communicate between a master flash unit and the remote units slaved to that main flash. The ability to change channels allows several master flash units to operate in the same environment without interfering with each other.

chromatic aberration An image defect, often seen as green or purple fringing around the edges of an object, caused by a lens failing to focus all colors of a light source at the same point. *See also* fringing.

circle of confusion A term applied to the fuzzy discs produced when a point of light is out of focus. The circle of confusion is not a fixed size. The viewing distance and amount of enlargement of the image determine whether we see a particular spot on the image as a point or as a disc. *See also* bokeh.

close-up lens A lens add-on that allows you to take pictures at a distance that is less than the closest-focusing distance of the lens alone.

color correction Changing the relative amounts of color in an image to produce a desired effect, typically a more accurate representation of those colors. Color correction can fix faulty color balance in the original image, or compensate for the deficiencies of the inks used to reproduce the image.

compression Reducing the size of a file by encoding using fewer bits of information to represent the original. Some compression schemes, such as JPEG, operate by discarding some image information, while others have options that preserve all the detail in the original, discarding only redundant data.

Continuous-Servo Autofocus An automatic focusing setting (AF-C) in which the camera constantly refocuses the image as you frame the picture. This setting is often the best choice for moving subjects. *See also* Single-Servo Autofocus.

contrast The range between the lightest and darkest tones in an image. A high-contrast image is one in which the shades fall at the extremes of the range between white and black. In a low-contrast image, the tones are closer together.

Creative Lighting System (CLS) Nikon's electronic flash system used to coordinate exposure, camera information, and timing between a camera's built-in flash (if present) and external flash units, which can be linked through direct electrical connections or wirelessly.

Custom Settings A group of different settings you can make to specify how the Nikon D90 behaves, such as the function of certain controls, electronic flash features, and other customizable attributes.

dedicated flash An electronic flash unit, such as the Nikon SB-900 Speedlight, designed to work with the automatic exposure features of a specific camera.

depth-of-field A distance range in a photograph in which all included portions of an image are at least acceptably sharp.

diaphragm An adjustable component, similar to the iris in the human eye, which can open and close to provide specific-sized lens openings, or f/stops and thus control the amount of light reaching the sensor or film.

diffuse lighting Soft, low-contrast lighting.

digital processing chip A solid-state device found in digital cameras that's in charge of applying the image algorithms to the raw picture data prior to storage on the memory card.

diopter A value used to represent the magnification power of a lens, calculated as the reciprocal of a lens's focal length (in meters). Diopters are most often used to represent the optical correction used in a viewfinder to adjust for limitations of the photographer's eyesight, and to describe the magnification of a close-up lens attachment.

equivalent focal length A digital camera's focal length translated into the corresponding values for a 35mm film camera. This value can be calculated for lenses used with the Nikon D90 by multiplying by 1.5.

exchangeable image file format (Exif) Developed to standardize the exchange of image data between hardware devices and software. A variation on JPEG, Exif is used by most digital cameras, and includes information such as the date and time a photo was taken, the camera settings, resolution, amount of compression, and other data.

Exif *See* exchangeable image file format (Exif).

exposure The amount of light allowed to reach the film or sensor, determined by the intensity of the light, the amount admitted by the iris of the lens, the length of time determined by the shutter speed, and the sensitivity of the sensor or film to light.

exposure compensation Exposure compensation, which uses exposure value (EV) settings, is a way of adding or decreasing exposure without the need to reference f/stops or shutter speeds. For example, if you tell your camera to add +1EV, it will provide twice as much exposure, either by using a larger f/stop, slower shutter speed, or both. The D90 offers both conventional exposure compensation and flash exposure compensation.

fill lighting In photography, lighting used to illuminate shadows. Reflectors or additional incandescent lighting or electronic flash can be used to brighten shadows. One common technique outdoors is to use the camera's flash as a fill in sunlit situations.

filter In photography, a device that fits over the lens, changing the light in some way. In image editing, a feature that changes the pixels in an image to produce blurring, sharpening, and other special effects. Photoshop includes several interesting filter effects, including Lens Blur and Photo Filters.

flash sync The timing mechanism that insures that an internal or external electronic flash fires at the correct time during the exposure cycle. A digital SLR's flash sync speed is the highest shutter speed that can be used with flash, ordinarily 1/200th of a second with the Nikon D90. *See also* front-curtain sync and rear-curtain sync.

focal length The distance between the film and the optical center of the lens when the lens is focused on infinity, usually measured in millimeters.

focal plane A line, perpendicular to the optical axis, which passes through the focal point forming a plane of sharp focus when the lens is set at infinity. A focal plane indicator is etched into the Nikon D90 on the top panel.

focus tracking The ability of the automatic focus feature of a camera to change focus as the distance between the subject and the camera changes. One type of focus tracking is *predictive*, in which the mechanism anticipates the motion of the object being focused on, and adjusts the focus to suit.

format To erase a memory card and prepare it to accept files.

fringing A chromatic aberration that produces fringes of color around the edges of subjects, caused by a lens's inability to focus the various wavelengths of light onto the same spot. Purple fringing is especially troublesome with backlit images.

front-curtain sync (first-curtain sync) The default kind of electronic flash synchronization technique, originally associated with focal plane shutters, which consists of a traveling set of curtains, including a *front curtain*, which opens to reveal the film or sensor, and a *rear curtain*, which follows at a distance determined by shutter speed to conceal the film or sensor at the conclusion of the exposure. For a flash picture to be taken, the entire sensor must be exposed at one time to the brief flash exposure, so the image is exposed after the front curtain has reached the other side of the focal plane, but before the rear curtain begins to move. Front-curtain sync causes the flash to fire at the beginning of this period when the shutter is completely open, in the instant that the first curtain of the focal plane shutter finishes its movement across the film or sensor plane. With slow shutter speeds, this feature can create a blur effect from the ambient light, showing as patterns that follow a moving subject with the subject shown sharply frozen at the beginning of the blur trail. *See also* rear-curtain sync.

front lighting   Illumination that comes from the direction of the camera. *See also* backlighting and side lighting.

f/stop   The relative size of the lens aperture, which helps determine both exposure and depth-of-field. The larger the f/stop number, the smaller the f/stop itself.

graduated filter   A lens attachment with variable density or color from one edge to another. A graduated neutral density filter, for example, can be oriented so the neutral density portion is concentrated at the top of the lens's view with the less dense or clear portion at the bottom, thus reducing the amount of light from a very bright sky while not interfering with the exposure of the landscape in the foreground. Graduated filters can also be split into several color sections to provide a color gradient between portions of the image.

gray card   A piece of cardboard or other material with a standardized 18-percent reflectance. Gray cards can be used as a reference for determining correct exposure or for setting white balance.

group   A way of bundling more than one wireless flash unit into a single cluster that all share the same flash output setting, as controlled by the master flash unit.

HDMI   High-Definition Multimedia Interface is a connection for transmitting digital audio and video information, including standard, enhanced, and high-definition video and multiple channels of audio. Nikon includes an HDMI port in the Nikon D90, D5000, and its more advanced models like the top-of-the-line Nikon D3x.

high contrast   A wide range of density in a print, negative, or other image.

highlights   The brightest parts of an image containing detail.

histogram   A kind of chart showing the relationship of tones in an image using a series of 256 vertical bars, one for each brightness level. A histogram chart, such as the one the Nikon D90 can display during picture review, typically looks like a curve with one or more slopes and peaks, depending on how many highlight, midtone, and shadow tones are present in the image.

hot shoe   A mount on top of a camera used to hold an electronic flash, while providing an electrical connection between the flash and the camera. Also called an accessory shoe.

hyperfocal distance A point of focus where everything from half that distance to infinity appears to be acceptably sharp. For example, if your lens has a hyperfocal distance of four feet, everything from two feet to infinity would be sharp. The hyperfocal distance varies by the lens and the aperture in use. If you know you'll be making a grab shot without warning, sometimes it is useful to turn off your camera's automatic focus, and set the lens to infinity, or, better yet, the hyperfocal distance. Then, you can snap off a quick picture without having to wait for the lag that occurs with most digital cameras as their autofocus locks in.

image rotation A feature that senses whether a picture was taken in horizontal or vertical orientation. That information is embedded in the picture file so that the camera and compatible software applications can automatically display the image in the correct orientation.

image stabilization A technology that compensates for camera shake, usually by adjusting the position of the camera sensor or (with Nikon technology) by re-arranging the position of certain lens elements in response to movements of the camera.

incident light Light falling on a surface.

International Organization for Standardization (ISO) A governing body that provides standards used to represent film speed, or the equivalent sensitivity of a digital camera's sensor. Digital camera sensitivity is expressed in ISO settings.

interpolation A technique digital cameras, scanners, and image editors use to create new pixels required whenever you resize or change the resolution of an image based on the values of surrounding pixels. Devices such as scanners and digital cameras can also use interpolation to create pixels in addition to those actually captured, thereby increasing the apparent resolution or color information in an image.

ISO *See* International Organization for Standardization (ISO).

i-TTL Nikon's intelligent through-the-lens flash metering system, which uses preflashes to calculate exposure and to communicate between flash units, using the camera's 420-segment RGB sensor viewfinder exposure meter.

jaggies Staircasing effect of lines that are not perfectly horizontal or vertical, caused by pixels that are too large to represent the line accurately. *See also* anti-alias.

JPEG A file "lossy" format (short for Joint Photographic Experts Group) that supports 24-bit color and reduces file sizes by selectively discarding image data. Digital cameras generally use JPEG compression to pack more images onto memory cards. You can select how much compression is used (and, therefore, how much information is thrown away) by selecting from among the Standard, Fine, Super Fine, or other quality settings offered by your camera. *See also* RAW.

Kelvin (K) A unit of measure based on the absolute temperature scale in which absolute zero is zero; it's used to describe the color of continuous-spectrum light sources and applied when setting white balance. For example, daylight has a color temperature of about 5,500K, and a tungsten lamp has a temperature of about 3,400K.

lag time The interval between when the shutter is pressed and when the picture is actually taken. During that span, the camera may be automatically focusing and calculating exposure. With digital SLRs like the Nikon D90, lag time is generally very short; with non-dSLRs, the elapsed time easily can be one second or more under certain conditions.

latitude The degree by which exposure can be varied and still produce an acceptable photo.

lens flare A feature of conventional photography that is both a bane and a creative outlet. It is an effect produced by the reflection of light internally among elements of an optical lens. Bright light sources within or just outside the field of view cause lens flare. Flare can be reduced by the use of coatings on the lens elements or with the use of lens hoods. Photographers sometimes use the effect as a creative technique, and Photoshop includes a filter that lets you add lens flare at your whim.

lighting ratio The proportional relationship between the amount of light falling on the subject from the main light and other lights, expressed in a ratio, such as 3:1.

lossless compression An image-compression scheme, such as TIFF, that preserves all image detail. When the image is decompressed, it is identical to the original version.

lossy compression An image-compression scheme, such as JPEG, that creates smaller files by discarding image information, which can affect image quality.

macro lens A lens that provides continuous focusing from infinity to extreme close-ups, often to a reproduction ratio of 1:2 (half life-size) or 1:1 (life-size).

Matrix metering A system of exposure calculation that looks at many different segments of an image to determine the brightest and darkest portions, and base f/stop and shutter speed on settings derived from a database of images.

maximum burst The number of frames that can be exposed at the current settings until the buffer fills.

midtones Parts of an image with tones of an intermediate value, usually in the 25 to 75 percent brightness range. Many image-editing features allow you to manipulate midtones independently from the highlights and shadows.

mirror lock-up The ability of the D90 to retract its mirror to allow access to the sensor for cleaning.

neutral color A color in which red, green, and blue are present in equal amounts, producing a gray.

neutral density filter A gray camera filter reducing the amount of light entering the camera without affecting the colors.

noise In an image, pixels with randomly distributed color values. Noise in digital photographs tends to be the product of low-light conditions and long exposures, particularly when you've set your camera to a higher ISO rating than normal.

noise reduction A technology used to cut down on the amount of random information in a digital picture, usually caused by long exposures at increased sensitivity ratings.

normal lens A lens that makes the image in a photograph appear in a perspective that is like that of the original scene, typically with a field of view of roughly 45 degrees.

overexposure A condition in which too much light reaches the film or sensor, producing a dense negative or a very bright/light print, slide, or digital image.

pincushion distortion A type of lens distortion in which lines at the top and side edges of an image are bent inward, producing an effect that looks like a pincushion. *See also* barrel distortion.

polarizing filter A filter that forces light, which normally vibrates in all directions, to vibrate only in a single plane, reducing or removing the specular reflections from the surface of objects.

RAW An image file format, such as the NEF format in the Nikon D90, which includes all the unprocessed information captured by the camera after conversion to digital form. RAW files are very large compared to JPEG files and must be processed by a special program such as Nikon Capture NX or Adobe's Camera Raw filter after being downloaded from the camera.

rear-curtain sync (second-curtain sync) An optional kind of electronic flash synchronization technique, originally associated with focal plane shutters, which consists of a traveling set of curtains, including a *front (first) curtain* (which opens to reveal the film or sensor) and a *rear (second) curtain* (which follows at a distance determined by shutter speed to conceal the film or sensor at the conclusion of the exposure). For a flash picture to be taken, the entire sensor must be exposed at one time to the brief flash exposure, so the image is exposed after the front curtain has reached the other side of the focal plane, but before the rear curtain begins to move. Rear-curtain sync causes the flash to fire at the end of the exposure, an instant before the second or rear curtain of the focal plane shutter begins to move. With slow shutter speeds, this feature can create a blur effect from the ambient light, showing as patterns that follow a moving subject with the subject shown sharply frozen at the end of the blur trail. If you were shooting a photo of The Flash, the superhero would appear sharp, with a ghostly trail behind him. *See also* front-curtain sync (first-curtain sync).

red-eye An effect from flash photography that appears to make a person's eyes glow red, or an animal's yellow or green. It's caused by light bouncing from the retina of the eye and is most pronounced in dim illumination (when the irises are wide open) and when the electronic flash is close to the lens and, therefore, prone to reflect directly back. Image editors can fix red-eye through cloning other pixels over the offending red or orange ones.

RGB color A color model that represents the three colors—red, green, and blue—used by devices such as scanners or monitors to reproduce color. Photoshop works in RGB mode by default, and even displays CMYK images by converting them to RGB.

saturation The purity of color; the amount by which a pure color is diluted with white or gray.

selective focus Choosing a lens opening that produces a shallow depth-of-field. Usually this is used to isolate a subject in portraits, close-ups, and other types of images, by causing most other elements in the scene to be blurred.

self-timer A mechanism that delays the opening of the shutter for some seconds after the release has been operated.

sensitivity A measure of the degree of response of a film or sensor to light, measured using the ISO setting.

shadow The darkest part of an image, represented on a digital image by pixels with low numeric values.

sharpening Increasing the apparent sharpness of an image by boosting the contrast between adjacent pixels that form an edge.

shutter In a conventional film camera, the shutter is a mechanism consisting of blades, a curtain, a plate, or some other movable cover that controls the time during which light reaches the film. Digital cameras can use both a mechanical shutter and an electronic shutter for higher effective speeds.

Shutter Priority An exposure mode in which you set the shutter speed and the camera determines the appropriate f/stop. *See also* Aperture Priority.

side lighting Applying illumination from the left or right sides of the camera. *See also* backlighting and front lighting.

Single-Servo Autofocus An automatic focusing setting (AF-S) in which the camera focuses once when the shutter release is pressed down halfway. *See also* Continuous-Servo Autofocus.

slave unit An accessory flash unit that supplements the main flash, usually triggered electronically when the slave senses the light output by the main unit, or through radio waves.

slow sync An electronic flash synchronizing method that uses a slow shutter speed so that ambient light is recorded by the camera in addition to the electronic flash illumination. This allows the background to receive more exposure for a more realistic effect.

specular highlight Bright spots in an image caused by reflection of light sources.

spot meter An exposure system that concentrates on a small area in the image. *See also* center-weighted meter.

time exposure A picture taken by leaving the shutter open for a long period, usually more than one second. The camera is generally locked down with a tripod to prevent blur during the long exposure.

through-the-lens (TTL) A system of providing viewing and exposure calculation through the actual lens taking the picture.

tungsten light Light from ordinary room lamps and ceiling fixtures, as opposed to fluorescent illumination.

underexposure A condition in which too little light reaches the film or sensor, producing a thin negative, a dark slide, a muddy-looking print, or a dark digital image.

unsharp masking The process for increasing the contrast between adjacent pixels in an image, increasing sharpness, especially around edges.

vignetting Dark corners of an image, often produced by using a lens hood that is too small for the field of view, a lens that does not completely fill the image frame, or generated artificially using image-editing techniques.

white balance The adjustment of a digital camera to the color temperature of the light source. Interior illumination is relatively red; outdoor light is relatively blue. Digital cameras like the Nikon D90 set correct white balance automatically or let you do it through menus. Image editors can often do some color correction of images that were exposed using the wrong white balance setting, especially when working with RAW files that contain the information originally captured by the camera before white balance was applied.

zoom head The capability of an electronic flash to change the area of its coverage to more closely match the focal length setting of a prime or zoom lens.

Index